Additional Praise for *The Fabric of the Future*

"Here is a timeless book, a book of healing for both women and men, a book to inspire, remind, and teach, a book filled with wisdom both feminine and universal. Enjoy just one essay each day and you will be richer by the season's end."

—**Dan Millman,** author of *Way of the Peaceful Warrior* and *Everyday Enlightenment*

"The most important book I've read in years. These sheroic women survey the landscape of the future and see a world in which women's wisdom takes its rightful place."

—**Varla Ventura,** author of *Sheroes: Bold, Brash and Absolutely Unabashed Superwomen from Susan B. Anthony to Xena*

"Within these pages many of today's most influential women illuminate the way to wholeness and a future full of possibilities. Their voices resound with the new warrior spirit of love, compassion, and respect for all life. Every page has a heartfelt message, a story and a song that will give hope for a resplendent tomorrow."

—**Fred Alan Wolf,** author of *The Spiritual Universe* and *Taking the Quantum Leap* and **Sonia Sierra-Wolf,** personal development consultant

"A breathtaking vision of where we are and where we are going that unfolds with depth and texture."

—**Will Glennon,** editor of *The Community of Kindness*

THE
FABRIC
OF THE
FUTURE

Women Visionaries of Today Illuminate the Path to Tomorrow

Edited by M. J. Ryan
Foreword by Ken Wilber
Preface by Patrice Wynne

CONARI PRESS
Berkeley, CA

Printed in the United States of America on recycled paper

Conari Press books are distributed by Publishers Group West

Library of Congress Cataloging-in-Publication Data

   The fabric of the future : women visionaries illuminate the path to tomorrow / edited by M. J. Ryan : foreword by Ken Wilber : preface by Patrice Wynn.
      p.   cm.
   Included bibliographical references and index.
   ISBN 1–57324–129–6
   1. Women—Religious life. 2. New Age Movement. 3. Sex roles.
   4. Ecology—Philosophy. 5. Two thousand, A.D. I. Ryan, M. J. (Mary Jane). 1952–   .
BL625.7.F33   1998
303.49—dc21   98–8504
                                                                          CIP

Cover design: Suzanne Albertson
Cover photo courtesy of SuperStock, Inc.

For Ana Li,
and all our daughters and sons

And I thought over again
My small adventures
As with a shore wind I drifted out
In my kayak
And thought I was in danger,

My tears,
Those small ones
That I thought so big
For all the vital things
I had to get and to reach

And yet, there is only
One great thing,
The only thing
To live to see in huts and on journeys
The great day that dawns,
And the light that fills the world.

—Inuit song

The Fabric of the Future

ACKNOWLEDGMENTS

First my thanks go to the women who contributed to *The Fabric of the Future.* They generously took time out of unbelievably hectic schedules to answer my questions of where are we going and what should we be doing. I know it was not easy for any of them to find the time and I am so glad they did.

Putting together an anthology of such busy, well-known women entailed a great deal of shuffling and organizing logistical details. I absolutely could never have done it without the assistance of Claudia Schaab, who kept track of all loose ends and didn't let anything slip through the cracks. I thank too all the wonderful assistants of the contributors. Many of you put up with seemingly endless games of phone tag with Claudia and me to facilitate the process. I am very grateful for your grace under pressure.

Several people provided invaluable suggestions as to contributors, including Dawna Markova, Brenda Knight, Patrice Wynne, Robert Welsch, Luisah Teish, Marianne Dresser, Sheridan McCarthy, Patricia Renton, and Carol Flinders. Thanks to you the anthology is more well-rounded and ethnically diverse than it would have been. Several angels, including Tami Simon, Joel and Michelle Levey, Jennifer Brontsema, Jay Kahn, Nancy Fisch, and The Rose, provided me with the contacts I needed to make this anthology happen—your generosity is greatly appreciated.

Thank you so much to Ann Foley, who compiled the wonderful resource guide at the back of the book. As usual, Ann, you did a phenomenal job!

A bouquet of thanks especially to Dawna Markova, for inspiration when my spirit was flagging, for quotes and concepts, and for our years of conversation; your thinking has informed and elevated mine so much.

A special thank you to Will Glennon, who proved to be essential in the working-out of the structure of the book. He has been a thinking partner of mine for twenty years and, as copublisher of Conari Press with me, shares my vision of a better world. It is he who has maintained all these years that it is women who will lead us into the future.

Finally, I thank you, the reader, for picking up this book and entering the conversation. It is ultimately all of us together who will determine how and whether we will survive. We need each and every one of us working toward a world that we would want to live in.

FOREWORD

T*he Fabric of the Future* is truly an extraordinary book, profound, wise, far-ranging, visionary, compassionate, often brilliant, always moving. And a book whose forty or so contributors are all women.

This in itself is not the least surprising. What is surprising, and more than a bit depressing, is that the vast wisdom of this rich diversity of female voices has to be presented in a book, instead of being an already accepted part of the fabric of the culture at large. And yet just that situation is, in a sense, the theme of this volume: The fabric of the future will necessarily incorporate the rich diversity of female voices, and it will do so in a more gracious, graceful, and generous fashion than does today's world, if livable future we are to have at all.

On the one hand, of course, men and women share a vast array of common and universal experiences: we are all born, we all die, and in between we laugh and love and loathe and cherish; we play, and work, and fight, and fear. We breathe the same air, are sustained by the same Earth, have our heads in the same sky, and wonder all about it. More technically, there appear to be many linguistic, cognitive, biological, and affective universals, which remind us daily that we are, finally, a common humanity interrelated with global commons and all of Gaia's inhabitants.

But within those profound commonalities, there are wonderful differences: between cultures, between individuals, and between the sexes. And we seem to be at an extraordinary and auspicious moment in human evolution, where many of these rich differences, previously undervalued or even devalued altogether, are now being unleashed. And this certainly seems to be true of those values that have traditionally been called "feminine."

Some theorists, of course, prefer not to speak of a difference between "male" and "female" values, believing that any differentiation between the sexes will simply lead, in the long run, to further disenfranchisement of women; and thus it is imperative that we solely emphasize gender equity, equal rights, and sexual equality. While I think that is mandatory as a *legal* agenda (all individuals, regardless of race, creed, or gender, stand equal before the law), surely there is room, within that legal freedom, to recognize and cherish the many values traditionally known as "female," if for no other reason than that those values are precisely ones that the modern world has so insistently overlooked. And values that, therefore, a future evolution will incorporate in a more balanced and graceful tomorrow.

—Ken Wilber, author of
A Brief History of Everything and
Sex, Ecology, and Spirituality: The Spirit of Evolution

PREFACE

An Imaginative Delphic Oracle

When I was a young girl in the '50s, I was mesmerized by the vision of the future—that far, far distant time at the end of the century—described with great fervor by scientists writing in popular magazines. One future scenario that was particularly memorable to me promised women the freedom to give birth in a sensation-free tent so that the pains of labor which my mother so vividly described could be circumvented by the time I became a mother-to-be. And, of course, with so much leisure time on our hands—every imaginable labor-saving device would be invented to ease my household chores—my only real challenge would be learning how to travel to distant lands with a baby stroller for my happiness to be complete as a new mother. How fortunate I was to be born at a time when babies would just pop out like cupcakes from an oven! How easy my adult life would be thanks to the men of science who were inventing the future!

Forty years later, I am living in the future that seemed so distant in the imagination of a prepubescent girl. What an amusing irony that as we enter the twenty-first century, women are choosing to endure the pain of birth naturally, recognizing the gifts of awareness, feeling, and consciousness in this most spiritually creative of all human activities. The scientists who were so all-powerful then seem so limited now in their understanding of human potential and women's contributions to culture: giving birth to a new world grounded in fierce compassion, respect for human, cultural, and natural diversity, and a generous, loving presence to the essence of life unfolding within us. For a future to be born.

In *The Fabric of the Future: Women Visionaries Illuminate the Path to Tomorrow*, you will not find wildly fantastic predictions on the life-changing nature of technology, the design of work spaces in outer space, or the sexual practices of mutant humans. Rather, with their listening eyes and vision-seeking hearts, these writers invite all of us to pursue a passionate optimism in a future grounded in the emerging, evolving, and enduring values of women's spirituality. Looking at the human condition through courageous eyes that have seen the world of human suffering, they remain steadfastly true to a life-giving vision of the world being born from the beginning of time.

As co-owner of GAIA Bookstore, I have hosted over a thousand authors speaking on the creation and celebration, substance and sustenance of human spiritual transformation. Many of these speakers are the women found in this anthology who, on fire with a personal vision, are reinventing their fields of endeavor with a passionate faith in the power of the feminine to awaken the life force within. Their writing articulates the sacred possibilities at the heart of medicine and science, psychology and politics, education and sexuality, family and work, friendship, creativity, and spirituality.

In collecting these visions of women leaders, *The Fabric of the Future* transports us to an imaginative Delphic oracle of the next century. In this anthology are some of the brightest beacons of female wisdom collected in one place to read, ponder, and invigorate our own unique contributions to the creation of a future world. On these pages is sound counsel, women's wit, and girlfriend energy gathered in a circle of women writing, women visioning, women creating. The future is in your hands.

—Patrice Wynne
Berkeley, CA

I

SWIMMING TOGETHER
THROUGH THE
WHITEWATERS OF CHANGE

"Who knows what form the forward momentum of life will take in the time
ahead or what use it will make of our anguished searching. The most any one
of us can seem to do is fashion something—an object or ourselves—and drop
it into the confusion, make an offering of it, so to speak, to the life force."

—Ernest Becker

For three years, I was part of a conversation group of nine people ranging
in age from the thirties to seventies who met weekly for two hours in a
living room. Often we talked about our purpose—why did we keep showing
up every Wednesday night and what were we supposed to be doing together?
But we also talked about the particulars of our lives—not so much for support
or "gossip," but to see if we could uncover some underlying patterns that
were true for us all. We were professionals and working people—dentists and
teachers and principals and book publishers and seamstresses and handymen
and psychiatrists—and what became clear over time is that each of us was
undergoing profound shifts. Some were self-initiated, the result of an inner
call: the teacher decided to become a teacher trainer, the seamstress decided to
look for work with more meaning, the handyman's body signaled that he
needed less physically challenging work. The rest of us were undergoing transitions that, in some sense, were the result of vast social changes. Health care,
education, publishing—all were industries experiencing upheavals that we
were very personally feeling the effects of. Over and over, we would conclude
the evening with the recognition that the old forms were breaking down and
the new had yet to emerge.

I began to notice that it wasn't just our group. Everywhere around me, I
heard stories of individuals wanting to pause in midstream to heed some vague
inner call to slow down, to stop; people spoke of experiencing a sense of waiting, that there seemed to be something wanting to emerge, but no one was
quite sure what it was or what she or he should do about it. They too seemed

to feel that our institutions were crumbling around us, and had a deepening sense of anxiety about the future. For all of us, there were both subtle internal kinds of changes as well as the need to respond to the external changes that were happening all around us.

In our group, each of us dealt with the changes in their own way, navigating the whitewater rapids as gracefully as they could. But I have never been the patient type. I became tired with all the breaking down—I wanted to know what was breaking *through*. More specifically I wanted to know what I could do to help the breakthrough happen. In times of change, says my friend Dawna Markova, two questions are always urgently asked: Who am I now and how do I connect to the whole? For me, the second was much more vital. I knew who I was, but I wanted to understand how the changes—interior and exterior—that I was experiencing related to the larger shift that was happening and what I could do to join my individual life to the great stream of consciousness that is flowing into the future. I'm a good kid; I'm willing to do my part— if I could only figure out what that was.

SURVIVING ON QUICKSAND

"In the absence of certainty, one must have courage. Courage requires overcoming our fear of the unknown....We are afraid of the letting go that chaos requires because we believe our world will fall apart without strict control. And yet the new science of chaos theory tells us there is an underlying order to the universe that does not require our control, and that chaos can be a gateway to quantum leaps in improvement."

—Daniel Kim

As we sit poised at the brink of a new century and a new millennium, there is little doubt that we are in the midst of a vast transformation: of business, education, and health care, of relationships to one another and to the Earth, and even of consciousness itself. As Norman Lear, the veteran TV and movie producer said recently, "I have developed a rather keen appreciation of the troubles and joys of ordinary families, struggling to do the best they can in our crazy times. There is no longer any dispute that the foundations of modern society ·... are being shaken to their very depths. We are living through a wrenching transition—economically, culturally, spiritually. The old certainties are gone and the new ones have yet to crystallize."

There has also been a great deal of conversation, in magazines and books, of what this shift might be; a great deal of talk, often phrased in very general terms, of "healing the planet" and "living more in harmony with natural rhythms." But the more I read, the more it seemed that there were precious little specifics about what we need to be doing in order to get from here to there, or what specific kinds of tools we need to navigate through these turbulent times. Shallow rhetoric seemed to abound yet true wisdom seemed elusive. Being a pragmatic New Englander, I was frustrated by the lack of specificity—what should I be *doing?* I decided to take matters into my own hands.

I resolved to ask the leading women thinkers of our times from as wide a variety of spiritual and philosophical orientations as possible one very pointed question: Practically, what do we need to be doing at this point in our psychospiritual evolution. I asked those skilled in the psychospiritual realms because I believe strongly, as Jean Houston articulates in her article, that "the action on behalf of the redeeming vision has never taken place in society until it has been played out in the soul." So I wasn't asking so much about forms and structures—about business and health care and government—as the evolving state of our psyches. I asked Buddhists and Christians and Taoists and Jews; Wiccans, astrologers, Tantric practitioners, and "New Agers"; Black women and white, Native American, Asian and Hispanic; Black and white Africans; lesbians and straights; artists, environmentalists, business consultants, therapists, and even a couple futurists. My emphasis on women was not because I wished to promote separation, but rather because I had the sense that it is primarily women who are leading the way of this social and cultural transformation, and women who are most actively in search of help in the process.

WE'RE ALL IN THIS TOGETHER

"There are years that ask questions and years that answer them."

—Zora Neale Hurston

I sent a letter that began with Zora Neale Hurston's quote above, articulating much of what I have said here. You hold the result in your hands—a tapestry that incorporates the warp and woof of each individual voice, yet amazingly creates a picture that is surprisingly unified in its broad strokes. I hope you enjoy seeing the common threads that weave through the pieces—many women, for example, have been influenced by one another's work and several give credit to Betty Friedan's *The Feminine Mystique* as being a pivot point in the transformation that is happening how.

But the strongest thread that unifies most all of the pieces is each woman's sense, no matter how she puts it into words, that what is trying to be born is a world in which what have been traditionally called "feminine" values—receptivity, intuition, empathy, relational thinking, etc.—are as honored and supported as traditional "male values" as linear thinking, action, differentiation, etc. Each woman articulates it differently, has a different emphasis or perspective, and many do not use the term "feminine" at all quite intentionally, believing that it only fosters a sense of division between men and women and that there are other, less loaded ways of discussing the same values. But if you think deeply about what each woman is saying, you will discover the thread there somewhere.

I began to believe that this "feminine" consciousness is indeed what is struggling to emerge in full bloom and that therefore it was no coincidence that I had asked women to be the contributors to this book. Then, one day, one of the people in my Wednesday night group said to me, "If you are doing a book on this, you must include Barbara Marx Hubbard. Come and hear her speak." And so I did—and came to see not only that the role women have to play in the future is nothing less than, as Hubbard puts it, evolutionary. As Hubbard and other contributors point out, we are at a unique place in human evolution. Never before have women lived so long past childbirth and never before have women en masse had the kinds of access to education, careers, and psychological awareness that they now enjoy. The creative potential that we women represent, with our different skill sets and values than men, is a force that has never before been unleashed in the world. Through her speech, which is adapted here, I began to see what my part might be—helping women deliver their messages to the world is not just my job as an editor, but my contribution to the great changes underway.

As you read through each woman's perspective, I hope you get a strong sense of the possible future. For as we face the challenges of our times, having a strong vision will be what keeps us going. Not one of the women here claims the future is guaranteed to be rosy. Rather, as Joanna Macy says so articulately, "There is no guarantee that we will make it in time for civilization, or even complex life forms, to survive." Thus, she continues, "I consider it an enormous privilege to be alive now, in this Turning, when all the wisdom and courage we ever harvested can be put to use and matter supremely." To harvest all the wisdom and courage we need, we need each and every one of us contributing.

That's why I also pray that *The Fabric of the Future* helps you find your own part in the possible future. I hope you are brought to new ways of seeing, understanding, and incorporating your own personal story into what is unfolding all around us. For this is not just a static reading experience—woman or man, you are being invited, indeed urged, to add your colors to the loom. As Jean Houston so eloquently responds to Zora Neale Hurston's quote at the end of her powerful essay, "These are the times. We are the people. And we are living in the answering years." May we find our way—together.

—M. J. Ryan

2

AT THE CROSSROADS: LIVING IN BETWEEN

"At the boundary, life blossoms."

—James Gleick

The pieces in this section set the stage and provide the context for where we are and how we got here. They unfold in broad, strong sweeps, viewing the evolution of humankind from a vantage point that allows us to see the effects of our historical choices. From this height we can also see the fine strong lines of something new emerging, a pattern beautifully capable of reweaving the tapestry of life.

We begin with futurist Barbara Marx Hubbard, who looks at the changes that have led us to this moment of psychological history and offers a profoundly optimistic view of how evolution itself is helping us through this transition. We then go wider with philosopher Jean Houston's mythic look at where we've come from and where we are going. We need myth, she claims, at times of breakdown and breakthrough; right now we are in a period she calls "the rising of the soul of the world."

Riane Eisler then asks us to consider how much the way our intimate relationships are constructed affects our social, political, and economic lives. We are being called on, she maintains, to reorganize those relationships into what she calls a partnership model, an equal partnership between men and women, with respect for what has been traditionally considered "feminine" values. Z Budapest encourages us to reflect on the way larger forces, specifically planetary forces, have been shaping the changes we've been experiencing in the last one hundred years.

"We are collectively giving birth to the intuitive, receptive, transformative, and enduring nature of our human potential," writes author Jamie Sams, while noting that this doesn't mean the transition will be easy. "In Native American legend, the time between worlds is described as the wobble," and so she offers daily practices to find "new points of balance."

While we are considering the big picture, let's be sure to include all of us, not just white middle-class folks, reminds Yoruba priestess Luisah Teish, who notes that even the notion of the new millennium comes from the Christian paradigm: "There are other cultures with different spiritual traditions and calendars." She also calls on us to make a "radical shift in conscience as well as consciousness."

Joanna Macy and Margaret Wheatley call us to the environmental aspects of the big picture, Macy notes that we must make an "epochal shift from an industrial growth society, dependent on accelerating consumption of resources, to a sustainable or life-sustaining society." Such a change requires a profound shift in consciousness. Wheatley names Gaia "the feminine energy that compels us to care about the future of Earth" and encourages us to give up our mechanistic view of life and tell a new cosmic story, one that fits more accurately the way life really works—namely, that the "purpose of life is to explore newness" and as such, we don't need to fear change or chaos.

We begin to narrow our focus a bit now and put ourselves into the picture. Anthropologist Angeles Arrien asks us to orient ourselves in these times of change by seeing where we are in relationship to eight gates of initiation. Jungian analyst Marion Woodman reminds us that we need to feel our way through this threshold time so that we don't simply succumb to fear. And Daphne Rose Kingma reminds us that ultimately the new millennium is about love, "but only if we are willing to become the artists who, *con amore,* create this new world."

Barbara Marx Hubbard, President of The Foundation for Conscious Evolution, is a futurist, author, speaker, and social architect. Her name was placed in nomination for the Vice Presidency of the United States on the Democratic ticket in 1984; she advocated a Peace Room in the White House to scan for, map, connect, and communicate what is working in America. Her latest book, *Conscious Evolution: Awakening the Power of Our Social Potential,* sets forth a spirit-motivated plan of action for the twenty-first century culminating in a vision of a "co-creative society"—what it might be like if everything works.

Awakening to Our Genius: The Heroine's Journey

Something radically new is happening with women. We feel it within ourselves as an upwelling of creativity, of frustration, of the desire to be more, to find life purpose, to express and evolve ourselves and our world. This sense of increased power and purpose is, I believe, a phenomenon of an evolutionary order, not merely an historical order. "Evolutionary" means it will lead to transformation rather than reformation or incremental improvement.

We happen to be the generation born when an unprecedented set of changes is occurring on our planet. Suddenly we have reached a limit to growth on our mother planet. We have to stop overpopulating and polluting, we must coordinate ourselves as one body, handle our own wastes, shift from nonrenewable to renewable resources, distribute food to all members, redesign failing social systems in education, health, finance, the environment. We are the first generation to be required to undertake these immense new responsibilities.

Yet there are no schools for managing a planet, no experts in planetary management to guide us, for no one has ever done it before. "Space Ship Earth came without an operating manual," as Buckminster Fuller said. My metaphor for this planetary change is that we are undergoing a "crisis of birth" toward the next stage of human evolution. It is dangerous, but natural. It has taken fifteen billion years of evolution, from the Big Bang to the present to develop a planetary species on Earth that is aware of itself as a whole and must become responsible for the future of the whole system. The entire story of creation has led to the birth of a species which must learn to cooperate and co-create on a planetary scale. If we can get through this next thirty years, we can see beckoning before us a future that can fulfill the aspirations of the human race. For the very powers with which we might destroy ourselves, especially in advanced science and technology, are, if properly used, the very same powers with which we can transform ourselves. This, as we shall soon see, is where women come in!

THE PERIOD OF OUR PLANETARY BIRTH

To place the rise of women in this evolutionary context, let's look at three key developments that happened in the 1960s as natural events heralding the emergence of the next stage of our evolution.

The first was the development of space travel. We left Earth alive, penetrated our biosphere, and set foot on a new world—the moon. We found that there are materials of a thousand Earths in our solar system in the moon and the asteroids. By stepping onto a new world, we saw that we are one world here on Earth, and that we have the possibilities of many new worlds in space—we have an immeasurable physical future. There are no known limits to our physical growth in a universe of billions and billions of galaxies. There is no resource shortage, no energy shortage, no space shortages for us in the future—if we can make it through this period of change.

More important for our immediate future, we looked back upon ourselves from outer space, saw our Earth as one body, and fell in love with ourselves as a whole. We loved our north and our south, our east and our west. This beautiful blue-water planet we saw had no nations, no divisions, no barriers—it is clearly one body and we are all members of it. In the same timeframe, the environmental movement awoke. 1969 was the lunar landing; 1970 was the first Earth Day. We saw that the environment is not outside ourselves. Rather, the environment is ourselves. It is our extended body.

We began to have a growing awareness that the Earth is a living organism and that we are all connected; we are all relatives; we are all part of one body. Millions began to feel this connectedness empathetically, as love for nature, for other species, for people in distant lands, for children everywhere. This sense of connectedness is a newer version of an ancient consciousness that the world is alive, that we are living members of a living body, animated by the same spirit. This mystical awareness of the past is becoming a practical necessity in the present. Because we are learning that if we do not take care of our soil, our water, our air, if we do not preserve and care for other species, if we do not recognize that we must handle our toxic wastes, stop polluting, forbid the proliferation of nuclear weapons, and so on, that we shall surely destroy our chances for a positive future, and even become extinct. And there is a time consideration here. We do not have hundreds of years to change. Even one more generation of polluting and overpopulating at the current rate may destroy our life support system for future generations.

The third movement that happened in the '60s was the rise of the women's movement, and it is no coincidence that a widespread emancipation of women's creativity arose at the precise time when the planetary system as a whole recognized its limits to one form of growth and its need to repattern its social systems and mature its consciousness if the human race is to survive.

Perhaps the most important new fact impinging on the future is that we are the first generation to be aware that there is a limit to population growth on this Earth. One more doubling of the population will be over ten billion people, and it is expected to happen within the next forty to fifty years—in the lifetime of the generations now alive. Such a doubling cannot happen again. We have been told since time immemorial to be fruitful and multiply. Now, suddenly in this generation, since the 1960s, we see that we must limit our populations in order to survive as a species. Yet it is estimated that three billion women will reach childbearing age in the next decade! We know that wherever women have sufficient economic development, education, and freedom, they choose to have fewer children. That maternal energy is being liberated, it is being experienced as the expanded desire to create, to self-express, to find meaningful work and life purpose.

And this brings us to the biggest change of all: Although there have been many great women in the past, never before has the creative genius of the woman been aroused and called forth collectively. We are being activated by an evolutionary drive of global proportions to shift from the massive effort to procreate up to maximum to a new effort. The energy that went into maximum reproduction, having five to ten children per family, is being liberated en masse. What is this creativity for? From the evolutionary perspective, this is the energy needed to carry us through this crisis of "our birth" to the next stage of human evolution.

LABOR PAINS

These great evolutionary forces are not abstract; they have been manifesting in our individual lives. I remember clearly how it happened for me. It was the 1960s and I was a housewife in Lakeville, Connecticut with five children. (I was a member of the last generation in the developed world to have that many babies without thinking—Margaret Mead called it "mindless fecundity.")

I had graduated from Bryn Mawr cum laude with a B.A. in political science in 1951. After graduation, I wanted to go to Washington and get a job. But instead I married at twenty-one and found myself pregnant. At first I was resentful. I had barely begun my own life. But in the seventh month, when the milk started to come in, I changed and began to long for the unknown child. I lost interest in the development of my "self" and became devoted to the care and nurturing of my child. I loved giving birth. I loved my children dearly and gave them all my time. But after each child was weaned, the same longing came forth—that there was something more I was born to do. Not knowing what it was, I had another child, and another and another, until I had five.

I began to experience a "strange" and unaccountable depression. What could it be? I had a husband I loved. I loved my children. I had a nice house. From the point of view of my culture in the '50s, I must be neurotic, selfish, sick, not to be happy. My depression deepened—until I came across two key books. The first was Betty Friedan's *The Feminine Mystique*. She had been sent out to do an article on women who seemed to have a nameless "problem." What she discovered was that the "problem" they had was a desire for an identity beyond their roles of wife and mother! They seemed to want to be individuals, persons. (It is hard to imagine this was only thirty years ago.) Friedan called this condition the "feminine mystique." It was a rising up of feminine identity, creativity, and expression—that had no name in our culture at all! It's very hard to remember how new this development is. From the point of view of our evolution, it is merely a blink of the cosmic eye.

The other book was Abraham Maslow's *Toward a Psychology of Being*. He had the genius to study well people rather than the sick. He discovered that every well person, everyone who was joyful, productive, and beneficent, had one thing in common—chosen work which they found of intrinsic value and self-rewarding, a vocation, a calling which they loved. He called such people self-actualizing. Suddenly I saw that my "problem" was that I had not yet found my vocation. I loved my children, but I was more than a mother. This was my wake-up call. I was not neurotic—I was underdeveloped! I put a plus sign on my frustration, and reinterpreted it as a positive growth signal, guiding me onward. I knew that in order to be fulfilled, I had to find my vocation and offer my unique gifts to the world.

In my search, I read deeply and found several other seminal thinkers who offered a basis of hope and a positive vision of our future that deeply attracted me. One of them was Teilhard de Chardin, the Jesuit paleontologist. He discovered "God" in evolution, and put forward the Law of Complexity/Consciousness, which put as simply as possible states that as a system becomes more complex, it jumps in consciousness and freedom, as from molecule to cell to multicellular animal to humans. Planet Earth is itself now becoming ever more complex, interactive, and interconnected. At some point, he foresaw, we would experience empathetically that we are in fact all members of one body, and there would be a collective jump in consciousness and freedom on Earth. It would be felt as the fire of love and the passion to participate creatively in the world. This thought awakened in me a flame of desire for greater fulfillment, not only for myself, but for us all.

Then I read Buckminster Fuller. He said we have the technology, resources, and know-how we need to make of this world a 100 percent physical success, without damage to the environment, without disadvantaging anyone. The human mind is designed to know the design of nature, he believed, and the nature of nature is regenerative and ever-increasing in knowledge. I began to see the possibility for a positive future for the whole human race. Instead of coming to some sort of final limits and end, we were actually at the threshold of an immeasurable future.

With all these ideas churning within me, one day while taking a walk I asked the universe a question: *What is our story? What is happening on planet Earth?* I knew it must be one story, for it was one Earth. With that question, I went into a slight daydreaming type walk. Suddenly, I had an "out-of-Earth" experience. My mind's eye was lifted into outer space. Floating as the astronauts did, I experienced our planet as a living organism struggling to coordinate itself as a whole. I felt the pollution choking our lungs, the hunger torturing our bodies, the weapons killing ourselves. I felt the pain in the whole system for one frightful instant in time. Then, a miracle seemed to happen. I felt as though I were seeing a few frames ahead in the movie of creation. In this moment of expanded reality, an unbearable pain intensified throughout the whole planetary body, very much like the pain before giving birth to a child. There was a flash of light, an unearthly light, the kind that the mystics see. It came from within us, and from beyond us. We saw the light together. The floodgates of our hearts opened. Love streamed forth. The barriers that separated us dissolved. The air cleared, the waters cleared. Healings abounded. I heard the inner words: "Our story is a birth. We are one body. What the avatars have come to tell us is true. *Go tell the story of our birth, Barbara!*"

That sense of vocation opened the floodgates of creativity within me. Suddenly I had a personal purpose that related to a larger meaning. I felt myself, and all of us, to be vital parts of an ever-evolving process. I understood the whole evolutionary story of creation as the story of the birth of a universal humanity—ourselves! I accepted my vocation—to understand, communicate, and help realize humanity's evolutionary potential to transcend current limitations and to co-create a magnificent future. (By the way, Maslow pointed out that the way most of us find our vocations is either through a peak experience where we transcend our small separated selves, and/or by finding at least one other person to emulate, someone whom we admire and love who can serve to awaken our own innate genius.)

In my case, that peak experience, combined with reading and deep dialogues with my artist husband and others, set me on my new path toward my second life, my chosen life. I became a storyteller and a futurist. My life transformed. I felt joy, purpose, challenge. I sought out people at the growing edge of every field and learned the incredible stories of our new capacities—spiritual, social, and scientific.

This growth within myself has made me a far better mother. When I was fifty, my children gave me a birthday party. I asked them, "What did I do well as a mother?" Their answer was that the gift I had given them was that I had found my own life purpose, and had "followed my bliss," as Joseph Campbell put it, while loving them and inviting them to be with me as a pioneering woman. They felt that having this kind of mother had inspired them to do the same in their own lives. Being more myself, I have more of myself to give. Now five out of five children have their own vocations and are as dedicated as I am.

My experience is a prototypical example of what began to happen to women since. But at that time, in the early '60s, the women's movement had just begun to attract the general public. Given the patriarchal nature of our society, it was necessary that the first phase of the women's movement was focused on the effort to secure equal rights, often having to protest, to fight against injustice. While this effort continues, especially in those parts of the world where male dominance is still the accepted way, there is now arising a second phase of the women's movement: from feminism to co-creation. This second phase grows out of the desire, intelligence, and power to co-create a new and better world. It springs from the recognition that we must be the change we wish to see in the world, that the inner work of personal and spiritual growth must now be extended into the outer world, creating a world equal to our higher values of love, inclusivity, nonviolence, and spirituality.

FROM PROCREATION TO CO-CREATION

Evolutionary forces are helping in this transformation. My understanding is that the sexual drive to procreate is expanding into the *suprasexual drive to co-create.* The life pulse of sexuality is animating our creativity, and awakening our genius to evolve ourselves and our world. Just as everyone of us has a genetic code, so each of us has a *genius code* which holds our unique creativity. In sexuality, we are attracted to join our genes to have a child. In suprasexuality, we are attracted to *join our genius* to give birth to our full potential selves, and to produce the work needed for the world. In this as-yet unexpressed creativity that the suprasexual drive releases lies the seeds of the better world. In our genius are the ideas, projects, and capacities needed to transform ourselves and our world.

Through the process of co-creation, we ourselves evolve. When we join our genius with others, we have moments of what we might call *a fusion of genius.* It happens when we get excited over a project and begin to resonate with others. It's explosive! We are thrilled, totally alive. We want to do more of it because by doing more of it we become more ourselves. Thus the acorn within us is given sunlight and water and feels itself unfolding, becoming the giant oak!

This force is felt as what I call *vocational arousal.* It can strike at any age, from eighteen to eighty. It's usually felt at first as frustration, as the desire to do more, to be more, as happened to me as a mother of five in my early thirties. It's the awakening of our passion to create, to discover what more we are born to do, and to give. It's the third great human drive: from self-preservation to self-reproduction to self-evolution.

This awakening which women have been feeling so strongly over the last thirty years is, from the evolutionary perspective, nature awaking within us for the survival and fulfillment of human life. Just as nature urges us to reproduce the species, now she is arising within us to empower us to evolve the species.

This is a monumental change. Throughout human history, most of us never had time to fully mature. We had the maximum number of babies, worked eighteen hours a day to survive, and died young, as did the men. But all this is changing. At the beginning of this century, the average life span was under fifty. Now it's almost up to eighty and rising every year, especially for women. Everyone over fifty is a member of the newest generation—in the past we would have been dead! It takes a long while to grow up. We've been given a whole generation of life to use in a new way. The purpose of our longevity is to mature enough to express our untapped potential for the building of a new and better world.

As we have fewer children and live longer lives with greater education, choice, and awareness, for the first time in human history the creative drive in the feminine is being called forth en masse. On the deepest level, we can see this call to self-express as the evolution of our spirituality. Our creativity is the *creator within us.* It is the spark of the divine encoded in our genius. When it gets aroused, we are activated not simply by the desire for a job, or to compete with men, but rather with the same love that we feel when we are pregnant with a child. We are pregnant with ourselves. We move from self-reproduction to self-evolution. What all the implications are of such a transformation are unclear. No one yet knows what a fully aroused co-creative woman can be in a culture which supports and needs her power!

However, we are at the threshold of the emergence of a new archetype on Earth—the *feminine co-creator.* The co-creative woman is one who is activated by spirit, awakened in the heart to express her unique creativity in loving action which evolves both herself and the world. Co-creative action is not sacrificial, it is self-actualizing. We have had many types of women—the mother, the mystic, the priestess, the artist, the healer, the pioneering woman. The co-creative woman is a synthesis of all of this and something more, something new, because the world condition in which we are emerging is new.

THE NEW HEROINE'S JOURNEY

The new heroine's journey begins when our unique creativity is aroused, when we commit to giving birth to our full potential selves with the same devotion with which we say yes to the birth and nurturing of a child, when we discover our vocation, our calling, and begin upon the path of realizing our full potential in the world through creative action.

To experience a vocation is like falling in love. It cannot be willed, it only can be surrendered unto. If we yield to a calling, we find that every aspect of our nature will be challenged and called forth. We will have to meet every obstacle and opportunity and overcome every immaturity and self-imposed limit within ourselves. We have to go the whole way in our own self-development.

To surrender to a vocation affects our intimate and personal lives. We can have now the "chosen child." Childbearing is not a necessity, it is a choice. Indeed, it is a vocation. Those who are called to have children should do so freely. But those who are not called to have children are equally important, for their creativity becomes available for the larger human family. Those young women in their thirties and forties who are deciding not to have children at all are a new breed. Their passionate love and caring is available for the world. They fall in love with their work, with their teammates, with their higher purpose.

Some young women, like two of my three daughters, for example, have chosen to have both a vocation and children. This requires deep commitment and patience, especially when the children are young. Yet out of this effort great women are emerging whose children have the advantage of their mother as an example of a co-creative woman whom they can emulate and use as a role model.

Surrendering to a vocation also affects our intimate partners, our spouses, our husbands, our mates. This is a most difficult challenge for many women. For when a woman becomes vocationally aroused and surrenders to a vocation, her beloved may feel displaced, no longer central in her life. Many women find their mates depressed, feeling diminished by their creativity. Often couples split up at this point, for a spiritually motivated, transformationally activated women is a powerful force. She usually wants a partner, she does not want to be alone, but it takes a very strong and sensitive man to be able to live with such an awakened feminine co-creator. For it is often a reversal of roles. Women are taking the lead in motivation and seem to know what to do, whereas many good men feel disoriented and lost. We need a whole new level of relationship work to deal with the "co-creative couple." The ideal for such a new form of coupling would be, I feel from my own personal experience, that when the woman's creativity is aroused, she is received in love by the man she loves, and is accepted, indeed loved, for her creative initiative and power. In turn, she draws forth from him his unexpressed creativity and he too becomes more fully himself through the union. She can be a strong woman without causing resentment in the man, and he can manifest his strength purified of aggression. For he no longer wins the woman through aggressive behavior. On the contrary, he wins her by his receptivity and adoration of her power!

The holy purpose of such co-creative coupling is, I believe, for each partner through the joining to give birth to their own and to each other's full potential. This is a high challenge and a great art to be learned by co-creative women and men. The model we seek is not a matriarchy but, as Riane Eisler pointed out in *The Chalice and the Blade,* a partnership among co-equal co-creators. Catherine Chardin calls this kind of relationship the Cosmic Couple. She believes that this form of union among co-equal co-creators is the basis of the new civilization. In such a union, each partner becomes whole, masculine and feminine joined within. Then they join, whole being with whole being, in nonpossessive and creative love, both sexual and suprasexual. In fact, sexuality itself is deepened and can become regenerative and recreative, rather than only procreative or recreational. (This is, of course, an ideal, not often an actuality.) Even now, we can see that the breakup of the old nuclear family may lead us toward far a richer form of union—the co-creative family. The heart of the new union is the new feminine archetype: the co-creative woman, joined by a co-creative man.

THE NOOSPHERE COMES OF AGE

Let's look at the world in which this co-creative woman is now entering. It is a world in which systems are breaking down everywhere. There is hunger, poverty, violence, crime, drug abuse, pollution, the destruction of our waters, the depletion of our soil, the spreading of toxic wastes. The problems might seem overwhelming.

To imagine how to respond to these immense new challenges we need first of all to recognize the enormity of our new powers. What is radically new on Earth is not ourselves as individual humans. We have not really changed very much in thousands of years. However, the social and technological environment into which we have been born has transformed, even in the last fifty years, since the understanding of the atom, the gene, the brain. We now have the actual power to co-create or to co-destroy our world, and we are entering the first age of *conscious* evolution, from passive to active participation in evolution itself.

These powers do not come from us as individuals; they are given to us by the maturation of what Teilhard called "the noosphere," coming from the Greek word *noos,* meaning mind. The noosphere is the thinking layer of Earth. We were given the geosphere, the hydrosphere, the biosphere, but human intelligence and creativity has engendered the noosphere. It consists of our collective consciousness, of our religions, arts, and cultures, of our constitutions, laws, social systems, and technologies—our faxes, phones, satellites, Internet, our rockets, our evolutionary technologies such as nanotechnology (the capacity to build atom by atom as nature does), biotechnology, cybernetics, astronautics, genetics. The noosphere can be conceived of as a superorganism, an organic, extended spiritual, scientific, social body of which each of us is a member. Through the noosphere, humans now inherit the powers we used to attribute to our gods. It is through the noosphere that we fly to the moon, map all the genes in our bodies, clone a sheep, flash our images around the globe via television with the speed of light; through this collective power we can build new worlds in space, or destroy this world on Earth.

GODDESSES OF THE NOOSPHERE

Women are awakening en masse to their creative genius at the same time that we have reached the limits to population growth, and in the same time frame of the maturing of the noosphere. It is our great task to apply our loving consciousness, our capacity to care for the whole, our intuition, and our compassion for life to the guidance of the new powers in the noosphere. Goddesses of the noosphere must now arise to guide this power toward the restoration of the Earth, the freeing of people from hunger and poverty, the liberating of unique creativity, the designing of win-win social systems, and the exploration of the further reaches of the human spirit and the universe beyond our home planet.

FROM THE HUMAN POTENTIAL TO THE SOCIAL POTENTIAL MOVEMENT

Women, in partnership with men, are called to lead from the human potential movement toward the social potential movement: to bring our values of caring, love, ecological sensitivity, nonviolence, gender balance, win-win and partnership models into the larger world. As the human potential movement studied human wellness, the social potential movement studies and fosters peaks of social creativity, solutions, breakthroughs, and projects that are already working to heal and evolve our world.

The social potential movement is still very young. If someone could wave a magic wand and say, "Okay, ladies, it's your turn—run the world!" would we know how to design the educational systems, the health care systems, the economic and social justice systems needed for a just, free, and regenerative society? These new structures are not yet mature. The social architecture for a peaceful, global civilization is not yet in place. For example, I believe that a major reason why Gorbachev was in such a terrible dilemma at the time of the breakup of the former Soviet Union was that he only had a choice between communism and the current form of capitalism. He did not have a third way. The social potential movement is discovering this third way. It is a holistic, synergistic, co-creative way that is still too new and unformed to run a world. This is not to say that new forms are not emerging. They are. But in general they are disconnected, underfunded, and largely unnoticed by the mass media which focuses more on breakdowns and violence than on breakthroughs and love. Thus, the purpose of the social potential movement must be to identify those breakthroughs, to map them, connect them, and communicate what is working through all media. Building on what is already working, we can begin to discover a design for a positive future, a social gospel for the twenty-first century.

A SPIRIT-MOTIVATED PLAN OF ACTION

One of the keys toward a more gentle, peaceful "birth" is to accelerate the connections among and support for positive innovations already happening. To aid us in this effort, my organization, The Foundation for Conscious Evolution has developed a Website called Cocreation to identify what is breaking through out of what is breaking down. We invite people to enter their projects, from the earliest stage of "I have a dream, I have a vision," to start-up projects and successful projects now underway, and finally to what Eleanor LeCain calls "golden innovation," projects now actually successfully transforming some aspect of society that can be replicated.

Such projects do exist. For example, in the fields of business and economics, micro-credit loans to the very poor (mainly women) are transforming poverty in Bangladesh, South America, and are rapidly spreading. Founder Mohammed Yunus said: "There is no need for poverty in this world." His goal is literally to eliminate poverty worldwide. In environment, we have, for example, the Natural Step. Originating in Sweden, it has developed the agreed-upon principles needed for a sustainable environment and has gained the support of an entire nation, and is now spreading to the United States and elsewhere. In crime rehabilitation, there is Delancey Street in San Francisco, where ex-criminals, drug addicts, and other people who have reached their very last chance learn to run their own businesses, take responsibility for each other, and accept no government funds. These and thousands of other such projects form the basis of the social potential movement. They all spring from the same principles of inclusivity, personal empowerment and responsibility, sustainability, caring, distributed power, cooperation, and co-creation. (We invite readers to check out our Website at http://www.cocreation.org and to enter your projects. Through the Website, you can find teammates, match needs and resources, and learn from what is already working.)

The Foundation for Conscious Evolution is also working closely with Women of Vision and Action (WOVA). WOVA is a global network to support women who are vocationally aroused to fulfill their visions in action. WOVA has developed a Wheel of Transformation which symbolizes all sectors of the social body calling forth projects and initiatives in every field. At the center of the wheel is One Source, symbolizing the creative spirit that connects all being. Vision Keepers surround the One Source, serving as pioneering souls to continue to support that which is breaking through. The interlocking circles represent a planetary DNA, an ever-evolving emergent design for a positive future, based on what is now working.

What works starts with our inner self awakened and ready to commit to doing and being our best, to giving our gift to the world. It moves into the transformation of our personal relationships as parents, spouses, and coworkers. Then it moves outward into our own vocations and callings in the world; then it moves outward into a myriad of projects and efforts that care for, heal, develop a better way; and finally what works results in golden innovations actually changing the world for the good.

I believe that even by the year 2000 we could foster an uprising of social wellness, an epidemic of social ease! This is the purpose of the great evolutionary energy now arising in women. This is the heroine's journey. We each have an opportunity right now to contribute to the evolution of ourselves, our species, and the planet as a whole. Everyone is needed. Everyone's genius fits into some evolving need of the whole system. In this sense we are all called to create a world in which each of us is free to be and do our best. The awakening of the co-creative woman signals the advent of the next stage of human evolution. If we can apply our creativity to the needs of the larger human family, there can be a peaceful transition toward a co-creative society in the third millennium.

Philosopher **Jean Houston** is the author of, among other books, *A Mythic Life* and *A Passion for the Possible,* and a friend and colleague of the late Joseph Campbell and Margaret Mead. Co-founder with her husband Robert Masters of the Foundation for Mind Research, she is an expert in the spectrum of human potential and has taught thousands of people the importance of "living in constant dialogue with myth." The following piece is based on a talk that she gave in 1995.

Living in One's and Future Myths

How often in the midst of the creative moment in which we now find ourselves do we feel the horizons expanding to mythic proportions, knowing ourselves as creators, celebrants of the mass of the world, willing participants in a "restorying" of life and its possibilities? A myth is something that never was but is always happening ... and that happening is upon us and within us, declaring its continued presence in whatever medium we choose to receive the news of our world. Myth is always about soul-making and about the pathos that accompanies the journey of the soul as it travels from outmoded existence to the amplified life in the kingdom. Thus it has much to teach us about where we are right now and where we are headed.

Daily, we see the flow of current events coursing through the runnels of time-deepened mythic themes. The continuing contention between North and South Ireland, between India and Pakistan, between the Israelis and the Palestinians, the interracial struggles of the South Africans recall the presence almost everywhere of the myths of the two contending brothers, Cain and

Abel, Osiris and Seth in Egypt, and among the West African Dogons of Mali, the contending siblings from the star Sirius, Nommo and Ogo. In the Mideast we find dragon kings guarding their lair of oil from pale, corporate princes; snorting fire from the latest and unnatural weaponry. Drugs seep into the veins of those who could be heroes, rendering them as pathetic and dysfunctional as those in ancient tales who are lured to sip the poison brew of mad magicians.

Then there are the money-mad—persons and countries alike—who are driven to endless seeking of an illusive Grail of endless material success because they have lost their inner spirit and look outward for all meaning, all identity. In this, they resemble Percival, who, in failing in his spiritual task, spent years in brooding pursuit of the Grail, doing knightly things with no passion and adding to the further wasting of the wasteland by his unconscious actions and quests. Then there is the remarkable way in which ancient myths—especially creation myths—prefigure in their storied content some of the most exciting speculations on the frontiers of science. Myths of chaos and the making of the world find their very liniments the discoveries of the new physics—the storm god, Marduk, blows his mighty winds into the body of the dragon goddess of chaos, Tiamat, and destroys her, but from her parts creates the world and its creatures. Similarly, chaos theory accounts for the raising of the wind or vibration of energy upon the chaos of unstructured molecular parts and particles to lure pattern into the making. Yahweh breathes upon the deep. The Egyptian god Kheper speaks his own name into the void and the earthmaker of the Winnebago Indians heats himself in a steam hut. With each, a new vibration is put into the inchoate and the world is called into being.

The stories of spiritual principals who are everywhere and all at once recalls the finding in quantum physics concerning the ways in which everything is part of everything else—every electron having knowledge and influence upon every other electron—and each one of us is ubiquitous throughout the great hologram that is our universe. And of course we *are* at the brink of a second genesis, soon to be able to create almost anything—and possibly anyone—we can imagine! (I sometimes wonder that some of these punk hair styles with pink, purple and green hair is not a prefiguration of what some of our future children will look like as they emerge from the womb.)

We look to our myths to discover what to do to recreate our world and, most importantly, what *not* to do to raise up monsters and apparitions. To call genetics and geologies into being is to play God. And so we return to the divine plays of myth to discover the scenarios that await us.

Whenever a society is in a state of breakdown and breakthrough—what I am calling whole-system transition, which we clearly are in the midst of now—it often requires a new social alignment which only myth, with its complex understanding, can bring. For it is the mythologically instructed community that can discover ways in which to mediate the shadow sides of self and society so as to not play out certain archetypal themes which today— if played out unchecked and unorchestrated—could destroy the world.

Joseph Campbell observed how mythology served four major psychological and social functions in any civilization. He said that first, myth provides a kind of bridging between one's local consciousness and the *mysterium tremendum ad fascinans* of the universe, the sheer, vast, overwhelming environment of being. It reconciles local historical space-time with transcendent realms and the eternal forms, the punctual everyday with the durative realm of the eternal.

Second, myth renders an interpretive total image of this relationship, giving in artistic and religious form the revelation to waking consciousness of the powers of its own sustaining source. Third, myth empowers the moral order, brings about a shaping and a conciliation between the individual and the requirements of his climate, geography, culture, and social group. You follow certain ethical precepts because Moses received them on the tablets on Sinai millennia ago. You're a Navajo because many moons ago Spider Woman laid an egg and from it the Navajo people emerged. You are perhaps an American because "four score and seven years ago...."

Now for those societies in whom the local mythology works, there is the experience of both accord with the social order and harmony with the universe. Being several times removed from that harmony by virtue of industrialization and the shattering of natural rhythms, we long for that universe we were once so intimately a part of, that realm of nature and deep belonging. Myth assures us, however, that the universe fits together, even though we live in towering glass houses and get our dogma from the editorials in the newspaper or the preachers on television. When mythological symbols no longer work, there's the sense of alienation from the society often followed by a desperate quest to replace the lost meaning of the once-powerful myths. So currently we are seeing quickie replacement programs—yoga, Eastern philosophies, macrobiotic diets, shamanic rituals, drumming—being tried on and often discarded like so many crosscultural garments that frankly don't fit our needs very well, as they too were grown in a different mythic soil. The demonic aspect of this can be the willingness to assent to the totalitarian embrace after all else fails. Or even the return to a primitivizing fundamentalism that reduces consciousness to a limiting, if comforting, notion of the way things work.

The fourth and most important function of myth is to foster the centering and unfolding of the individual in integrity with himself, the microcosm; his culture, the mesocosm; the universe, the macrocosm; and finally with the pancosmic unity, the ultimate creative mystery which is both beyond and within himself and all things.

THE RISING OF THE SOUL OF THE WORLD

These days, I myself come to myth by way of walkabout. *Walkabout* is a term used to describe the manner in which aboriginal people of Australia track their songlines, that is, the patterns that the great creative ancestor gods have left on the landscape as they created the world and its occupants in the mythical time known as the "Dream Time." Walking hundreds, sometimes thousands of miles in a year, the aboriginals sing and chant the story which describes the events that took place in Dream Time in the area through which they're passing. In doing this, they believe that they call the power of the original sacred creation back into land and plant and animal, as well as partaking of that power themselves.

My present walkabout causes me to travel sometimes as much as a quarter of a million miles a year, jetting, busing, boating, donkey-riding, and yes, even walking. Why do I do this? It's not simply a matter of my professional life as a planetary circuit rider for the development of the possible human and the possible society. It is because everywhere I am seeing not only the harvesting of the world's potentials but the harvesting of the great mythic stories. It is as if we are in a time of radical restorying. It is as if the soul of the world is rising.

I think there is much to be gained by reconsidering the ancient neo-Platonic notion of psyche as the *anima mundi*, the soul of the world. In this time of whole-system transition, it is crucial that we be able to hear psyche speaking through all of the things and events of the world. Psyche speaks to us in myths. Myths do not ground our experiences; rather, they open them to dynamic reflection and movement. They open the questions of life to transpersonal and culturally imaginative reflections. And what is so fascinating is in this crosscultural exchange of myth, something strange is happening.

I remember some years ago, I was sitting in India in a little village on a Sunday. On Sunday, it seemed that much of India closed down to watch on the one television set that each village had the *Ramayana,* the great mythic drama of Sita and Rama and Hanuman, and the rescuing of Sita from the demon Ravana. The *Ramayana* is a gorgeous, opulent epic and it was presented with all the skills and arts of India. As I was sitting on the ground watching with the other villagers, the little old Brahman lady who owned the television set sat down next to me and said, "Oh, I don't like Sita." "You don't?" "No, she too passive. She just sits there waiting to be rescued by Rama. We women in India are much stronger than that. My name is Sita; my husband's name is Rama. He is a lazy bum. If anything happened, I would have to rescue him. We got to change the story so that Sita becomes much more of a heroine. Sita's got to be part of the rescue. We got to change the story." I protested: "But Madam, the story is at least 3,000 years old." To which she responded: "All the more reason why we have to change it." The other ladies sitting around nodded in agreement while their men looked sheepish.

This extraordinary television production was followed by the American series *Dynasty.* Watching it, I felt terribly embarrassed. For here was this schmaltzy stuff being portrayed all over the world as an essential part of Amercian life. Seeing my embarassment, the old lady said: "Don't be so embarassed. Can't you see it is the same story?" "Really, how is that?" I asked in some astonishment. "Well, you got the good lady, you got the bad lady, the Joan Collins lady, you got the good man, you got the bad man. You got the beautiful house, the beautiful palace. You got the traveling through the air in interesting way. You know, you got the drama, you got the good and evil. It is the same story. Yes, indeed." And they were right! But they saw it in the larger mythic context. Because they had the *Ramayana* they had a much richer sense of the deeper meanings inherent even in our silly little soap operas.

THE MYTHIC LIFE

To be true to myth, we must recognize its autonomy, the great stories and actions of the soul functioning within each of us, seemingly quite apart from our own directives or even awareness. Like certain works of art, mythic figures emerge as spontaneous creations, full and richly detailed realities, glimpsed in dreams and visions in moments when the walls between the worlds are let down, leading one from the existentiality of the personal, particular concerns and frustrations of everyday life to the personal universal, with its broadening context and more universal formulation. By engaging in myth you become identified with one or another great archetypal persona.

Because I believe it is vital for us to begin to see our lives in mythic terms, in my seminars all over the world, I take a mythical figure, like Rama or Sita, or a story of a historical being who has through time and legend been rendered mythical, like Jesus or Gandhi, and show how we can see the experience of our own lives reflected and ennobled within the story of that great life.

When actively engaged, these stories lead from the limitations of the personal, particular problems and drama of our life to identity with and fulfillment in the personal-universal drama, with its broadening context and more universal formulations. One becomes Isis and Osiris. With Percival, one takes on the quest for the Grail. One adventures with Odysseus. One assumes the passion and the pathos of Psyche and Eros. One searches for the beloved of the soul with the Persian mystic teacher Rumi. Gradually you discover that these stories are your stories. They bear the amplified pattern of certain rhythms and cadences in one's own life.

You assume the mythic character who is yourself writ large and symbolic happenings appear in undisguised relevance to your personal life and problems. After having been Percival and Isis and Odysseus and Rumi and Christ, one comes back to one's own life enhanced, often with the ability to say, "I have the strength, the depth, the capacity, the wisdom, and the purpose. I will prevail." Your personal journey of transformation is then taken with a powerful sense of identity with the mythic character who can assume the aspect of oneself writ large. In other words, you may not do the work of consciousness in yourself but, by God, if you are attached to a god or an archetype who has a powerful, profound, and pithy story, you will engage in that story. And because of the resonance of the archetypal story with the deep story in yourself, you will be more inclined to do the profound work of the psyche.

But this is not just a way to do personal work. I've also taken leaders of a society and worked with them in a retreat center. Together we would work within the framework of their own cultural mythology. In India, for example, we would work with the *Ramayana* or with the life of Mahatma Gandhi, weaving processes, exercises, and moods of inquiry in such a way as to deepen both their personal unfolding and the betterment of their society. They find in the myths codings for new ways of being, new styles of education, new forms of social development. And what's more interesting is because the personal self has been amplified, they have the courage and the sense of community to carry on and to fight bureaucracy, because bureaucracy is ultimately boring and can rarely withstand the passion and energy of those who have renewed vigor and vision.

This is powerful work. Because if you hang in there with the larger story for three months or six months or a year, eventually your persistence—because you are holding a larger story—prevails.

THE NEW MYTH

There are many myths rising now, but one of the most important is a brand-new version of the hero and heroine's journey, a new and noble journey we must take in search of the possible human in ourselves and others. Once we have found this new possibility we can create the possible society—and, in T. S. Eliot's great lines, "redeem the time, redeem the unread vision of the higher dream." But it first requires inner work because the action on behalf of the redeeming vision has never taken place in society until it has been played out within the soul, especially the soul that allows itself the journey of what I call *palingenesia,* a Greek word that means "constant birthing, being reborn at every moment." This refers to the opportunity to experience new birth on all levels and in all forms of life, inviting a new and deeper reality to enter into time and to be made into a vital part of our daily lives. So *palingenesia* means a rebirth of ourselves and of a larger dimension of reality out of the womb of time.

The soul is the place where the role of the hero and heroine are reconsidered. Traditionally, the hero, according to Joseph Campbell, is the man or woman who has been able to battle past his or her personal and historical limitations to new emergent human forms. One's visions, ideals, and inspirations come pristine from the primary springs of human life and thought. Hence, they are eloquent not of the present disintegrating present society and psyche, but of the unquenched source through which society is reborn. So in becoming hero or heroine, we undertake the extraordinary task of dying to our modernity and being reborn to our eternity. How many of you have done that in the course of your life? How many of you have tried to transcend the little local self and cultural inhibitions, and have sought to journey instead to source your own eternity?

Through the journey of the hero or heroine, you enter archetypal places where the patterns demand, indeed require, divestiture of the old self. It's like Inanna going down into the depths of another world, divesting herself of the different symbols at her authority. It is even like the passion play of Jesus of Nazareth. And then, after the divestiture of the old self, continuing to travel deeper until you reach the eternal place of sourcing and resourcing.

Thus there are two great works for a hero/heroine to perform. The first is to withdraw from everyday life, to the causal zones within to reach that source; the second is to return to everyday life carrying the knowledge one has gained in the depths and put it to use to redeem time and society.

For the first, you go within to seek the great patterns, stories, forgotten magic, and knowings of earlier or ever deeper phases of one's existence to discover the seedings and the codings of evolution to come, and of structures within the self that remain unfulfilled and unfinished. These are often seen as the hidden potentials of the hero/heroine mythologized as secret helpers.

What a task this is. What a glory might be the result. Joseph Campbell once said "if only a portion of that lost totality could be dredged up into the light of day, we should experience a marvelous expansion of our powers, a vivid renewal of life; we should tower in stature. Moreover, if we could dredge up something forgotten not only by ourselves but by our whole generation or our entire civilization, we should indeed become the boon-bringer, the culture hero of the day, a personage of not only historical but world historical moment."

Now I believe that these forgotten or neglected things cannot be thought of as dead and buried but, more profoundly and accurately, as deep codings of the Source, the infinite within, what I have referred to as the "entelechy." *Entelechy* means the dynamic proposiveness that's coded in each one of us: it is the entelechy of an acorn to be an oak tree; it's the entelechy of a baby to be a grown-up human being; it's the entelechy of you and me to be God only knows who or what. And it may be at this time, on the eve of global civilization—and a global mind, as my old friend Teilhard de Chardin suggested, the "noosphere"—that perhaps we are coming to an entelechy of society such as we've never known before.

It's not for nothing that we are seeing the crumbling and crashing and trashing of old ideologies. Maybe we are at the end of history, or rather history as the contention between various isms and ideologies that were useful in their day because they created sufficient stuff to move the world into its planetary phase. But we may be at the end of this kind of contending history. I don't mean the wishy-washy hopes of certain New Agers but rather a dynamic sensibility that we are just beginning to get the senses of in our own psychic lives but not yet in our social lives.

Indeed, this is a great and perhaps one of the most dangerous times in human history. Because suddenly we're being emptied of old cultural beliefs—and what does it mean? I was talking to some old South American Marxists a couple of days ago. They said, "You cannot believe what it means to us to have had the collapse of Russian socialism and Marxism, because it means that it has collapsed not just all over the world but in ourselves and we are left empty, we are vacuums."

These are the times to begin to find the Source and begin to discover new potent social, political, psychological, spiritual forms so that we do not fall back into the first totalitarian embrace that comes along. These are the times. We are the people. And what we are trying to do, all of us now in these times, is to uncover our depths, to get past the vacuum, to have the courage to cleanse, purify, prepare our souls for the difficult task of becoming an instrument through which the Source may play its great music in time and space. As hero/heroines, we are all now the agents for the next dispensation, the inspiration for the bringing of culture and consciousness to its next possibility. Because the hero/heroine's journey is always about the deepening of culture, the universe in its unfolding enters more fully into the local culture. As such, we are agents of the entelechy, the great purpose of life.

Now this heroic role of being an instrument for deepening is vastly different from the traditional concept of the hero as the warring, beleaguered, and shame-ridden male adolescent. Rather, this hero/heroine must be a mature and compassionate adventurer who joins the complexity of her or his local space and time to the eternal domain of consciousness. This is one who risks the uncovering of painful knowings in order to transmute them to higher and more integrated patterns of culture. The hero/heroine is the quester for the possible human and, as fully and he or she can, an exemplar of that possibility.

She or he is always mindful, however, that the quest does not end with the vision or the example but must continue into high service of cleansing and releasing the toxic patterns of the old society and engendering the unfoldment of the possible society. Thus the hero/heroine always lives in a time of dyings, the dyings of the self, of the social sanctions, of society's forms, the dying of standard-brand religions, standard-brand governments, economics, psychologies, relationships. She or he, however, discovers the courage to undergo new birth and then serves as midwife for the continuum of births necessary to redeem both time and society to a higher level.

This describes the second great task of the hero/heroine, as many of the mythologies and records of the spiritual journeys of humankind tell us—which is to return right back to the world after the journey of transformation. So Plato tell us that the philosopher after his illumination in the world of eternal realities must go back into the cave of ordinary society. So Jesus comes back from the desert and Buddha returns from his ascetic meditations. All are deeply changed and from this state they begin teaching the lessons they have learned of *palingenesia,* of life renewed and deep.

One of the best stories I know about this is a very funny joke which says that in Des Moines, Iowa, there is a Mrs. Rosenberg and every year she takes a trip. This year she goes to her travel agent and says, "Listen, I want to go to the swami of the year, Swami Anandanandananda." And he says, "Mrs. Rosenberg, do you realize what's involved? You have to take five planes and then you've got to take an old bus and then you've got to take a yak cart and then you've got to walk for weeks and then you've got to wait in line for a month, and then you're only allowed to say three words to him." "That's all right," she responds. "I've got to go see him." So she takes a plane from Des Moines to New York and New York to Paris and Paris to Athens and Athens to Delhi and Delhi to Kathmandu, where she finally gets on a broken-down bus and goes way up, skirting the kingdom of the Hunza. Then she gets on a yak cart for weeks, and then she walks, and walks, and walks, and then she waits, and waits, and waits. She finally gets up to the front of the cave in which the swami of the year, Swami Anandanandananda, is meditating. His disciples are chanting and the air is filled with incense. A man in yellow robes comes to her and says, "You may only have three words with the great swami." "That's all right, I just need three words." She enters the cave. There he is, the beautiful swami, with great coils of black hair, and a great black beard, his eyes rolled up in his head in *samadhi.* She leans over and says to him: "Morris, come home!"

THE HEROIC JOURNEY

The dearth of heroes in our time—or what is worse, the media's treatment of them as banal—has created a dangerous trend, for we lose the high and holy service of those who would bring us the new births, the next steps. But perhaps one could also argue that it is right for the heroic tradition to be in abeyance for now; perhaps it is necessary for that image to die to its old forms, so that it can be remythologized, and reborn in the light of the Earth's spirit calling us to a new humanity. This new form of heroine is one that takes into account the rise of women to full partnership with men; the impossibility of war; the incredible complexity of current social forms; the rapidity of communication; and the need for a global sensibility.

But when you look at the classical form of the hero's journey, just remember what it entails. Campbell looked at 240 of these forms and he said that it generally tends to follow a certain pattern. First, you have the call to adventure. Now the call is not necessarily, "You-hoo, you're it." Often it's a blunder. You make an immense mistake: you marry the wrong person, go to the wrong school, enter a profession that is not appropriate at all, and from the blunder you fall into the depths of yourself. Because you are so wounded, you are rendered vulnerable and available, and in this state you can more readily make all kinds of connections, with allies—unlikely people, unlikely ideas, different societies and ways of being.

Then, with these allies, you cross the threshold of existence that separates your little local self and the expanded reality that is awaiting you. Often, there follows a period in which you are rewoven for a time in the belly of the whale: you may take up a spiritual practice or go into therapy or in some way pursue paths of regeneration. Then, when you feel ready, you center upon the larger challenge, which is called the Road of Trials or Road of Adventures. The Road of Trials can almost kill you or it can be extraordinarily exhilarating and uplifting. You take on all kinds of challenges you did not know you had the wherewithal to do—until finally you enter into the very depths of yourself where often you find the Beloved of the Soul or even what I refer to as the godself within. Here at the nether reaches of the inner journey you are given or discover a skill or an insight known as the boon. After gaining the boon, there is a magic flight back, back across the threshold, and you return as master or mistress of at least two worlds, able to carry the message and power of the deep world into the world of space and time.

THE TRANSHISTORICAL SHINING THROUGH

So this is the great initiatory journey. As I have indicated, it goes way beyond the personal. Those like James Hillman and others in the school of archetypal psychology are suggesting something that the ancient neo-Platonists knew—

certainly the Gnostics knew—that it is not psyche which exists in us but we who exist in psyche. And that the life of psyche is existent within the realm of God.

In my book *The Search for the Beloved,* I show that many traditions of sacred psychology tend to map three major realms of experience: the first is what I perceive as the realm of the factual historical. I call it "this is me" and I often draw it as little connected boxes of those attributes that give us things like age, gender, profession, etc. The second is the realm of the mythic and symbolic, which I often draw with broken lines, because it has very leaky margins; I call it "we are." And finally there is the realm of the unitive or Source level. That I draw as a great chaotic swirl which is named "I am" in honor of the great statement in the Bible as to His/Her self-identity: "I Am that I Am." The most familiar realm is the "this is me" realm. That refers to everyday ordinary existence. It's bounded and limited by geography, space, calendrical time. When we operate in this realm, we're guided by habit patterns, cultural codings, personal conditionings. Certainly the first two brains, the reptilian-amphibian brain, the old brain, and the old mammalian brain or limbic system, are a part of "this is me." Our reality in the "this is me" realm is structured by definition of gender, physical characteristics, name, local identity, profession, family, other relationships and affiliations—all of which terminate upon your death. "This is me" is the mask we wear, the persona of our everyday existence. It reflects the categories of our curriculum vitae and of our biography. Many of us never quite accept "this is me" as the final statement of who we are, and so we perpetually yearn, as the Gnostics did, for the self from someplace else.

Whenever the "this is me" is seen in and only for itself, without archetypal engagement, it is a cul-de-sac, a world without poetry, art, music, inspiration—without the sacred. Limited to the objective, definable and measurable, we would be stuck in existence all too graphically described by the seventeenth-century philosopher Thomas Hobbes (sometimes called the father of Materialism): "squalid, nasty, brutish and short."

Beyond the realm of "this is me" lies the realm of "we are," the residence of symbols, guiding archetypes, and myths, durative and enduring in an eternal world outside of time and space, as well as thoroughly transhistorical. The "we are" realm functions as the contact point for sacred time and space, the container of that which never was but is always happening.

In times like ours, in which humanity feels that it is approaching the end of history, this transhistorical realm really pulses through. Indeed, virtually every culture has tapped into this archetypal realm to acquire the energies of the stories that illumine rites of renewal and social transformation. For example, since the "we are" realm is the residence of creation myths and the energies of origins, many cultures have their priestesses, priests, and rulers enact the creation myth at the time of the new year. They play the parts of the gods who conquer the principles of chaos, restoring order and recreating the world. In this way, they bring the great durative time of creation and the deeper reaches of the psyche into the punctual circadian time of everyday. Thus, nature is restored and the psyche of both community and the individual is granted the healing powers of new life.

The third realm exists beyond and also within the other two realms—the "I am" being itself pure potency—a realm of love and organicity, the very stuff of reality. It is the realm many know as "God." I do not mean the gods; the gods live in the "we are," but rather God as the unity of being. This is the "I Am" of the "I Am that I Am" in Exodus—not to be confused with the "I" of the human ego. And it is the explicit inclusion of this realm that differentiates sacred psychology from many of the more secular psychologies, like those of the Freudians or the behaviorists, which may tend to avoid, exclude, and even deny this dimension. Sacred psychology assumes that the inherent yearning in every human soul is to experience union with this ultimate reality.

Each realm has its own reality. That is to say, while each is reflected within you, each exists independently of you. You are not only the center of reality—regardless of what various popular psychology may say. Neither do you singularly create all you behold and experience. Nor can you escape from any part of reality. The ancient Sanskrit metaphor of Indra's Net and the modern formulation of quantum physics remind us that we are all woven together. The human challenge is to become fully aware of, full participants in, and fully conscious co-creators of the historic, the mythic, and the unitive realms, especially in times like ours when we are invited by the very depths of being to become co-creators of the future. As Zora Neale Hurston has said: "There are years that ask questions and years that answer them." I would add that these are the times. We are the people. And we are living in the answering years.

Riane Eisler is best known as the author of *The Chalice and the Blade: Our History, Our Future,* which has been translated into sixteen languages and hailed by anthropologist Ashley Montagu as "the most important book since Darwin's *Origins of the Species.*" Her more recent book, *Sacred Pleasure: Sex, Myth, and the Politics of the Body,* probes such basic issues as pain and pleasure, sex and spirituality, and their relation to economics, politics, and the possibilities for our future. Born in Vienna, Eisler grew up in Cuba and obtained degrees in sociology and law at the University of California. She is cofounder of the Center for Partnership Studies in Pacific Grove, California, lectures widely about her cultural transformation theory, and has published in numerous journals ranging from *Political Psychology* and *Behavioral Sciences* to the *UNESCO Courier* and the *Human Rights Quarterly.*

Reclaiming Sacred Pleasure: From Domination to Partnership

When I was a little girl and my parents and I had to flee Nazi Europe, I asked myself the kinds of questions many of us have asked at one point or another in our lives: Does it have to be this way? Does there have to be so much brutality, so much pain, so much violence, so much hurtfulness? Years later, in the course of my research, I asked further questions: Why don't we have a more equitable, peaceful, and caring world when we humans have such a profound yearning for love, beauty, and justice? Why haven't we been able to get rid of both war and the war of the sexes? Why, when seeking pleasure and avoiding pain is the most basic human drive, do so many of our stories idealize and even sacralize the infliction or suffering of pain? What can we do, both personally and through social and political action, to change all this?

My books *The Chalice and the Blade* and *Sacred Pleasure* address these questions. Here I want to focus on our foundational relations—our intimate relations, our sexual relations, our parent-child relations—that involve what I call the politics of the body.

I focus on these primary relations, which entail intimate bodily touch, because it is through these relations that we are unconsciously conditioned, on the most basic neurological and cellular level, to either accept fear and the threat of pain as normal, or to expect relations based on the mutual giving and receiving of pleasure. What we thus learn about our intimate relations not only profoundly affects our day-to-day personal lives, it also profoundly affects the construction of our families, our religions, our education, our politics, our economics.

In other words, whether we learn to have relations governed primarily by domination and submission, by chronic violations of human rights, or by respect for human rights in our sexual relations and our parent-child relations does not happen in a vacuum. It happens in a larger social and cultural context that both affects, and is affected by, our intimate lives.

For example, for some years now we have been hearing a great deal of talk about leaving behind the dysfunctional family based on control. But the point is that our parents did not invent these kinds of relations; they learned them. These traditions of domination were passed on from generation to generation in earlier societies governed by despotic kings, societies where the male head of household had absolute authority, societies where pain and the threat of pain was the primary means of maintaining social order.

Similarly, in some quarters, for example the so-called Promise Keepers, we still hear that men have to "wear the pants"—that is, that they must be dominant in their relations with women. It even used to be said—as it is still said in some cultures today—that a man beating a woman or even killing her if she shows any romantic interest in another man is justifiable, as it is his traditional prerogative to control the woman he "loves."

Such dominator traditions are appropriate for a system of human relations where rigid rankings of domination—be it man over woman, man over man, tribe over tribe, or nation over nation—are enforced through pain or the fear of pain. But they are not appropriate for what we humans most want: trust instead of fear, love instead of hate, pleasure instead of pain. The cultivation of such attributes requires a different system of social, economic, political relations: one that I have called the partnership model. Societies that orient to this model are more equitable and nonviolent. Foundational to the partnership model are families and religious, educational, economic, and political institutions that promote equal partnership between the two halves of humanity: women and men.

THE STRUGGLE FOR OUR FUTURE

Most of us are still used to thinking of the struggle for our future in terms of the conventional labels of right versus left, capitalist versus communist, or secular versus religious. But if we look at this struggle from the new perspective of what I have identified as the partnership and dominator social alternatives, we begin to see a larger dynamic that includes not only relations in what is conventionally discussed as politics and economics, but also our most intimate personal relations. Specifically, we see that the normative ideal for intimate relations is very different depending on the degree of orientation to either the dominator or partnership model.

In societies or periods where we find rigid rankings of domination—whether on the basis of gender, race, religion, caste, class, or ethnic origin—we also see gender relations characterized by a painful "war of the sexes" and parent-child relations in which children painfully learn that their parents' orders must never be questioned. This is not coincidental. It is because these intimate relations are foundational to the construction of the entire social system.

Also foundational is how a society or period constructs its sacred stories, teachings, and images. For instance, the teachings of Jesus and some of the earlier Hebrew prophets that we should do unto others as we would have them do unto us—teachings about caring, compassion, and nonviolence—are religious teachings that would support a partnership way of living. But at the same time, be it in Western or Eastern religions, there are also teachings about fighting "holy wars" to kill "infidels" and "sinners" and "honor killings" of women suspected of the slightest sexual independence. These kinds of teachings are appropriate for a dominator rather than partnership society—a society such as the theocracies of ancient history and despotic Middle Eastern so-called fundamentalist regimes today.

This is why the struggle that we see today in our world is not something that can be understood by using old categories such as religious versus secular, capitalist versus communist, or right versus left. For instance, one can see dominator regimes on both the right and left, the most blatant examples in recent history being Hitler's Germany and Stalin's Soviet Union. And despotic regimes can be both religious or secular, communist or capitalist.

The struggle for our future hinges on the outcome of the underlying struggle between the partnership or dominator model for human relations in all spheres of life, from our families to politics and economics. It is a struggle that we need to actively engage in. And it is one that we see played out all around us in the current struggle over gender roles and relations, parent-child relations, family organization, and sexual relations.

On the one hand we are bombarded by a barrage of images constantly linking sex with violence and domination. This is not only in pornography, but in mainstream entertainment. Children sit glued to their television sets watching body parts flying all over the place, watching people being hacked to pieces, blown up, beaten—and if the hero prevails by using all this violence, he gets the girl. So even here we see this linking of romance, of sex, with domination and violence.

On the other hand, there are millions of people spending millions of dollars going to workshops, seminars, and retreats, buying books, video cassettes, audio cassettes, to learn how we can have more caring, more mutually satisfying, more mutually pleasurable relations—to relearn how to love and even how to touch in more partnership ways.

But how did we get to this place where we have to relearn how to love and even how to touch? Why do we have to relearn how to have more meaningful, more pleasurable, more mutually satisfying relations instead of hurtful ones? Has there never been a time when the partnership model prevailed in human society?

RECLAIMING OUR HIDDEN HERITAGE

We are all familiar with the version of history that tells us we have no choices. War and the war of the sexes, chronic violence and misery, so this story goes, have been with us since the dawn of civilization and even before. They are just human nature.

But thanks to what the British archaeologist James Mellaart calls a "veritable revolution in archaeology," a new story is beginning to emerge. It is that the first cradles of civilization are not only much older than was previously thought, but that they also seem to have been organized differently from what came later. This is what we are learning from scholars such as UCLA archaeologist Marija Gimbutas, Greek archaeologist Nicolas Platon, and others, including myself. These findings are challenging the conventional interpretations still generally taught today, as the new data do not fit into the old theories about human history and prehistory.

While my research has focused primarily on what is generally called early Western civilization—Europe and the Middle East—the same pattern has been found by scholars in other areas. For instance, in China, a cross-disciplinary team of scholars at the Chinese Academy of Social Sciences in Beijing applied my Cultural Transformation Theory to China and in 1995 published a book called *The Chalice and the Blade in Chinese Culture,* which is available from the Center for Partnership Studies in Pacific Grove, California.

Rather than chronically violent and warlike, the earliest cradles of civilization, going back 10,000 years to the beginning of the Neolithic or first Agrarian Age, seem to have been more peaceful. This is the first element of the partnership model.

In the archaeological record, we find for these early cradles of civilization few indications of destruction through warfare, few indications of fortifications. That is not to say that there was no violence. But it was not built into the system; it was not institutionalized nor idealized. Therefore, we also do not find in the very extensive art of these societies the kinds of images that we are so used to: images that idealize so-called heroic warfare, images that idealize hallowed rulers dragging their prisoners back in chains, images that, like the stories about the Greek god Zeus's many rapes of both goddesses and women, link sex with domination and violence. In fact, the images of sex, of the human body, of man's body, of woman's body, and of how two bodies should relate are primarily life-affirming, pleasure-affirming images. They are images in which sex, the human body—matters we have been taught to associate with the obscene—are actually part of the sacred.

The second thing we see is that while there are some differences in status and in wealth, as Mellaart writes, they are not extreme. In other words, while they were not ideal societies, they were more equitable.

Third, just as they did not view sex the same way as we have been taught, their spirituality was not one that places man and spirituality over woman and nature. The way that they imaged the powers that govern the universe was not as we have been taught, as an armed male deity—Jehovah with his thunderbolt, Zeus with his sword (actually Zeus has both a thunderbolt and a sword, so that if we didn't get that the highest power is the power to dominate and destroy the first time, we get it the second time). Rather, they imaged the powers that govern the universe more in terms of the power symbolized since remote antiquity by the Chalice or Holy Grail: the power to give life, to nurture life, and to illuminate life. They imaged the earth as a Great Mother from whose womb all of life ensues and to whose womb all life returns at death, like the cycles of vegetation, once again to be reborn.

But—and this is very important—this Great Goddess had both divine daughters and divine sons. Moreover, one of the central stories in this earlier, more nature-based religion that saw all of nature as interconnected and as imbued with what we call the divine, was the sacred marriage of the Goddess with her divine lover.

This takes us to the fourth element of the partnership configuration: that these were not matriarchies, or societies governed only by women. That was the interpretation made by nineteenth-century scholars when evidence of these earlier societies already began to surface as archaeology was still in its infancy. They actually were societies where a partnership relationship between the two halves of humanity—women and men linking, interconnected—was primary. That is not to say that there were no rankings. But they were what I call hierarchies of actualization rather than domination. These are more flexible hierarchies in which power is not viewed so much as power over as power to and power with: the kind of power described in the progressive management literature today as inspiring and supporting, rather than controlling, others.

SEX AND SOCIETY

For some people, findings about earlier societies that were more peaceful and equitable—in other words, societies that oriented more to the partnership model—are shocking. But actually, we have long had information about the existence of societies where women were not dominated by men and where qualities and actions still stereotypically labeled as "feminine" (whether they reside in women or men) were highly valued.

To begin with, when archeology was just emerging as a science in the nineteenth-century, archaeologists found that for thousands of years there were societies where a Great Goddess was worshiped—although, as noted above, they mislabeled the societies as matriarchies. But long before then, we had many clues to the existence of these societies. In fact, we find these clues in some of the world's best-known and most ancient stories. Talking about these stories is a good way of spreading awareness about our hidden partnership heritage—and showing that we have alternatives for our future.

The best-known story in Western civilization is the story of Adam and Eve. What does it tell us? It tells us that there was a time when woman and man lived in harmony with one another and with nature. Where was it? It was in a garden. Of course, the Neolithic societies, the first agrarian societies, planted the first gardens on this earth.

The story speaks of an Earthly Paradise. This does not mean that these early societies were ideal. Only by comparison with what came later, after the shift to the dominator model, were they remembered as ideal in folk memory.

That same story also gives us clues to this shift—which the archaeological evidence shows took place during a very violent, chaotic period in our prehistory, beginning in Europe and the Middle East about 5,000 years ago. In this story, we learn that when Eve seeks knowledge independently, a male deity decrees that henceforth woman be subservient to man. And in the very next story, the story of Cain and Abel, we learn that now brother kills brother. So there it is: war and the war of the sexes, the shift to the dominator model.

When I was a child, I always wanted to know what it was like before the "henceforth" spoken of in the Bible. And once again we can find clues to that if we look at some of our earliest stories. A particularly revealing source are some of the first known writings of Western civilization: the writings from ancient Sumer called the Hymns of Inanna.

Inanna was the Sumerian Queen of Heaven and Earth, the goddess of love and procreation. In the Hymns of Inanna we read of her sacred marriage to the god-king Dumuzi. It is an erotic, sacred hymn, sexual and tender. We read, "He put his hand in her hand. He put his hand to her heart. Sweet is the sleep of hand-to-hand. Sweeter still the sleep of heart-to-heart."

This then was a story that celebrated the pleasures of love, the pleasures of sex, the pleasures of the body as part of *sacred* literature! But by the time the Hymns of Inanna were rendered to cuneiform—inscribed on clay tablets (which is why they were preserved)—there was great disequilibrium throughout the fertile regions of the world. Wave after wave of nomadic pastoralist invasions were coming in from the more arid, less hospitable areas of the globe, areas where, if you will, the Earth was not a good mother. And after each wave, after the destruction they brought, when civilization resumed its course, it was in a very different direction: in a dominator rather than partnership direction.

This is manifested by the myths that we begin to get later (though we don't have space to go into them here, many can be found in *Sacred Pleasure* and *The Chalice and the Blade*). Suffice it to say that by the end of the Middle Ages, some very peculiar things had happened to the ancient sacred marriage between the Goddess and her divine partner.

OUR DOMINATOR INHERITANCE

What we now find is not called the sacred marriage but the mystical marriage. And this mystical marriage is very different from the ancient sacred marriage in two critical respects. First, the role of the Goddess—the female part—has been completely written out. It is now a mystical marriage between an all-powerful male god and his male priesthood.

As Luther wrote, "God chose for his son the Church as his bride." And when individual mystics write about this mystical marriage, they also write of it as a very unequal union. Most of these mystics whose writings we have were men, so again, it is still a marriage between males, with no females in it.

But there is another drastic change—one also characteristic of a shift from partnership to domination. Now instead of celebrating the pleasures of the body, the pleasures of sex, the pleasures of love, these mystics write about punishing the body, about violence to the body, about control and domination over the body. They flagellate themselves, they wear hairshirts, they lie on beds of nails, they tattoo their bodies with hot irons. In short, they torment their bodies—but they still write about all of this in erotic terms.

So we see that a radical transformation of both myth and reality has taken place. We see that the shift from a partnership to a dominator model of human relations has resulted in what I have called the pleasure to pain shift. It is this dominator baggage that we need to leave behind if we are to reclaim sex, love, power, and pleasure, if we are to reclaim what we humans most want and need: caring connections, mutual relations where pleasure rather than pain can be primary.

Now before going further, I want to clarify what I mean when I say pleasure. I'm not talking about pleasure in that frantic sense of "fun" through which people, in an addictive sense, compulsively seek escape from pain in dominator societies. I am talking about pleasure in the sense of satisfying what we all deeply yearn for, both women and men—which is love, caring, mutually satisfying intimate relations, and a feeling of safety—which you can never have in a dominator relationship. A dominator relationship is a lose-lose game for everybody. Not only do the dominated feel unsafe, but so do those who dominate because of this volcano underneath them, and also because there is always the danger of other dominators displacing them. With this mind-set, all you get is the mentality of: If I don't control, somebody will control me.

This myth that the only alternative to being dominated is to do the dominating is, of course, one of the cornerstones of the system that we are trying to leave behind. Which is why it is so important for us to reexamine how, with the shift from a more partnership-oriented to a more dominator-oriented way of living, came also a fundamental re-mything—a process which, as I detail in my books, quite literally stood reality on its head. We now find myths idealizing brutality and cruelty as "heroic," demeaning the characteristics that were henceforth to be associated with women and "the feminine" as "soft" and "wimpy," that is, unsuitable for "real men." We find myths justifying at every turn in-group versus out-group thinking and actions, as well as a social structure in which only a small elite of men control the wealth and the mass of people live in poverty. In short, we find a social structure in which the in-group of "mankind" and the out-group of the female "other" is taught every child from earliest infancy as a template for all other in-group versus out-group relations, be they the "superiority" of a race, religion, or ethnic group over another.

None of what we have been examining is to say that we need to leave everything in our myths behind. Rather, we need to carefully reexamine our myths, using the templates of the partnership and dominator models. We need to understand the historical context in which they arose. We then need to sort out those elements we want to reinforce and those that we want to leave behind.

From this new perspective, we can see that stories such as the expulsion of the primal woman and man from Paradise for Eve's "sin" in seeking knowledge independently have served to maintain a dominator model. The domination of one half of humanity over another—now said to be divinely ordained—serves as a model for all other rankings of domination. And just as woman was presumably put on earth solely to serve and help man, this serves as a model for relations between "superior" groups with other "inferior" or "dangerous" groups which were, like women, presumably put on this earth solely to serve their masters.

Moreover, we can also see that neither war nor the war of the sexes are inevitable except in societies or periods orienting primarily to the dominator rather than partnership model. The reexamining and sorting out of ancient myths that have presented to us a dominator model as the only human possibility is one step to help accelerate the shift to a less painful, more peaceful, equitable, and pleasurable way of living.

THE SHIFT FROM PAIN TO PLEASURE

There are many other things that we can and need to do in terms of personal action and in terms of social and political action—because it is all melded together—to accelerate this shift. Or, I should say, to complete this shift—because we are already in it to some extent or we couldn't be talking about these kinds of things, or we would be burned at the stake.

A critical lesson is that in addition to being more peaceful, pleasure-oriented, and equitable, with a more nature-based and immanent spirituality, a key part of the partnership configuration is that rather than being male-dominated, women themselves and the values we have been taught to associate with women and the "feminine" are accorded high value.

Indeed, one of the central findings from my work is something that, once articulated, seems perfectly self-evident. This is that the way that a society organizes the relations between the two halves of humanity—which is what women and men are—not only profoundly affects our day-to-day relations, our life options as women and men; it also profoundly affects the kinds of families we have (whether they are partnership or dominator oriented), the kinds of religions we have, the kinds of laws, education, politics, economics—and whether so-called feminine values and activities, such as nonviolence, caring for children, and cleaning up the environment, can be given economic priority.

This is extremely important if we are to cut through the political confusion of our time and begin to see political choices as either fostering partnership or domination. For example, currently we are being told that there is enough money for activities that are in the dominator model stereotypically associated with masculinity—for example, weapons for fighting wars, even though they cause terrible pain. There is, we are told, enough money to build more and more prisons—once more for punitive activities stereotypically associated with the male head of household in dominator families. But there is, so we are told, no money for feeding children, for child-care centers, for nurturing activities, or for cleaning up our environment—which are partnership values that, in dominator thinking, are stereotypically considered feminine activities. When we begin to see the world in this way, we can begin to reinforce with our votes and with our dollars the kind of society we wish to create.

I want to emphasize two points here. First, the orientation to a partnership or dominator model is always a matter of degree in any society. In other words, we are not talking of absolutes.

Second, none of what we are dealing with is a question of anything inherent in women or men. Look at all the men who today are redefining fathering, nurturing children, doing what used to be considered "women's work." They're diapering their babies, they're feeding their children. You talk to these men and they say, "It feels so good, I have so much pleasure from these more 'feminine' activities." At the same time, women are becoming more assertive, a stereotypically "masculine" trait in the dominator definitions of masculinity and femininity.

In other words, we've got to be very careful about this whole thing about the "deep masculine" and the "deep feminine" that is marketed today in New Age Jungian clothes. What we are talking about is not masculine or feminine in any essential way—it is part of both women's and men's shared human repertoire.

THE STRUGGLE FOR OUR FUTURE

What else can help us in this transformation to partnership? First, we need to be aware that there has been an underlying dynamic in modern history: the tension between the forward movement toward a partnership way of life and the dominator systems' resistance, as well as periodic regressions toward a more rigid dominator model. We can then see that some of this regression today comes under the guise of religious fundamentalism—which is in fact dominator fundamentalism. It is the reimposition of a way of living in which men control women, a small group of men controls all of us (including our intimate relations and how we think), and violence is again built into the system and justified as divinely ordained in holy wars, in violence against children, against women, against those one disagrees with.

We need to be aware that we have choices and to make others aware that they do, too. We need to help others become aware of what we see all around us: that human relations can be structured in ways that are mutually pleasurable or in ways that are very much based on fear and the threat of pain—relations where even pleasure becomes distorted.

We can also begin to see that some of what is pulling us back towards the dominator model—and this is a very important point—comes not only from the right; some of it comes from people who consider themselves liberals and who are in almost every other way trying to help complete the shift to a partnership society. The people who are really trying to pull us back to the dominator society recognize the centrality of intimate relations, of relations that involve touch, of sexual relations, of gender relations, of parent-child relations, to the kind of system they believe is divinely ordained—one based on rankings of domination, on fear and force and pain. But many people who are on the liberal side still do not see these connections. They fail to recognize that images linking sex with violence and portraying sexual violence as natural, even pleasurable, have everything to do with our pain orientation.

Many leaders from the religious right condone, and even command, violence against those they perceive as "enemies" and argue that since we are inherently evil the only way that we can be governed is by strict controls, by punishments. By contrast, many people from the liberal side condemn violence and domination. But the moment that violence and domination are put together with sex, the moment there is a nude body in the picture, they think it's fine—arguing that images constantly linking sexual relations (and by implication, male/female relations) with violence are harmless.

They fail to recognize that this constant linking of sex and violence, sex and domination—what I call the erotization of domination and violence—is actually one of the linchpins of a dominator model. And they insist on this even though there are many social scientists, men like Linz, Donnerstein, and Penrod, who have in their experiments come to the same conclusions I have in my research: that through a process of emotional misattribution, these images condition men, and to some extent also women, not only to become insensitive to domination and violence but to actually get sexually aroused by it.

There are even studies by social psychologists that show something that we are seeing in our own time: that when there is an intensification of images eroticizing violence, linking sex and violence, Don Juan–type stories of men who are heroes but who brutalize women, as in Clint Eastwood or Arnold Schwarzenegger films, that this is a predictor of periods of movement towards more violence, towards a more repressive system—in other words, toward dominator regression. And that's what we have been seeing today.

So we need to understand that these images are not a question of freedom of expression. Quite the contrary: this constant bombardment experienced by both adults and children, in music, in videos, in movies, in video games, of the linking of sex with violence and domination, is very dangerous.

I am not advocating censorship. But people who make money from these images must be held accountable for the consequences. Moreover, we have to educate ourselves and others to the negative consequences not only for our intimate relations, but our social system as a whole. For on an unconscious, almost neural level, the erotization of domination and violence serves to condition us to accept relations of domination and submission not only as normal, but even as desirable.

We hear a great deal of talk about the modern sexual revolution. There has been a real sexual revolution: the recognition that there is nothing wrong with our bodies (we all get one); that sex is not dirty (everyone has sexual urges); that sex is not evil or sinful (though sexual violence and domination are); that women as well as men have sexual urges and have a great capacity for sexual pleasure; and that we are all entitled to education about sexuality, including education about family planning. That is all part of the movement toward the kind of sexuality that goes with a partnership rather than dominator model. So also is the recognition that some people are homosexual, as well as something scientists are beginning to examine: what Masters and Johnson call the pleasure bond, the giving and receiving of sexual pleasure, as an important basis for intimate relations.

But there is also a great deal going on that is part of the pull back toward the kind of sexuality appropriate for a dominator rather than partnership model of sexual relations. Not only this constant erotization of violence and domination through movies, CDs, and video games, but also the making of sex dirty again by associating it only with pre-adolescent dirty talk, by constantly using slang sexual terms, as insults, as swear words, to characterize something ugly, something that we're angry about.

ORGANIZING FOR ACTION

In our attempts to help move society from dominator- to partnership-based, there are many actions we can take, from writing letters to networks, advertisers, and publishers telling them that we will not buy their products if they broadcast, publish, and sponsor images and stories eroticizing domination and violence, to working to substitute for such images healthier, more pleasure-directed images of human sexuality. We need to remember that the far right has organized very effectively—exerting enormous influence even though they are only a small percentage of the population—but they are far less concerned about violence than about sex. So we also need to support positive sex education as well as work against education for violence and domination.

We need to become partnership fundamentalists. So much of what is today being called religious fundamentalism, has, if you really think about it, very little to do with the teachings of Jesus—teachings of caring, compassion, empathy, and nonviolence, of equality between men and women. These are partnership teachings, stereotypically feminine values. Instead, what these leaders of the so-called Christian Right preach is domination, hate, violence, anger, punishment, and fear—the staples of the dominator model. In fact, of course, Jesus taught nothing of the kind.

On the contrary, Jesus violated the norms of his times—norms such as those we find today in Iran and other Muslim fundamentalist states, norms of strict sexual segregation, designed to "keep women in their place." Jesus stopped the stoning of a woman—a practice that we see today also in these religious dominator nations. Jesus freely associated with women and never taught anything about strengthening male power over women. On the contrary, he taught that men should no longer be able to throw out a wife at will—which is why he preached against divorce (which only men could unilaterally obtain, as is still the case in some religious dominator societies today). He also said nothing about keeping women out of the priesthood. In fact, we know from the official Scriptures that some of the leaders in early Christian communities were women and we know from the Gnostic Gospels that Mary Magdalene was a major figure in early Christian leadership.

We need to untangle what is going on in our time and reclaim some of the emotionally laden words and ideas being misused by dominator fundamentalists. We are being told that we need to go back to the traditional ways of doing things. I often say, "I'm really a very traditional person, except I go back to much older traditions." What the word *traditional* has become is a code word for dominator relations.

We also need to understand what this whole thing about family values is about, and to reclaim both family and values for a partnership way of relating. Family values, as used today by dominator fundamentalists, is *not* about valuing families. It's about pushing us back to a male-headed, male-controlled family where women can manipulate but can't assert themselves (which, again, is a wonderful recipe for misery for both women and men) and where children are taught from very early on the fundamentals that will make them fit into a dominator society: that caring touch is also coercive touch and that love is conditional on absolute obedience to orders, no matter how unjust or how painful they may be.

If we look at the dominator psyche, we begin to see why there is today a whole literature on denial. Because people in dominator families have to repress their feelings of anger and frustration. And then, since they can't express them against those who have caused them pain, they deflect them by scapegoating others rather than taking responsibility for their actions. That is what we seeing today as part of an organized dominator regression. Incited by demagogic leaders under the guise of morality and religion, we see the scapegoating of minorities, immigrants, women (poor women, in particular), gays—groups that are perceived as weak and groups that are perceived as being feminine (which in the dominator mind is the same as weak).

Using the partnership and dominator models as tools, we can recognize these patterns and go beyond the religious rhetoric to the realities. And we can get past old-fashioned categories such as right versus left, capitalist versus communist, religious or not religious, and become conscious participants in the modern Partnership Movement.

FULL PARTICIPATION OF MEN AND WOMEN

A key part of the Partnership Movement agenda goes to the matter of how the roles and relations between the female and male halves of humanity are socially constructed. As I mentioned earlier, such choices not only affect our day-to-day lives within our families and communities, they also affect all of our life choices as women and men. They profoundly affect everything about a society, from what kind of family we have, whether it's an authoritarian or democratic family, to what kind of religion, politics, and economics we have.

Do we want a religion where half of humanity can't get into the priesthood and therefore are deprived of moral authority—of the authority to assert what is right or wrong, including what is done to us? Or do we want one where all members of our species can assume spiritual leadership? Do we want a politics in which half of humanity only has token representation in a "democracy," or a real representative democracy? Do we want an economics where we always seem to have money for what is stereotypically associated with men—weapons, war, prisons—and never seem to have enough money for so-called women's work—feeding children, caring for people's health, caring for our environment—or one where these life-sustaining and life-enhancing activities are given the highest social and economic priority?

We need to vigorously work not only against gender discrimination, but against any gender stereotypes that stand in our way. Certainly violent behaviors are not masculine, much less heroic. They are mean and hurtful behaviors. And being submissive is not feminine. It is what people who have been socially, legally, and culturally disempowered in societies orienting closely to the dominator model are forced to do. By stripping such dysfunctional behaviors, which support relations based on domination and submission, from notions of masculine and feminine, we can leave them behind and instead reinforce positive partnership-promoting traits and behaviors. By doing this, we not only move toward gender equity but also facilitate the movement to a society where the American ideals of democracy, social justice, and community can be realized.

THE NEW POLITICS OF PARTNERSHIP

Ultimately what I am talking about is extremely political once we get used to thinking of politics in terms of the Partnership Movement countered by dominator model resistance and regression. If we really look at what has been happening since the eighteenth-century Enlightenment, we see that it has been a time of cumulating challenges to one form after another of entrenched traditions of domination, countered by dominator resistance and periodic regressions. We aren't taught history that way, unfortunately, which makes it hard for us to see—and this is important in a time of dominator regression such as ours—that we have actually been moving, in starts and stops, toward a partnership model for the last 300 years.

First we see the "rights of man" movement. What was that? It was a challenge to the so-called divinely ordained right of kings to rule over their subjects in despotic ways. Monarchies were, at least in some world regions, replaced by republics. If we look at the antislavery movement, the abolitionist movement, and then the twentieth-century civil rights and anticolonial movements, we see that they challenged the "divinely ordained right" of one race to dominate, even enslave, another. Indeed, all the modern movements for greater social and economic justice have been movements against economic oppression and domination. Even the ecology movement is a challenge to traditions of domination: to man's once celebrated "conquest of nature," which at this stage of technological development is about to do us in. Finally, we are beginning to regain the consciousness that everything in nature is interconnected and that nature was not created just for us to exploit, that we need to be in partnership with nature.

From this larger perspective, we can see that we have made many gains. But we can also see something else, something that has made it very difficult for us to hang on to, and build on, these gains.

Most of the energy of these changes has gone into what I have called the top of the dominator pyramid: the so-called public sphere of economic and political relations from which women and children were excluded; in other words, to what was once aptly called the "men's world." Until recently, the foundational relations—parent-child, woman-man, sexual, intimate relations, relations in the so-called private rather than public sphere—have not received as much attention. Yes, in the past 200 years we've had the feminist movement, which challenges the "divinely ordained" right of men to rule over the women and children in the "castles of their homes." But it is still vigorously resisted and even many liberals fight it or ignore it, failing to understand its foundational importance to any real and lasting progress toward a more equitable and less violent society. And without true gender equality, the foundations remain for chronic dominator regressions.

BUILDING THE FOUNDATIONS FOR A PARTNERSHIP WORLD

The exciting thing about our time is that we now stand at the threshold of an integrated stage in the cumulating Partnership Movement. Many so-called "private" issues are becoming political issues, issues that we didn't even talk about not so long ago. For example, we are beginning to have a children's rights movement, getting away from the old notion that the male head of household (and his wife by delegated power) has absolute authority over children. We used to hear, "spare the rod and spoil the child." Today we call it what it is: child abuse. We used to hear, "if rape is inevitable, relax and enjoy it." Today we recognize that this is a crime of violence. But it's not only a crime of violence, it's a way of maintaining domination by one half of humanity over the other through terror.

If a man beat a stranger, he used to be sent straight to jail, but if he beat somebody he said he loved, someone that he had a sexual relationship with, at best he was walked around the block until he cooled off so he could do it again. Today we are recognizing this for what it is: another tradition of domination.

Once we recognize what those dominators who want to pull us back have long recognized—that gender relations and parent-child relations are foundational relations—then we can move toward an integrated politics of partnership. And precisely because we're at the threshold of such an integrated politics of partnership—a politics that focuses on partnership intimate relations, on partnership gender and sexual relations, on a democratic family— there is also intensification of the dominator systems' resistance. If we recognize that living systems seek to maintain themselves, and that dominator systems maintain themselves through violence, then we can be more effective and we can stop being so disheartened, as so many people are today. Then we can take full advantage of this time of social disequilibrium—which is the only time transformative change can take place—and focus not just on the crisis but on the opportunity to move from a reactive to a proactive integrated partnership political agenda.

This is not to say that we will inevitably break through. But we have already made tremendous progress despite enormous resistance and intermittent regressions—and we need to teach that to our children. We need to teach children our real history, including the struggle of women for freedom from horribly oppressive traditions and the struggle to free children from horribly oppressive traditions.

This is hardly a struggle against men. Boys and men suffer terribly in a dominator society. Men must fight in chronic wars, be wounded, die. If they are sensitive they are despised as sissies, as weak sisters. So men in rigid dominator societies have to deaden their empathy, deaden what makes them human. Of course, many men have always refused to do this. But now we are seeing it in the open, with men increasingly challenging the notion that male violence is heroic, that "real masculinity," as in the *Iron John* story, means killing an opponent and therefore getting to mate.

As I have emphasized, working to change how we relate in our personal intimate relations is not enough by itself. We also have to work together to change society. Sometimes when I speak I say, "trying to heal yourself in a dominator society is like trying to go up on a down escalator." You spend your life trying to heal, instead of being able to realize your incredible human potentials. So we always come back to organized legal, social, and political action. And, yes, to changing our economics.

Why should a society give so little real economic value to the work without which it could not go on, the essential "women's work" of caring for children, of caring for the elderly, of caring for people's health in a family, of maintaining a clean and healthy home environment? Right now, as we shift from an industrial to postindustrial society, we will soon see a redefinition of what is productive work, because we are seeing fewer jobs in what has traditionally been described as work. So we have a window of opportunity: a unique chance for social and economic inventions that give economic value to this essential work of caring and caretaking. To this end, I have recently been involved in founding a Clearinghouse for Economic Inventions that recognize the value of caring work. A concept paper on this can be found on the Center for Partnership Studies Website (http://www. partnershipway.org).

Finally, we also have an opportunity, in this time when there is so much talk of a new spirituality, to take a new look at what is sacred and what is profane. Many of the images that are our heritage from our five-thousand-year dominator detour sacralize the infliction or the suffering of pain. As is appropriate for a dominator model, they are about a vengeful God, about divine retribution, about terrible punishments, about saints and martyrs, pierced, incinerated, tortured. And it is not just in the West. For example, in the *Mahabharata* we read about deities hacking each other to pieces. Why should that be part of the sacred? The reason is that in a dominator model of society the sacred is associated with fear, with fear of pain from those who dominate—beginning with punitive angry gods.

That takes me to the title of one of my books: *Sacred Pleasure.* The notion may sound heretical to some. But in a partnership society, we can associate the sacred with pleasure rather than pain, with wonder rather than fear. We can celebrate the miracle, the wonder, of the enormous pleasure that has been given to us by the grace of evolution, uniquely, I think, of all species, not only when we are loved but when we love, not only when we are touched in caring ways, but when we touch another—a child, a lover, even a pet—in a way that gives pleasure.

That is what we need to sacralize. Then we can move to a world of very different myths and realities. There will still in this world be myths sacralizing suffering, as pain and death are part of the cycles of nature and of life. But, as

I write in *Sacred Pleasure,* "there will be many more myths about the awe, wonder, and ecstasy that has been given us to feel, including the joy, awe, wonder, and ecstasy of physical love." There will in this world "be stories about how we humans are conceived in delight and rapture, not in sin. There will be images spiritualizing the erotic, rather than eroticizing violence and domination. And rather than myths about our salvation through violence and pain, there will be myths about our salvation through caring and pleasure."

Z Budapest is an internationally known author, lecturer, and feminist activist. Her books include *The Holy Book of Women's Mysteries, Grandmother of Time, Grandmother Moon, Goddess in the Office, Goddess in the Bedroom,* and *Summoning the Fates.* Through The Women's Spirituality Forum (WSF) she organizes biannual festivals called Goddess 2000. She lives in Oakland, California.

Harmonizing with the Fates

Before all else, know that we are always in deep and energetic transformation. Always. Not just at the end of a millennium, but in the middle of it and at the start of it—always. These constant transformations do not depend on our particular way of counting of time: a millennium doesn't really exist, except in human calendars.

What does exist are celestial wheels within wheels, the universal bodies of the ancient Zodiac, the planets of Pluto and Neptune and Uranus. Layered like a wedding cake, the Sun and Moon, the planets Venus and Mars, color, modify, define, and express each other with their influences on Earth and its inhabitants. Some wheels of life are turning just now, some already have turned, some will begin to turn at any moment. These forces in concert were called many things—Divine Providence, Fate, the Astrological Ages. All these names denote a kind of order, a dependable system which we don't quite fully understand but that we know is present.

In *Summoning the Fates,* I explore these forces in great detail. This article will only touch lightly on the most obvious features of destiny.

Life is complex, yet mysteriously organized. Even the chaotic parts are in a kind of order. There are signposts, both within and without. To perceive their guidance we have to pay close attention. The burden of educating ourselves how to see and understand this guidance is upon ourselves. One weekend class will not give us all we need to navigate through our times, it's only a start. To have a conscious life, you need to follow the heavens, follow your feelings, notice the ebbs and flows as they affect you personally. Consciousness is hard work. Many of us don't have the kind of time to develop it. Many of us just go through life and discover its twists and turns of fate only afterward, when we look back.

In the old days, checking in with your soul was called *prayer.* Daily prayer, in the morning and at night, is a time to turn your attention within. Teach the practice of prayer to your children; it's a mind-relaxing skill, and it allows the inner picture to synthesize. It doesn't matter what name you use for God; it only matters that you feel you are talking to God, to your conception of the divine. Then you will be linked with that energy. The flow will be with you.

Women of today are experiencing unease; they feel a big change is coming again. They don't know what the new world is going to be like, so they worry, especially when they see institutions that they have worked hard to build dismembered, such as Affirmative Action, which was the open door to a career for many women. All of the business world is transforming with the new Information Age. The invention and widespread popularity of computers has just begun exerting its influence on our everyday lives, just like a hundred years ago when we felt change through the impact of the automobile and, at mid-century, television.

But back to the wheels.

A significant change we had in recent history that is still powerfully influencing our times and lives happened in 1962. The sub-age of Aquarius arrived. Not the Great Age of Aquarius the popular song announced, but its little sister, a sort of sentinel or forerunner. This sub-age will last 179 years. (How is a sub-age counted? A great year takes 25,820 years, or approximately 26,000 years, to travel through all the zodiac signs. This is the precession of the equinoxes. If you divide 26,000 by twelve you get the Ages of the Earth. These are huge blocks of time lasting a couple thousand years. Divide one age by twelve and you get a sub-age, 179 years, a number more within our grasp.)

This new sub-age of Aquarius is potent; it heralds the values and feelings of the coming Great Age which will arrive in the twenty-fourth century. This sub-age, these precious 179 years, is a window of opportunity—you can smell it, you can play with it, you can seed with it the big one. Aquarius is all about communication, electronics, new inventions, quick changes, a holistic understanding of the world, a humanitarian point of view coming into focus.

The new Aquarian consciousness jumped out at us first from popular music. The Beatles synthesized black R&B into rock and reached the world with it. Truly Aquarian, they brought in a human point of view on women—they wanted to hold our hand, a simple, honest, romantic idea. This had always happened in real life of course, but never in songs about love which were always lofty, unrealistic.

The Beatles ignited young women with an ecstatic passion that drove them to scream their ecstasy at the stage. Girls screamed all through the concerts, they wept, they emoted shamelessly as if possessed. Like banshees they screamed out their uninhibited, first-born, Aquarian joy. Nobody knew why. It didn't make sense. Eventually the fans extreme response drove the Beatles off the performance stage—the poor dears couldn't even hear themselves play! As musicians it was embarrassing to be the object of such passion. At some level they must have known it wasn't only for their talent—it was their on-the-dime Aquarian timing. The entire message of the Beatles was passionate, loving humanism.

Characters like the spinster Eleanor Rigby had never been portrayed in songs before—all the lonely people, The Nowhere Man, The Taxman—these were all recognizable people with very human concerns. And the Beatles spoke about love, not mystical but human, the kind where we get jealous, admit to hurting each other, and make up. The kind where we want to stay together "'til we're sixty-four." At the time, this all seemed very, very far away. Four young men were given license to be playful, to sport long hair; they clowned around, they lived in a "Yellow Submarine," and got high like the rest of the young world.

And the Beatles brought in wisdom way beyond their years. "The love you take is equal to the love you make" was an awesome phrase to hear, when we hadn't heard anything honest or informative about love in ages. Through music we started feeling and acting different. Some of us lived plugged into the music. And that's how the future started, Virginia.

The second big wheel that overlaps our times is Pluto. This planet defies generations and their concerns. As Pluto moves through the zodiac it brings in the consciousness of each particular sign. Why? It's a mystery how the most recently discovered planet, this long distant relative in our galaxy, has such power over us.

Pluto was in Leo from roughly 1939 to 1957. (It's important to note that the ages don't begin on the dime, their edges sort of overlap one another. Their effect is cumulative on the generations who live through them, who become the repositories of the many layers of influence they bring.) This brought the prevalent values about power and domination to center stage, made them public. Pluto brings in the dark side, stirs up the manure around power, exposes the depths. Historically, terrible dictators have ruled under this time, and violence was seen as "teaching a lesson." As we reached the sub-age of Aquarius, this changed into the need to redirect and humanize power, introduce love into it, make power into "Flower Power." Favorite slogans of the sub-age of Aquarius were "Power to the people," "Stop the War," "War is unhealthy for children and other living creatures." It was still about power, but good Aquarian power.

This was followed by Pluto in Virgo (approximately 1957 to 1972). Virgo is the only female human sign in the zodiac. Virgo likes to improve health, and be kind to women and children. My favorite time. The Women's Movement, fueled by the abortion rights and health movements, came into being. It brought with it lifestyle changes: herbal teas and vegetarianism, meditation and inner reflection, science, healing, culture, and getting along as the crowd did at Woodstock, where a huge number of people existed together without fighting. Virgo highlights femaleness, mediation, mellowness, analysis, the sciences, health, and food. Fighting is not one of her passions.

Women demanded to be equal partners in everything, from culture to spiritual life. We reclaimed the dignity of women, the strength of women, and the higher status of women. In the public eye, there had been very little discussion of women; TV shows had only male characters who supposedly represented all of humanity. Females were thrown in just to support the male characters. Actresses played either young chicks, old hags, or victims.

But under the influence of Virgo, the fact that there was one female role to every ten male roles was criticized for the first time. The lack of representation in the houses of power, Congress and the Senate, was also noted for the first time, and derided. The force was with women. This consciousness, as all others, stayed after the Plutonian visit, as a kind of residue, a layer of insight. This is the reason that feminism today is still part of the fabric of our lives. We synthesized it from our times.

Meanwhile the sub-age of Aquarius deepened, incorporating this new Virgo conscience with political analysis and female-highlighted awareness, repairing the lack of female visibility. Television grew up. Talk shows started to become more popular; a staged showdown between a chauvinist pig and a tennis star named Billie Jean King was televised. King rose to archetype status when she whooped the cocky guy, whose name is forgotten in the annals of the sport. In mythic fashion, Billie Jean King, in her white skirts and splendid athletic body, was carried into the court on a litter borne by clad, Chippendales-type of men. That was a crowning ceremony for all woman. We were empowered ritualistically, once and for all.

Today we take it for granted that there are anchorwomen on the news, female reporters, female representatives, and Secretary of State Madeleine Albright, who represents the United States to the world, enjoying the equal status with prime ministers and kings. I remember a time when we had to write letters to TV stations pleading them not to call women's events at the Olympic Games "girls' events." We wrote: "The athletes at the Olympics all seem to be older than twelve years old. If you call them girls' events, then call the men's events 'boys' events.'" This worked because Aquarius had already pried open the minds of the public, and then Virgo could slip in with her fair corrections. The TV station staff never replied but we noticed that the media began using the dreaded word "woman" more often.

A Plutonian visit lasts from ten to fifteen years. These smaller universal waves we do catch because we live though them. The bigger ages elude us because we don't get to see when they begin; our existence is much too short to witness their reality. In the Great Ages we're just "staffing" the times. But my generation is lucky because we did feel the stirrings of the sub-age of Aquarius which heralded the future. Because communication is Aquarius's main strength, the media, especially television, started taking up public education, confrontation, town hall mythos. Thinkers, writers, actors, celebrities, and regular folks shared their stories. Phil Donahue ruled the TV waves; expressions of disagreement became acceptable in public forums.

The next Plutonian age was in Libra (roughly 1972 to 1984). In this time women went to the courts and fought for justice, became lawyers themselves, fought for equal opportunity in employment and for equal pay. We had a female

Supreme Court appointee, even from the conservative Reagan presidency. Secretaries stopped making coffee; women created their own networking system and mentored each other as equals. Civil rights became law; women started winning in court. Gender and racial equality were discussed as legitimate concerns. The great Aquarian personality Oprah Winfrey ascended her throne in public consciousness. With full humanitarian sensibility and the generosity of a Leo, she embraces the entire world. Oprah is the new measure of standard for female behavior. She's teaching the world to be fair, to be honest, to heal, to read.

The most recently completed Plutonian visit was in Scorpio (around 1984 to 1995). This Zodiac sign looks at death and suffering, sexuality and its shadows. Scorpio exposes that which is hidden, and a lot of shadows came to light in this time. The notion of family was liberated; we discovered that the isolated nuclear family was not such a good idea after all. Remember the televised freak shows? The very bottom layers of society had vast public access, confessing to their crimes (I killed my mother and sister), lust (I cheated on my husband with his brother), perversion (I had sex with my daughter or son), abuse (I molested my little boy or girl).

The freak show, it seemed, would never end. Mrs. Bobbitt cut off her husband's penis, and the world shook. This was truly a Scorpio moment. Suddenly women had teeth and knives and guns. The flood of exposés was overwhelming. Church fathers who abused altar boys, bishops who had children—everybody was suing everybody else, airing the dirty linen in public, confessing, weeping. And many were going to jail. Justice was raining down like never before.

The final showdown was the O. J. Simpson trial. His case had everything—an aging arrogant athlete with sagging charm, a beautiful young ex-wife, her face bashed in. The returning abused wife, the little children who inherited the mess. It had black female jurors nursing a deep wound from the racist LAPD that was just waiting to be vented. The trial was used to get even with the police.

But it was the Aquarian sub-age and the whole world was watching. Scorpio stirred up the media with this ongoing true-life soap opera. It was a daily show. Women watched. We knew. There will be no one who will defend us. Women, we are on our own.

The big issue really was sex and violence—male sexuality and possessiveness. This is the great unfinished business of our species. When will somebody finally dare to ask the question: What about the men? Why is it that only among humans do males attack and kill females? The human male rapes children, buys them as slaves, maintains a multibillion-dollar business in child prostitution. How can we humanize male sexuality and not shame all men? How can we separate out rapists from brothers? The thorny question of the men still stands.

Life is complex. If you didn't finish Libra business when you were supposed to, it spilled over into Scorpio and then all hell broke loose. With Scorpio, psychotherapy was elevated into religious ritual, our language finally and permanently taking on its concepts and terminology. We all talk about "denial" when something is real but we say it's not. We talk about our "inner child" and our "inner wild woman," all kinds of inner beings housed with us—it's crowded in there! And the final insight, that childhood is everything—well, most everything. If you hurt a child, you'll pay for it when he/she grows up.

Repressed memories, false repressed memories, and the power of sexuality came home to roost. Rape trials finally convicted rapists; mothers fought against hazings; drunk drivers were put away. Scorpio was a long road for the collective consciousness to travel but we made it and came out the other end. Its lessons are still reverberating in our society and culture. The Scorpion prurient taste hasn't gone away; in fact we have become addicted to exposés. We want more. The tabloids have ascended to legitimate status, and scoop respected publications when it comes to gossip.

Something had to be done. How do we pull out of this spin into darkness? It took a triple female sacrifice: Jon-Benet Ramsey, the young nymph; Diana, Princess of Wales, the Maiden grown to Queen of Hearts; and Mother Teresa, the all-compassionate Crone.

Jon-Benet's gruesome death was "unsolved" (reinforcing the fact that women get no justice). She represented how vulnerable we are. Diana's accidental death was blamed on aggressive paparazzi and the tabloids who pay them too well. Her death said to us: Beauty demands to be witnessed, and is loved and hated at the same time. We kill what turns us on. When Diana died, we realized how short life is, we faced our own mortality. She was the Fairy Queen. Mother Theresa was a pragmatist who chose to save humanity. The ultimate servant of God—no man has ever done what she has. Her death told us: Be compassionate, every one of us is God.

All three deaths disturbed our collective soul deeply. All three women were *us,* somehow. We emptied the cup of grief to the bottom. And with the message of compassion we have arrived in the Plutonian Sagittarius (about 1995 to 2008). This is the half-horse/half-man image. Good Chiron, the wounded healer and centaur. We can assume that animal rights will be in the forefront. Already a new television network, Animal Planet, is slowly replacing the freak gossip shows. Animals will be treasured and their wisdom gleaned in this short ten years.

Sagittarius likes women, sexuality that is robust but not violent. High goals to chase in medicine, teaching and learning, ritual and religion. This phase in our history will be peppered with medical discoveries. The dreaded virus—AIDS, herpes, the common cold, and other beasts we could not shake—will be defeated now, finally. We shall honor our inventors who have conquered a high goal; human interests will be highlighted once again.

Youth will be trusted, elected, and promoted—but not for their beauty. Youth will take on vigorous endeavors for the common good. Sports will have to become more civil, and remunerated more realistically. Women again will win the Olympics for the U.S.A. The elderly, the aging "Flower Children" who were the first bloom of the sub-age of Aquarius, will be taken care of by society. Good health care and retirement care will be made available.

This age is fun. All religions that provide solace and appreciation for the human spirit will flourish. Religions that are punitive, fear-oriented, all hell-fire-and-brimstone, will diminish. If it's boring, it won't fly.

After this fun age, we will enter Plutonian Capricorn (roughly 2008 to 2012). This sign highlights the Earth, structures, and institutions, and also spasms, as in birth and even orgasms. This age will usher in the first new institutions of the twenty-first century which will replace old models. Business will be rearranged, life will be less centralized. The Information Age—a code name for Aquarius—will totally bloom in Capricorn.

Our work will be connected from all points of the globe. Business will take place where you are: bosses online only, parents working while rocking the baby. All those Plutonian visits will be finally finished here in Capricorn. Pollution will decrease as we use Earth-friendly energy sources, such as solar energy, windpower, and the energy of ocean waves. Capricorn will be a time of serious studies, less partying than in Sagittarius. Humanity will mature, incorporating all the past lessons, synthesizing all Plutonian visits. The body, as Earth herself, will be honored. Health consciousness will reach a kind of old-fashioned mode, with readily widespread knowledge of good health habits and exercise, and healthy foods being sold on the streets, memories from our Virgo past.

A new conservatism may also emerge here, which will closely resemble the hippie rebels of the past. Few of the original "Flower Children" will be around to see it come full circle, but if we do, we shall lift our medical marijuana joints in the air to celebrate.

With each age, the best policy is to follow the spirit of the times. So right now don't worry about the millennium, tend to the humanistic Sagittarian age that is here right now. This is more real than the coming turn of the century. This is a time when the soul and her needs will take center stage. Practice some form of spirituality. For women, a Goddess consciousness or fate consciousness is right. For men, finally learn to follow women as leaders. Oh, yes—it will be an "in" thing, you see. Women are way ahead in the soul department. We have been at it since the Plutonian Virgo, when men were just getting around to contemplating female orgasm and finding the G spot. Women had already begun worshiping the goddess, writing a lot of books about it, and calling on the four directions in circles.

Soul care, inner life, intuitions, instinctual leadership, improvisations— these are all skills for Sagittarius. You cannot succeed here unless you are in touch with your body, your inner animal, and can brighten your spirit. Instead of repressing our animal nature, it's time to investigate it, see how we can synthesize the animal and soul natures of our species better. It's a noble fate marriage; we are all spouses. Sagittarius will want to climb the heights of imagination. Entertainment must be soulful and instructive again. The Scorpio age of anger and rage is over. Fueled with the growing Aquarian vibration, this can be a wonderful time.

Around 2008 it will turn into Plutonian Capricorn. And even beyond that, the wheels within the wheels are turning. "All things must pass" said the inscription to the Fates. Our species is weathering the changes, and we are discovering that we are made of stars and that our destination is life returning.

Jamie Sams is a writer of Seneca, Cherokee, and French descent. The author of, among other works, *Earth Medicine, The Thirteen Original Clan Mothers,* and *Animal Medicine,* she has created three foundations that are supported by the royalties from her work, one of which is dedicated to preserving the wisdom of her teachers and her Native American ancestors by putting those teachings in written and audio form for all of the Children of Earth. The others provide scholarships for Native Americans, books for schools and Native Americans in prisons, and assistance for Native American youth projects and the Family Service Centers on Reservations. Ms. Sams has dedicated her life to learning from the Elders who were her teachers and to walking those lessons in her own life, faithfully remembering the words of her teachers in order to offer those gifts of wisdom to humankind.

Messages for the Women of the Millennium

Our traditional Native American greeting in the Seneca language is *Na:weh Skennio*—thank you for being! Whether you know it or not, each of you represents a spark of inspiration within the Great Mystery. You are needed. You touch the lives of many and are responsible for changing the lives of others for the better. For all that you do and for who you are, I thank you for being.

The Native American prophesy of my elders has spoken of the millennium and the end of the present era of time called the Fourth World of Separation. We are now beginning a new era of time that is called the Fifth World of Illumination and Peace. Our prophesy tells us that the Earth Mother will endure the climactic changes and shifts that are already occurring. Since the Earth Mother is changing her form and image, we are also being given the opportunity to change ours. How we see ourselves and our effectiveness in the world is totally dependent upon our abilities of imagination and determination. As women, we are asked to see these changes through eyes of wonder, not through the helpless eyes of fear. We are asked to see the metaphor for the changes occurring in the natural world as simple reflections of the empowered feminine aspect within humankind. We are collectively giving birth to the intuitive, receptive, transformative, and enduring nature of our human potential. Embracing that potential is a choice. Having the courage to endure and to go through the transformation process tests us on all that we have ever known and insists that we apply our experience and hard-earned wisdom moment by moment.

Transformation and change can pertain to our body's health, our personal sense of integrity, our willingness to take charge of our lives, or our ability to respond to and to authentically use the gifts of wisdom that we carry. The most important aspect of changing our image for the millennium is to move beyond any former ideas of separation, en masse, becoming living extensions of the Earth Mother's unconditional love. Any judgments we harbor against ourselves or another must be relinquished, allowing all past resentments or unfinished business to be healed and brought to closure if we are to take our places as empowered human beings who have the ability to dream a dream that all people and living things can equally share.

Women are sources of inspiration to others and have inspired great works of art, music, and literature throughout time. The word *inspiration* comes from the Latin and means to inhale the divine or to take spirit within the self. When we take in that spirit, we are then forced to exhale or we die a little. When we are inspired, we funnel our creativity into fashioning something of beauty, whether it is dance, art, music, or making a meal for our families. When we finish, we exhale our creations, sending them into the world to be shared with others. Creativity is present in everything we do and is fueled by the amount of life-force we are willing to embrace.

Human beings can live without food, without water, without shelter, and without companionship for a while, but we cannot live without the breath of life for more than a few minutes. Every time we inhale, we are given the gift of spirit or life-force that fuels our imaginations. Einstein said, "Imagination is everything." What we are being asked to reclaim at this time in our Earth Mother's history is the basic idea that women can be imaginative and inspired and, therefore, inspire others to create a world that will serve the next seven generations of humankind. Nothing is impossible if we can imagine it, dream it, and work toward that end.

During these changing times we can access the wonder of life if we are in sync with ourselves and with the rhythms of the Earth Mother. If our efforts are not coming to fruition, we are simply out of sync. To remedy being out-of-sync, we simply need to enter *Tiyoweh,* or the stillness. No one knows better than Native people how to find strength in retreat. Our warriors would wait in silence until the time was right before they chose to attack and win a battle. Our women have retreated to a moon lodge to rest and gather their strength before returning to the strenuous duties of caring for a family or clan. When we retreat and find the stillness, we change the pattern of our breathing. When we relax and breathe deeply, we are given the gift of inspiration and renewed life-force that can change the patterns of our daily life, how we see others, and how we see ourselves. From a renewed viewpoint, we can access solutions that would have escaped our notice when we were overwhelmed. Taking time for ourselves is of paramount importance.

Before menopause, women have thirteen menstrual flows a year. There are thirteen moons during a calendar year and thirteen is the number of transformation. In the tradition of my two Kiowa Grandmother teachers, each moon has a Clan Mother who is the keeper of the rites of passage that mark human growth cycles. These Clan Mothers offer wisdom and practical daily rituals that allow us to remain in balance during the best and the worst of times. These are the thirteen daily guidelines that I would like to share:

1. Focus on positive, happy thoughts.
2. Be kind and merciful with yourself and all living things.
3. Be good to your body.
4. Follow your heart and honor your inner-knowing.
5. Quiet your mind.
6. Cherish every act in life as an expression of your creativity.
7. Let go of stress and tension.
8. Drop all judgments.
9. Be grateful.
10. Breathe deeply.
11. Connect with the Earth.
12. Allow, allow, allow.
13. Savor the art of being.

These basic guidelines may sound simple to some, but to authentically accomplish them on a daily basis is no small task. In Native American legend, this time between worlds is described as the wobble. Like newborn colts trying to find their legs, human beings will have to learn to find new points of balance. The scientific community has explained this phenomena as being related to the hertz level, which is the measurement for electrical impulses that run through the planet. As we approach the millennium and until the year 2012, the hertz level of the Earth will be escalating. In 1986, the hertz level was 7.2 and in March 1997 the hertz level became 9.9. By the year 2012 the Earth Mother's electrical impulses will reach 13 hertz. That means that the electrical impulses that run through the Earth and through our bodies will be affecting our emotions. Finding a daily balance will be imperative if we are to remain effective.

On the other hand, that same influx of mounting energy supports our ability to develop the higher mind and intuition. We are being given an opportunity to go beyond our limitations and to become the vision of ourselves that reflects our potential. The challenge we are facing is becoming our highest potential and inspiring others to do the same. We are being provided with the usable energy that we need. If we do not fear it, but rather embrace the power surges of energy and the changes we experience as a gift, we will transform and thrive. Each woman has an individual healing and growth process that is as unique as her role in life. When we use these thirteen guidelines daily, our progress will be inspired and can furnish us with priceless rewards.

Forming a personal creed is another practical way of finding and maintaining our balance in changing times. The personal creed is no more than a set of promises that we make to ourselves which are simple reminders of our commitments to our personal growth processes. An example might contain the following: "I promise to honor my feelings and to be as present as possible at all times. I promise to show appreciation for all that life offers me. I promise to use integrity in all my thoughts, words, and actions. I promise to be loyal to myself and to those I love. I promise to look for ways to resolve issues that appear in my life. I promise to be respectful of the beliefs and lifestyles of others and to release any judgments I hold regarding anything I do not fully understand. I promise to support the rights of human beings to find happiness in their own ways. I promise to listen to others and to my own inner-knowing. I promise to celebrate the life I am living. I promise to seek the positive aspects of every situation and discover what I can learn from cherishing every joyous and disruptive situation I encounter."

Each woman will find her own way of making a personal creed and as she changes, she can add to or delete the parts that no longer apply. In this way, we are allowing ourselves to grow and to expand the application of our personal creeds. Personal integrity and serenity are accumulated over time with the maturation process. As we maintain personal balance, we find that wise aspects of ourselves are emerging and those parts of ourselves become an inspiration to others, even if we are not aware of our influence. Becoming a role model for others is not "the goal." If we live our lives, behaving as if every moment matters, our influence radiates into the lives of others because we are being. We are walking our talk. Doing is a secondary purpose that allows our actions to speak for us, but when we are being who we are and honestly living with inspired integrity, we automatically inspire the imaginations of everyone we encounter.

Having a sense of humor is one of the most important tasks that we can embrace during these changing times. Seriousness makes us morose and endangers the amount of life-force that we can access. Laughing at our personal antics is Good Medicine. It is healthy to laugh at how we tend to become myopic, getting wrapped up in our lives and how we lose the bigger picture. We thrive when we can shed the armor of too much seriousness. When we can see the cosmic joke of how we have meandered into circumstances that force us to acknowledge our humanness, we shake off our unwanted self-importance. Sometimes we must learn to laugh at our ridiculous tendencies to become puritanical and to think that we are being spiritual if we deny ourselves the smallest bit of slack. That tightrope has nothing to do with authentic spiritual integrity. Human pleasures can be whittled away by adopting belief systems that disallow many of the simple joys of being human.

We can dare to be different. We can dare to be irreverent and to be happy. Many spiritual women are seeking to become the light or to embrace the light and yet in the process they have become so rigid that they have created entire belief systems that make simple human pleasures an endangered species. "Lighten up" can take on a whole new meaning if we honor our right to embrace more than low-fat diets, meditation, celibacy, and puritanical group thinking that scoffs at anyone who embraces life with gusto. Step back and look at how certain medical advice has been disproved over the past ten years and how we all believed everything we were programmed to believe on the evening news medical report. Where is our inner-knowing about what is right for us individually? Wise women can dare to know for themselves and allow others to find what is right for them and we can laugh at the ridiculous one-size-fits-all type of advice that is being touted for the masses. This example of our times is a perfect set-up that allows us the opportunity to discern the value our inner-knowing. It is hilarious that we have become such lambs when we are striving to become lionesses, empowered by the wisdom found in our own healing processes.

Reclaiming the belly-laugh can cure a world of woes. There is nothing that is sadder than a person who cannot see the beauty of a sunset without fearing what tomorrow will bring. Worry about the future keeps us from being present in the now. When we worry, we leak life-force on nonexistent woes and we project our fears into a future time and place that has not yet appeared on the horizon. Life-force is precious and when we are not consolidating our energy, using it for productive, present-time endeavors, we are wasting the gift of life-force. When we catch ourselves doing that, we need to laugh at our fears and refuse to give them authority over our creativity. Destructive tendencies can masquerade themselves in many forms. Using our imagination and life-force to mentally create a future world of pain, anguish, scarcity, and bogeymen is the ultimate self-sabotage. We betray ourselves and all other human beings when we entertain doom-and-gloom thinking. Being creative can also mean that we are willing to outwit our fears by becoming visionaries and dreamers who hold the dream of a bright future for our planet. We can dispel our tendencies to be regretful of the past or fearful of the future by focusing on the now. Nothing brings us back to the present as quickly as a good laugh! When we are fully present we are able to catch the wave of synchronistic energy that fuels the manifestation of our dreams.

Throughout the ages, women have been considered to be mysterious. We become more mysterious when we have enough of ourselves present to empower our lives. Observers sense a quality within us that cannot be defined. When chaos appears on the horizon and we glide through the modern minefields of human life with ease, they sit up and take notice. Life will always test us on our weaknesses. The challenge is to learn how to maintain balance in every situation without abandoning ourselves, our integrity, or the multifaceted purposes we have for being on the Earth Mother at this time. The unequaled opportunities that we are being given to make a difference in our world are priceless. The feminine aspect of humanity is emerging and coming into balance with the male demonstrative side of our natures. This transformation process allows us to embody our visions of ourselves and to dream a dream that honors every aspect of life, every culture, every race, every living thing, and our places within the whole without empowering the same ideas of separation we have endured during in the Fourth World. As we move through the time period called the wobble between worlds and welcome the millennium which is the Fifth World of Illumination and Peace, our first step is to find the qualities of illumination and peace within ourselves. Then we can give those qualities their birth and share our newborn dream for humanity with all living things.

Luisah Teish is a writer, performer, priestess of Oshun, and ritual designer. She is the author of *Jambalaya: The Natural Woman's Book of Personal Charms and Practical Rituals* and *Carnival of the Spirit: Seasonal Celebrations and Rites of Passage.* She teaches Women's Rites of Passage, Femmyth, and Ritual at the University of Creation Spirituality, John F. Kennedy University, and New College of California. She has performed mythplays and folkstorytelling in the United States, Canada, Europe, Australia, and New Zealand, and is a marketwoman with ASHE, an Oakland, California-based cooperative economics group.

Sister, Can You Paradigm? or, Whose Millennium Is It?

Speaking as an African American woman I cannot entertain the idyllic notion that the coming of the millennium will make all our concerns magically disappear on the gossamer wings of white-robed angels, simply by flipping a page on the calendar.

Nor can I accept the idea that the millennium will bring about the end of the world. Many people are waiting to be lifted up to heaven in a religious rapture, or by first-class reservations on the Mothership. These beliefs are, in my opinion, simply projections of hatred of the Earth and fear of the future. And it's a great way to excuse oneself from taking responsibility for the consequences of our actions.

I am writing this article because I can and must, see, believe in, and struggle for a better tomorrow. And I feel that the discussion on the subject can be improved and enriched if the voices of those of us who have faced violent genocide and sexist oppression for more than a millennium are heard.

In the Black community we have a phrase: "Sister, let me drop a dime on you." The act of "dropping a dime" on a sister means that we let her in on a secret. Often this is done by asking her a question she hadn't asked herself. We give her a "wake-up call," (a phone call used to cost a dime) by pointing out an irony. Or we "break it down" for her by providing information that will enable her to have an informed opinion, or to make a sound judgment. If you drop enough dimes at the right times she may change her perspective entirely.

I cannot speak for *all* African American women, and would not presume to do so. But I can and will speak as *an* African American woman whose attitudes and experiences may reflect those of other working-class women of color. In writing this article, I am speaking to *all* women who are willing to have the conversation. Listen for the dial tone, sister, as I drop a dime on the new millennium paradigm.

WHOSE MILLENNIUM IS IT?

The first dime comes in the form of a question. Whose millennium is it?

The millennium measures time by the solar calendar and the birth of Christ. This is a mythological reference point. The assumption that "the solar millennium" reflects *universal truth* is simply another manifestation of the Christian paradigm which has been imposed upon the world. There are other cultures with different spiritual traditions and calendars.

The millennium myth is, I feel, a child of "The Post Man." Somewhere there is a mysterious band of men, magicians perhaps, who *determine* when an era of struggle becomes "post," then declare it to the world through the media. I have lived through the "post-Civil Rights Era" while fighting for my civil rights. Someone declared that we had arrived at the "post-Feminist Era" while I was still trying to protect my body and crying to have my voice heard. Now I'm told to think of my self as living in the "Post Modern Era"! What is that about? For me this label "post" is a media *MAN*ipulation, an attempt to make us believe that a particular set of ideas, values, and struggles are dead. I think that the magicians, the governments, the corporations, and the institutions are causing our affirmative actions to magically disappear! Sister, somebody's yanking my *change*. If the "post man" *is* related to the millennium magicians, I have reason to be suspicious.

Most cultures have their own means of measuring time. Usually these measurements are connected to celestial activities such as the phases of the Moon. I have a little more faith in this because the Moon has always been there and She shines on all of us regardless of location, religion, or culture.

If we wish to create a global community, I think we should become familiar with a wide range of the cultural interpretations of celestial events such as the Chinese zodiac, the Mayan Calendar, and Gede, the West African astrological system.

In some cultures, time is measured by occurrences in nature (such as the swelling of the river Nile in Egypt) or significant animal migrations (the swallows in Capistrano). Perhaps in the future our calendar should be marked by the unnatural occurrences of our times such as destruction of the rainforests or the extinction of the elephants.

Cultures also mark time according to historical events: the establishment of a village, an exodus from oppression, or a life-altering creation such as the advent of agriculture. The importance of events such as these seem to have impact everywhere. If we are to have success in evolving a global culture, we must become familiar with the history and learn to respect the spiritual practices of all the world's cultures.

There I go again, advocating respectful multiculturalism. But I have some reservations based on past experience.

The Harmonic Convergence of the late '80s was hailed as the beginning multiculturalism of great spiritual enlightenment. But the '90s have been characterized by the same practices of exploitation and cultural appropriation that existed prior to the convergence. In my opinion, the so-called "modern primitives movement" of the last decade has been an insult. The sacred symbols and practices of African, Native American, and Asian people have been usurped without respect or compensation. These symbols have been stripped of their true meaning and reduced to the fleeting diversions of Western spiritual adolescents. This is disheartening to me, as a woman of color. If the millennium is going to be any better than the '90s, shouldn't we start rehearsing for it now? This is a "company call."

Since I don't subscribe to blind faith, and my vision is blurred by the present reality, I can only speculate on the nature of the new millennium.

I think it will have meaning for the global community if Western cultures are *willing and able* to make a radical shift in *conscience* as well as *consciousness*.

SISTER, CAN YOU PARADIGM?

Many well-intentioned women speak of themselves as midwives to a "new age." They believe that this new age will bring about a "new consciousness." I'm told that we will develop new relationships to nature, to ourselves, and to spirit. They say we will "shift the paradigm." I would like to believe in their belief.

But it seems to me that shifting the paradigm requires a *conscience* as well as a consciousness. The shift must carry a sense of responsibility for correcting the injustices of the past; for understanding how and why atrocities are committed; and it must include a means for avoiding repetition of past crimes. In short, there must be a willingness and an ability to *imagine* ourselves as *different Beings,* and from that imagining to think and act differently.

So sister, let me drop this dime....

I ask you now to picture a *mermaid.* Do you see an image of a creature who is half woman and half fish? No doubt she is white-skinned, with long flowing hair, and the lower half of her body is that of a fish with colorful scales and a magnificent tail. This is the typical, acceptable image of this mythological creature. Thanks to folklore and the magic of Disney, most of us see her this way.

Shift. Reverse the biological construct. Make the top of this creature a fish and the bottom a human. Make her skin as black as night! What is your response to this? Does this make you uncomfortable? If it does, ask yourself why? Perhaps it is because we have been conditioned to imagine things in a white Western way. Perhaps we can relate to "others" only when they look "just like us"; when we are assured that they have the same "head" as we do (that they think in the same way); and that their "tail" (their instincts) can be benevolently controlled by us.

The assumption of the twentieth-century has been that the West would dominate the world and that the rest of the world would *attain* something called *equality* by mimicking the ways of the West. Then we can all luv each other. But that kind of love is void of respect. It is a plugged nickel, a cheap shot that has led to war, disease, pollution, and depression. I can't use it.

I maintain that the biggest challenge in the new millennium could be a change of habit. We could change from a dominating commodity culture into one of true exchange in which we learn from each other in humility and respect. I do think it's possible. But it's up to us.

SISTER, CATCH THIS DIME....

1. I imagine that human beings could interface with beings from other dimensions without waging war. But we'd have to give up fear.
2. I imagine that humans could preserve the beauty and balance of nature. But we'd have to give up greed.
3. I imagine that humans could realize true kinship. But we'd have to accept that we all evolved from Africa and that we are all equally human.
4. I imagine that every culture has a gift to share. But we'd have to practice humility in order to learn from each other.
5. I imagine that women, men, and children could live in peaceful communities. But we'd have to respect the divine in each other.

I can imagine a future that will be as radically different from the past as my mermaid is from Disney's.

Sister, can you paradigm? Can you, can you really?

Joanna Macy, Ph.D., is a teacher of deep ecology, Buddhism, and general systems theory living in the San Francisco Bay Area and known worldwide for her workshops at the interface of spiritual breakthrough and social action. Her books include *World as Lover World as Self* and *Rilke's Book of Hours,* with Anita Barrows. Her *Coming Back to Life,* a manual on her group work, will appear in late 1998, and *Widening Circles,* a memoir, in 1999.

The Great Turning

I imagine that future generations will look back on these closing years of the twentieth century and call it the time of the Great Turning. It is the epochal shift from an industrial growth society, dependent on accelerating consumption of resources, to a sustainable or life-sustaining society. There is no guarantee that we will make it in time for civilization, or even complex life forms, to survive; but it is clear that there's no alternative, because we are now, in systems terms, "on runaway," consuming our own life support system. I consider it an enormous privilege to be alive now, in this Turning, when all the wisdom and courage we ever harvested can be put to use and matter supremely.

Lester Brown of the Worldwatch Institute says that, while the agricultural revolution took centuries and the industrial revolution took decades, *this* ecological revolution must happen within a few years. At the same time, it will be, of necessity, more thorough-going—involving not only our political economy, but the attitudes and habits that sustain it.

Scientists—at least those who are not in the pay of the corporations—see more quickly than politicians that there is no technological fix. No magic bullet, not even the Internet, can save us from population explosion, deforestation, climate disruption, poison by pollution, and wholesale extinctions of plant and animal species. We are going to have to want different things, seek different pleasures, pursue different goals, than those that have been driving us and our global economy.

New values must arise *now*, while we still have room to maneuver—and that is precisely what is happening. They are emerging at this very moment, like green shoots through the rubble. It's not in the headlines or the evening news, but if you open your eyes and fiddle a bit with the focal length, you can see it, like a faint green haze over things, intensifying here and there in pools and pockets of grass, cress, clover.

The Great Turning is occurring on three simultaneous levels or dimensions. Recognize how they are gaining momentum through your own life.

On the most visible level are holding actions in defense of Earth, including all the political, legislative, and legal work required to slow down the destruction, as well as direct actions—blockades, boycotts, civil disobedience, and other forms of refusal. Work of this kind buys time. It helps save biological and cultural systems, and the gene pool, for the sustainable society to come; but it is insufficient to bring that society about.

This first level is wearing. You can get stressed out of your mind by both the urgency and increasing violence against activists. In point position, you take a lot of punishment; and when you step back to take a breather, you often feel as if you are abandoning ship. But to the extent you still care what's happening to the world, you're probably just slipping back to continue the work of the Great Turning in another form—the way the head goose, when she's tired, slips back and flies in the windstream of others, and another flyer takes her place.

The second or middle level of the Great Turning addresses structural causes of the global crisis and creates sustainable alternatives. Only a couple of years ago, it was hard slogging to raise any opposition to, or even interest in, GATT (the Global Agreement on Trade and Tariffs); people's eyes glazed over. But now they are rapidly becoming aware of the rape of the world, and the attack on democracy, built into corporate privilege. Novel types of teach-ins demystify economics, engage the practical imagination. At the same time, new social and economic arrangements are mushrooming, from local currencies, local marketing and consumer cooperatives, to eco-villages and renewable, off-the-grid energy generation. They may *look* fringe, but they hold the seeds of the future.

These nascent institutions cannot take root and survive, however, without values to sustain them. They must mirror what we want, and think we are. *That* paradigmatic shift—at the third, most basic level of the Great Turning—is happening all around us. Some see it as an influx of spirit from above, others as "hitting bottom" in our doomed and addictive society. Either way, we are opening our senses to the web of relationships, the deep ecology, in which we have our being. Like our primordial ancestors, we begin again to see the world as our body and (whether we say the word or not) as sacred.

We hardly have words for the cognitive, spiritual, and perceptual revolution that is occurring now at a stunning rate of speed. These lines from the late California poet Robinson Jeffers catch some of its flavor:

> I entered the life of the brown forest,
> And the great life of the ancient peaks,
> > the patience of stone,
> I felt the changes in the veins
> In the throat of the mountain,
> > and, I was the streams
> Draining the mountain wood; and I was the stag
> > drinking:
> > and I was the stars,
> Boiling with light, wandering alone,
> > each one the lord of his own summit,
> > and I was the darkness
> Outside the stars, I included them.
> > They were a part of me.
> > … how can I express the excellence
> I have found, that has no color but clearness;
> No honey but ecstasy.…

We can't tell which will happen first, the final unraveling of life on Earth, or the moment when the elements of a sustainable world cohere and catch hold. But even if the Great Turning fails to carry this planetary experiment onward through linear time, it still is worth it. It is a homecoming to our true nature.

Just a thousand years ago, a theologian wrote a poem. Amid the apocalyptic fears and hopes of the first millennium, he experienced and expressed a new vision of the holy—not as a remote, justly angry judge, but as an immanent presence, creative and loving. Now, at the end of the second millennium, we can receive his poem and let it speak to our own inklings of that which presses within us to be born. So attend now to Symeon the Theologian (949–1022), knowing that where he said "Christ" and "God," I am substituting "Earth" and "planet." (The original version can be found in translation in *The Enlightened Heart* edited by Stephen Mitchell.)

We awaken in Earth's body
as Earth awakens our bodies.
And my poor hand is Earth, she enters
my foot, and is infinitely me.

I move my hand, and wonderfully
my hand becomes Earth, becomes all of her
(for our planet is indivisibly
whole, seamless in her planethood).

I move my foot, and at once
she appears like a flash of lightning.
Do my words seem blasphemous? Then
open your heart to her,

and let yourself receive the one
who is opening to you so deeply.
For if we genuinely love her,
we wake up inside Earth's body

where all our body, all over,
every most hidden part of it,
is realized in joy as her,
and she makes us utterly real,

and everything that is hurt, everything
that seemed to us dark, harsh, shameful,
maimed, ugly, irreparably
damaged, is in her transformed

and recognized as whole, as lovely,
and radiant in her light,
we awaken as the Beloved
in every last part of our body.

Margaret J. Wheatley writes, speaks, and teaches about the new story. Before accepting this assignment, she was a consultant and professor for many years. If you are interested in exploring her version of this story in more detail, please read her books: *A Simpler Way,* co-authored with Myron Kellner-Rogers (1996), and *Leadership and the New Science* (1992). She lives in the mountains of Utah, where Gaia speaks out clearly.

Reclaiming Gaia, Reclaiming Life

Queen of Heaven, Goddess of the Universe,
the One who walked in terrible chaos
and brought life by the law of love
and out of chaos brought us harmony.
From chaos She has led us by the hand....

—written of Ishtar, Goddess of Babylon, 5000 B.C.E.

In the new millennium, who will be this goddess? Who will lead us by the hand through our terrible chaos? Who will bring us to life by the law of love?

Throughout all time and in all societies, this goddess has been known. In some cultures she has been honored, in others reviled, but she is always present at the dawn of creation. In the origins of Western thought (600 B.C.E.), she appears in Hesiod as *Gaia,* one among the creation trinity of Chaos and Eros. It is Gaia who reaches into the void that is Chaos and pulls forth life. It is Gaia who works with the creative impulse that is Eros and creates the world. She is the created universe, the mother of all life, the great partner of chaos and creativity. In modern science, she is planet Earth, a living being who creates for herself the conditions that nourish and sustain life. And in this millennial era, Gaia is us. She is the feminine energy that compels us to care about the future of Earth. She is the feminine sensibility that inspires us to dream of harmony among all beings. She is the feminine voice that yearns to speak through us of the law of love.

I hear Gaia speaking quietly and forcefully through many women these days. But while her voice is clear, too many of us question what it means. Instead of celebrating our clarity, we ask, "Am I crazy?" Some of us feel so out of place that the question escalates to: "Am I from another planet?" The Tibetan teacher Trungpa Rinpoche described a dark time as one in which people forget who they are, lose confidence, and so lack the courage to speak. Courageous acts are born only from the self-acknowledgment of our goodness. How, then, will we speak of Gaia if we believe we're crazy?

It is time to stop feeling crazy. It is time to acknowledge that we represent *the new sanity*. This new sanity—which is the ancient teachings of many peoples—can tell us how to be with life in a way that blesses, nurtures, and creates. It can tell us how to extend our Gaian reach into the genuine chaos of this age and from it secure the wisdom that will transform us.

In my own work, I am seeking to bring the Gaian voice I hear into organizations of all varieties. How can we create organizations worthy of human habitation, where life flourishes and creativity is a delight? How could we organize human endeavor if we understood how our Gaian planet has organized herself? In asking these questions within organizations, I hope to have us realize that we have choice in how we organize, that there are other beliefs and methods available to us that are far more life-sustaining than our current practices. I know that I am giving new voice to beliefs that were once widely known. I also know that I am speaking them into a world that effectively deposed and banished them from public speech about 300 years ago when the image of a clockwork, mechanical universe gained hegemony.

A few years ago, as the Gaian voices competed with those that told me I was insane, I discovered a new role for myself and all those haunted by ancient images of peace and possibility. I discovered that I could describe myself as the teller of a new story, a new cosmic creation story.

I was introduced to the critical nature of this teller-of-new-stories role in reading the work of physicist Brian Swimme. Brian, partnering with Thomas Berry, has spent the past several years developing a new story of the universe. They believe that only by creating a new cosmic story can we usher in a new era of human and planetary health. (For more details, see their book *The Universe Story*.)

Lest you believe that cosmic stories belong only to physicists or theologians, their idea of a cosmic story is one that answers such questions as: What's going on? Where did everything come from? Why are you doing what you do?

Gaian voices answer these questions with a new story that differs in all ways from our old cosmology. Because Gaia's story is about life, I know that as women we embody a profound sensibility to this story. And I have come to believe that it is our responsibility to lend our voice and authority to this new cosmic story that Gaia is sharing with and through us. I would like to contrast in some detail the new and the old stories. My hope is that in seeing the great polarities between these two, you will feel that you have no choice but to give voice to the new.

The old story is a story of dominion and control, and all-encompassing materialism. Western culture has been developing this story far longer than 300 years, but it was in the seventeenth century, with the advent of modern science, that it became all-encompassing. Modern science promised that it was within human province to understand the workings of the universe and to gain complete mastery over physical matter. This promise grew from the image of the universe as a grand, clockwork machine. If the world was a machine, we could understand it through minute dissection, we would engineer it to do what we saw fit, and we would fix it through our engineering brilliance. This hypnotic image of powers beyond previous human imagination gradually crept into everything we looked at: our bodies were seen as the ultimate machines; our organizations had all the parts and specifications to assure well-oiled performance; and in science, where it had all begun, too many scientists confused metaphor with reality and believed life *was* a machine.

This dream still wields immense power over us. For every problem, we quickly leap to technical solutions, even if technology is the initial cause of the problem. Science will still save us, no matter the earthly mess we've created. In our bodies, our greatest ills, perhaps even death, will vanish once we conquer the challenges of genetic engineering. In most endeavors—in science, health, organizational management, self-help—the focus is on creating better-functioning machines. We replace the faulty part, re-engineer the organization, install a new behavior or attitude, create a better fit, recharge our batteries. The language and thinking is all machines. And we remain seduced by this image because it's the only vision that promises us we can conquer life's cyclical nature, our one hope of escape from Gaia's incessant demands for creation and destruction.

This story of complete dominion over matter was accompanied by control's necessary partner, fear. We seek to control that which we fear. When it resists our control, we become even more afraid. We seek to find other, more successful means of controlling it. We become entangled in a cycle of exerting control, failing to control, exerting harsher control, failing again. The fear that arises from this cycle is notable in many of us. It is especially notable in our organizations. Things aren't working as we had hoped, our control is failing, but we know of no other way to proceed. The world becomes ever more fearsome as we realize the depths of our ignorance and confront our true powerlessness. Yet it is from this place, from an acknowledgment of our ignorance and lack of power, that the call can go out for a new story.

But the old story has further dimensions worth noting. This story has had a particularly pernicious effect on how we think about one another and how we approach the task of organizing any human endeavor. When we conceived of ourselves as machines, we gave up most of what is essential to being human. We created ourselves devoid of spirit, will, passion, compassion, even intelligence. A machine has none of these characteristics innately, and none of them can be built into its specifications. The imagery is so foreign to what we know and feel to be true about ourselves that it seems strange that we ever adopted this as an accurate description of being human. But we did, and we do. A colleague of mine, as he was about to work with a group of oil company engineers, was warned that they had "heads of cement." He cheerfully remarked that it didn't matter, because they all had hearts, didn't they? "Well," they replied, "we call it a pump."

The engineering image of ourselves has led to organizational lives where we believe we can ignore the deep realities of human existence. We can ignore that people carry spiritual questions and quests into their work; we can ignore that people need love and acknowledgment; we can pretend that emotions are not part of our work lives; we can pretend we don't have families, or health crises, or deep worries. In essence, we take the complexity of human life and organize it away. It is not part of the story we want to believe. We want a story of simple dimensions: people are machines and can be controlled to perform with the same efficiency and predictability.

It is important to recognize that in our experience, people never behave like machines. When given directions, we insist on putting our unique spin on them. When told to follow orders, we resist in obvious or subtle ways. When told to accept someone else's solution, or to institute a program created elsewhere, we deny that it has sufficient value.

When we meet with such nonmechanical responses, we've had two different options. We can criticize our own leadership, or we can blame everyone else. If we as leader are the problem, perhaps it's due to poor communication skills; perhaps we aren't visionary enough; maybe we chose the wrong sales technique. If our colleagues (or children, or friends) are the problem, it must be that they lack motivation or a clear sense of responsibility, or it could be that this time we've just been cursed with an obstinate and rebellious group. With so much blame looking for targets, we haven't stopped long enough to question our basic beliefs about each other. Are expectations of machine-like obedience and regularity appropriate when working with other people?

Trying to be an effective leader in this machine story is especially exhausting. He or she is leading a group of lifeless, empty automatons who are just waiting to be filled with vision and direction and intelligence. The leader is responsible for providing everything: the organizational mission and values, the organizational structure, the plans, the supervision. The leader must also figure out, through clever use of incentives or coercives, how to pump energy into this lifeless mass. Once the pump is primed, he/she must then rush hither and yon to make sure that everyone is clanking along in the same direction, at the established speed, with no diversions. It is the role of the leader to provide the organizing energy for a system that is believed to have no internal capacities for self-creation, self-organization, or self-transcendence.

As I reflect on the awful demands placed on leaders by the old story, I wonder how anyone could survive in that job. Yet the mechanistic story has created roles for all of us that are equally deadly. It has led us to believe that we, with our unpredictable behaviors, our passions, our independence, our creativity, our consciousness—that we are the problem rather than the blessing. In fact, our rebellious and untrustworthy natures are the very reason we need to create organizations as we do. How else could we structure such recalcitrance into vehicles of efficient production?

In this story, such key human traits as uniqueness, free will, and creativity pose enormous problems. Machines are built to do repetitive functions that require no thought and minimal adjustment. Conformity and compliance are key values. Creativity is unwanted, because it is always surprising and therefore uncontrollable. If we tolerate creative expressions, this leads to unmanageable levels of diversity. A machine world is willing to sacrifice exploration for prediction. Guaranteed levels of performance are preferable to surprising breakthroughs. In our machine-organizations, we try to extinguish individuality in order to reach our goal of certainty. We trade uniqueness for control and barter our humanness for petty performance measures.

It is one of the great ironies of our age that we created organizations to constrain our problematic human natures, and now the only thing that can save these organizations is a full appreciation of the expansive capacities of us humans.

So it is time for the new story. Our old one, with its alienating myths, is eating away at us from the inside, rotting from its core. Fewer of us can tell it with any conviction. Increasing numbers of us have heard the Gaian voice and seen in our experience ways of being together that celebrate and affirm life. More and more we are in conversations where we speak of the great forces of life—love, purpose, soul, spirit, freedom, courage, integrity, meaning. The new story is being born in these conversations. We are learning to give voice to a different and fuller sense of who we really are.

The new story is a tale of the primal trinity of Gaia, Chaos, and Eros. Once our machine glasses have been set aside, we can see life's ebullient creativity and life's great need for other life. We see a world whose two great organizing energies are the need to create and the need for relationships. We see a world where there is no such thing as an independent individual and no need for a leader to take on as much responsibility as we've demanded in the past.

As I develop some of the major themes of this new story of life, I draw first on the work of modern science. However, science is only the most recent voice. We hear Gaia's story in primal wisdom traditions, in today's indigenous tribes, in most spiritual thought, and in poets old and new. It is a story that has never been forgotten by any of us, that has been held for us continually by many peoples and cultures. Yet for those of us exhausted by the old mechanistic tale, it feels new. And it certainly opens us to new discoveries about who we are as people, as organizations, and as women.

For me, one of the most wonderful contrasts of the old and new stories came from thinking about a passage I read in Kevin Kelly's book *Out of Control.* As he reached for language to describe life, he moved into sheer exuberance. (I always pay attention when a scientist uses poetry or exuberant language—I know that something has touched him or her at a level of awareness that I don't want to ignore.) Kelly was trying to describe the ceaseless creativity that characterizes life. He said that life gives to itself this great freedom, the freedom to become. Then he asked, "Becoming what?" and went on to answer: "Becoming becoming. Life is on its way to further complications, further deepness and mystery, further processes of becoming and change. Life is circles of becoming, an autocatalytic set, inflaming itself with its own sparks, breeding upon itself more life and more wildness and more 'becomingness.' Life has no conditions, no moments that are not instantly becoming something more than life itself."

Kelly's passionate description of Gaian processes that inflame, breed more life and wildness, create more deepness and mystery, stand in stark contrast to the expectations we have held for one another. Contrast Kelly's description of life with the lives we describe when we design an organizational chart. The contrast between the two is both funny and sobering. Could we even begin to tolerate such levels of passion and creativity in our organizations? But can we survive without them?

In the 1960s, the great American poet A. R. Ammons told the same story in different and precise language in *Tape for the Turn of the Year:*

> Don't establish the
> > boundaries
> > first
> > the squares, triangles,
> > boxes
> > of preconceived
> > possibility,
> > and then
> > pour
> > life into them, trimming
> off left-over edges,
> ending potential:
> > let centers

        proliferate
        from
    self-justifying motions!

In both recent science and poetry, we are remembering a story about life that has creativity and connectedness as its essential themes. As we use this new story to look into our organizational lives, it offers us images of how we could be together that are both startling and enticing. It offers us images of organizations where our diversity—our uniqueness—is essential and revered. It offers us an arena big enough to embrace the full expression of our infinitely creative human natures. And for the first time in a long time, it offers us the recognition that we humans are, in the words of physicist Ilya Prigogine, "the most striking realization of the laws of nature." We can use ourselves and what we know about ourselves to understand the universe. By observing with new eyes the processes of creation in us, we can understand the forces that create galaxies, move continents, and give birth to stars. No longer intent on describing ourselves as the machines we thought the universe to be, we are encouraged now to describe the universe through the life we know we are.

As we look at life through the lens of human nature and human desire, we are presented with some wonderful realizations. Our own desire for autonomy and creativity is reflected in all life. Life appears as boundlessly creative, searching for new possibilities and new capacities wherever it can. Observing the diversity of life forms has become a humbling experience for many biologists. At this point, no one knows how many different species there are, or where the next forms of life will appear, except that now we even expect them to appear elsewhere in our solar system.

Life is born from this unquenchable need to be. One of the most interesting definitions of life in modern biology is that something is considered alive if it has the capacity to create itself. The term for this is *autopoiesis*—self-creation—from the same root as poetry. At the very heart of our ideas about life is this definition: Life begins from the desire to create something original, to bring a new being into form.

As I have read about and observed more consciously the incredible diversity of life, I have felt witness to a creativity that has little to do with the survival struggles that we thought explained everything. Newness appears not for simple utilitarian purposes but just because it is possible to be inventive. Life gives to itself the freedom to become because life is about discovering new possibilities, new forms of expression. Two Chilean biologists, Francisco Varela and Humberto Maturana, observe that life responds not to "survival of the fittest," but to the greater space of experimentation of "survival of the fit." Many designs, many adaptations are possible and organisms enjoy far more freedom to experiment than we humans, with our insane demand to "get it right the first time."

The freedom to experiment, to tinker oneself into a form of being that can live and reproduce, leads to diversity that has no bounds. In my own telling of the Gaian story, I believe that the very purpose of life is to explore newness, that newness is a primary value embraced by all life, a primary force that encourages life into new discoveries. The need and ability to create one's self is a force we see quite clearly in human experience but which we have greatly misunderstood in our organizational lives.

The second great force to add to this cosmic story is that life needs other life. Life needs relationships in order to exist. Gaia is not lonely. It is impossible to look into the natural world and find a separated individual. As an African proverb states: "Alone, I have seen many marvelous things, none of which were true." Biologist Lynn Margulis expresses a similar idea when she comments that independence is a political concept, not a biological concept. Everywhere life displays itself as complex, tangled, messy webs of relationships. From these relationships, life creates systems that offer greater stability and support than life lived alone. Organisms shape themselves in response to their neighbors and their environments. All respond to one another, co-evolving and co-creating the complex systems of organization that we see in nature. Life is systems-seeking. It seeks organization. Organization is a naturally occurring phenomenon. Self-organization is the powerful force by which Gaia created herself through relationships, creating all the living systems we see. She knows how to organize from the inside out, from partnering with neighbors rather than from imposition and control.

These self-organizing systems have the capacity to create for themselves the organizations that we thought had to be provided to them. Self-organizing systems create structures and pathways, networks of communication, values and meaning, behaviors and norms. In essence, they do for themselves most of what we believed we had to do to them. Rather than thinking of organization as an imposed structure, plan, design, or role, it is clear that in life, organization arises from the interactions and needs of individuals who have decided to come together. We see the results of these relationships in the forms that arise; but it is important, especially because we are so easily seduced by material forms, to look past these manifestations to the desires for relationship that gave birth to the forms.

It is easy to observe the clash of the old and new stories in many places, but one arena where it is painfully visible is in organizations that we create to fulfill some special purpose, some important call. People came together in response to the call; they joined because they knew that more was possible by organizing together than by staying alone. Their dream of contribution required an organization to move it forward. These human desires—to find meaning in one's life, to bring more good into the world, to seek out others—are part of the new story.

But the clash with old beliefs and images occurs as soon as we embark on the task of creating an organization. We move back to machine ideas about structures, roles, designs, leaders. We create organizations from the outside, imposing these limiting designs on the rich desires of those who have come together. We sever relationships by creating boxes; we ignore meaning by focusing on procedures. Over time, the organization that was created in response to some deep call becomes a rigid structure that impedes fulfilling that call. People come to resent the organization they created because now it is a major impediment to their creativity, to their faith, to their purposeful dreams.

Gaia holds out different images of organization—she teaches us that when we join together we are capable of giving birth to the form of the organization, to the plans, to the values, to the vision. All of life is self-organizing and so are we. But her new story also details a process for organizing that stands in shocking contrast to the images of well-planned, well-orchestrated, well-supervised organizing. I can summarize the organizing processes of life quite simply: Life seeks organization, but it uses messes to get there. Organization is a process, not a structure. The process of organizing is difficult to chart because it happens in many places simultaneously within messy and expanding webs. It involves creating relationships around a shared sense of purpose, exchanging and creating information, learning constantly, paying attention to the results of our efforts, co-adapting, co-evolving, developing wisdom as we learn, staying clear about our purpose, being alert to changes from all directions. Living systems give form to their organization, and evolve those forms into new ones, because of exquisite capacities to create meaning together, to communicate, and to notice what's going on in the moment. These are the capacities that give any organization its true liveliness, that support life's desire to self-organize.

In the Gaian story, we are introduced to a world where life gives birth to itself in response to two powerful forces: the imperative to create one's self as an exploration of newness, and the need to reach out for relationships with others. I could similarly describe these as the force of Chaos, where creativity and freedom abound, and the force of Eros, where we are impelled to create through attraction. These forces cannot disappear from life. Even if we deny them, we can never extinguish them. They are always active, even in the most repressive human organizations. Life can never stop asserting its need to create itself, and life never stops searching for other life.

We fail to acknowledge these unstoppable forces of life whenever we try to impose direction and control. But life always pushes back against our demands for obedience. When this happens, instead of learning about life, we tend to see others' "difficult" behaviors as justification for a more controlling style. I believe that most of the failures and discontents in our organizational lives can be understood as the result of this denial of life's forces, and the pushing back of life against a story that excludes them.

As an example of these competing forces, think about how many times you have engaged in conversations about "resistance to change." I have participated in far too many of these and, in the old days as a consultant, when I still thought that it was me who was "managing" change, my colleagues and I always were thoughtful enough to plan a campaign to overcome this resistance. Contrast this view that humans resist change with Kelly's images of life as "further processes of becoming and change . . . circles of becoming, inflaming itself with its own sparks, breeding upon itself more life and more wildness." Who's telling the right story? Do we, as a species, dig in our heels while the rest of life is engaged in this awesome dance of creation? Are we the only problem, whereas the rest of life participates in something wild and wonderful?

The old story asserts that resistance to change is a fact of life. In a world that sought stability and control and feared chaos, change has always been frightening. But Gaia has always partnered with Chaos and Eros. Resistance is not a fact of life but evidence of an act of insult against life. Life is in motion, constantly creating, exploring, discovering. Newness is its desire. Nothing alive, including us, resists these great creative motions. But all of life resists control. All of life pushes back against any process that inhibits its freedom to create itself.

In organizations of the old story, plans and designs are constantly being imposed. People are told what to do all the time. As a final insult, we go outside the organization to look for answers, returning with experts that we offer up as great gifts. Yet those in the organization can only see these external and imposed solutions as insults. Their creativity has been dismissed, their opportunity to discover something new for the organization has been denied. When we deny life's need to create, life pushes back. We label it resistance and invent strategies to overcome it. But we would do far better if we changed the story and learned how to invoke the resident creativity of everyone. We need to work with these insistent creative forces or they will be provoked to work against us.

And most organizations deny the systems-seeking, self-organizing forces that are always present, the forces that, in fact, are responsible for uncharted levels of contribution and innovation. These fail to get reported because they occur outside "the boxes of preconceived possibility." There is no better indicator of the daily but unrecognized contributions made by people than when a municipal union decides to "work to rule." These unions are prohibited from going on strike. But they have developed an effective form of protest against problematic working conditions. They work only according to the rule book. They *only* follow policies and job descriptions. Even though the rule books and policy manuals were designed to create productive employees, as soon as they take them literally, cities cease running, effective civil functioning stops. What they demonstrate so forcefully is that no organization can function on the *planned* contributions of its members. Every organization relies intensely on its members going beyond the rules and roles. The organization relies on its members to figure out what needs to be done, to solve unexpected problems, to contribute in a crisis situation. But although organizations depend on this self-organizing activity, leaders seldom acknowledge it.

We also deny these system-seeking forces when we narrow people to self-serving work, when we pit colleagues against one another to improve performance, when we believe people are most strongly motivated by promises of personal gain. If we deny people's great need for relationships, for systems of support, for work that connects to a larger purpose, they push back. They may respond first by embracing competition, but then lose interest in the incentives. Performance falls back to pre-contest levels, in both children and adults. In organizations driven by greed, people push back by distrusting and despising their leaders. In organizations that try to substitute monetary rewards for a true purpose, people respond with apathy and disaffection.

It is possible to look at the negative and troubling behaviors in organizations today as the clash between the forces of life and the forces of domination, between the new story and the old. Once we realize that we cannot ever extinguish these creative forces, that it is impossible to deny the life that lives in our organizations, we can begin to search for new ways of being together.

We who live in the new story can help others understand themselves differently by the way we are with them. We can trust their humanness; we can welcome the surprises they bring to us; we can be curious about our differences; we can delight in their inventiveness; we can nurture them; we can connect them to one another. As Gaia has trusted us, we can trust them to create wisely and well. We know they have the best interests of our organization and our community at heart; we know they want to bring more good into the world.

We who hold this story feel both its beauty and its promise. What might we create if we lived our lives closer to the spirit of life? What might our organizations accomplish if they trusted and called on that spirit? I want us to be telling this story in every organization we engage with. When we hear the old story from a boss, a counselor, a politician, I want our voices to emerge with what we know to be true. I want us to stop being persuaded away from the deeper realities we know. I want us to feel the new sanity that we hold within us, and to give it voice.

We have been given a new story. When it is time for a new story to emerge, holding onto the past, whether from self-doubt or fear, only intensifies our dilemma. We experience daily the failures of the old story, and if no one voices an alternative we descend into a profound sense of lost.

So what is asked of us, the tellers of the new story, is our voice and our courage. We do not need to create a massive training program, a global-wide approach, a dramatic style. We only need to speak our story when we are with others. We need to break our silence and share the Gaian vision we have come to know.

If this story had been given to you, it is time to tell it, wherever you are, to whomever you meet. Brian Swimme compares our role to that of the early Christians. They had nothing but "a profound revelatory experience. They did nothing—nothing but wander about telling a new story." As with these early believers, we need only become wanderers, telling our new story.

Through our simple wanderings, we will "ignite the transformation of humanity."

And, in *Evolution Extended,* Brian Swimme leaves us with a promise: "What will happen when the storytellers emerge? What will happen when 'the primal mind' sings of our common origin, our stupendous journey, our immense good fortune? We will become Earthlings. We will have evoked out of the depths of the human psyche those qualities enabling our transformation from disease to health. They will sing our epic of being, and stirring up from our roots will be a vast awe, an enduring gratitude, the astonishment of communion experiences, and the realization of cosmic adventure."

What a wonderful promise. Gaia has invited us into the telling.

Angeles Arrien, anthropologist, author, educator, and corporate consultant, lectures internationally and conducts workshops that bridge cultural anthropology, psychology, and comparative religions. She is the founder and president of the Angeles Arrien Foundation for Cross-Cultural Education and Research, and the author of *The Four-Fold Way* and *Signs of Life* (winner of the 1993 Benjamin Franklin Award).

Transformation in the Millennium

"The salvation of this human world lies nowhere else than in the human heart,
in the human power to reflect, in human meekness and human responsibility."

—Vaclav Havel, President of Czechoslovakia
in his address to the U.S. Congress

As the millennium approaches, Vaclav Havel reminds us of what is needed in our human psychospiritual development in order to remedy the global crisis of character, courage, and weak-heartedness that is present in the world today. How do we follow what has heart and meaning? What are the tools that encourage reflection? How do we make choices that support courage, character, service, and effective leadership? How can we take responsibility and create a world that is healthier, happier—with less violence, apathy, and despair?

In the Lakota tradition, according to Billy Mills in his book *Wokini,* there are eight lies of Iktumi, the trickster or liar figure, that have the ability to jeopardize happiness and ruin a person's life. These are Iktumi's ancient invitations to self-deception:

1. If only I were rich, then I would be happy.
2. If only I were famous, then I would be happy.
3. If only I could find the right person to marry, then I would be happy.
4. If only I had more friends, then I would be happy.
5. If only I were more attractive, then I would be happy.
6. If only I weren't physically handicapped in any way, then I would be happy.
7. If only someone close to me hadn't died, then I could be happy.
8. If only the world were a better place, then I would be happy.

None of these illusions are true in relationship to our happiness and salvation. At work and at home, we obsessively strive for as many of the eight illusions as we can, things Iktumi tells us will make us happy. Once these goals are attained, we are often stunned to find ourselves still without satisfaction, meaning, or happiness. Ceasing to strive for meaning and happiness, according to Iktumi's ways, allows us to open and become liberated from our own fear and false attachments. Take time to reflect on which of the eight lies have driven your personal and professional expression in different areas of your life.

Gandhi reminds us of an important leadership principle that can serve us well in staying liberated and fully expressive in a meaningful way in all sectors of our life. He states that "Power, privilege, and position are great resources. Use them well. Do not become attached to them; for when we do, we begin to lose our moral fiber."

Regardless of where we find ourselves making a contribution or being connected to our creative fire, nothing will be accomplished that has meaning unless the lies of Iktumi are dismantled, and the priority of happiness is connected to values that support our moral fiber and reinstate the right use of power, privilege, and position.

At this time in history, humanity is undergoing an initiation. Collectively, at some level, all of us know that we are being initiated into a new world. The Dalai Lama reminds us of the motivation we must carry as we go through this initiation: "We must have a pure, honest, and warm-hearted motivation, and on top of that determination, optimism, hope, and the ability not to be discouraged. The whole of humanity depends on this motivation."

Universally there are eight gates of initiation that are important for us to identify to maintain clear motivation and dismantle the eight lies. Each of these gates are all present in different parts of our lives. Each gate prepares us to come into the fullness of our authentic selves without bringing forward any of Iktumi's lies. To help us identify and work with these eight gates of initiation, I have placed these gates within the oldest healing and teaching art found in all cultures, *storytelling*. Cross-culturally, story is a tool of reflection and discovery. Story opens us to discover where we really are in our journey rather than where we think we are. As we go through these eight universal gates, review which gates are most prevalent in your life. Which ones are the easiest or most challenging for you at this time? How can the application of this information be used to help us as we are collectively initiated into the new millennium?

THE STORY OF THE EIGHT GATES OF INITIATION

In the not-so-far-away land, in very ordinary time—in the time, east of the sun and west of the moon, where stories are older than pine needles on a tree—a little gnome with green boots and a rust felt hat taps his foot on the root of an old oak tree, saying, "You know, we all come through the silver gate, and we all go out the gold gate, and there are many gates in between." Let us approach each of these gates in turn.

THE SILVER GATE: BIRTH AND NEW EXPERIENCES

The silver gate represents all that is *new* in our lives—whether it is a new belief, a new relationship, a new interest, a new creative project, a new experience. At this gate, we are required to consider, What's new in my life? How can I attend to what is emerging in my life? Just as we tend to babies with deep love, care, and attention, we need to bring those same qualities to the process that we're all involved in at this time. We need to trust and preserve what is new, without pushing or holding back. In many ways, the twelve labors of Hercules or Inanna's passage to the underworld offer the archetypal prototypes of what is necessary to birth something new in our interior and external lives at this time in history. The silver gate is present at any conception, furthers in the gestation process, initiates in its laboring, and triumphs in birth. What mental, emotional, physical, and spiritual births are being conceived, gestated, labored, and delivered for each of us personally and collectively? These processes announce the presence of the silver gate in our lives.

THE WHITE PICKET FENCE GATE: CHANGING IDENTITIES

We then come to the white picket fence gate. It asks us to drop our teeth so our face will change. Cross-culturally, this gate is about changing identities. Every culture of the world creates masks, and what are masks but cultural recognitions that we are constantly letting go of old parts of ourselves so new parts can emerge? At this gate we must consider, "What deeper or more amplified identity am I urged to release or allow to emerge at this time? How can I trust the instinctual authenticity that waits and wants always to emerge?"

And she looked into the mirror and saw squirrel ears, cat whiskers, a pig's snout, one side fur, the other side scales, webbed feet, turtle hands, she thought to herself, "Oh my God, I'm changing."

THE CLAY GATE: RIGHT USE OF SEXUALITY AND SENSUALITY

At the clay gate, we are confronted by what is always changing and shifting yet never comes into form. Behind this gate, an old wizened male gnome holds a bowl with thick white liquid in it, and an old wizened female gnome holds a bowl with thick red liquid in it. The bowl with thick white liquid is given to every young lad coming through this gate, and the bowl with thick red liquid is given to every young maiden coming through this gate. As every young lad and as every young maiden comes to this gate the old wizened male and female gnomes say, "Now you've entered a mystery you'll never understand." The clay gate is the gate of our initiation into sensuality and sexuality, that mystery we will never understand.

And he came through the back door with his black sombrero and his black snapping eyes, and he challenged all with his charisma and contagious smile to meet his gaze. When you looked closely you saw silver bullets across his chest, and tucked in between the silver bullets were dried wildflowers. He looked around and there was only one face that would hold his gaze, a silver-haired woman with doe-brown eyes. He took off his hat and threw it across the room. It landed at her feet, and the whole room stood up and cheered, "Viva Zapata!"

This kind of instant recognition of another or an attraction often reveals itself at the clay gate, the gate of sensuality and sexuality. This gate is always changing because our relationship to sensuality and sexuality is always changing. The expression of our sexuality is very different in our twenties and thirties, in our forties and fifties, and in our sixties, seventies, and eighties—the sensuality of coming to our senses, using common sense, enjoying touch, sounds, tastes, aesthetics, and true beauty. At the clay gate we inquire, "How can I express my sexuality as an expression of love that is alignment with my emotional integrity? How can I re-beautify the Earth? How can I walk in my beauty? How can I come to my senses and use my common sense?"

THE BLACK-AND-WHITE GATE: RELATIONSHIPS, INTIMACY, AND COMMITMENT

And then we come to the double gate, the black gate with the white knob and the white gate with a black knob. At this gate there are no gnomes, there are only torches of fire. We cannot go through this gate alone; we are required to go through it with at least one other person.

The fire roars and says we will be burned and humbled at this gate. This is the gate where we are required to drop pride and fear, to learn about intimacy, commitment, and deep loyalty. We release betrayals, self-deceptions, and many of Iktumi's eight lies at this gate.

The art and craft of relationship is learned at this gate, not only the relationship with self but the relationship with a significant other and the relationships we have with collectives, organizational groupings, and teams. This is the gate where once again we remember who we are as humans: we are of the Earth—*humus*, out of this root word come the words "human," "humor," "humility," and "humiliation."

At the black-and-white gate we learn about love; here we're forced to know that the only way to come home to spirit is to allow our love nature, Eros, to be stronger than fear. Easy to say, difficult to practice. We need to bless those who challenge us to be fully loving; they mirror to us where we may withhold our love by being closed-hearted, half-hearted, and weak-hearted. They are great teachers for us, and remind us that the greatest remorse for human beings is love unexpressed. At the black-and-white gate, we are faced with the questions, "Who am I currently learning from about love at the black-and-white gate? What do I know about love? What am I learning about love? Where do I not fully express my love in my life at this time? What gets in the way of my expression of love?"

THE RUSTIC GATE:
CREATIVITY AND OUR LIFE DREAM

The rustic gate, loose on its hinges, opens up to a great green meadow filled with wildflowers and deep valleys surrounded by huge mountains. In the meadow is a huge bonfire that takes no wood. In the center of this meadow is a large boulder where a gnome wags his finger at anyone coming into the meadow, and says, "You won't find your way out of here unless you leave a project in the great green meadow. You won't find your way out of here unless you reconnect to the creative fire, the fire that takes no wood. You can't find your way out of here unless you leave your dream in the great green meadow."

At the rustic gate in our lives, we are challenged to see where we are with our creativity and work: "What parts of my life are asking me to reconnect to the creative fire, the fire that takes no wood? How many projects have I left in this meadow, finished or unfinished? What parts of my dream have I actually manifested in my life—the great green meadow? Am I doing work that I love?" The Persian poet Rumi paid this tribute to creativity when he wrote:

*Today, like every other day, I wake up empty and frightened. Don't go to the door of the study and read a book. Instead, take down the dulcimer, **let the beauty of what you love be what you do.** There are a thousand ways to kneel and kiss the ground, there are a thousand ways to go home again.*

Rumi reminds us that today, like every other day, we may wake up empty and frightened. Today, we may have forgotten who we are. When we feel alienated, separated, isolated, that is not a time to take a detour. Don't go to the study and begin to escape into a favorite mystery novel or TV. Instead, take down the dulcimer, a symbol of our life dream, our heart song. Let the beauty of what we love be what we do. This is our reminder in the great green meadow, with the rustic gate, loose on its hinges. There are a thousand ways to go home again; there are a thousand ways to kneel and kiss the ground; a thousand ways to reconnect to the creative fire, and our life dream.

THE BONE GATE: AUTHENTICITY AND CHARACTER

Next we come to the bone gate, surrounded by large vats, where the sky is filled with ashes that fall into the vats. When we go through this gate, anything that's unnatural in our nature is totally shredded and the ashes fill the air. This is the gate where we are absolutely required to come back home to the authentic self, to model character, and to drop the false self system that is fueled by pretense, performance, editing, rehearsing, or hiding.

Gertrude Stein would invite contemporary artists and writers to her Paris salons, and would note at the bottom of her invitation, "Please remember that no one real is boring." In other words, please leave your false selves at home. Remember, no one real is boring. At the bone gate we confront who or what is asking us to return to the authentic self, to tell the truth, to stay in our integrity, and to value character development. There comes a time in the spiritual journey where our patterns of denial and our patterns of indulgence become more painful than truly being ourselves. This is when we begin finally to risk telling the truth about who we really are. At the bone gate, the sky is filled with ashes of the shredded false self, and the ashes drop into large vats around the gate—so that we can reclaim the authentic self and release all eight lies of Iktumi. We look again to see, "Who or what is challenging me to be fully authentic, truthful, and real? Where am I avoiding being who I truly am at this time? What gets in the way of trusting myself completely?"

THE NATURAL GATE: HAPPINESS, SATISFACTION, AND PEACE

Deep in the heart of the forest, surrounded by a beautiful desert where two trees arch, we meet the natural gate. It is said that every woman of the world comes out of an elm tree and that every man of the world comes out of an ash tree; and that all other trees that we know and love are said to be their children. A powerful shaft of light comes down between these two trees, where they arch and touch each other. When we arrive at this gate, warmed by the light and comforted by the balance of the elm and the ash, we have the experience of deep contentment, satisfaction, and happiness.

The natural gate requires that we review where in our lives we are experiencing deep contentment, satisfaction, and happiness. When have we experienced those states in the past? Whenever we experience happiness and peace in our natures, we are at the gate where the medicines of joy, laughter, play, fun, and humor flourish. Victor Borge reminds us of the natural unity found at this gate when he said that laughter is the shortest distance between two people.

The natural gate requires us to consider, "What makes me happy, who makes me happy? What satisfies me? How do I satisfy myself? How do I savor wisdom found in silence? What nourishes peace in my nature?" This is the gate where we experience a sense of peace that often comes in deep quietude, stillness, or contemplation. The experiences of solitude are those in which we feel filled by silence, rather than empty or alone. At the natural gate we come home to the deep spiritual essence of who we are—in satisfaction, peace, and contentment.

THE GOLD GATE: DETACHMENT, SURRENDER, AND LETTING GO

While sitting within the natural gate, feeling the light, we become mesmerized by our new awareness. Gradually we are drawn up, up, up towards the light to find ourselves at the gold gate. Here we are asked to surrender, and to let go of our attachments. At the gold gate, we learn about detachment, the capacity to deeply care from an objective place. This is the gate where we learn about dying and letting go. We practice the art and craft of dying every night when we put ourselves in bed, access a deep trust, and let go into the mystery of night, into formless form. Dying is the process of letting go and surrendering.

The gold gate is the place where we learn about surrender, about letting go, about detachment in different parts of our life. We practice the art and craft of dying when we say goodbye to people that we will be separated from for some time. We practice the art of dying whenever we complete something that had meaning and significance for us. At this gate we're asked to totally trust, to give up control, which is the opposite of trust. Wherever we are trying to stay in control, controlling others, or controlling the situation, we are attached and nontrusting. The gold gate requires that we look at the attachments that are necessary to release from our lives and to seriously consider what needs to be released and surrendered in life to become more effective.

Finally, we come full circle in our story to the gnome with green boots and a rust felt hat, tapping his foot on the root of an old oak tree, saying, "We all come through the silver gate, and we all go out the gold gate, and there are many gates in between."

Globally, we are at the silver gate, the birthing gate. We are at a time in history where collectively we are laboring to give birth to a new world. Simultaneously, we will be required to dismantle and let go of Iktumi's eight lies at the gold gate, while we experience and gather resources from all the other gates in between.

Transformation in the millennium ultimately will require that each individual follow Buddha's sage advice:

> *However young the seeker who*
> *sets out upon the way*
> *Shines bright over the world.*
> *But day and night the person who is awake*
> *Shines in the radiance of the spirit.*
> *Meditate, Live purely, Be quiet.*
>
> *Do your work with Mastery*
> *Like the Moon,*
> *Come out from behind the clouds!*
> *Shine.*

Marion Woodman is a Jungian analyst, a graduate of the C. G. Jung-Institut, Zurich, Switzerland. She is the author of several books on feminine consciousness, including *The Pregnant Virgin, Addiction to Perfection,* and *The Ravaged Bridegroom.* Her most recent book, with Jill Mellick, is *Coming Home to Myself.*

Crossing the Threshold: Fear or Feelings

It is December 31, 1997. New Year's Eve is not one of my favorite celebrations, never has been. The old year with all its surprises and disappointments, triumphs and mistakes, has become a friend—congenial, undemanding. A new year stretches ahead, fresh as white snow, pristine, perfectly void. New Year's Eve 1999 flashes through me, a whole millennium, pristine, perfectly void, daunting. Advertisements already invite me to the greatest parties, the greatest champagne, the greatest ways of passing into oblivion in greatest style on that greatest of New Year's Eves. That is not my idea of style. If I am going to stride elegantly through Threshold 2000, I have some heavy baggage to leave behind between now and then.

As I look around me and within me, I think the biggest wound in our contemporary psyche is fear. What cripples us from daring the New Day is unconscious fear, the worst kind of fear, fear without content. As I see it, it is fear of dependency, fear of the loss of personal freedom that permeates so many relationships—personal, national, and international. With the globalization of the economy, more and more people are being forced from the land and the small businesses that have been their families' security, their psychological mother, for generations. Now many of them are eking out an existence in factories or corporate jobs in which they take no pride and find no self-worth. Others in the so-called middle class are faithfully working hard, centred in their professions and home, only to discover that the savings which they have always trusted, indeed their whole security base, their mother, is threatened by a stock market crash, a freefall that can be manipulated by cyberspace billionaires.

The fear evoked in the loss of basic security triggers nonverbal, infantile fear. Nothing is more frightening than absolute dependence. Someone or something has the power of life and death in an absolute sense. That fear—spoken or unspoken—is intensified when individuals are separated from their mother land and their mother body. The reliance on reason and technology has split head from body in our culture; therefore, many individuals cannot depend on their own body to be their own ground of feeling. In this splitting, polarization creates an unnatural psychic situation—a death mother on one side separated from an idealized mother on the other, death separated from life, life from death. In natural life, nothing is polarized; life and death are one. Their unity minimizes fear.

If, for example, we think of our total dependence during the nine months we spend in our mother's womb, our emergence from that cosy container or prison can be experienced as birth or death. We are forced from the womb that has been our sole sustenance into an unknown world. However, our faculties that have been forming for nine months—ears, eyes, lungs—all are suddenly necessary to this new reality. Death in one world is birth in another. Spiritually speaking, this is known as rebirth. If we can hold that shifting perspective, death and birth, negative and positive mother are no longer polarized. They move from contradiction to paradox: what appeared negative appears as potentially positive.

In order to move through thresholds gracefully, we have to come to this detached focal point. Then we ask the question: In this death, what is struggling to be born? Without this perspective, the sense of dependence on that which is no longer dependable is as overwhelming as death, and fear becomes fight, flight, or freeze.

The core of initiation festivals is the letting go of what is now, in the natural progression of life, dead, and the recognition that the new life is present in potential ready to flower into new life. The awareness of our failure to recognize the fundamental rhythms of life, death, and rebirth can help us to accept the reality of the death of the old making way for the new. Surely, the greatest teaching of 1997 lies in the tragic death of Diana, Princess of Wales. In her death, what is struggling to be born? The collective love that poured out following her death has to find meaning in a new outpouring of the feminine love that can confront existing patriarchal institutions, permeate their rigidity, and bring forth something new. Surely as the wave of love for Diana swept around the Western world and met with the wave of love for Mother Teresa that swept around the Eastern world, surely as they swept Earth together, something new was born. Most of us were droplets in that magnificent wave, and something in us was changed. Instead of carrying the depression of our lost feelings in our lost bodies, we are now responsible for bringing our grief and fear and love to consciousness, for re-creating them and integrating them into our lives. If we can even work on that possibility, we can be free to move as whole human beings, thinking *and feeling*, into the new millennium.

Daphne Rose Kingma is the bestselling author of eight books on the psychospiritual aspects of love, including *True Love, Love for a Lifetime, A Garland of Love, Weddings from the Heart,* and, most recently, *The Future of Love.*

A Profound Infusion of Love

There is an ancient expression that an artist works *con amore* with God in the creation of every work of art. What this means is that the divine energy flows through him or her and that this energy, love, is what brings the work of art to life. In this last century, we have quietly drawn toward the possibility of infusing our lives with more love. But we have not yet become artists of love to the full dimension of that possibility.

As we approach the millennium, we are now being called to this great work. We are being invited to an opening of our hearts and a deeper awareness of our souls, to an experience of the energy of love which is, in fact, our essence and to infuse it into every arena of our existence.

What this means, very simply, is that we need to love more. We are being called to more conscious love, more kinds of love, more capacity to love, more freedom to love, more valuing of love, more trusting that love will carry us to where we need to go, more capacity to feel the love that is constantly being offered to us in a myriad of forms—by lovers and strangers, by plants and animal and trees, by flowers and children, and by the gentle Earth itself. We are being asked to become creators of the changes through which subtly, and with beauty, our world will become ever more infused with love.

A PERSONAL UNDERTAKING

This infusion of love is a personal undertaking. It requires, first of all, that we awaken to the necessity of allowing love to operate at every level of our lives. Love, by now, is a necessity. This is because at no other time in history have we been more thoroughly subjected to the circumstances that insist upon love—the stressful complexity of our daily lives; the ways we have already compromised the well-being of our planet; the longing in our hearts for a meaning to our existence that goes beyond the daily and the ordinary; an already burgeoning awareness that we are spiritual and not merely physical or even psychological beings.

Over the last several centuries we have moved steadily through the various epochs of our human evolution—from survival and conquest to rational thought and technological grandeur. Our frontier, now, is our own inner being—discovering our spiritual essence, accessing the love that resides in each of us, and offering it as a gift to the world.

We have a magnificent metaphor for the presence of love in our midst. Our fabulous technological ingenuity has created a world that is now linked by a pulsating electronic web, a global nervous system which demonstrates in a very concrete way that as a body of humanity we are all beautifully linked together, that we are all incredibly connected. We accept "the Web" as a miracle of technology, but the real challenge now is for us to see that it is love that is truly the web of our connection, that we are all of a piece as human beings and spirits, that we share the same joys and woes, that we partake of the same eternal spiritual destiny.

It may seem almost simplistic to say that what the world needs now is more love. In one form or another, we've been talking about love for centuries. We've heard hundreds of songs and poems and seen multitudes of works of art that talk about love and how it makes us feel and what it can do for us. The truth is all those poems and songs aren't wrong. What they are really saying in their romantic, passionate, heartbroken way is that love really is the energy that creates and sustains our world.

But now we are being called upon to expand our definition of love, to understand it and embody it in all of its richness and complexity. It is about the love that passes all understanding, that the new millennium will teach us— but only if we are willing to become the artists who, *con amore,* create this new world.

In order to become the creators of a world that is truly infused with love, we must begin by becoming aware of the many ordinary and beautiful forms of love that already exist in our lives. The most familiar of these is the love that we experience in our intimate relationships. Here we become acquainted with love, we discover its power to excite and delight us. We learn how much love feeds us, how lost and unlike ourselves we feel when we aren't being loved.

Because we "fall in love" and have the experience of some kind of ecstatic sensation which is categorically different from every other life experience, we have all had at least a taste of love, a moment, a glimmer of knowing what it feels like to be loved.

But in the course of a lifetime we will experience many kinds of love: not only romantic love, but the love of friendship, the love of our parents and children. What is most significant is that in all of these experiences we are connected by more than the forms of these *particular* relationships. We are affected by the *love* in them. And as we are loved, well or badly, we learn more about the nature of love itself. We learn to give love because it has been given to us—or because of its painful absence. If we have been loved well, that generosity spills over, and if we haven't, that void of love becomes in time either bitterness or the birthplace of our own compassion. Through loss and love, we become lovers ourselves.

Love is an energy. We don't experience it in the abstract. We experience it through the medium of our relationships. And so it is that the infusion of love that is being asked for above all is an enriching of all our relationships, our relationships with our spouses and lovers, with our parents and children, with the people with whom we work, and even with our enemies and strangers.

AWAKENING EMOTIONAL AWARENESS

We have just passed through a century that taught us a great deal about our relationships. As the century opened, Freud introduced us to the magnitude of who we are as emotional beings. He acquainted us with the fact that our emotions, whether or not we're aware of them, are constantly running our lives. The fact that there is an emotional component to our lives is a thread, a sturdy cord that runs throughout the twentieth century, bringing us to new levels of awareness about how we operate as human beings and showing us that we have a consciousness that goes far beyond the information that we receive through our five senses.

With his help and the help of others, we have learned that our relationships aren't just a pairing up for the survival of the species. We have discovered that they are the vehicles for our emotional healing and that as human beings, we become ourselves through them. Our emotional bodies are formed and transformed through our relationships. They are formed by the relationships of childhood, and transformed by all the experiences of love we have as we live out the challenges and obligations of our adult romantic relationships.

The future possibility of our relationships is that now, through them, we will discover even more the exact nature of love. We will discover it not only as a property that arouses our feelings of anger, fear, happiness, and sorrow, but we will come to know it also as a property of the spirit—that is, of the dimension of our beings that is soul.

The journey to the soul begins with loving ourselves. For many of us the love of self is the foster child of all our endeavors to love. We often put ourselves last on the list of those to whom we extend the hand of our own compassion. We must love ourselves now because all true love springs from a loving awareness of self. As self-love grows we can venture toward loving another, and as we see the impact of our love on others, our capacity for self-love also increases. In this way we create an ever widening spiral of love.

You can begin this process in your own life by recognizing that you are a self, a unique and beautiful, unrepeatable person who deserves all the encouragement and recognition and care you would give to the best of your friends. What is it about your own being that is most in need of comfort, recognition, or healing? Is it your body that you have forgotten? Your spirit you have ignored? Your emotions that you have denied and held in abeyance? Is it your talents, your beauty, your strength that you've overlooked? Whatever it is, begin now to honor yourself.

Self love is part of the process of infusing the world with more love because when we love ourselves, we also become more able to love others.

And when we do, we see that our love is returned. We see that we are connected to others, and we become ever more aware of the mysterious orderly beauty of our lives. We learn the generous nature of love, and this, in time, leads us to an awareness of our souls.

EMBRACING OUR SOULS

When we speak of our souls, we are talking about the eternal dimension in each of us, that energy of spirit that comes into the human frame when we take on life. We are not just personalities but actually spiritual beings who have taken on the journey of human life. As souls we're just here for a visit. We're here to experience love as it operates in this human dimension, to learn about love through the human relationship experience.

So it is that our second undertaking becomes infusing our relationships with this soul dimension of love. In order to experience this larger spiritual dimension, we must, first of all, do our emotional work. That is, we must learn what happened to us in our childhoods and then learn how this has affected our behavior as adults. What does it mean, for example, that you grew up in poverty? Or that your father was an alcoholic? That your mother never held you? That the brother born before you died in infancy? How have these facts affected your behavior? Your relationships?

We must do this work because as long as we're involved with unresolved emotional issues we will remain unconscious about our spiritual selves and be unable to give our attention to the matters of our spirit. Until we resolve the issues that are generated by a particular level of experience, we will stay stranded at that level.

Each of us is in a different place on this journey of emotional resolution. Some of us are just getting acquainted with the fact that we are emotional beings. Some of us have resolved our relationships with our parents, but are still emotionally unaware in our relationships with our mates. Or, we may be good lovers but hurtful, unconscious parents to our own children because we haven't yet developed the lack of self-focus that allows us to be truly generous in our parenting.

It doesn't matter where you are on the scale of development. You can still contribute to the infusion of love. What matters is that wherever you are, you have the courage to ask yourself: What is the next step that I need to take in order to mature my love? Is it to resolve your issues with your parents? To become more conscious of your emotions in the intimate relationship you're having now? Is it to take on the challenge of finally becoming a parent? To learn how to love yourself better?

LOVE IN ALL DIMENSIONS

These questions are all inspired by what we commonly call our "relationships," that is, our familiar forms of being connected. But I believe that we are also being asked to bring love into every arena of our human experience, to see it not only as a property of our intimate lives, but of every aspect of our experience.

What would it mean, for example, if we asked ourselves to conduct our work with love? How would our behavior change? What different beliefs would we hold? We might see that the work we're doing isn't just a transaction that has a bottom line financially, but is one that involves human beings who, just like us, have histories and feelings. While justice or logic might say that the contract or the money is the bottom line, as participants in the infusion of love, we will see that it is the well-being of the people who are conducting the business that is the bottom line.

When we enter the world of work with our hearts open, we may not make as much money; we won't be quite as sure that we're "right," we may not be furthering the capitalist dream. Operating from the principle that every business transaction we make whether with a corporation or a single human being involves not just the gross national product, the corporate sales revenue, or even another person's billfold, but other human beings who are being affected, emotionally and spiritually, positively or negatively, by every transaction that we make, we will certainly be participating in the infusion of love.

Recently I was part of a complex business transaction in which all three parties were harmed by the arising of a series of unforeseen circumstances. As we muddled through the consequences of these unexpected developments, there was a choice about whether or not we would all go to lawyers, have a nasty fray, and win at all costs, or open our hearts, look at the situation that we had created together and see that we needed to share the consequences. We chose to do the latter. Rather than coming out of this transaction with bad feelings and bitterness, we completed it with a feeling of newfound closeness and admiration for one another—you might say, with love.

REFRAMING POLITICS

This same love must also begin to operate in the world of politics. In the political arena, too, we are being called upon to change our motivations, deepen our values, come from our hearts, and recognize that our laws exist to serve people and cannot simply be the reframing of a number of abstract principles that we think represent the way things ought to be. As long as we govern ourselves by principles that don't acknowledge our hearts or bow to the fact that we are spiritual beings, we will continue to create outcomes that will eventually lead to chaos as our souls react with a vengeance because our deeper needs are not being met.

SURRENDERING TO THE DIVINE

To infuse the world with love, we must also deepen our relationship with God. The more we surrender to God—the Divine, the Force, the Source, the ultimate, the ground of being, the alpha and the omega, love, whatever that word may mean for you—the more we shall see the beauty and order, the meaning of things.

In the past century, we have learned a great deal about our awesome powers as human beings. We have cloned animals and split genes, created medicines that cancel depression and invent childbirth after menopause. We have become almost godlike in our power. Indeed, our ability to tamper with the natural order of things is by now so developed that at times we can almost fantasize that we are the creators of life. But we have also learned about our limitations, seen the dark side of our creativity, come face to face with our ability to destroy—Auschwitz, the atom bomb, Three Mile Island, Chernobyl. But in spite of all our achievements, the actual creation of life still eludes us. And the fact that it does reveals our true place in the universe.

Surrendering to the divine is bowing to the power beyond us. And to the degree that we bow before that huge mysterious energy, to that degree precisely shall we come ever more into a state of tranquility and beauty—of love—with one another.

RECLAIMING THE EARTH

It's no secret that the Earth, our dwelling place, is in a state of disrepair and that, as a majestic being in its own right, its very survival is in question. We have been very hard on the vibrating, beautiful planet that has been given to us as the landscape in which we may unfold the origami figures of our human lives. We easily take for granted how gracious and easy our lives have become because of the gold and oil and jewels and grass and trees that the Earth has offered up so generously. But now, we must learn to live in the knowledge that nature can no longer give us her love unless we return it with our own most tender care. We must infuse the earth with our love.

A few years ago I drove to Los Angeles after the major earthquake that shattered Northridge. Driving along the freeway that I had driven down so many times before, I looked across at the mountains coated with a heavy, funereal curtain of smog. They had almost vanished from sight; their beauty was utterly obscured. It was as if the mountains themselves were announcing that they could no longer be mountains, could not any longer bear up under the unrelenting insults that had been heaped upon them. For just a minute as I saw them, I got the message: Nature isn't going to cooperate with us any more. Unless we give back, the Earth itself will become our enemy. We must plant trees; we must purify the waters; we must cleanse the air.

The labors of loving the Earth are many. None of us singlehandedly can save it, but we can all do our part. Whether your part is as simple as picking up the trash in your own front yard, cleaning up a section of the freeway, or consciously, consistently recycling every single wrapper, lid, newspaper, can, or cardboard box, you must do it. We must also love the Earth by promising that we will not, simply for the sake of our own self-indulgence, require that she give up the last of her virgin largesse.

A GLOBAL WORK OF ART

The infusion of love that is being asked for by the new millennium is a global work of art that begins with each of us in the chambers of our own hearts. Insofar as we are willing to participate, each one of us to become a channel through which more love can pour, to that degree will we see a spiritual blossoming of love in our midst more radiant than we have ever seen. For as we undertake each of these practices of love we will see more and more that as human beings we are all beautifully interwoven into a single consciousness.

As we love ourselves more, as we deepen our relationships, as we change our business practices and refine our politics, as we nurse the earth back to life, we will see that love is what we have come here to do, love is who we are. Not only will we be receivers of love as a blessing on our own path, we shall be working *con amore* with God in creating a new world.

3

THE EMERGING PATH:
QUESTING FOR WHOLENESS

"Some day, men and women will rise, they will reach the mountain peak, they will meet big and strong and free, ready to receive, to partake and to bask in the golden rays of love. What fancy, what imagination, what poetic genius can foresee even approximately the potentialities of such a force in the lives of men and women."

—Emma Goldman

These essays draw us in for a closer look at what is emerging. By definition they are painted in the soft, translucent brushstrokes of watercolor, for this is the still-forming present and the unformed future. We are led into the world of seeing what can just begin to be seen, allowing our imaginations to put substance and content into the patterns. These pieces give us a focal point, something to concentrate on, a location to watch for what is emerging and to lend our support when possible.

Taken as a group, the picture that emerges of the future is one with a greater sense of wholeness, a wholeness that comes from incorporating the feminine aspects of humanity that have been ignored or even repudiated in the past to balance the masculine aspects that have been ascendent for so long.

We begin with medical intuitive Caroline Myss, who reminds us that our childhood as a species is now over and that we are being given the opportunity to become spiritual adults. In order to do that, we must see we are responsible for co-creating our lives and that we all, no matter our religious tradition, are facing the same challenges and being given the same opportunities for wholeness.

Joan Borysenko then narrows the focus slightly to the issue of the emerging feminine principle. She refers to it as the spirit of Ishtar, who journeyed to the underworld "to redeem the male principle, that the two could co-create through love." Echoing the theme of wholeness she writes, "In the ancient tradition of India, the *shakti*, or creative feminine energy, can only rise when it comes into balance with the male energy. I believe that women, the collective earth-goddess Ishtar, are coming back from the darkness to sanctify that sacred union of male and female energies that will once again give birth to passion and purpose, refructifying the Earth and bringing hope to all our children."

Gayatri Naraine further examines the feminine principle, calling it "the clear, cool spring that can give life to humanity's arid wasteland; the sacred water from which to draw purpose and meaning," while Sue Patton Thoele examines our "deep and holy hunger" for the Sacred Feminine and offers practical tools for bringing her into daily life. Native American Paula Underwood talks about this principle in her people's terms, calling on women to become Clan Mothers, nurturers who are responsible for the community at large in the very way mothers are responsible for their children.

Therapist and author Jean Shinola Bolen looks at this force as it is manifesting in older women, echoing Barbara Marx Hubbard in recognizing the power of this age of women as they bring their wisdom to the world: "It would be a mistake to assume that they will be invisible." Carol Flinders takes the discussion of the feminine principle into the joint worlds of politics and soul, calling on feminism to find its spiritual roots in order to wake the "sleeping giant" of the women's movement.

Then Carol Parrish-Harra and Woodene Koenig-Bricker look even more closely at the feminine face of God. Parrish-Harra examines the way women are re-forming the Christian church to include the feminine principle and points to the rise of the worship of Sophia, Kuan Yin, and Mary as examples. Koenig-Bricker looks at the Holy Spirit as the feminine principle of God and asks us to recognize how Spirit is moving through us and how we limit her work in our lives.

The divine feminine is not all sweetness and light, however, reminds China Galland and Flor Fernandez, and in order to find wholeness we must embrace the other side as well. In China Galland's penetrating article on the rise of the Black Madonna, she writes, "Whoever this Dark One is, whether she appears as Virgin, Mother, Crone, or Queen, she is found underneath tradition after tradition: the Aztec Goddess Tonantzin at whose site Our Lady of Guadalupe, the Patron of All the Americas, appeared in Mexico; *La Pachamama*, the source of all life beloved by the people of the Andes; *Maria Lionza,* the mountain goddess of Venezuela; the African Goddess Isis of Egypt whose worship spread throughout Europe up until the second and third centuries C.E.; the Hindu Kali carried from India by the Gypsies on their migrations; the Orishas brought from Africa to Brazil.... This Dark One who champions all that is left out also symbolizes what must be included now." Fernandez echoes that theme in her piece. "Are you willing to take a journey not packaged in a Club Med mentality but one of wonder, honoring, and blessing the disruptions that you encounter along the way that are your best teachers?... We cannot pretend to be fully enlightened until we are willing to be endarkened."

Artist and poet M. C. Richards comes at the embracing of opposites from a different perspective, but wholeness is her quest as well as she asks us to see separating and connecting, war and peace, as part of one dynamic, inseparable. "Can we come to a state of awareness in which Peace and War come into center to enrich the forms of our relationships and intentions?" she asks. And Tantric teacher Margot Anand also urges us beyond duality, urging us to fully develop both our inner man and inner woman so that we can incorporate both aspects.

In our final contributions to this section, Cheri Huber and Sue Bender ask us to consider that we are already whole, just as we are. We need to see that "our True Nature is goodness," writes Huber, and accept what is. From acceptance "many possibilities become available to me that might never have done so had I persisted in my conditioned responses."

Caroline Myss, Ph.D., is an internationally sought-after speaker on spirituality and personal power. The author of *Anatomy of the Spirit, Why People Don't Heal and How They Can,* and *The Creation of Health,* she is widely recognized for her work teaching intuitive diagnosis and is a pioneer in the field of energy medicine. She lives in Chicago. For her full explanation of the relationship between chakras, the Christian sacraments, and the Kabbalah, see *Anatomy of the Spirit.*

Made in the Image of God

Ever since I got my first medical intuitions, I have been aware that they are basically about the human spirit, even though they describe physical problems and even though I use energy terms to explain them to others. *Energy* is a neutral word that evokes no religious associations or deeply held fears about one's relationship to God. It is much easier for someone to be told "Your energy is depleted" than "Your spirit is toxic." Yet most of the people who come to me have, in fact, been in spiritual crises. I have described their crises to them as energy disorders, but doing so was not as helpful as discussing them in spiritual terms, too, would have been.

I ultimately did incorporate spiritual language into my energy descriptions after I realized the congruencies between the Eastern chakras and Western religious sacraments. It happened suddenly, during one of my workshops on energy anatomy. As I was giving the opening lecture, I drew seven circles on the blackboard, lined up vertically to represent the power centers of the human energy system. As I turned to face the empty circles, I was struck by the fact that there are not only seven chakras but also seven Christian sacraments. In that moment I understood that their spiritual messages are the same. Later, as I researched and explored their similarities more deeply, I learned that the Kabbalah, too, has seven corresponding teachings. These three traditions' congruencies led me to see that spirituality is far more than a psychological and emotional need: it is an inherent biological need. Our spirits, our energy, and our personal power are all one and the same force.

The seven sacred truths that these traditions share lie at the core of our spiritual power. They instruct us in how to direct the power or life-force that runs through our systems. In effect, we embody these truths in our seven power centers. They are part of our internal physical and spiritual guidance system, and at the same time they are a universal, external guidance system for our spiritual behavior and for the creation of health. Our spiritual task in this lifetime is to learn to balance the energies of body and soul, of thought and action, of physical and mental power. Our bodies contain an immanent blueprint for healing.

The Book of Genesis describes Adam's body as created "in the image of God." The message in this phrase is both literal and symbolic. It means that people are energy duplicates of a Divine power system of seven primary energies whose truths we are meant to explore and develop through this experience called life.

When I realized that the human energy system embodies these seven truths, I could no longer limit myself to an energy vocabulary, and I began incorporating spiritual ideas *in* my intuitive diagnoses. Because our biological design is also a spiritual design, the language of energy and spirit used together crosses a variety of belief systems. It opens avenues of communication between faiths and even allows people to return to religious cultures they formerly rejected, unburdened by religious dogma. People in my workshops have readily adopted this energy-spirit language to address the challenges inherent in their physical illnesses, stress disorders, or emotional suffering. Seeing their problem within a spiritual framework accelerates their healing process because it adds a dimension of meaning and purpose to their crisis. They are able to help themselves heal; they co-create their health and re-create their lives. Because all human stress corresponds to a spiritual crisis and is an opportunity for spiritual learning, you can gain insight into the use, misuse, or misdirection of your spirit, your personal power, in almost any illness.

The source of human consciousness, spirit, or power is considered Divine in most religious and cultural traditions, from the ancient Greek and Hindu teachings to the Chinese and Mayan. Most every culture's myths recount Divine interaction with humanity in stories of the gods mating with human beings to produce godlike and half-godlike offspring. These offspring embody the full spectrum of human behavior—from great acts of creation, destruction, and vengeance to petty acts of jealousy, rivalry, and pique, and transcendental acts of metamorphosis, sex, and sensuality. The early cultures that created these divine mythologies were exploring their emotional and psychological natures and the powers inherent in the human spirit. Each culture expressed its own view of the transformations and passages of the universal spiritual journey—the hero's journey, in Joseph Campbell's parlance.

Among God stories, however, the Jewish tradition is unique, because Yahweh is never depicted as being sexual. God is referred to as having a right and left hand, but the description never continues "below the waist." Unlike other spiritual traditions, the Jews transferred only limited human qualities to Yahweh, maintaining a more distant relationship with their inaccessible Divine.

When Christianity appeared on the scene, however, its then still-Jewish followers gave their God a human body, calling him Jesus, the son of God. The Christians' great heresy, for other Jews, was to cross the biological divide and begin their new theology with a biospiritual event—the Annunciation. In the Annunciation the angel Gabriel announces to the Virgin Mary that she has shown great favor with the Lord and is to bear a son and call him Jesus. The implication is that God is the biological father of this child. Suddenly the abstract Divine principle in Judaism called Yahweh was mating with a human woman.

Christians made Jesus' birth into a "biological theology" and used Jesus' life as evidence that humanity is made in the "image and likeness of God." Jews and Christians alike believed our physical bodies, particularly male physical bodies, to be like God's. More contemporary theological writings have challenged that biological likeness, revising it into a spiritual likeness, but the original notion that we are biologically made in the image of God remains, nonetheless, a major literal and archetypal aspect of the Judeo-Christian tradition.

The thread common to all spiritual myths is that human beings are compelled to merge our bodies with the essence of God, that we want to have the Divine in our bones and blood and in our mental and emotional makeup. In belief systems around the world, conceptions of the Divine's spiritual nature reflect the best human qualities and characteristics. Since at our best we are compassionate, then God must be all-compassionate; since we are capable of forgiveness, then God must be all-forgiving; since we are capable of love, then God must be only love; since we try to be just, Divine justice must rule over our efforts to balance right and wrong. In Eastern traditions Divine justice is the law of karma; in the Christian world it underlies the Golden Rule. We have woven the Divine, one way or another, into all aspects of our lives, our thoughts, and our actions.

Today many spiritual seekers are trying to infuse their daily lives with a heightened consciousness of the sacred, striving to act as if each of their attitudes expressed their spiritual essence. Such conscious living is an invocation, a request for personal spiritual authority. It represents a dismantling of the old religions' classic parent-child relationship to God and a move into spiritual adulthood. Spiritual maturation includes not only developing the ability to interpret the deeper messages of sacred texts, but learning to read the spiritual language of the body. As we become more conscious and recognize the impact of our thoughts and attitudes—our internal life—upon our physical bodies and external lives, we no longer need to conceive of an external parent-God that creates for us and on whom we are fully dependent. As spiritual adults we accept responsibility for co-creating our lives and our health. Co-creation is in fact the essence of spiritual adulthood: it is the exercise of choice and the acceptance of our responsibility for those choices.

Managing our power of choice is the Divine challenge, the sacred contract that we are here to fulfill. It begins with choosing what our thoughts and attitudes will be. Whereas choice once meant our ability to respond to that which God has created for us, it now means that we are participants in what we experience—that we co-create our physical bodies through the creative strength of our thoughts and emotions. The seven sacred truths of the Kabbalah, the Christian sacraments, and the Hindu chakras support our gradual transformation into conscious spiritual adults. These literal and symbolic teachings redefine spiritual and biological health and help us understand what keeps us healthy, what makes us ill, and what helps us heal.

The seven sacred truths transcend cultural boundaries, and at the symbolic level they constitute a road map for our life journey—a road map imprinted in our biological design. Again and again the sacred texts tell us that our life's purpose is to understand and develop the power of our spirit, power that is vital to our mental and physical well-being. Abusing this power depletes our spirit and siphons the life-force itself out of our physical bodies.

Because Divine energy *is* inherent in our biological system, every thought that crosses our minds, every belief we nurture, every memory to which we cling translates into a positive or negative command to our bodies and spirits. It is magnificent to see ourselves through this lens, but it is also intimidating, because no part of our lives or thoughts is powerless or even private. We are biological creations of Divine design. Once this truth becomes a part of your conscious mind, you can never again live an ordinary life.

We are simultaneously matter and spirit. In order to understand ourselves and be healthy in both body and spirit, we have to understand how matter and spirit interact, what draws the spirit or life-force out of our bodies, and how we can retrieve our spirits from the false gods of fear, anger, and attachments to the past. Every attachment we hold on to out of fear commands a circuit of our spirit to leave our energy field and, to use a biblical phrase, "breathe life onto earth"—earth that costs us health. What drains your spirit drains your body. What fuels your spirit fuels your body. The power that fuels our bodies, our minds, and our hearts does not originate in our DNA. Rather, it has roots in Divinity itself. The truth is as simple and eternal as that.

The truths contained in the scriptural teachings of the different religious traditions are meant to unite us, not separate us. Literal interpretation creates separation, whereas symbolic interpretation—seeing that all of them address the identical design of our spiritual natures—brings us together. As we shift our attention away from the external world and into the internal one, we learn symbolic sight. Within, we are all the same, and the spiritual challenges we face are all the same. Our external differences are illusory and temporary, mere physical props. The more we seek what is the same in all of us, the more our symbolic sight gains authority to direct us. Merging Hindu, Buddhist, Christian, and Jewish spiritual traditions into one system with common sacred truths constitutes a powerful system of guidance that can enhance our minds and bodies and show us how to manage our spirits within the world.

One of the architects of the new medical synthesis called psychoneuroimmunology, **Joan Borysenko,** Ph.D., is the author of *Minding the Body, Mending the Mind, A Woman's Book of Life: The Biology, Psychology, and Spirituality of the Feminine Lifecycle* and *The Ways of The Mystic: Seven Paths to God.* She is a licensed psychologist, cell biologist, and the cofounder and former director of the Mind/Body Clinic at New England Deaconess Hospital.

Rebuilding the Holy Temple: The Feminine Principle of Resurrection

In ancient Babylon, the Archetypal storyteller says, there was a beautiful young savior-god named Tammuz who died and was brought back from the underworld by his lover, the earth-mother goddess Ishtar. As in the story of the Greek goddess Persephone, who likewise spent time in the underworld, the crops failed and the life-force ebbed when Ishtar dwelt in the darkness of exile. There was no lovemaking, no passion, no living creature was born and the earth was plunged into mourning. This story exists in many forms in the mythology of Sumeria, Greece, Egypt, and throughout the Mediterranean.

The Jews adopted this tale to refer to the destruction and rebuilding of the Holy Temple. The two Temples of Judaism were both attacked in the Hebrew month of Tammuz (June/July), and the dove that Noah sent out to search for dry land after the Great Flood found no resting place in this month. During Tammuz, Moses came down from Mt. Sinai with the Ten Commandments, only to break the tablets when he discovered that his people had lost faith and were worshiping a golden calf.

Tammuz is a month of mourning, and we are in a kind of global Tammuz now as the advent of the millennium encourages a stock-taking of where we are personally in the making of our souls, and where the world is as a crucible for the enduring values of love, charity, and creative evolution. Tammuz contains the recurrent themes of building and destruction, death and resurrection, which are the heartbeat of the universe. But the story of Tammuz contains something more, namely the role of Ishtar, the feminine principle, in bringing about the resurrection of the world.

Our planet is in a global dark night of the soul, a time of death and mourning which sets the stage for the resurrection. Grandmother Earth is crying out, running a potentially fatal fever as global warming warns us of her precarious health. AIDS is decimating the population of Africa and continuing to spread in the United States and other countries. New viruses are being liberated as the rainforest continues to be relentlessly destroyed. Holocausts continue in Eastern Europe and Africa. Famine is a way of life in large parts of the world. Racism and religious hatred, old and sad stories, become more threatening as nuclear armaments salvaged from the breakup of the former Soviet Union find their way into the hands of the highest bidders, many of whom are in the powderkegs of Africa and the Middle East. Some might say that hatred and violence have long held sway in the world, but we live in a new era where the triple threats of overpopulation, environmental destruction, and weapons with the potential to end life on Earth loom over us.

Beginning in the 1960s, the spirit of Ishtar began to emerge once again from the underworld where she had voluntarily journeyed to redeem the male principle, that the two together could co-create through love. The 1960s were witness to a sudden revitalization of culture, an awakening that bubbled up through five seemingly disparate wellsprings. The first was the appearance of the feminist movement and the publication of Betty Friedan's *The Feminine Mystique*. The second was opposition to the Vietnam War and to the senselessness of violence as a way to bring about peace. The third was the birth of the environmental movement with the publication of Rachel Carson's classic, *Silent Spring*. The fourth was the advent of humanistic psychology and a growing interest in spirituality, meditation, and healing. The fifth was psychedelic experimentation and a sudden breaching of what Aldous Huxley, borrowing from William Blake, called the Doors of Perception.

Sociologist Paul Ray has chronicled the growth of a new segment of American culture, which did not exist before the early 1970s, which now numbers 44 million strong, or 24 percent of the population; he calls this newly emergent group Cultural Creatives (CC). Twenty million of this group (10.6 percent of Americans) are "Core Cultural Creatives" who embody values based on psychological healing, spiritual growth, community, feminine values, preservation of the environment, love of religious and cultural diversity, and service. The female/male ratio in this group is two to one. Twenty-four million (13 percent of Americans) are "Green Cultural Creatives" whose major interest is environmental preservation, but who have less of an interest in spirituality and psychology. The Green Cultural Creatives appear to take their cues from the core CCs, who are leading-edge thinkers and innovators with a major motivation to heal and transform the world.

I was delighted when Ray's survey was published because it provided an answer for the frequently asked question, "Where have all the flower children of the 1960s gone? Have they sold out to the very culture they sought to transform?" I was one of those flower children, and what I have been doing for thirty years is growing up, learning about the world, falling on my face and getting up again, and figuring out some way to make a positive difference in the world. Sociologically, our culture is aging. I was born in 1945, technically a year before the baby boom, and I find myself in midlife surrounded by a huge groundswell of women and men whose values were forged in the 1960s. We're finally of an age to have a voice in politics, medicine, sociology, psychology, spirituality, religion, and, certainly, the economy.

As I approach the menopausal, wisewoman age, like other women I am coming into my power. Boundaries are better. It's easier to say "no" to what saps me personally and what is unkind to others and the Earth. And as the estrogen and progesterone levels in my body and those of my cohorts decline, our relative testosterone levels are rising. We're feisty, mouthy, and have the balls to take on the system and create change. We Cultural Creatives have done enough personal healing work so that our emerging voices are strong, loving, and insistent rather than bitter or stagnant. As a group, midlife women are coming back from the underworld, having reclaimed Tammuz both as their own male aspects, and as an inspiration to men to reclaim their feminine aspects, as reflected in Paul Ray's data.

In the ancient tradition of India, the *shakti*, or creative feminine energy can only rise when it comes into balance with the male energy. I believe that women, the collective earth-goddess Ishtar, are coming back from the darkness to sanctify that sacred union of male and female energies that will once again give birth to passion and purpose, refructifying the Earth and bringing hope to all our children.

Gayatri Naraine is a member of the Brahma Kumaris World Spiritual University and has practiced Raja Yoga meditation for the past twenty years and is dedicated to integrating its principles and values into contemporary life. Since 1980, she has served as representative of the Brahma Kumaris at the United Nations in New York. Her responsibilities include attending United Nations conferences and organizing major international outreach projects, such as the "Global Cooperation for a Better World" that asked hundreds of thousands of people in 129 countries: "What is your vision of a better world?" and "Living Values: An Educational Initiative," a partnership between global educators, UNICEF, and UNESCO currently being implemented in more than fifty-seven countries.

The Feminine Principle

Personal growth and human development are perhaps two of the more popular banners flapping in the breeze at the eve of the twenty-first century. So what's new? Aren't these two old chestnuts that humanity has been chewing over throughout history? The issues may indeed be the same but what is new is the emergence of a suppressed part of the human dynamic that can be called the *feminine principle*. This principle does not cater to a prejudiced belief in the superiority or inferiority of one group compared to another. Nor does it seek to replace male chauvinism with female chauvinism. Its aim is to allow the blossoming of a full and balanced personality that is at once vigorous and serene in an era of both light and might.

The feminine principle is a subtle energy which has remained untapped within the psyche of both men and women. It is merged in the essence of our spiritual identity and is marked by qualities attributed to the more gentle side of the human being—care, respect, trust, patience, loyalty, love, honesty, empathy, and mercy. When this principle is understood and realized, it is a force so powerful that it awakens us to new realities and realigns us to the true purpose and meaning of life. Both men and women possess this feminine principle but throughout history it has often been equated with emotion, weakness, and vulnerability and, in the context of social, economic, and political issues, flushed from the mainstream of development to a backwater and then labeled as "women's issues." The feminine principle was thereby controlled and crushed by the iron hand of patriarchal power, which almost invariably demanded nothing less than the sacrifice of intuition at the altar of rigid logic, the suppression of gentleness for the sake of brute strength, and the compliance of women with the dominance of men.

If the problems which have arisen through the suppression and control of this principle are to be corrected in a way that will last, then this must be done through a change of consciousness rather than a reversal of positions or roles: a change of consciousness which takes its birth from a base of spirituality and not from a base of sexuality. The feminine principle, this untapped subtle potential which lies at the core of our being, must now be realized to restore a balance between intellect and intuition, facts and feelings, reason and realism.

At the brink of the new millennium, in the midst of the most turbulent of times, the feminine principle is the clear, cool spring that can give life to humanity's arid wasteland; the sacred water from which to draw purpose and meaning.

LESSONS COME FROM HINDSIGHT

Looking back at the twentieth century, one may say that the progress of women has been slow and laborious, for up until the '60s women were best known for their roles as wives, mothers, sisters, nurses, and secretaries. As women's liberation movements asserted that women were also entitled to human rights, the international community responded with a series of women's conferences that have contributed to the great strides made in putting women's concerns high on the global agenda. Yet most women who managed to claim the positions they deserved in the world did so at the expense of the feminine principle and were either caught in the power play of sexuality or achieved their positions only by developing an iron-fisted control over others. While such measures were doubtless successful in the short term, any individual who has to compromise on who she is, and knowingly or unknowingly deny herself access to the source of her own strength, will sooner or later succumb to the trap of exploiting, manipulating, and discriminating against others—the very evils she sought to dispel. Deprived of the strength that comes from within, these are the only tools available to a person living outside the borders of their own being.

Twentieth-century women will be remembered as pioneers of a hard and perilous path to freedom and liberation. Their efforts brought phenomenal breakthroughs and taught significant lessons. The starting point was action-oriented and was influenced by characteristics associated with the left hemisphere of the brain—courage, determination, will-power, and advocacy. The result was the formation of an international network of women's organizations and groups whose fingers are on the pulse of political, social, and economic changes, and who know how these impact the lives of women all over the world. Faced with the paradox of some material and professional success but very little emotional and spiritual fulfillment, such women continued to feel a sense of inner depletion and a lack of self-worth and self-esteem. Recognizing that the advancement of women was an uphill task, a whole of many parts, it became apparent that progress on the outside had to be nurtured by growth on the inside. Soon, programs on self-development and personal growth began to mushroom. Conferences, seminars, and forums were replaced by dialogues, discussions, and conversations. The significant lesson learned was the patience to trust that whatever happened was part of a process that would lead to a successful outcome and the rediscovery of characteristics such as intuition, creativity, spirituality, nurturing, sustenance, care, love, and compassion. This shift in consciousness became the backbone of their stories.

In many ways, Dadi Janki, co-administrative head of the Brahma Kumaris World Spiritual University, embodies these lessons. In her statement to the Fourth World Conference on Women in Beijing in September 1995, she said, "In the India in which I was born nearly eighty years ago, no girl could ever imagine that she would come to speak before an international gathering of world leaders and share a platform with them. The strict social structures and family systems of those days were expected to lead me into a life of obedience with the wishes and desires of others and my formal preparation for life was limited to three years of schooling. The fact that I stand before you today as the co-administrative head of an organization with branches in over seventy countries worldwide and about 400,000 members is the direct result of a process of spiritual education that has empowered me to break the bondage of centuries of discrimination.

"Like many of you here today I wanted to serve others and not just live for myself or those immediately around me. The awakening of the self and the discovery and realization of my potential enabled me to overcome external bondage and develop self-confidence, kindness, and compassion. The message that I share with you today is that it is these qualities that are needed in all walks of life and that spirituality is the means to achieve them. An unshakable conviction of my own spiritual identity and a deep loving relationship with God are the basis of my self-respect. They have also given me personal independence and empowerment and are the foundation of all that I have achieved."

VISION COMES FROM FORESIGHT

Women of the twentieth century have developed guidelines and set standards for women of the twenty-first century to pursue and develop further. The feminine principle, which has come to be seen as the light at the end of the tunnel in the latter years of the twentieth century, will become a natural way of being in the future. Trust, respect, and wisdom will lie at the heart of authentic leadership by women and men; integrity and high moral standards will sustain it. Power will no longer lie in the hands of others who make decisions for us, but within the hearts of each one of us. As natural leaders, we will lead from the core of our inner strength and will follow our own inner principles, conscience, and truth, thus creating our own disciplines.

It will be an integral part of the awareness and attitudes of women responsible for the growth and development of children that every child has the right to participate fully in all areas of society and to equality of opportunity. These guardians of humanity's future will ensure that the worth of an individual is not determined by gender and will bestow the love and respect with which the true self of each young person may flourish. To a great extent, it lies in the hands of women to master a process that will rescue us and succeeding generations from being restricted by discriminatory attitudes, abusive patterns of physical and emotional behavior, and the limitations we may have put on ourselves. This will be the *sine qua non* of our ultimate freedom.

In preparing for life in the next millennium, it is often young women who seem to have the greatest challenges to face. Will they inherit the same mental models as their mothers or will they use the feminine principle to mold and shape themselves as women of the twenty-first century, thereby blazing a new path along which others may also walk? Here is one such young woman, a medical student at George Washington University Medical Center in Washington, D.C.:

My name is Alexandra and I was born in Haiti. Growing up I always marveled at the thought that in the year 2000 I would only be twenty-five years old. This implied that I would be old enough to remember the old century and young enough to be open to all that the new one would bring in scientific discoveries, innovative ideas, and lifestyle changes.

While being very aware of the fact that the year 2000 is very close, I still have to pay attention to the present. I have to face challenges now because it is only by doing so that I could even fathom being strong enough to not be engulfed by the tidal wave of the twenty-first century. The biggest challenge that I am faced with at the present time is going through medical school and keeping my inner being still intact. I remember that one of my mentors once told me that I had to do my best to 'hold on to my soul' as I went through the process of becoming a doctor. This truly is not an easy task in an environment that progressively dehumanizes by constantly subjecting one to the sometimes unbearable pressure to succeed, to do better than your peers, to learn more information than you ever thought existed and use it in an appropriate way. At the same time, they are asking you to be empathetic, compassionate, and respectful to patients at all times. I realized that to protect myself from simply going through the motions of life and becoming dry inside, I had to stay very close to the feminine attribute of being able to continually give of one's self. I saw that I had to be giving and caring first to myself, to not allow myself to simply switch to a survival mode that ultimately can transform into clinical depression. This idea of nurturing the self allows me to create a world inside where no one can come in and move things around according to their belief system or values or lack thereof. This keeps the soul safe and steady and so becomes the place I draw from to be able to give the compassion that patients need.

My apprehension for the twenty-first century is that as women get more and more acknowledgment from society as to their ability to do well in professions traditionally held by men, they will move away from that principle of giving and nurturing, seeing it as a sign of being too feminine, and so a sign of weakness. As for myself, I believe that it will not be possible for me to be a good physician if these attributes are lacking, especially in the twenty-first century. For one thing, we will be asked more than ever before to think about everything on a global scale. It is as if as women we will no longer be mothers or sisters, but 'world mothers' and 'world sisters.' As information grows to phenomenal proportions in the twenty-first century and is disseminated throughout the world, we might feel closer to each other and yet so far apart, interacting with the information and not with each other. Maybe what will be valued will be that moment of connection with another human being at the physician's office. This will require simplicity on my part so that I can be a clear receptor that does not filter too much of what I hear through my beliefs but simply listens with the intention of wanting to understand and help. Spirituality is the tool that I use on an every day basis to bring back simplicity and stillness so that I can become a clear receptor.

WISDOM COMES FROM INSIGHT

"Who am I
always keeping an 'eye' on 'I'?"

At the confluence of the two millennia, one of the most challenging insecurities to be overcome is that felt by people in relation to themselves—the question: Who am I?

By using the feminine principle as the premise to explore this mystery, we can embark on our journey of discovery from a perspective of faith in one's self. We are often reluctant to look within ourselves because we lack the confidence to come face-to-face with the person we fear the most—our own true selves. Spiritual knowledge gives a deeper level of understanding that can remove the fear of the unknown and open the door to insight. Insight gives the spiritual clarity to recognize the self and the inner strength to accept the self, including our present limitations. Insight also serves as a searchlight with which to see through the layers of limitations we have acquired by overemphasizing the temporary or physical aspects of our identity and focus on the realization of our original and eternal identity—"Who I am always." To identify with the inner self is the method to free myself from the confines and constraints of the physical limitations. Faith in myself elevates and divinizes my intellect and opens my third eye of wisdom. This is the kind of faith that creates trust and gives me the courage to accept the past, enjoy the present, and create the future I want. It is this wisdom that women must embody. This wisdom is born from the depth of a spiritual consciousness and has been remembered as *shakti*—will-power received directly from God. Such wisdom, when brought into action, has a truly transforming effect on our lives, and the lives of those around us, bringing about integration with integrity.

Using the feminine principle to bring about integration with integrity is the most powerful tool now at our disposal. The practice of returning to one's original identity and remembering "Who I am always" as we play our different roles and honor our various responsibilities is crucial as it enthrones us on our seat of self-respect. When our subtle inner abilities are integrated in the wholeness of our being and allowed to be expressed with the support of self-respect, actions are performed with a high level of integrity.

The feminine principle has often been mistaken for femininity on a physical level and so respect for inner beauty has often yielded to an obsession with beauty that knows nothing deeper than the skin. A woman's worth comes from the original and innate qualities of the soul: truth, love, purity, joy, and peace, and it is from these values that a woman's beauty is derived and radiated through her features. To believe in the beauty of one's innate worth and to see the self in the context of this eternal reality, rather than just the transitory physical appearance, gives a tremendous boost to one's self-esteem and self-confidence.

To feel is a basic human trait, yet when it comes to expressing our feelings in a particular relationship, our passion for a task or admiration for a piece of art or music, often we either overindulge ourselves and lose our sense of reason or we suppress ourselves with the fear of being rejected or of being too emotional. Something somewhere has gone wrong with feelings and so we need to understand deeply what true feelings are. Feelings are linked to motives, intentions, desires, and expectations, and I can control the way I feel when I am in touch with these. I am empowered when my feelings are based on the strength of what is true to me and come from respecting and believing in myself. I am disempowered when I allow external influences to create doubts and fears in the way I feel, causing me to look outward to validate my own feelings. Looking outside myself is the way to let loose waves of victimization, uncertainty, and insecurity and so feelings are often suppressed and never dealt with. This suppression of feelings leads to depression as I am unable to trust my own feelings and I am reluctant to talk about them, fearing being misunderstood, criticized, or rejected. Staying close to my own truth, innate values, and inner strength enables me to trust my feelings. I am responsible for the way I feel and I have the capacity to remove any painful feelings and to create pure feelings in their place.

Capacity building is the art of balancing feeling with reason. This balance is especially needed in areas of trust, honesty, loyalty, and love. Reason tells me that when I begin to cultivate and nurture any of these values, my own insecurities, fears, and doubts will arise to test the strength of my commitment and to stretch my capacity. Every test has a benefit merged in it. What needs to be understood during these battles is that I must not shrink my capacity to trust just because someone betrays this trust, or my capacity to be honest just because someone lies to me. It is so easy to be influenced by someone else's behavior and to internalize their weakness in a way that causes me to lose faith in my own capacity and to waver from staying in alignment with my own values. This is where space is required to maintain healthy and long-standing relationships and not to become so wrapped up in another that I lose all sense of who I am. This stepping back to maintain my own independence and integrity nurtures my growth and increases my capacity to exercise free-dom of choice rather than succumbing to the pull of external influences or the expectations of others.

As Anne Frank said, "How noble and good everyone could be if, at the end of the day, they were to review their own behavior and weigh up the rights and wrongs. They would automatically try to do better at the start of each day and after a while, would certainly accomplish a great deal. Everyone is welcome to this prescription: it costs nothing and is definitely useful."

It has been observed that a woman's intuition guides her ability to make decisions, almost like a sixth sense. However, intuition on its own is not enough for effective decision-making. It is only when motives are clean and devoid of selfish desires that the intuition can give clear signals to help make objective decisions. These subtle abilities must be applied or expressed in rela-tion to facts and not fancy or imagination. Walking the tightrope of daily life can also challenge our ability to make decisions with integrity. This is why it is so important to periodically keep an "eye" on "I" to see whether my actions, words, thoughts, and values are in alignment with my principles. If they are not we must use our sense of self-worth to allow us to delay the deci-sion and, if they are, then that alignment gives us the authority to take a stand, make the decision, and be committed to it.

As it is written in *Living Values: A Guidebook:* "When motives are based on right values in accord with fundamental and natural laws, we think, speak, and act in ways which guarantee success, accomplishment, and peace of mind."

Within the heart of the human soul, a new world is waiting to be born. The gift we can, and must, offer—to ourselves and to each other—is to rekin-dle within ourselves the flame of the feminine principle and then to keep that flame glowing strong and steady in our souls, sustaining it with the oil of pure feelings, faith, and determination. A commitment to live by this principle is a commitment to ignite the spirit of the twenty-first century in the hearts of all humanity. If I don't make this commitment, who will?

Psychotherapist **Sue Patton Thoele** is the author of *The Courage to Be Yourself* and *The Courage to Be Yourself Journal, The Woman's Book of Spirit, The Woman's Book of Courage, The Woman's Book of Confidence, The Woman's Book of Soul, Heart Centered Marriage, Autumn of the Spring Chicken,* and *Freedoms After 50.* She and her husband Gene live in Boulder, Colorado, and have four adult children, a son-in-law, and one grandson.

A Deep and Holy Hunger: Reclaiming the Sacred Feminine in Daily Life

What is the birth cry of the new millennium? I believe it is a deep and holy hunger, an impassioned call to all people, but women in particular, to reclaim and act from the soft power of the Sacred Feminine within our hearts. This inspired call resonates with the assurance that "Love is the answer." Not syrupy, sentimental, Hollywood love but an empowered, compassionate, and hardworking Mother-love that willingly opens her arms and heart to all. In reality, that love is within each of us yearning to flow freely from us as a blessing to both individuals and to the whole.

Our hearts are the rivers through which God's love flows. They are the eminent domain of divine energy and possess an intelligence greater than any other aspect of our being. Love emanating from our heart-center is a powerful force that unleashes the very creative energy of the universe. In order to make this forceful and fruitful love a reality one of the things we are called to do is rescue the Sacred Feminine from exile, reconstitute her within ourselves, and act with her compassion and passion toward those in our lives.

WHAT IS THE SACRED FEMININE?

At her core, the Sacred Feminine is love and the primary teacher of relationship. Since all of life is one form of relationship or another, our lives can only hum with the song of love if they are filled with the Sacred Feminine voice, for she *is* the song of love. She is the harp upon which the strings of compassion and connection quiver. From the Feminine comes the sweet music composed as we love those with whom our lives are intertwined in a complementary and cooperative manner.

To be effective we must, of course, have a *balance* of both masculine and feminine energy. However, at this point in history, the scale needs to be weighted toward the feminine aspects of our being, for the Feminine carries the heart-energy of compassion and connection capable of satisfying our deep and holy hunger for sacred partnership with ourselves and those we love. As Marion Woodman, Jungian analyst and contributor to this anthology, says, "The task of the feminine is to contain, as the mother contains the baby. The eternal feminine is that loving, cherishing, nurturing principle which looks at the life that is becoming and honors it, celebrates it, allows it to grow into its full maturity."

Without such supportive love we cannot mature in a healthy way. As we begin to embrace the nurturing Feminine and provide a shelter of love and acceptance for ourselves and those to whom we relate, we will be encouraged to develop into the beautiful beings that we are meant to become. Of course, none of us can sustain this all-encompassing feminine stance of loving at every moment, but we can, by choosing the feminine, heart qualities we want to be primary in our lives and becoming educated about them, create an atmosphere in which love flourishes and we can grow into fruitful maturity.

Familiarizing ourselves with these qualities encourages us to come from the heart of love. Incorporating the Sacred Feminine qualities into our daily lives can act as a plumb line while the pendulum of gender confusion, prevalent in the last several decades, swings toward the core awareness that reverence and respect for all people, all beings, is essential for the well-being of the whole.

QUALITIES OF THE FEMININE

The Feminine is the embodiment of heart energy. Her key qualities are compassion and the ability to accept and honor the process of whatever is happening. Perhaps this is often easier for women because we are physically and emotionally programmed to honor the cycle of conception, pregnancy, and birth and to welcome and include whomever may be born from that long, mysterious process.

Contrary to the idea that women are overemotional, the Sacred Feminine is well grounded emotionally and has the capacity to bring all of her energy to exactly where she is in the moment. Feminine energy accepts the paradoxes of life and realizes at some basic level that there is unification possible within even the most disparate incongruities. Feminine energy also resonates with and deeply connects with the Earth and all of her children, feeling for and with them.

The following list of feminine qualities, the songs of the Sacred Feminine, is by no means complete. You will be able to add many of your own.

THE FEMININE IS ...

Inclusive: recognizing the value and worth of all people and things;

Honoring of Process: able to allow circumstances, ideas, and experiences to unfold;

Empowered: with steeled softness she champions the weak and vulnerable and stands firm for what is right;

Intuitive: holistic, accessing immediate perception rather than rational thinking;

Compassionate: empathetic, warm, openhearted;

Complementary: lives in concert with others, augmenting the whole with her presence;

Connective: desiring to link hands and hearts;

Cooperative: able to work with others without needing to be in control;

Diffuse: perceives and understands a wide range of stimuli;

Relational: interested in preserving and deepening relationships;

Gentle: able to live gently with herself and others;

Receptive: open to receive the new, different, and wondrous;

Empowering: awakens others to their potential;

Forgiving: realizes that we are all imperfect and that non-forgiveness dams the natural flow of spirit;

A "Be"-er: introspective, drawn to the spiritual and the philosophical;

Healing: carries the ability to heal body, mind, and spirit through a talent for listening deeply to her internal, inherent wisdom.

Pondering these attributes helps us recognize and respect our innate talent as women to usher into all situations the energy of love and acceptance. As with everything—and much to our chagrin at times—the revolution of compassion, caring, and kindness exemplified by the Sacred Feminine needs to begin within ourselves. As the song says, "Let there be peace on earth, and let it begin with me." A revolution of love. A revolution of respect. A revolution of acceptance, tolerance, and inclusion—all of these values must first be nurtured in our own hearts and souls, and in our intimate social groups, if they are to be transformative for the whole. Only a daunting idea if we cast our glance too far afield. First, and always foremost, we need to extricate *ourselves* from the dungheap of disrespect and dismissal, and honor who we truly are. Why is this so hard? Because devaluation of the Sacred Feminine has been rampant for centuries. But we are now being called to "rescue the damsel in suppress."

FREEZE-DRIED FEMININE POWER

Over the last several hundred years, our society, both consciously and unconsciously, has attempted to freeze-dry feminine power, stow it safely in a corked jar, and bury it in the remote recesses of a dark cavern. As well as trying to silence women's intuition and wisdom, society has denigrated the Sacred Feminine qualities of cooperation, inclusion, receptivity, and compassion, to name only a few, by relegating them to the second-class areas of servitude and sacrifice.

As much as I'm sad to admit it, the attempts to bury the innate spiritual qualities of the Sacred Feminine were certainly successful with me. For many years, my sense of spiritual and personal power lay dormant and I felt no sense of connection to a divine being or to the divinity within myself. Although I tried to act out the values of the Feminine by loving, caring, and supporting others, my service sprang mostly from fear and a sense of obligation rather than flowing freely from my heart. I did what I *should* do and neither embodied the values, spoke with the voice, nor radiated the joy of the Sacred Feminine. She was hidden, safely freeze-dried in my heart, buried under mounds of false beliefs, societal injunctions, and visceral fears.

From talking with friends and working with clients, I know that my barren experience was not unique.

But thankfully, we are now moving into a time when many of us—men and women alike—can and are renouncing the sacrificial voice of subservient fear and are reclaiming the Sacred Feminine without being subjected to rejection, abuse, persecution, or projection. And when we are faced with these negative responses, we're finding the courage to speak out anyway.

THE REEMERGENCE OF THE SACRED FEMININE

But we have considerable *relearning* to do in order to rescue feminine energy in ourselves and our relationships. For the centuries that our world has been parched by the mind-oriented patriarchy and all that is fertile, emotional, and intuitive—all that is *feminine*—has been labeled as suspect at best, and abnormal or demonic at worst, much of our innate nature has been overpowered and stifled. However, unable to be destroyed, the moist, rich, fruitful *feeling-ness* of the Feminine has been stored in the womb of our semiconscious yearnings, waiting to return. The time is now ripe.

Having plumbed the depths of masculine domination for the last several centuries and found it devoid of the qualities that make our hearts sing, we are again ready to welcome an equilibrium of masculine *and* feminine energy into our lives. Thankfully, in the evolving spiritual climate, the Sacred Feminine is being encouraged to emerge from her cave and take her rightful place in our hearts and in our sorely beleaguered world.

By far the most important indicators of the return of the Sacred Feminine are those stirring within our own hearts. Such stirrings may come in the form of little nudges to invoke a female power or deity while praying, intuitive flashes that we have the courage to voice and act upon, acts of kindness, love, and wisdom that effortlessly bubble from us, feeling intensely connected to nature, joyous bursts of creativity, or soft, silent whispers that come during dreams or meditation.

One such whisper came to me during meditation. I had just finished writing *Heart Centered Marriage* and was in the creative lull that I often experience following periods of concentrated work. These times are usually uncomfortable for me. I feel like a drained pond that lies baking in the sun, arid and purposeless. (Being a "good girl" raised on the Midwestern adage "Idle hands are the devil's workshop," I rarely remember, unless prompted, that rest and refilling are positive and purposeful.) In order to assuage my feelings of fruitlessness I decided to ask during a meditation what my purpose and goals were now that my current project was completed. Although I'm not a wildly psychic person who regularly receives a lot of "phenomena," unexplained yet very clearly, a message was delivered: *Pour water upon my women.*

Because I was already deeply committed to reclaiming the Sacred Feminine Voice in myself, relationships, and the world in general, I felt the message pertained to revitalizing and reintroducing feminine values. But there seemed to be more that I wasn't understanding and I asked to be shown the significance of the enigmatic message. One source of understanding was a conversation with a dear friend. She was telling me that her adult daughter only seemed to relate to her when she needed something. "It's as if she freeze-dries me and puts me on a shelf until she needs something. Then she takes me down, reconstitutes me with her tears, and fully expects me to help her." I answered, "And you do, right?" She moaned, "Yes ..." and we laughed in recognition.

While musing about that conversation, it dawned on me that I had freeze-dried the Divine Mother within myself every bit as effectively as society in general had dried and buried her. With that awareness came many tears. As the tears changed from torrents to trickles, I fell deeply and passionately in love with the desire to reconstitute the Sacred Feminine in my personal life. Along with that passion came a deep commitment to bring the Sacred Feminine center stage in my writing, speaking, and group work. *Pour water upon my women.* I now know what the message means and I'm pretty darn sure I know who sent it.

EMBRACING THE SACRED FEMININE

How can we pour water upon our spirits and reconstitute the Sacred Feminine within us? Because each of us is unique, there are limitless ways to discover the special spiritual gifts that we bring to this life and to offer them in relationship. Even though there are myriad possibilities for embracing the Divine and embodying her in our lives and hearts, I want to share a few of the ones that have helped me and the women with whom I work and play. Incorporating the following ideas into our lives has helped us move closer to the Sacred Feminine Voice and, as a result, have more joyous and compassionate relationships. Although our ways and rituals will not necessarily be yours, maybe they will plant a seed or strike a cord within you inspiring your own unique and beautiful songs to the Divine Feminine residing in your heart.

1. Becoming Aware of and Relating to the Sacred Feminine

Luckily, it isn't hard to become aware of the Sacred Feminine now. The idea that Spirit encompasses, and undoubtedly surpasses, both masculine and feminine qualities is prevalent in the hearts and minds of many people. For instance, referring to God as Mother/Father no longer causes gasps of shock in most instances. It is an idea that's time has come. This is great. But it is not a place to stop. Awareness is the first step but not the destination.

Embracing and embodying the Sacred Feminine attributes is our intention. This is our calling, the journey of our soul toward clear expression of its authentic self.

Keeping sacred feminine symbols around me helps remind me of my relationship to a God with whom I can identify. Praying to, reading about, and meditating on a benevolent and all-loving female figure feels very grounding to me and to many of the women I know. If you haven't already, you might want to choose a time when you can be undisturbed and open yourself to a visit from your inner Divine Feminine. One way to do this is to close your eyes, breath deeply and evenly, and thank yourself for giving yourself the gift of a quiet moment. As you relax, ask for a meaningful symbol of the Sacred Feminine to come to you. If the symbol or person who appears doesn't feel totally caring and benevolent, ask it/her to leave and invite the perfect, right symbol to be with you. Please don't be discouraged if nothing happens at first. Sometimes it just takes a little practice for us to open to the wisdom within.

Some women relate to the Feminine by cultivating beautiful gardens in which they work, rest, and connect with Mother Nature. I have a friend who creates fabulous quilts honoring certain goddesses. Loving energy vibrates from these works of art which she uses as both a meditative discipline and a source of income. Other women relate to the Feminine Beloved by swimming with dolphins, consciously being with children, basking in solitude, writing haiku poetry, painting pictures that appear to them in dreams, washing woodwork, asking for comfort when vulnerable, doing volunteer and church work, and taking care of ill or invalid loved ones. It doesn't matter how we connect with the Sacred Feminine. It only matters that we do and that we embody her love and spread it.

2. Center in Our Hearts

By far, one of the most effective means of spreading love is to center our attention in our hearts and learn to act from them. Researchers are now discovering that our hearts are, indeed, the rivers through which the love of God flows, and the flow from our hearts contains transformative energy. But, as mystics and lovers have known for eons, the wonderful reality is that heart energy can be tapped at will. We can *choose* to move into our hearts and alter not only our feelings and the situations in which we find ourselves but also the very atmosphere around us.

Research being conducted at the Institute of HearthMath in Boulder Creek, California is providing compelling evidence that activating heart energy harmonizes the body/mind connection, reduces stress, and increases well-being physically, emotionally, mentally, and spiritually. Turning our attention to our heart enables us to draw upon its core feelings of appreciation, forgiveness, courage, kindness, peace, compassion, and love to name only a few. Certainly sounds like Sacred Feminine attributes to me.

Although it would be wonderful if we were aware of our hearts at all times, it's especially important to turn to them in times of stress. One way to do this is to simply put our attention on them. Sometimes it helps to place your hands over your heart as you quietly imagine yourself breathing through it. After breathing in this manner for a little while, bring into your awareness a situation or person about whom you can honestly feel love or appreciation. Allow this feeling to expand in your chest. If you do not *feel* or *see* anything during meditative processes like this, it's okay. Merely *think* or *imagine* what you would like to feel. Now that you're centered in your heart, ask it what, if anything, you should do to respond to the feelings that you were experiencing before tuning into your heart. With practice you will be able to receive messages consistently because our hearts yearn to share their wisdom and compassion with us.

Interestingly, I was tickled to learn a fact about the physical workings of the heart which was corroborated by a cardiologist friend. *The heart pumps to itself first.* Before circulating blood to other parts of the body, the astute heart makes sure that it has received what it needs to keep working efficiently. Wouldn't we be wise to take that example to heart, so to speak, and allow divine energy to flow to us first and then *through* us to those given into our care and acquaintance?

A highly effective way to center in our hearts is to say a small prayer or blessing at the beginning of our day stating our intention to live heartfully. I might say something as simple as, "You through me, please." No matter what we want to say or who we feel comfortable saying it to, as long as we are desirous of being an instrument of love and peace, we will be embracing and embodying the Sacred Feminine by opening our hearts and sending forth blessings. First, to ourselves.

3. Heal Our Pain

One of the most powerful ways to relate to the Sacred Feminine is to allow her to help us gently and constructively move through our pain, learn from it, and become a more compassionate person as a result. Safe in the arms of the Sacred Feminine, our souls, seared by pain, can be sanctified.

Pain and crisis are a part of the human cycle. We ascend, flourish, bear fruit, and then, seemingly as an answer to the law of gravity, we arch in a plateau, descend, and die to the wounded part of us. Because feminine energy is deeply aware of and in tune with cycles, crisis and pain are most often handled best by the Sacred Feminine within us. She, in her wisdom, knows that pain is followed by rebirth. When a part of us—an old pattern, an expectation, a role—is washed away in the alchemy of crisis, new parts of our being are conceived and born. Trauma and transformation walk hand in hand.

Grief and loss require a feminine response. Healing is a *process*. It can't be fixed or solved by *doing* and can only be soothed and healed through *experiencing* the feelings involved, and a safe shelter is essential to the healing process. Friends and family can provide such shelter, but if they are not available or we don't want to ask for outside support, allowing ourselves to crawl into the lap of the Divine Feminine, who loves us beyond reason and from before time, is our best solace.

4. Patience with the Process

Because we rarely leap effortlessly over the hot coals of our pain and woundedness, we need to open our hearts to ourselves and thereby enhance our ability to honor and remain patient with the process of processing. Learning patience is one of my hardest lessons, and I won't be surprised if I'm still at it until the day I die—maybe beyond, who knows. So, I am very amused by a poster I once saw: Two vultures are hunkered down on a limb. One turns to the other and says, disgustedly, "To hell with patience! Let's go kill something!" Love it. I can certainly remember many times when my patience ran thin and I wanted to *do* something, *anything* in order to alleviate the pain of waiting. But the darn part about losing patience with the process of our own growth, healing, or with circumstances out of our control is that it's usually ourselves we rush to kill, isn't it?

In lieu of trying to *make* something happen, the Sacred Feminine way is to adopt the awesome power and strength of that most feminine of all elements, water. She yields while waiting for resolution and inspiration, knowing without a doubt that she will eventually reach the source. At times when we struggle mightily with our humanness, ricocheting from confidence to insecurity, or dissolving from strength into a puddle of dependence, the Sacred Feminine smiles at us fondly, knowing that this, too, shall pass. I confess that I sometimes find this as annoying as I do comforting. But it does help when I touch base with her during trying times and ask her to ooze through my resistance as only water can.

5. Live Gently with Ourselves and Others

There is nothing so strong as true gentleness. If each of us became a smidgen more gentle each day, the planet would be blessed with both the strength and the compassion of the Sacred Feminine.

When first entertaining the concept of being gentle with myself, the very idea seemed blasphemous. Of course I expected myself to be gentle with others, but wasn't I supposed to be my own hardest taskmaster and severest critic? No. In reality, learning to be gentle with ourselves enhances our ability to come from our hearts with greater love, trust, and respect for others. Embraced by a nurturing, sensitive *self*, we make much safer friends and family members for others. Treating ourselves harshly bruises our hearts. A bruised heart is more likely to treat others in a bruising way, or at least wish it could.

Most of us really want to choose gentle awareness and action for, inherently, we have gentle hearts. If we don't feel gentle-hearted, it's probably because we have been wounded and are protecting ourselves from the pain of our injuries. The core of our being is filled with the spirit of love and, when we can act from this gentle reality, we feel so much better about ourselves, more authentic, more able to express the soul of our true Selves.

I believe that we sincerely want to be gentle but we often don't know how. Sometimes all we need to cultivate a gentle attitude are some small reminders. I have a magnet on the refrigerator with my business card logo, *Live gently with yourself and others*, written on it. It's a little cue to the subconscious, a gentle jolt to help put me back on track when I've lost sight of my commitment to live gently.

What would be a good reminder for you? Maybe a little note by the phone or in your checkbook? Or an agreement with friends to ask, "Is that gentle?" when you're hard on yourself or accept too many commitments. As you think about it, you'll know how you can welcome the art of gentleness into your heart and home. Living gently creates an aura of peace in our lives— a down comforter of support for ourselves and those with whom we are in relationship.

6. Create Little Rituals of Love

Rituals speak the language of the soul. During meaningful ritual, divine energy is absorbed not only by our brains but in our hearts and souls as well. Creating and taking part in ritual and ceremony, whether a tiny, solitary blessing or a grand pageant, opens our hearts, connects us with our community and makes us more accessible to ourselves, others, and to the Beloved.

Profoundly valuable are blessing ceremonies. In them we intentionally sprinkle divine grace upon the blessed. Blessing someone or something lifts it into the care and light of God. As we bless, our spirits are also lifted.

Nothing is too minuscule or too magnificent not to benefit from being blessed. We can bless the ill and weary, the food we eat, dead animals along the road, our faces—wrinkles and all—war-torn countries and the children suffering in them. Blessings can be very simple—a silent inward bow, a gentle touch, the murmuring of a few heartfelt words, a few minutes of deep listening, a sincere thank you. As we bestow blessings, we offer our good wishes and open our heart as a conduit for the divine to flow through.

Probably one of the most valuable little rituals of love that we can do is adopt an attitude of gratitude. Gratitude catapults us directly into our hearts and bathes our souls in grace. There are myriad ways to incorporate gratitude into our days and nights. They could include using "Thank you" as a mantra during meditation, jotting gratitudes in a journal, taking grateful-breathing breaks at work—breathe in deeply and, as you exhale, give thanks for something that you consider a little boon. Both body and soul benefit from breathing breaks. We do not have to wait for grandiose blessings before giving thanks. For instance, right now I am feeling grateful that my cat came in before dark. One of the most profound gratitude rituals that I've heard of is to make a conscious decision to be thankful for three new and different things each day. I tried it. It's very easy for the first week or so....

Powerfully transformative is the practice of being grateful for things, situations, and people that we consider negative, painful, or harmful. The mere act of being willing to be grateful for pain and irritation changes the energy of the feelings and brings us closer to the accepting and inclusive soft power of the Sacred Feminine.

GATHERING AT THE WELL

Embracing the Sacred Feminine within us is both our birthright and responsibility. For she is who we are. Uncovering our true selves takes immense courage. Shoveling from our consciousness the heavy and pervasive layers of misconceptions and false beliefs heaped upon us during the last several hundred years is not an easy task. Equally difficult is our need to sort through the confusion of reactions and defenses we've employed against inequality and societal limitations. Whether societal or self-imposed, both limitation and rebellion can dump very large barrels over the light of our true selves. And that is the call, isn't it? The deep and holy hunger to reclaim and act from our authentic spiritual selves; to reconstitute the Sacred Feminine Voice and values within all women so that we may bestow her blessings on our world.

Spirituality is simple. Fundamentally, we are spiritual beings with soul as our essence and love as our most basic quality. We've forgotten. I continue to forget on a daily basis. Consequently, it seems to me that a huge spiritual lesson for most of us is to re-remember, to re-evolve into simplicity of spirit, and invite the natural, inherent essence of our Selves back to the fore of our lives, to "become like little children."

I believe women are being called to birth this all-important spirit-memory. In order for our relationships, our lives, and perhaps our very planet to thrive, we must free our spiritual essence from the closet to which it has been relegated. Only then can love flow continually into our hearts from the divine and overflow onto others. Women are inherently vessels of love, and through our love and spiritual connection, we can rescue the parched and perishing within and among us.

We cannot do it alone. Realizing this, countless women are gathering together right now. Through tears, rituals, honoring, acknowledging, and learning from each other, we are healing our wounds and opening our hearts to our birthright as daughters of the Sacred Feminine. We are remembering and connecting with our own inherent spiritual core and with the core of others. Rising from the ashes of injustice, domination, and fear, we women are reclaiming our heritage as essentially spiritual beings who are learning and growing through human experience. Since you are reading these words, I have no doubt that you are already dipping your chalice into the well of soul.

The new millennium is an exciting time in human history. Women everywhere are gathering at the spring-fed wells of our beings to reconstitute the Sacred Feminine within us by pouring the water of our spirits on each other, to share our hearts, to join hands as we move toward more completely expressing our boundless love, magnificent wisdom, and compassionate intuition. To these limitless wells, each of us carries her *own* container. Each of us fills her *own* jar. And, each of us is also called to walk with her sisters and brothers along the way, providing support, guidance, encouragement, inspiration, and love.

So vast is the nature of the Sacred Feminine that we can never fully fathom it. We can simply experience her grace by immersing ourselves in her healing presence and embracing her qualities as our own. By living in and acting from our hearts—the eternal home of the Beloved—we will become her arms reaching out with compassion to guide, comfort, empower, and to initiate the changes necessary to create the loving world for which we hunger.

Paula Underwood, M.A., is the Developer and Director of The LearningWay Company (TLC), a nationwide award-winning program used in education, corporate learning, and health services. TLC is based on Paula's lifelong training in an ancient Iroquois methodology for learning, organization, and health. Her first book, *Who Speaks for Wolf*, won the Thomas Jefferson Cup for quality writing, has since been declared an environmental classic, and "The best book I know of on Systems Thinking!" Paula is consistently praised for her ability to apply Ancient and enduring Wisdom to the apparent chaos of rapid change. Herman Miller, the Lafeber Company, and Xerox number among her corporate clients.

Clan Mothers in the Twenty-first Century

The Clan Mother years are a traditional time for realigning your life—old enough for your children to be grown, young enough to still be active. It is for this reason that my father and I chose this time for me to begin the principle task of my life, writing down in English the ancient treasures which my family has carried with it for the last five generations.

In my tradition it is understood that not all women are physically or emotionally prepared for motherhood. Motherhood is not asked of them. Other meaningful tasks are found. In general, however, it is understood that just as it is natural for women to raise and bear children during a certain period in their life, it is equally natural for them to move on to a different purpose later on. With the first part of their adult life they raise individual children, gathering Grandmother Wisdom as they go. With this next period in their lives they take responsibility for the whole People, for the whole community. I see many women around me moving from a period of time when they focus on their own careers, which is a way of paying attention to the individual, they have moved on to a focus on how they can help the whole people. This is again moving into Grandmother Wisdom.

As we in the Western world come to this stage in our lives, untrained as we are in understanding Grandmother Wisdom, many of us are surprised by what happens to us, surprised by the calling we feel to pay attention to the good of the whole people, to the well-being of Earth herself, surprised at the changes that seem to be evoked from us for this purpose.

My life path was different from this.

In my tradition every attempt is made to identify what we call "task people" early in life, so that they may be prepared for the difficulties that probably lie ahead of them. They will receive that degree of training, that kind of training, that will make their life easier in as many ways as possible, because it is well understood that Task People will have a difficult life at best.

My own task as the next generational Keeper of the Old Things began at the age of two and three when my father was already training me for memory, so that later on—if I chose to do so—I could retain and carry with me all of the Old Things that we have so far preserved.

My Father would do this by asking me what someone had said, again and again, until I remembered verbatim whatever had been spoken. He would do this by suddenly crying out, "Oh, look at that!" And then gently turning me around. "What, what?" I would answer. "What did you see?" he would reply. "Well, what did you want me to see?" "What did you see?" "Well ... what are you looking for?" "What did you see?" Until at last I learned when anyone cried out, "Look at that!" to take a photograph with my mind that I could examine later and recite what was in the photograph.

This is not, you understand, usual training for absolutely everyone, although some memory training would be traditionally included for every individual. It is for those who have a particular need for it. This training, you see, requires attention, time, and energy—from both the learner and the one she is learning from.

In this way, by the time I was twelve my father had well prepared me for the life that lay ahead. My task was clear—to wait until I lived long enough to gain some Grandmother Wisdom, to write down everything that I had learned from my Father in English, the language of the broader Nation, so that it might be shared, as my Grandfather's Grandmother had asked, "with all Earth's children with Listening Ears."

Yes, my task is clear. How to do it was another matter.

For this reason, my father emphasized again and again, how critical it was that I learned the Western way—"Learn the dance" he would say. "Learn the system. If you don't understand the system, if you don't understand the dance you will trip over your own footsteps."

And so, as I moved into the Western world and lived there increasingly, I focused on government, I focused on how people lived together in this Nation, on this Earth. It was and is necessary that I understand these things, you see, or how could I choose the proper words in English?

From the age of twelve to the age of forty-two I concentrated on learning the Western way as an enthusiastic participant. In my tradition one of the many sayings is, "That thing you choose to do, do that thing with a whole heart and stint in no way." During all this time I gave little or no thought to my responsibilities for the Old Things. My task was different now. My task was to understand the society in which I existed *well enough* so that I would be a good ambassador from the Ancestors to the present circumstance.

Life found me marvelous ways in which to study. While I worked on my degrees at George Washington University, my part-time work took me to Capitol Hill where I worked in various positions for the Congress, learning to understand that fascinating institution better and better as time went along. By the time I finished my Bachelor's degree, I was working for the Senate Foreign Relations Subcommittee on Disarmament under the chairmanship of Hubert Humphrey. It is that subcommittee that laid the groundwork that enabled the disarmament treaties that followed.

Later I worked for the International Monetary Fund and I learned to understand better and better how that organization and the World Bank enable and encourage the kind of economy we have chosen for ourselves in the Western world.

After my children were born, I still sought understanding in my community and began many years of work with the League of Women Voters, moving on later to the Overseas Education Fund, a sister organization to the League that worked overseas training women and women's organizations in the possibilities of community organization, law, and economics. That organization still exists under the title "Women, Law, and Development International."

Now I drew closer to the age forty-two. Now it was time to shift my focus from only studying the Western way, from only learning what it means to be a child of the Western way. Now it was time to remember the Old Things.

And I began. I wrote out the first of the ancient Learning Stories—Stories designed to enable each individual to teach *themselves* how to learn—on a yellow legal pad. I began to record the thousands of years of Oral History on a book of blank pages a friend of mine, Ann Schrogie, gave me with the admonition, "Now sit down and start writing!" I still have that book.

Now the confusion set in.

You see, when I was a child my Father would stand me on my left foot and say, "Answer this question in the manner of the People." And I understood what he meant. I understood the depth of perception, the image-ic way of thinking that was so important—and I would answer him.

Then he would stand me on my right foot and say, "Now answer this question so your mother would understand it." My mother who was *only* Western, my mother who would not hear the words of the People with any great understanding.

And when I had accomplished this task as well he would stand me on both feet and say, "Now what do you see?"

Such was the pattern my life followed. For the first many years of my life I stood on my left foot and thought in the ways of the People. For the next many years of my life I stood on my right foot and thought in the ways of my mother's people. Now, I was confronted with the third task, standing on both feet, learning to hear both realities at the same time and speaking from one to the other—in patterns both could understand.

There is an old saying which delights me greatly, "You too can be an overnight success ... and it only takes fifteen years hard work!"

That was how it was with the Old Things—learning how to share them, learning what to say; learning to share them in ways that could be understood. Years ... *years* were spent in reading selections from the Oral History as I wrote it down ... to groups of loyal friends who would patiently hear me and tell me whether or not they understood.

In the work I had done with the Overseas Education Fund they called this *field testing*. For years I practiced this field testing, reassuring myself that once my first task had been accomplished—the task of writing these things down in English that I myself found accurate—the second task was also accomplished—to test whether or not anyone at all could understand what I was saying.

These then were years of tremendous confusion, valiant struggles in trying to communicate, constant searches for words and phrases that work. Sometimes someone would ask me a question. I knew I knew the answer—

but could find no way to say it in English! Two or three *years* later—sometimes—I would finally find a way.

I answer more quickly now, most of the time. But as is often true between cultures, between languages, what may take two or three words in English or two or three words in my ancient tongue, may take pages to explain in the other idiom.

What I am telling you is that although I had a great deal of training that prepared me for this task of the second half of my life, and although I carefully prepared myself, the transition is still difficult. I knew exactly what I was supposed to do. I had no clue whatsoever as to how to do it! That was the great experiment.

Or as my Father used to say, "Time to step off the mountain and learn how to fly."

Many friends helped me and help me still when they give advice and guidance, tell me what they can and cannot understand. Where would we be without the greater community which allows us to better see ourselves and the effect of what we are doing?

So Life led me where it intended to—often in spite of my valiant efforts to "succeed." And gradually, step by step, I gave up all pretense of trying to "succeed," forgot even my basic purpose of failing to go bankrupt, and finally let Life take me where it needed me. Let Life present me with the opportunities she had designed.

I learned, you see, to be Native American again.

In the Western tradition, we worry constantly about wasting time, about making good use of time. In Native American traditions, in general, time is not even a factor. It is not even considered a real thing, but something invented by man to torment himself. Instead, in my tradition, the focus is on making very efficient use of energy. So you watch, you wait, until things seem to be falling together … and there is where you put your major effort. There is where you apply your own skills and purposes. In that way, you make maximum use of who you are in the context of what exists around you.

As I increasingly did this, strange things began to happen. Possibilities began to coalesce that I never would have dreamed of. I had no ambitions for myself, you see, except to do my task to the best of my ability and fulfill my commitment to the Ancestors to stay around for ten or fifteen years to answer questions.

My continuing question is, "When does that ten or fifteen years begin, only when I finish writing everything down?" I've been writing since the age of forty-two, I have reached the age of sixty-five and I'm not quite finished yet.

Of their own nature, the Ancient Things evolved themselves into an educational program, not because I planned it that way but because teachers immediately saw the value of learning in what was now before them. *Who Speaks for Wolf* won an award I didn't even apply for—the Thomas Jefferson Cup. And the value of this LearningWay was recognized by corporations, because they too want to learn. Health and healing came next. All these many ways of applying this Ancient Wisdom, all these many varying yet similar questions to answer, and I'm answering still—answering today, through these words that I write down for you.

You see how it is? How all my life I have had a left foot and a right foot view—in effect, two eyes to see the world with. One eye is Western. One eye is Native American. And between the two of them, they lend a depth of perception that would otherwise be missing.

Ever since I took economics in 1956, I have applied these understandings to the things I was learning at the university; I apply them still. The media use of information as merchandise worries me. It is not in the manner of the People, not in the manner of how Clan Mothers handle these things.

Ah! There's another subject. Let's talk for awhile about how those who are chosen to be Clan Mothers live out their lives. This is, you see, what I think we are all doing to a certain extent, we Women of the Millennium. We are teaching ourselves to be Clan Mothers.

ON THE NATURE OF CLAN MOTHERS

So many tasks that are ignored or inadequately done in our society were, in my tradition, the responsibilities of the Clan Mothers. It seems to me that, in our society, we have "killed the Clan Mothers," so to speak, without replacing them.

I do not mean to say or even to imply that the social circumstance described in the enclosed is the ideal toward which we must gravitate. That circumstance, too, has its difficulties. The degree of monitoring necessary to keep the system functioning is staggering! Clan Mother is truly a more-than-full-time job. As, by the way, is the task of being a Representative of the People (called "Chief" in English).

It seems to me useful to look at how this flow of energy was monitored and enhanced by Responsible People, specific individuals in a Nation of people, all of whom saw themselves as responsible—responsible for their own decisions, their own actions, and responsible to one another.

We know now that an ounce of prevention is truly worth a pound of cure. To be more fiscally specific, $1 spent on prevention is estimated to be worth $8 spent on correction. And we have yet to learn that lesson!

This treatise on the Nature of Clan Mothers is designed in the Native way, pithy comments that may well deserve some thought before moving on. In the Western way, we carry that thought forward on the threads of our words, filling the air or the page with commentary designed to give the listener, the reader, time to consider. In the Native way, you say what you have to say, then let silence give the space necessary for consideration, knowing that whether or not anyone considers your words, whether or not they agree, both are their responsibility. You only bring potential fuel to the fire of their thoughts.

For an excellent example of how the tasks of Clan Mother proceed, see the TNT video, *Broken Chain*, which shows the men leaders interacting with their Clan Mothers in a wonderful and precisely accurate way. The only thing that is missing from this video presentation is a demonstration of how Clan Mothers acquire their information, including a sharp sense of the thinking of the People, which is always the consensual base of their authority.

THE RESPONSIBILITIES OF NURTURANCE

Nurturance …. and protection …. form an Interactive Circle, one assuring the other. Together they assure the continuance of the People. Protection is the Warrior task. Some Warriors will be women. Nurturance is the Clan Mother task. Some men are natural nurturers. This interaction is one reason why we say, "That council which lacks male wisdom, that council which lacks female wisdom, lacks too much."

But we speak today of nurturance, the task of all women in the house and of those who work with them, the task especially of Clan Mothers. Their task is to make sure everyone has adequate nurturance and protection, a task which exceeds winter preparations and palisade walls. For nurturance must be gathered for Body, for Mind, and for Spirit—and presented to the People at times and in ways they can accept. Truly a task requiring Wisdom.

Care for the Body,

Respect for the Mind,

Nurturance for the Spirit.

Clan Mothers are chosen over the decades. Listening Ears and Careful Eyes are requisite, as it will be their task to gather consensus, to engender health. It is essential that they be able to know the general thinking of their group most of the time ... and be able to ask when they do not know.

Consensus, you see, is nothing at all you sit down and gain before set of sun. It is an ongoing process that is never begun because it never ended. Only from time to time particular foci are necessary. Consensus toward certain decisions being required, a clan council may be called and all invited to speak.

And yet, even before the time to speak-and-listen, Clan Mothers and those who work with them have been gathering information, gathering understanding of the issues at hand, presenting this carefully culled and sorted bounty to the People for their consideration. Information they do not have they have sent for. Reports have been checked and cross-checked, the views of many being always preferable to the view of one or a few. In other words, they are responsible for the quality of the information they present, as well as the content. And never, *never* do they speak merely to be first! They speak as appropriate for the well-being of the People. Minds filled with inaccurate, unchecked information tend to make poor decisions. Minds filled with more accurate, verified information do better. Inquiring minds ... want good data....

You see how it is? How Clan Mothers perform most of the tasks of today's media? And lay much of the groundwork necessary for effective self-governance? You see how it is much of this goes undone in our present society?

Care for the Mind. Care for the Body. It is the task of Clan Mothers to monitor the health of the People—as individuals, as a group. It is their responsibility to notice when anyone at all is moving *away* from health, and to focus on this change before something small grows into something large. Maintaining health is considered preferable to curing sickness. That which is eaten will be changed accordingly, before any loss of health is too great. Perhaps rest is required, perhaps activity. Ways will be found. Perhaps someone loses self-respect for too little is asked of them. More will be asked. The dysfunction will be identified as soon as possible. A way will be found to move toward health, at least a little.

Health for the group. No individual is treated outside of the well-being of the whole group. The entire interaction of everyone together is studied for clues, for any need for change. For every individual is part of the broader group and cannot be merely removed therefrom, healed, and returned without any other effort. Health for each. Health for all. Health together.

Clan Mothers ... and those who work with them! You see how it is, these tasks are nothing at all Clan Mothers are expected to do alone. For "those who work with them" truly includes, from time to time, each and every one of the People. It is the Clan Mothers' task to notice the need, or to recognize it when anyone at all points it out. It is their task to identify some remedy, to find a source, to see that it is done. It may be your task or mine, the actual doing.

Care for the Body. Respect for the Mind. Nurturance for the Spirit. Each of these aspects of responsibility relate to the People Together, as well as to each of the People. Nurturance for the Spirit comes through those ceremonies which remind us of the value of this aspect of Life. It comes through wise gratitude for Life's many gifts. It comes through celebration and renewal of relationships—the Web of Life in which we each belong, to which we each are connected, that which we nourish, that which nourishes us.

And in each of these ways, how do we assure the continuance of the children's children's children? And after them the children? How do we encourage adequate stability, interacting with a capacity for effective change? For if Life changes, and we do not, where will we be then? Who will we be then? Will we be ... then?

The Council of the Community is a men's council. These men have been chosen by the Clan Mothers. The Clan Mothers have been chosen by the People. The Council of Clan Mothers is a women's council. Both must approve all community decisions. Clan Mothers gather the concerns of the people, identify which of these most need attention, and ask the men's council to address these issues, which they must do.

> **And never, *never* do they speak merely to be first! They speak as appropriate for the well-being of the People.**

The Community Council, having reached consensus, gives that consensus back to the Council of Clan Mothers. If they approve, then there is agreement. If they do not approve, no agreement has been reached and the process begins again. In this way, all aspects of the community have spoken, have been heard, and all agreement—or lack thereof—identified. In this way, little enforcement is ever necessary.

Care for Body, for health. Respect for Mind, gathering information and agreement. Nurturance for Spirit. These are Clan Mother tasks. Let us seek out a way where we are now to see that these tasks begin to be accomplished.

TWENTIETH-CENTURY CLAN MOTHERS

While I was still living in Washington D.C., I worked with LaDonna Harris at Americans for Indian Opportunity (AIO). LaDonna founded AIO and was president of that useful organization. I was responsible to her for evaluating Indian educational programs. LaDonna was responsible for everyone who walked in her door.

After I had been working with her for five or six years I asked her one day if I could tell her about something I had learned. A willing listener, she!

"You know," I told her, "when I first began working here I knew that you were Comanche and I absolutely didn't know what to expect! I had always heard that the Comanche were a very warlike people, so I didn't know what you would be like.

"I discovered, to my amazement, that you were just a regular everyday Clan Mother, just as I would expect you to be! Responsible for the people, responsible for helping them in relation to themselves and with one another. You are the Responsible Person.

"And then I realized that everything I learned about the Iroquois I learned from my father. Consequently, I was impervious to the learnings presented in the educational system. On the other hand, everything I thought I knew about the Comanche I had learned in the white man's school! I had learned that the Comanche were fearsome and warlike.

"But," I said, "you are a Clan Mother, the kind of Clan Mother I'd expect to find!"

By this time LaDonna was laughing heartily.

"I hope I didn't offend you, LaDonna!"

"Paula," she replied, "you don't offend me a bit. I had the same reaction to you!

"You see, you're the first Iroquois person I had ever gotten to know and I had always been told that the Iroquois were fearsome and warlike. But I discovered very quickly that you are simply a regular all-around Clan Mother. That's just how you function."

So we learned together—LaDonna and I—a number of things. We learned together that "Clan Mother" is something that is understood throughout Native America. And we learned the difference between our own understandings of our own traditions—and the understandings promulgated in school.

I tell you this story because I think we have already begun the time when we are rebuilding the Nature of Clan Mother. I suspect that most or all of the women in this book either are or are learning to be Clan Mothers in their own right, Clan Mothers to their own group.

My own group consists of those who still study the Ancient Way with me, who seek to learn under the aegis of The LearningWay Company, under the aegis of The Past is Prologue Educational Program. Some become Certified Trainers, Keepers in their own right of some of the Ancient Understandings. They come by to hear stories, to sit around the fire for awhile and listen to the possibilities, to plan together a life that is somewhat different from the life we have been leading.

For this is surely a time of great change, surely a time when every possible seed of Wisdom we can find should be settled gently into fertile soil to see what may yet grow.

In my tradition, one of the many sayings is, "Wisdom is wisdom, the source cannot matter."

Our task, especially as Clan Mothers, is to recognize the Wisdom that lies before us, sometimes hidden, sometimes lying on the open sand. To recognize that Wisdom and to share it in effective ways so that we may weave together a world that is wiser, a world that creates without destroying, a world that is sustainable, even unto the Seventh Generation and far, far beyond.

So you see how it is? My transition has not been from one way of living to a new way of living I have never thought of before. Instead, my transition has been back and forth between two approaches to life, gradually and increasingly learning to balance between them. And I find great value in this. Native American wisdom, you see, pays attention to precisely those elements that the Western way forgets to remember. In this way, it is not wiser than the Western way, but is instead a perfect augmentation to it.

And remember that as Americans, each of us is at least a little bit, sometimes a great deal, Native American already. Or, as my father used to say, "Daniel Boone taught us to be Pioneers, and who do you think taught Daniel Boone?" Many of our customs, many of our words, and certainly our focus on freedom, our form of government, come, at least in part, from Native American traditions. Many know that the Iroquois Great Law of Peace was a substantial influence and in one sense a bedrock of the United States Constitution. Clearly English law was another bedrock, it's just that there were more rocks than one.

If we fail to understand these Native American influences on us as we built our nation, we cannot truly understand our history or our nature as a nation, not unless we understand this aspect of our national growth.

Only to the extent that we understand the circumstance in which we live, only to that extent can we be effective as leaders, as Clan Mothers, as Keepers of the possibilities of our children's Future.

I am still learning how to live up to my responsibilities as Clan Mother in my own particular circumstance.

I invite you to join me in this exploration.

Now,

Kind thoughts come.

ON THE NATURE OF FEMALE WISDOM

The Old Ones say ... that any Council Circle which lacks Male Wisdom ... any Council Circle which lacks Female Wisdom ... lacks too much. And I see how it is so.

And yet we know that the mere inclusion of persons who are male or female does not guarantee either wisdom. For we know that some of those who are male, some of those who are female, follow the complementary way. It is their nature.

Wisdom therefore tells us to use great care in selecting representation. Forget neither Wisdom! Ensure its inclusion!!

And yet, what is here? What wisdom do we seek? What may we consider Wisdom in the nature of that half which is Male, that half which is Female?

Forest and Path. Path and Forest.

Perhaps it is the general nature of that half which is Male to think in terms of Systems. If so, then let us remember that any System is selected out of the true Wholeness of Life and therefore will lack Wholeness.

Perhaps it is the general nature of that half which is Female to think in terms of Attitude. If so, then let us remember that Attitude addresses the Wholeness of Life, includes it in possibility, and yet of itself carves no selected Path through the Forest.

And so we say that Female Wisdom keeps the House, the source of Nurturing, including all the children in it.

And so we say that Male Wisdom walks the threads of connection between one House and the Other, between one Community and the Other, designing the connective Pattern.

Now—as we regard how we have organized ourselves, which Wisdom have we most forgotten?

For I tell you now that any System at all can be misused, any Plan at all misfunction—and so it will be without an Attitude which Nurtures the health and well-being of all the People in their wondrous diversity, the well-being of Earth and all her children. For Earth is a House which must also be kept.

And I tell you now that Attitude without devised System leads Nowhere of its self, but can and will tell us which Path to choose.

And that Path will vary. No one Plan, no one System can meet the needs of all Earth's children. Do Bison and Otter live in the same way? Do they both offer service to Life?

Let us, therefore, cherish and respect Diversity. Let us require no sameness of the human race, no human monoculture. For we have learned how susceptible to general death any monoculture may be.

And yet there may be some sharing of General Vision—a willingness to respect diversity and the needs of nurturance, a willingness to respect our own limitations and our great need for further learning.

The Old Ones say that we are here to Learn.

And tell us there are Many Paths to that Learning.

Kind thoughts come.

Jungian analyst **Jean Shinoda Bolen,** M.D., is a psychiatrist in private practice and clinical Professor of Psychiatry at the University of California, San Francisco. She is the author of seven books, including *Goddesses in Everywoman, Crossing to Avalon,* and the forthcoming *Goddesses in Older Women,* to be published in Fall 1999/ Spring 2000.

Wisewomen at the Crossroad

Two significant events are about to intersect: the millennium approaches and a huge generation of women's movement-empowered women are entering the third phase of their lives. Baby-boomer women at fifty are energetic, younger in spirit and vitality than any generation before them, used to having options, reinventing themselves. Many are alumnae of women's consciousness groups and have an adult lifetime of supportive woman friends. There has never been such a generation of women, and this at a time when the excesses and limitations of patriarchy are known, when men behaving badly in high places and close to home make it increasingly obvious that the male gender does not seem inclined to be caretakers of the planet or their portion of it.

We are in the archetypal realm of Hecate, Goddess of the Crossroad, whenever we arrive at a significant juncture or major fork in the road. Here we may encounter ghosts of the past and have intimations and hopes for the future. Hecate is an archetype of the wisewoman and crone, midwife and medium. She was a pre-Olympian divinity, a mysterious and minimized goddess, a shadowy presence whose influence through women has been denigrated and feared. In Old Europe, offerings were left for her at forks in the road, where it was said she could see all three ways at once. She could see where you were coming from and where the two roads could take you. Or her inner gaze could see past, present, future. Or know of heaven, earth, and underworld. Insight, intuition, and vision are contemporary expressions of the archetype of Hecate, which matures with age and experience. When women grow older and enter the third phase of their lives, around fifty years old, there is a shift in archetypes as well as in hormones. We come into the age of wisdom and for many of us, priorities shift. It's a personal time of menopausal transition that coincides with an archetypal time of expectation, when there is an openness to change.

On the eve of this millennium, the possibility exists for the first time in historic memory that older women will come into their own in positions of influence. An estimated forty million baby-boomer generation women turn fifty in the few years preceding and following the year 2000, joining those women's movement-women who led the way a decade earlier. This could very well constitute a critical mass of women of wisdom, authority, and action who may determine the direction that humanity will take. What we do or fail to do at this liminal time will not only shape the course of our personal lives, but collectively will affect the third millennium and with it, the future of the planet.

I believe that a grass-roots collective consciousness-raising is quietly occurring among women, individually, in small and large groups, and globally and universally. Consciousness-raising occurs whenever women become aware of an absence of compassion or loyalty or justice, for them as women or as wives or lovers or mothers or sisters or friends or colleagues, especially when that was naively assumed to be there. It begins with seeing injustice and perceiving how power is misused, and then realizing that there are other ways of thinking and doing. It involves growing wiser, redefining oneself and the competency of women, and then doing something about what needs to be changed.

Once women see their situation clearly, whether to do something or do nothing about the situation arises. How outraged versus how disheartened matters, especially in young women. With age, women often act with more deliberation and commitment to see something through. Women inspire each other much more by what they do and what they have done, or survived and even thrived doing, than by what they say another woman ought to do.

Whenever one woman identifies with another, it becomes possible for her to imagine doing something similar herself. Since the women's movement, there is a whole generation of women who not only have learned to trust and identify with each other, but have resources of information and referral sources for all manner of undertakings. When something arises that needs to be changed in a personal or institutional situation, to act and act effectively becomes an option. This is the immediate background of women approaching their fifties, who will step into the third phase of their lives as we enter the next millennium. It would be a mistake to assume that they will be invisible.

Women at the 1995 United Nations Women's Conference in Beijing and the 1996 World Population Conference in Cairo gave us a preview of the emergence of what the policies and priorities would be when there is a critical mass of women with influence to change the world. A common realization is that if this world ever becomes a good and safe place for all children, it will then be safe for their mothers and, by extension, for all women and men.

Until now, there has *never* been a significant number of women who have had authority in the work world as well as in the household. Never before did women who had education, positions of privilege, and authority also see themselves as sharing concerns, vulnerabilities, and experiences with each other and with all women everywhere, as we do now.

There has been patriarchy, hierarchy, and rule by men with power, class, and privilege for as long as we know from history. War has been the determining act, and property what has been fought over. Whether nations or gangs, the dominant male archetypes have defined others as either stronger or weaker, with contempt for and oppression of the weaker. Weaker people became property or chattel, defined clearly as one's inferiors and often seen as "other," especially when there were gender or racial differences. Dehumanizing inferiors or projecting qualities or fears onto them, and then fearing their retribution usually followed. There is very little room for compassion and empathy in institutions or individuals under such circumstances.

Disempowered as a group and as individuals, women have not been in a position to influence the patriarchal culture until the last few decades of the second millennium. The ideological message came through the writing and demonstrations by feminists in the mid-1960s. Judicial and legislative efforts followed, which led to affirmative action and to a change in the climate and culture in education and in the workplace, so by the time the baby-boomer generation arrived, schools, professions, and corporate positions that had been virtually closed to women a scant decade or two before were open. The status quo has been undergoing change ever since, with change and backlash.

When women's movement literature was being written and women's consciousness-raising groups were meeting, I was in my medical training years, isolated from the real world by the demanding hours. Betty Friedan's *The Feminine Mystique* and the *Report of the Commission on the Status of Women* that had been appointed by President John F. Kennedy had just been published and were causing controversy. Demonstrations by radical feminists had no relevancy for me. The then-status quo allowed for a token number of women and we felt privileged to be where we were.

As a reader, I gradually became influenced by women's movement literature that had entered the mainstream through a number of anthologies published by major publishing houses and by reading *Ms. Magazine.* But it was not until I became pregnant and was in labor and delivery that I had the archetypal experience that made me aware that I was no different than every woman throughout history who had ever been in this powerful, painful, vulnerative, and transformative experience. This personal physical experience was an initiation that provided me with further insights into the archetypes of the collective unconscious that I was growing to appreciate more and more through my work as a psychiatrist and in my training to be a Jungian analyst.

In 1984, my book *Goddesses in Everywoman: A New Psychology of Women* was published. My own experiences, Jungian archetypal psychology, and a feminist perspective came together in this book. It provided words and images through which women might define themselves and what deeply mattered to them. Archetypes are collective tendencies like other human talents and abilities; the strength and depth of them vary from person to person and, like any other attribute, the development of any particular one depends upon environment and support for its development and growth. Some of these archetypes were supported by the women's movement. Others are expressed through women's traditional roles. Some are greatly influenced by hormone and bodily changes; others are not. *Goddesses in Everywoman* became a classic, one that has been of special value to women in their early- and mid-adult years, because knowledge of archetypes help us to know ourselves. If we make choices about what we do that rings true to our archetypal depth rather than to others' expectations, then what we do and who we are come together and a meaningful life can then result.

I am now working on *Goddesses in Older Women: The Third Phase of Women's Lives*, which will be published just months before the Year 2000. This time I am writing about archetypes that can come into full expression when a woman is around fifty years old. Just as physical and hormonal changes influenced archetypes earlier at this stage in life, there are major archetypal shifts as we approach and pass through menopause. They are archetypes of wisdom and action, of compassion and outrage. I begin with Hecate but of necessity go outside the Olympian mythology. In Greek myths, as in every Western culture since then, older women are either virtually invisible or disempowered. There are no powerful and angry goddesses of any age in Greek myths as there are in Egypt or India, for example, and only traces exist of a pre-Olympian Greek goddess who was older and sexual, even bawdy. Yet women over fifty are often at their most personally interesting, sexually expressive, and most understanding, or else they are at that place in their lives when enough is enough. To learn of these archetypes gives women images, names, stories, and ultimately meaning to whatever is inarticulately stirring deeply in their psyches.

I have learned that the world changes one person at a time, but that change becomes increasingly easy the more and more there are who do change. A woman who makes a major change in herself by recognizing qualities that are true for her can tap into a preexistent archetype that is new for her, which becomes a source of psychic energy, of feelings, and of images that arise in dreams and metaphors from the collective unconscious. This is how women experienced themselves as they identified with goddess archetypes in *Goddesses in Everywoman*. This is how a similar interior experience will follow the recognition of archetypes in older women, also modeled on goddess figures that are already patterns in the collective unconscious.

A second concept, akin to the collective unconscious, can account for a change in a culture's attitude and values, which would need to take place for there to be a major shift in the next millennium. This is the morphic field hypothesis proposed by the theoretical biologist Rupert Sheldrake in a series of books. It's a simple-to-grasp idea: the way we do things and perceive reality is based on commonly held assumptions or habits which can be changed when a critical number of individuals change.

Each person who changes a perception and acts accordingly contributes to the pattern which others add to and tap into when they similarly change. It becomes increasingly easy for such shifts to occur the more members of the human species have already done so, until what was once new or even previously unthinkable becomes the way things are.

It is the archetype of Hecate who informs us that we are on the threshold of great change. As we grow older, even without conscious awareness that we are learning about cycles, patterns, and timing, we are. Body knowledge has been a teacher, the seasons have been classes, and personal life has provided experience through which we acquired such wisdom. At a personal psychological and physiological level and in our relationships, we come to realize—after having lived long enough—that we seem to know when we are at the threshold of change or at a boundary crossing. We may even be able to read the signs.

We also know from experience that after a transition time, we will be different or things will be different or a relationship will never be the same. There are propitious or pregnant or decisive moments in each person's personal life—and in history—when outcome can be affected by what was done or not. Metaphors reflect what we know: there is a last straw, a hundredth monkey, something that tips the scales, a little Dutch boy who put his finger in the hole in the dike, a critical mass or a critical temperature, a time when opportunity knocks, once.

It is the intuitive and visionary Hecate in me and in the editor and other contributors to this anthology that recognizes that this millennial threshold is such a moment in historical time. There is a stirring in the psyches of a generation of women's movement-influenced older women, one that calls on us to be an influence, to say what we know, to enter the phase of the wisewoman, whose concern is for other generations and the greater good. In relationships and in institutions, when change is threatening, there may be desperate efforts to keep the upper hand, a last-ditch resistance that is a natural part of the transition itself. Hecate, as archetype of the midwife, knows about transition as the last stage and the most intense, knows that it will take that final great push to cross that threshold and overcome the resistance.

Once over the physiological boundary into menopause, the years of potential biological childbirth are over. In this phase, the only "babies" we may birth will grow out of our spirit, intelligence, experience, and imagination—metaphoric offspring of who we became by living this long. If enough of us do what we know in our bones matters at this juncture, history may retrospectively know much further down the road we took, that the fate of humanity was at the crossroad with us.

BY SAYING WHAT YOU KNOW IS TRUE OR RIGHT YOU CHANGE YOUR WORLD

Gloria Steinem used to end her talks by urging her audiences, "Promise that you will do something outrageous, every day," and then as we wondered about the scope of such a charge, she would say in a gentle voice, "For example, tell him, 'pick it up yourself.'" With that simple a phrase, a major change in a woman's significant relationship could begin. It could be a fork-in-the-road moment, when an egalitarian evolution or personal revolution began. It was one of Steinem's pithy comments that made me think about how transformation of culture depends on shifts in perception and small acts of courage on the part of ordinary people.

The women's movement and psychiatric observation made me realize the destructive effect of patriarchy—or hierarchy in relationships and institutions, including the family. If it is not safe to express what we perceive or what we feel, then power, not love, is the ruling principle in that relationship. If we are punished for this in an intimate relationship, we are not in a safe relationship; instead we are in our own private version of patriarchy.

Cultural assumptions change one person at a time. Therefore, if—finally, at fifty—a woman gets fed up with obeying someone else or carrying out directives that run counter to her own wisdom and compassion, her interior change marks a significant beginning. When she speaks up or acts on what she knows, she is challenging the patriarchal underpinnings of her personal life or the old way business is done and making it possible for others to change and evolve. You don't have to join a cause or take on a giant; you have to say what needs to be said, what is true for you, where you are. Sometimes this is welcomed as a contribution; it's you finally acting like a full participant or partner in the relationship. Or, you may be taking as big a step in your personal life, as Martin Luther did when he nailed a list of his perceptions of abuses on a church door, an act which would lead to the Reformation.

Evolutionary changes may be brought about when women speak up about new ways to do things. Women juggle roles, tasks, budgets, they keep track of children and adults and what they need; they have to be flexible because somebody may be sick, or somebody may change plans. Women as a gender have a lifetime experience in adaptability, flexibility, making do with what one has—whether it's food on hand, time, or money—in ways that men as a gender usually have not. Community problems or planetary ones may be issues that women's ways of thinking and relating may help solve. Women also have paid attention to people and, as a gender, are likely better at sizing up the character of a person. Input into leadership, a voice about selection of which men or women are best suited for a task—in these ways, a woman whose voice is that of an elder may make a major difference if listened to. Whether in forefront or in the background, if enough women in this phase of their lives speak up and are listened to, transformative changes in society will result.

A CIRCLE IS A SOURCE OF SUPPORT

The women's movement grew out of consciousness-raising groups, and consciousness-raising groups grew into the women's movement, round and round: something new grew out of women telling each other true stories, real feelings, and finding strengths, vulnerabilities, character, anger, and courage to act, in each other and in themselves. They shared books, articles, information, experience. The same phenomenon is happening in cancer support groups, which may extend life or contribute to remissions and healing. Women in these groups survive twice as long as women who do not. Such is the sustaining energy that women can provide each other.

Around fifty, most women have more time for themselves and for friends. It is a time when the idea of a women's circle often strikes a chord. Sometimes such a group begins to support a friend with cancer. Increasingly, it is motivated by a wish to be in the company of women who have spiritual and psychological depth.

Sometimes they call themselves councils, sometimes wisdom groups, sometimes crone circles. Sometimes they begin as dream groups or book groups. Regardless of their beginnings, they usually become a place to "check in," and thus everyone in the group knows what is currently important to each other. Such groups become a place where women witness each other's lives and serve as role models for aspects of each other. Support to be themselves grows out of the practice of meeting together and being real.

After fifty, what to do with the rest of our lives does come up. Especially when we become aware of how short and precious life is and we wonder why we are still here, when cancer, AIDS, and other life-threatening illnesses have taken contemporaries. Then, the wish to make a difference, or to live life fully, or to give back may come into consciousness. To become an elder, to make a contribution, to be a mentor, or to be creative may become issues. There is sometimes a tension between a husband who looks forward to retiring, and his wife who wants to now become more involved with something that competes for time with the leisure and travel he envisions. What to do at this juncture is often a personal crossroad for women.

If blessed by good health, the baby-boomer achiever generation of women is likely to enter the third phase of their lives with vitality, material and psychological resources, and a sense of possibility that menopausal women have never had before. Lacking role models in their mother's or grandmother's generation, women look to each other to see what may be possible for them. The networking that younger women do grows into a mature version of knowing who to trust and how to get things done. Whether it is to run for political office or find a good oncologist, massage therapist, divorce lawyer, or whomever, women at fifty know people who know people. There is often also an extended network of friends who are the "old girl network."

A circle can be a place to incubate the idea of what to do next. The circle can act as a vision-carrier for its members, holding possibilities without judgment or fear. In doing so, the circle becomes an incubator for new growth: it might be that you have yearned to go back to school for a particular reason, or want to start a business or a nonprofit, or enter politics, or go on a meditation retreat or a trek, or write poetry or a book, paint, join a choral group, or take up an instrument; what you are considering may also be the first step in making a major change in your life, and it may be your contribution to changing the world.

A circle can be a sanctuary in a true sense. *Sanctuary* is derived from a root word meaning "sacred," which is a place for divinity to dwell. When a circle of women is the form, one way the invisible structure of the group can be imagined is as a wheel with a spiritual center. Christina Baldwin, in her book *Calling the Circle*, has developed very practical ways of forming and sustaining a spiritually centered circle. Barbara Marx Hubbard has been describing and inspiring the formation of resonating or co-creative circles as part of a larger planetary vision of action for well over a decade. Circles as a form are cropping up all over—even in business, in government, and in churches where there is hierarchy. Every circle is quietly subverting the up-and-down linear chain-of-command form.

AN INNER LIFE IS CENTERING: AN ARCHETYPAL WISEWOMAN LIVES THERE

Someone who is perceived by others as a wise elder or crone is a woman whose influence comes from who she is, not from power in the world, accomplishments, prestige, or position. When a woman comes into the phase of the crone and is considered a wisewoman people who see her as such usually are perceiving a quality of her soul and character. She has an inner connection with the archetype of the wisewoman, which she personifies in her particular way. Sometimes a woman still looks the part, but increasingly the resemblance is only an inner one. What others know of her is that she has had her share of the joys and suffering of life, that she has lived and learned, forgiven and let go of unimportant details, and doesn't concern herself with neurotic dramas. She is not perfect, she is human. There is an inner serenity, however, that she can always return to, because she has an inner life. There is a center within.

Increasingly women personify this center as an archetypal wisewoman or goddess. In the Christian tradition, the Holy Spirit is within her. The dove as a symbol is common to both goddess and Counselor, with peace as its attribute. Solitude nourishes this aspect of the psyche, so that taking time out to go inside and be spiritually replenished is needed. Sometimes, a few quiet moments of prayer or meditation can be restorative of the connection. The wisewoman archetype can be like an inner gyroscope that is centering. When a woman is in the world, doing her part to make a difference, her strongest ally is inside when she is exposed to intense personal encounters that are off-centering. She finds outer support and the means to tap into a collective spiritual source if she has a spiritually supportive, regularly meeting group. (One's religion, Nature, a personal intimate, a therapist, can be other sources of centering.)

Any woman who wants to bring about change, to do good or do right, or make something better, will become involved with people. She may be provoked by some and drained by others. The relationship orientation that draws women to work with people or help them also makes them vulnerable to be emotionally infected or contaminated by some encounters. Its hard for most women to be impersonal, and that difficulty is both a gift and liability.

Wisdom comes from a combination of having had enough experience with whatever it is to not be drawn off-center by what another person does or feels, and by being able to go inside and find a wisdom and serenity there, a center in the midst of outer emotional turbulence and difficult circumstances. The inner wisewoman provides perspectives for reflection to balance outer involvements. She is there, as a still point in the psyche of the activist.

Carol Flinders, Ph.D., coauthored *Laurel's Kitchen* in the 1970s and continued writing about natural foods and vegetarianism until 1993, when she published *Enduring Grace: Living Portraits of Seven Women Mystics* and, in 1997, *At the Root of this Longing: Reconciling a Spiritual Hunger and a Feminist Thirst*. She has taught in several departments at U.C. Berkeley and is currently affiliated with the Graduate Theological Union. She lives with her husband and son at the headquarters of the Blue Mountain Center of Meditation.

Feminism Reimagined: A Civil Rights Movement Grounded in Spirituality

"The feminist revolution will not be an overthrow, but a transformation."

—Gerda Lerner, *Why History Matters*

I love the traditional Italian way of bringing in the New Year: At the stroke of midnight, windows fly open and the sound of crockery smashing on pavement forms a raucous counterpoint to the pealing of church bells. All year long, householders have kept every chipped cup, every cracked plate or bowl, and now they hurl them out into the street, singly and deliberately, while everyone laughs like children at the absurd racket, the delicious unruliness of it all.

It's hard to resist drawing a millennial metaphor. Imagine what it would mean if we could lay hands on every bad idea, every cracked master plan or patched-together policy and just *throw it out*. NAFTA, GATT, the Inquisition, silicon implants, Manifest Destiny, nuclear reactors, the Crusades, Lunchables, television.

But, of course, the allegory is flawed. Profoundly so. All the while I'm exulting at the disappearance of corporate medicine, for example, or call-waiting, or the divinely sanctioned right to bear arms, my neighbor would surely be having his or her own kind of fun getting rid of Roe v. Wade, the Marshall Plan, and e-mail.

No, it doesn't work. Tempting as it is to look at that string of zeroes and see in it a kind of cosmic reprieve, a literal "naughting" of all those wrong moves, the truth is that as we straggle into the twenty-first century, we will carry our history with us—all of it. We will go on drinking from chipped cups and eating from bowls with hairline cracks because we're stuck with them until (perhaps there is hope for the metaphor after all!) we provide ourselves with new and better ones.

And surely we can. The precious beginnings of a different kind of world are not impossibly hard to imagine, and each of us needs to be imagining them—strenuously. But we don't have to start from scratch. Important as it is to recall all those wrong turns, it may be even more crucial to identify the women and men who know, or knew, what a right turn looks like. Two such figures come readily to mind, people whose lives and teachings are of inestimable value to women in particular. Both have shaped profoundly my own thinking about the international women's movement.

Before I read historian Gerda Lerner's brilliant two-part work, *The Creation of Patriarchy* and *The Creation of Feminist Consciousness*, I was in a state of more-or-less perpetual frustration with regard to feminist thought and action: it all seemed to be taking place within a historical vacuum, which only seemed to confirm the argument that contemporary women were asking for something that was utterly without precedent and therefore inconceivable. Lerner was not the first scholar to suggest that human culture has not always been male-centered and male-voiced. For decades, archaeological and anthropological evidence had been mounting, suggesting that prior to what we commonly regard as "civilization"—the rise of agriculture and the city states, roughly—deities were feminine as well as masculine and the whole female domain was seen as both mysterious and sacred. But Lerner *was* the first scholar, it seemed to me, to offer a convincing picture of the stages by which patriarchy probably established itself, and this struck me as tremendously important. Thanks to her, one could actually see them—those critical wrong turns—right there in the historical record.

Drawing on the history of Assyrian civilization in particular, Lerner describes two developments that she sees as pivotal to humanity's transition from a relatively balanced, inclusive way of life to one that marginalized women in a host of ways. The first of these was the gradual commodification of women's sexuality and reproductivity that appears to have taken place as agriculture replaced the gathering/hunting mode of life. Large-scale farming required a large labor force, and this meant that children came to be regarded more and more as field-workers-to-be and their mothers as "breeders" by the men who organized and headed up the work. The second milestone was the division of women by class that occurred when the so-called "veiling laws" were introduced late in the second millennium B.C.E. Women who were married to property-owning men were now required to wear veils when they were in public, while slaves or prostitutes were just as adamantly forbidden to. The veil marked a woman as chaste and therefore privileged: its absence signaled her utter vulnerability.

Shorn now of full human dignity, pitted against one another by laws that made it dangerous for them to act in solidarity, women were severely undercut. Yet, Lerner tells us, they retained a very real measure of power and authority until one final and immensely important step was taken. In order for women to be brought fully into submission, the connections they had enjoyed with the sacred had to be severed entirely. Female deities had to be discredited and their centers of worship destroyed. The aura of sanctity that had pervaded domestic work had to be stripped away and the work itself trivialized. Finally, women had to be barred from holding any significant role within religious institutions.

In order for civilization "as we know it" to unfold, all traces of the sacred feminine were erased and women were relegated to the dim outskirts of the culture. The history of early Christianity is instructive in this regard. The life and teachings of Jesus Christ were without question woman-friendly, as was the vital, inclusive, home-centered church that sprang up in his name. But within a few hundred years after his death, the pervasive misogyny of the Mediterranean world had caught up and remade the fledgling church in the image of Imperial Rome.

Lerner's work on the development of patriarchy revealed to her something she had never fully grasped before, and that was "the significance to women of their relationship to the Divine and the profound impact the severing of that relationship had on the history of women." This insight in turn allowed her in her next book, *The Creation of Feminist Consciousness,* to appreciate and document "the depth and urgency of the search of Jewish and Christian women for connection to the Divine, which found expression in more than 1000 years of feminist Bible criticism and religious re-visioning," and to conclude finally *"that religion was the primary arena on which women fought for hundreds of years for feminist consciousness."* (Emphasis mine.)

Learning how profoundly important "connection with the Divine" actually was to our feminist foremothers was, for Lerner, a momentous discovery—one whose implications contemporary feminists haven't even begun to take in. Nineteenth-century feminism, for example, takes on a very different look when we take seriously the innumerable links between the suffrage movement and various "alternative" religious movements that came into existence around the same time or somewhat earlier—movements that were characterized by inclusiveness, intuition, spontaneity, tolerance ... and female leadership. It would appear that the women *and* men who fought for women's rights drew substantial inspiration and strength from their religious commitments and communities. They were most certainly the same women and men who fought for the abolition of slavery, and for essentially the same reasons.

Lerner's analysis of the first stirrings of feminist thought and action compels us to look with new eyes at the contemporary women's movement—in particular, at its resolutely secular tone and outlook. For *if* we have good reason to believe that women could only be fully subordinated when they had lost access to the sacred—and *if* we can see that, conversely, as soon as women did find their way back into connection with the sacred, as mystics, prophets, scriptural authorities, healers, etc., they began very swiftly to reclaim the authority and power that had been stolen from them, then surely we have to wonder whether contemporary feminism has not left something vitally important out of the mix. The movement is stalled, say many commentators— is indeed, by journalist Leonard Pitt's account, "a sleeping giant"—and one can't help wondering whether this paralysis might not have something to do with the fact that religion itself and everything associated with it has been made marginal to feminist discourse.

Obviously feminists have had good reasons for keeping religion out of their politics. Mainstream organized religion has done little to advance the cause of women's liberation, and historically, religious convictions have done more in this country to promote divisiveness than solidarity. So it has made sense up until now to envision the women's movement as a civil rights' movement—the full and just expansion of democracy, but nothing more.

And yet if we reflect at all upon the Civil Rights movement of the '60s, we have to recognize that it was rooted and grounded in a passionately felt amalgam of African and Christian spirituality—in a belief in the sanctity, and *therefore* the dignity, of every child, woman, and man.

The fact is, Lerner's analysis also compels us to look at patriarchy itself with new eyes, and to see that those first "wrong turns" were not merely violations of civil rights but rather crimes against the human spirit, perpetuated down through time in all our social—and religious!—institutions. The opposite of patriarchy is not matriarchy at all (one keeps wishing this had become obvious). At the core of patriarchy, ideologically fundamental to the nation-state, is the belief that one builds a "self"—becomes more fully human— through competition and acquisition, a creed that culminates in standing armies, colonial expansion, and ridiculously large buildings that tower over slums, a creed which is nothing more, at bottom, than materialism itself. The antithesis to this belief system (and I suspect that only when feminism recognizes this and acts accordingly will its paralysis be cured) arises out of a radically different understanding of "self" and its construction ... "a perspectivity," in the words of contemporary feminist scholar Ellen Messer-Davidow, "that confers self all around," and that is most plainly visible in figures like Saint Catherine of Genoa or the Dalai Lama.

One might even argue, then—to push things just a little further—that it wasn't just the sacred feminine that patriarchy set itself against, it was in a very real sense sacredness itself. Because if the testimony of the mystics— Christian, Hindu, Buddhist, Sufi—is to be taken seriously at all, then what characterizes the Holy is wholeness, and experiential knowledge of the indwelling divinity of all creatures—and there is simply no place in that view of things for the oppression of one sex, or race, or class by another. The very worst and most threatening aspects of contemporary civilization—the worship of technology and proliferation of weapons, the growing disparity between rich and poor, the wholesale destruction of the Earth itself—all grow directly out of the mental set that first decided it was okay to "other" women and count them as less than fully human. And if our religious leaders aren't particularly effective in opposing these threatening developments, it's because what passes for religion under patriarchy has imbibed patriarchy's fundamental commitment to "othering," often treating spirituality itself as something very like a commodity.

In suggesting it is time to begin seeing feminism as a civil rights movement *grounded in spirituality*, I'm not suggesting there is anything wrong with continuing to press through our courts and legislative bodies for equal pay, for equal access to jobs, adequate health care, etc. All of those imbalances are symptomatic of misogyny and none should go unchallenged. But we need to see through them to the attitudes that have rationalized them, and address those attitudes as well.

What would it *look like* if women were to ground their feminism in spirituality? It would look like a great many things—does now, in fact, because certainly many women are beginning to see their feminism in this light. Some are seeking to recapture or re-create the forms of prepatriarchal spirituality, immersing themselves in the imagery of female strength as an antidote to the imagery of female dependence and depravity so ubiquitous in contemporary media. Others are securing a measure of detachment from the sheer turbulence of political activism by adopting the meditative practices of non-Western religious traditions. Still others—and their resourcefulness can be breathtaking—manage to find in their own inherited faiths, despite dauntingly patriarchal elements, the spiritual nourishment they need as women.

But what I find even more intriguing is the fact that many women whose first commitment is to political activism are discovering along the way that the work *in and of itself* has a powerfully spiritual dimension. In *Visionary Voices: Women on Power,* for example, Papusa Molina, founding member of Women Against Racism and director of the Women's Center at University of Iowa, thanks Luisah Teish, author, dancer, storyteller, and initiated Yoruba priestess, for giving her back "the practicality of spirituality."

"Spiritual beliefs are rooted in the welfare of the community," she maintains. "Teish helped me realize that my political work was spiritual work. By liberating people, by liberating myself, I was liberating my spirit, and the spirit of the people. And the more I understand that, I realize again that spirituality cannot be an individual thing."

In other words, when women live out their commitment to connection, inclusiveness, the sacredness of all life, working on behalf of children, the elderly, the Earth itself, and one another, they often feel they really are rehabilitating the sacred—affirming it over and against the narrow and damaged version of religion that is propounded by denominational churches, with their commitment to hierarchical authority, otherworldliness, and the systematic compartmentalizing of life. The selflessness, the austerity, and the communality of resistance work kindles a kind of flame.... One thinks of the heroine of Alice Walker's *Possessing the Secret of Joy* and the banner that is the last thing she sees before she is killed by a firing squad: "The Secret of Joy ... is Resistance."

The feminist who discerns this golden thread in the fabric of her political activism has a choice to make. She can feel her way little by little into this astonishing new paradigm, making it up as she goes along—or she can realize that she doesn't need to reinvent the wheel. For she stands, after all, in a lineage; she has predecessors, among them some of the most remarkable people who've lived, and she can draw deeply, if she chooses, upon their experience.

There would be no better place to start than with the life and teachings of Mohandas K. Gandhi (who certainly would have preferred to be known as such, rather than as "the Mahatma," the "great-souled one"), because nobody has explored the complexities of politics as religion, or religion as politics, to the depth that Gandhi did. And yet nothing he did looked much like what most of us think of as religion. He was associated with no church, temple, mosque, or synagogue. Indeed, he playfully spoke of the prison where he was repeatedly incarcerated, Yervada Prison, as Yervada Mandir—Yervada Temple—because it was only when he was in prison that he had the leisure for prayer and study of scripture.

"I could not be leading a religious life," Gandhi maintained, "unless I identified myself with the whole of mankind, and that I could not do unless I took part in politics." From the very outset, when he took on the government of South Africa on behalf of its Indian population, his politics were shaped and informed by his spiritual convictions. In the present context, I can only touch upon what that meant, but in so doing I hope to convey something of the significance Gandhi's "experiments with truth" may hold for contemporary women.

Gandhi rejected the use of violence as a means to achieve political ends, claiming that in fact every violent act plants the seed of another. The principle is not, after all, so very recondite. Anybody could grasp it who has lived observantly in the family context, and I suspect that, consciously or not, most women do. We speak today of "cycles of abuse" as if they'd been discovered by contemporary social scientists, but the understanding that cruelty perpetuates cruelty, which was foundational to Gandhian nonviolence, was a commonplace in Buddhist and Hindu religious teachings. Gandhi's real genius was simply that, like all great mystics, he was utterly inept at compartmentalizing life, and imagining that what doesn't work in one sphere will work just fine in another.

Having rejected violence as an instrument of change, Gandhi looked around for an alternative, and found it close at hand, in the methods by which his own wife regularly brought *him* around when he was oppressing her, which, by his own admission, he certainly did. Instead of retaliating, he saw, one could take suffering upon oneself, not masochistically or sullenly, but in such a way as to effectively "mirror" the injustice, making it visible to the oppressor and palpable to his or her conscience.

When he began trying to meet violence with nonviolence in the political arena, he found very quickly that being able to regulate his emotional responses—fear, anger, resentment—was crucial, and, furthermore, that he could actually make himself more courageous, patient, and secure through spiritual disciplines—very simple practices, like eating foods that were nutritious instead of merely those he liked, or building periods of prayerful silence into his day. One can see this perception playing itself out on a large scale in Gandhi's views on colonialism. If Indians were going to throw off their British rulers, he reasoned, they would have to free themselves first from economic dependence upon them—for a colonized people are not held in place merely by military force. There are always "perks." Indians must, for example, rebuild the cottage industry that had once produced all of their own fabric, and they must wear it, too, instead of purchasing British-made textiles. In doing so, they would not only reaffirm the dignity of their own ancient culture, but also acquire a new confidence in themselves—specifically, in their capacity to make small personal sacrifices in the service of a larger ideal, letting go of a here-and-now pleasure when it meant bringing the dream of a free India closer to realization for their children and grandchildren. For India to become truly free and capable of governing herself, it wasn't enough that the well-to-do city folk be liberated. The plight of the desperately poor villagers would have to be relieved, and purchasing homespun cotton, or *khadi,* would help achieve that. But in subtler ways doing so would also strengthen wealthier Indians, teaching them that they could exchange the pleasures of consuming—the illusory freedom of being a shopper in a richly furnished marketplace—for the joys of connection and community.

Gandhi saw the futility of challenging outward forms of colonial oppression without at the same time beginning to dismantle the internalized forms—the complex of beliefs, inbuilt by centuries of institutionalized racism, in one's own *inherent* unworthiness. The antidote to this slow-seeping poison was a passionate belief in the unity of life, which he cultivated in himself through prayer and the study of world scriptures. He saw that all religions are imperfect, because all of them took shape in particular cultures with particular limitations, but he also insisted that they are all "true," insofar as they sprang in the first place from someone's deep experiential understanding of unity and that their core beliefs are, in fact, extraordinarily consonant with one another. At nightly prayer meetings, attended by all his coworkers, he was as likely to request hymns like "Abide with Me" as he was to ask for a traditional Hindu *bhajan,* and to sing along with rapt intensity—this despite the longstanding and unutterably insulting presence in India of thousands upon thousands of Western missionaries come to convert "the heathen."

Feminism has no better friend or more ardent champion than Gandhi. I've never seen it noted, for example, that when he was in South Africa launching his first nonviolent campaign against institutionalized racism, he wrote an editorial urging his followers to emulate the British suffragettes who had chained themselves to the gates of Parliament. Gandhi drew women into the top leadership positions of the Congress Party, and he railed against the men of India continually for their subjugation of women, comparing it openly to their own subjugation by Britain. But his relevance to contemporary women doesn't stop there at all. He actually carried out a revolution that was "not an overthrow, but a transformation," providing us with a historic model we can build upon.

The importance of that model really can't be overstated, because one of the real sticking points for would-be feminists all along—one of the reasons the movement has not attracted the large numbers of women it should have, or held all it *has* attracted—is the oppositional paradigm that we've inherited from patriarchy itself—the winner-take-all model that assumes a champion and a challenger, one who is victorious, and one who is vanquished. Women feel themselves to be too profoundly connected with men—as wives, mothers, daughters, coworkers even—to embrace that model for anything resembling a sustained campaign. Our loyalties to one another can be strong, but not so strong as to overshadow those other connections altogether. And what the Gandhiian model tells us is *that they don't have to.* The real rallying point, the ground we can hold, and really must, is the understanding that patriarchy is poisoning the lives of our sons and husbands and lovers, as well as our own. Gandhi knew the British well enough—had lived in England for several years—to have seen how their basic decency had been blurred over and transmogrified by their long tenure as a colonial power. And we know the men in our own lives well enough to have seen what misogyny, or even just the simple, unquestioned assumption of male privilege, has done to them.

The other problem with that pervasive "oppositional paradigm," of course, is that it's been the only one generally available to men, too, so when women speak of the need for balance and fairness, men hear only a call to battle and a challenge to their own hegemony and they react accordingly. Persuading them that "something else may be going on here" will be the task of every one of us—daughters, wives, mothers, and, thank goodness, a fair number of male allies as well—who sees that indeed it is. And merely talking about it isn't enough. We must live it. "The moment the slave resolves that he will no longer be a slave," Gandhi told his people, "his fetters fall. He frees himself and shows the way to others. Freedom and slavery are mental states."

What took several thousand years to put in place won't come down in a decade. No question but that we're looking at a long, long struggle. But there could be no better preparation for that struggle than to immerse ourselves in the study of Gandhian nonviolence.

Rev. **Carol E. Parrish-Harra**, Ph.D., was propelled into spiritual awareness after a near-death experience in 1958. In 1978, she founded Sancta Sophia Seminary for the study of the ancient wisdom teachings, Agni Yoga, Kabbalah, Esoteric Christianity, spiritual sciences, astrology, and many other metaphysical subjects. Sancta Sophia is located in Sparrow Hawk Village, a spiritual community begun in 1981 by Dr. Parrish, her husband, and a friend, in the foothills of the Ozark Mountains near Tahlequah, Oklahoma. The author of ten books and numerous teaching tapes and articles, she is an international lecturer and member of the Network of Religious Futurists.

She Who Leads Happily Across

Each of us is familiar with the presentation of three faces of woman:
young and innocent;
empowered and well-defined;
elder and wise.

Nowhere in modern society is there more questing than in the lives of awakened women. Contemporary women recognize their unlimited potential. We are on the move; the energy of the divine feminine stimulates and lifts us toward a future yet unborn, and each of us becomes a component of her expression. Yes, we are magnificent.

As Woman garners her strength, she creates adventures and understanding with fresh new dreams. She most often takes form through those who dare to stretch their wings. We ponder her mystery, seeking to find ways to express— in words, songs, paintings, babies, hopes, jobs, or causes.

A near-death experience in 1958 set my inner nature free in a world with little comprehension of spirituality or the power of light-filled moments.

Without words or concepts to guide me, I foundered in a world of values that forbade new awareness. Struggling to bridge my conventional role of good Catholic wife and mother with the spiritual reality I had encountered ever so briefly, the experiences I needed to link inner and outer slowly emerged. When I sat quietly and contemplatively after the children were in bed, I discovered first a rewarding peace, then a comforting presence. I found that I was not alone.

Reconciling dichotomies is a major work of contemporary women. We are learning to use our hearts and minds, our creativity and our rational capabilities at home and in our new public positions as we role-model for those who follow: our daughters, their daughters, our collective daughters.

How we as women embrace and master life as we approach the twenty-first century is the focus of this book. Each contributor has found that strength, encouragement, and challenge helped forge her foundation. From personal perspectives, we face the millennium hoping to share words of clarity for those ready to move forward and transcend the past. We no longer hesitate, looking wistfully to others for the rules; we take the lead, challenging forces which once held us in restriction. Woman's way is to tell stories that call others to new awareness.

A preponderance of this new energy is called by many names; I use *divine feminine,* meaning "sensitive, creative, supportive." The nature of the feminine is to linger, endure, and embrace; it is often called Aquarian which implies humanitarian and universal. Native people say to become a "true human" is every person's goal. The time rapidly approaches when we will see beyond gender and acknowledge wholeness as the great goal.

The society of the past half century has been shattered by wave upon wave of falling thoughtforms. Equality is now demanded; mere promises are no longer adequate. No double standard, for it is too painful; glass ceilings demand shattering. The long-forgotten seed of spirit planted within human consciousness is bursting into bloom.

Currently, women are busy creating spirituality out of religion. Based on the experience of another, religion looks backward; spirituality looks to the future, to what we can be. Religion defines dogma and what is acceptable; spirituality acknowledges inner nature and begs its maturity.

We are in the midst of the Second Reformation of the Christian Church. In one hundred years, we will wonder why women moving into church prominence was so disturbing, for we know that Christ was served by holy women as he was by male disciples. The church of the third millennium will emerge as the church of the Mother and the Father—strong yet tender, healed and whole.

As we approach new frontiers, we are responding to impulses leading to Renaissance II—a flowering of fresh ideas, a new worldview. Spirituality is the next stage of that blossoming. Just as crystallizations of the Dark Ages once held individuals in a limited state, the Renaissance set the Western world free to begin a new cycle of ideas and philosophies. In the same way, spiritual will is carrying us beyond the entrapment of mechanistic thinking to reconcile and harmonize ancient wisdom and ever-expanding science. We must realize an expansion of consciousness in order to coordinate heart and mind, discover our unique inherent gifts, and claim both intellect and intuition. Wherever polarities exist, we seek to find a higher consciousness from which to view life—from a balanced, centered position, if you will. Awakened woman is ready to make her contribution. Sophia is her name.

The recognition of Sophia, as she is called in Proverbs, helps each world religion honor its feminine deities as personifications of wisdom, beloved in their own ways: Mary, Mother of Jesus; Nefertiti, Queen of the Nile; Kuan Yin, the Bodhisattva of Compassion; Isis; Venus; Athena; Ishtar; and Astarte. As each religious path or cultural pattern serves a collective, each advances slowly toward a worldview, bringing order to a seemingly random universe. As we consider what may be the end times as referenced by Christian Scriptures, we see disintegration all about us. Wisdom warns us not to conclude that this is the end of the planet, but of a worldview. Endings beg new beginnings, and the divine feminine responds.

THE EMERGING FEMININE ENERGIES

Visualize the emerging feminine energies as a fine mist penetrating ever so gently. The effects are nearly undetectable, like the delicate fragrance of freshness—vague, pleasant, refined. It enfolds us. Its physical influence is sensitive and peaceful; emotionally, the feminine *feels* pleasant, like a sunset or a warm, light rain. The greatest obstacle to this energy is mental. Not wanting to be absorbed by an encircling cloud of tranquility, the rational mind rebels, demanding independence and reward—from self and others.

Even as we admire sensitivity, nurturing, serenity, and encouragement, ego-mind ascertains that "soft" is not as acceptable as "strong," "casual" not as alluring as "chic," "natural" not as commanding as "earthy," "sensual" not as powerful as "sexual." We know the basic needs for mothers—homes, nature, the quiet of evening—yet as a society we have been motivated by conquest and intellectualism.

As we progress into the future, women can count on several factors:

- We will be challenged time and again.
- Humanity needs us, and we are to be role models.
- We must dare to be clear in our own ethics, even if misunderstood.
- As we progress, we keep one hand in the hand of a trusted confidant or therapist to help us wipe away the residue stirred.
- We must continue to love and forgive those who cannot understand.

To be positively feminine, a woman cannot be anti-male, nor can a true man be anti-woman. The time approaches when, valuing their differences, opposites will admire and honor one another. And an age of peace and accord and the wise use of creative powers will ensue.

Sophia, one of the names for God in the Scriptures, means "wisdom" in the original Greek of the Bible. Here exists divine validation of the holy feminine spirit—eternal co-creator with God who has been on the world stage from the beginning of time. In Proverbs 8:22 we read, "The Lord created me [Wisdom] as the first of his creations, before all of his works," and verses twenty-seven through thirty continue to affirm her participation. In fact, all of chapters eight and nine narrate the role of Wisdom (Sophia) in creation, as she formulates and orders the world, manifesting divine will. Wisdom delights to interact with humankind, teaching us her ways. Of greatest significance is that, as a gift of the intuitive heart, wisdom has been a guide, a goal, and a pathway for the homeward-bound soul among the discerning of all ages.

Feminine virtues—soft, loving, yielding, nurturing, and, above all, compassionate—are epitomized in the legend of Kuan Yin from the Chinese tradition:

Long ago an emperor and empress ruled the land well, but they were childless. They went to the Western Mountain and prayed for children. Thereafter three girls were born but no sons. The Emperor decided that when his daughters married, he would choose one of their husbands to succeed him. The youngest daughter, Miao Shan, became their favorite, and they decided to make her husband emperor. However, Miao Shan said, "I only want to sit alone and pray to become perfect; to care for the ill and to help the poor. I do not want to wed."

Her father became so angry he cast Miao Shan out to perish in the cold from hunger. She did not die. Her family begged her to change her mind, but she asked only to go to the Nunnery of the White Sparrow. The emperor allowed her to enter the nunnery but ordered its mistress to assign her the most menial tasks to discourage her from becoming a nun.

Miao Shan cheerfully carried out her hard chores. This report further angered the emperor. He ordered the nunnery to be burned to the ground, but Heaven must have taken pity on Miao Shan, for rain extinguished the fire.

The emperor then ordered his troops to seize her and behead her. When the empress begged the emperor to win their daughter back with music and feasting, Miao Shan was not tempted. On her execution day, a miracle: the axe shattered to smithereens as it touched her white neck. A tiger spirit is said to have carried her away to the underworld where she prayed until the underworld became bright with light.

Returning to Earth, she sought a quiet place to pray for perfection. For nine years, she meditated on the island of Pu To. By thinking only pure thoughts, she became perfect.

About to enter the Kingdom of Heaven, Miao Shan stopped at the gate. Wails of the poor, troubled people made her turn back to help. Because of her great compassion, from that time she has been called Kuan Yin, meaning "she who hears prayers."

While this lovely legend dramatically portrays the attribute of the divine feminine we call "compassion" (Kuan Yin is known as the Bodhisattva of Compassion), it also expresses great inner strength, though strength has long been deemed a masculine attribute. So we add to the well-acknowledged feminine energies—*nurturing, loving, flexible*—others less widely recognized: *inspiring, creative, long-enduring, intuitive,* and *playful.*

In eras of equality, male and female are of mutual significance. In our time, we experience misused masculine power. Evidence suggests that woman overreached her power in times past and triggered a wide swing of the pendulum. As we create an age of enlightenment, we work to re-create gratitude for feminine influences that express through both male and female.

Consider the symbolism of the "Tree of Life" of the kabbalistic tradition. On the feminine pillar, *Binah,* the sea, is filled with potential—the forms, or seeds, for all that can be. On the same pillar but on a lesser level, the stern mother, *Geburah,* trains and disciplines—with tough love, when necessary. Below that level on the feminine pillar, *Hod* is instinctual intellect—that inner knowing so often recognized as woman's intuition. There is so much more to each of us than meets the eye!

THE FEMININE STRENGTHS

Contemplation and meditation, as spiritual technologies, increase our realization of the benefits that accrue as humanity regains respect for the feminine principle. Through these tools, we will rediscover a natural reservoir of healing, comfort, tenderness, sensitivity, and protection. Strengthening our appreciation of feminine dignity and purity encourages women and men to reestablish worthy spiritual role models, thus empowering the woman of the future. With renewed appreciation, we will welcome feminine strengths in both genders. A return to sensitivity will reshape values and bring balance and wholeness.

So much mental rationale has been developed in our world that, as we prepare for the twenty-first century, we must now consciously stimulate an equal amount of sensitive love—compassion, rich with wisdom—to compensate for today's indifference. Extreme masculine or feminine traits push us toward overexpression. The absence of love for divine principles shows in competition without compassion; brute force; power without temperance, mercy, or nobility; war; and lack of appreciation for emotions, nature, and the well-being of the Earth. We must manifest the love humanity needs to *think with the heart and feel with the mind.*

It is interesting to note how Genesis, likely an early interpretation, is being reevaluated. Well-known Bible authority David Freedman of the University of California wrote recently in *Biblical Archaeology Review,* "The age-old scriptural image of woman being made subordinate to man may be the result of a mistranslation of the Hebrew word 'ezer' (Genesis 2.18) as 'helper' or 'helpmate.' The word actually has roots indicating it should be translated as 'a strength' or 'a power' and that the word 'kenegdo' used with it, though usually translated as 'fit,' should be translated 'equal.' *This would have made the Genesis account read that woman was created as 'a power equal to a man' instead of a 'helper fit for man.'*" (My emphasis.)

In ancient history, humanity revered the Divine Mother as goddess, giver of life, personifying the nurturing spirit that gave life. Later, Isis came to honor and immortalize the natural bond between mother and child. Then

Mary, Mother of Jesus, embodied this divine principle for Christian and non-Christian alike.

Peter Roche de Coppens writes in *The Nature and Use of Ritual for Spiritual Attainment,* "Short and simple as it is, the Rosary is one of the most important spiritual documents containing profound esoteric knowledge and a series of integrated and practical exercises designed to establish a breakthrough between the conscious and the superconscious, to fill the human aura with spiritual Light, and to harmonize human self with Spiritual Self.

"Mary, therefore, represents the ideal woman, the perfection of the female principle, and the incarnation of the eternal feminine aspect, a part which we all have within our being."

The long-hidden face of the divine feminine has endured in traditions worldwide. Buddhism's White Tara symbolizes the highest form of spiritual transformation. Tara is revered as "she who in the mind of all Yogis leads out of the darkness of bondage"—the primordial force of self-mastery and redemption. While on the lower plane she is known as Shakti, on the higher she is Tara "who leads happily across." Especially venerated in Tibet, she is considered the Mother of Buddhism. She leads the souls across the river of *samsara* ("reincarnation" or "worldly illusion" in Sanskrit) to the far shore which is *nirvana.* Her emblem, as illumination, is a book resting upon a lotus blossom, her hands forming a circle signifying the inner contemplation of the true doctrine. She is also called "Dolma"—the Saviouress, the Great Goddess of Mercy. Maya, the fantasy, the enchantress, delights in imprisoning all creatures; Tara, true spirituality, sets them free.

As we seek to appreciate the divine feminine and the emerging Sophia-wisdom—the intuitive knowing stirring more and more significantly among humanity—the challenge of acknowledging human divinity as feminine disturbs our age-old consideration of divinity only as masculine. Gradually, we realize that if God is whole and absolute, s/he must be of both genders, and we are forced to face our limited conceptions about holy reality.

Even as we are challenged and stirred by such daring thought, the goddess herself must be restless—perhaps saddened as well. From every corner she seeks to make herself known. Whether through appearances of Mary, the whispered inner knowing of Sophia, or the return to goddess religions such as Wicca and Isis, our world must confront the swing of the pendulum to the feminine. Since many are still uncomfortable with subjects dear to the Lady's heart—sexuality, birth, death, intuition, healing, play—polite society is thrown into many challenging areas. She seems to have her foot in the door of every arena, from the office and laboratory to sports and politics, as well as spiritual circles.

It is important to realize our goal is integration and balance of the divine in both the masculine and the feminine. Our social structure has functioned in a driven, success-oriented, competitive mode for centuries, and now a surge of interactive approaches challenges this achievement style. Women who dared enter the world of business, science, or higher education seventy-five to one hundred years ago did so at the risk of being stripped of their femininity or told to "park it at the door—emotion does not belong here."

Today, active listening is encouraged. Suggestions and ideas travel from ground level (foundation) up. Workers buy companies and find new ways to implement their ideas. Interactive styles are "in"; even for the President of the United States, the John Wayne approach has been retired.

What initiated such change in these few years since the women's movement began? Can we not see there is more at work here than just cultural shifts? Esoteric philosophy suggests a cosmic current is affecting our planet, and perhaps it is time to stand back and observe. Many believe humanity advances by utilizing first one set of skills or qualities, then another. Historically, we trace the last few ages from hunter (masculine) to agriculture (feminine) to conquest and industry (masculine). Having penetrated a new level on the spiral, we ascend again toward honoring feminine values.

Long ago, most of society shifted from tracing family lineage from matriarchal to patriarchal, from ownership by women to ownership by men. Only in this century have women captured the right to vote in our country, initiating their movement toward renewed value and the right to be heard. Modern history records the achievements of men, barely mentioning noted women and their contributions of the last millennium. Authors and poets were forced to write under pseudonyms to get published. The feminine gender was disdained.

Now we watch the tide turn. We are challenged to see what has long been denied. All of life is supporting this balancing. Planetary consciousness demonstrates its femininity distinctly:

- Earth continually adjusts to create a fertile environment to sustain the "seeds" of life.
- Mother Nature adapts her creatures to her environment.

- As a last resort, the enduring, long-suffering planet turns to tantrums and storms to cleanse, to begin life anew.

Societies themselves may be labeled masculine or feminine. The more rational, rigid, and ambitious the culture, the more it is considered masculine. The more instinctual, comfortable with emotions, and respectful of natural laws, the more a unified collective is regarded as feminine.

Cultures of the East project concepts of unity; of the West, separatism. Eastern religions and spiritual traditions recognize the relationship of every part to the whole, while the West dissects, analyzes, and rationalizes hows and whys. Thus, while the East cultivated philosophy, yoga, and castes, the West exalted science, art, and organized religion. While the East attuned to inner, invisible precepts, the West prized outer, visible power and status.

Like dawn and dusk, planetary cycles come and go. The dawn is overtly powerful—that is, masculine—but covertly contemplative; the dusk is overtly soft—that is, feminine—but covertly vigorous.

Women and highly sensitive men—feminine in nature—are used as instruments of impression repeatedly. Since the mid-nineteenth century, a swelling of information has spilled into the educated and articulate of the world. Messages from spirit and transmissions from holy ones in the higher world stir minds and set new currents into motion. Phenomena erupted: from Helena Blavatzky—saint or sinner, according to one's perspective—to the Fox Sisters of New England, to Alice Bailey and her service as an amanuensis for The Tibetan.

Wise Ones, or ascended beings, also provided guidance and instruction to Helena Roerich. Her inspired transmissions, *Agni Yoga,* offer data of a cosmic nature, addressing the changing period our planet would be entering and speaking to those deemed ready to receive. The Agni Yoga teachings gradually were shared with a small number who started adapting new thoughts and lifestyles, practicing meditation, and deepening their spiritual disciplines. As they observed the acceleration of change in the outer world, they contemplated the Agni writings for keys to holistic living.

Roerich, a Russian aristocrat and Theosophist (1879–1955), preferred absolute anonymity; her writings were published unattributed and remain so today. Two books of her letters, stepping down the teachings to students, have been published, but the bulk of transmitted material only now is becoming known. Much guidance concerning the future is given, with great emphasis upon cultivating an appreciation of the work, the teachings, and magnitude of the divine feminine.

Here are some Agni Yoga thoughts from the world of spirit, compiled in *Woman*, which was published by the Agni Yoga Society in 1958, regarding the impact of the divine feminine:

1. The approaching great epoch is closely connected with the ascendancy of woman. The future again offers woman her rightful place beside her eternal traveler and coworker, man. Buddha held woman in the greatest esteem, and stated that she could achieve, as well as man, the highest degrees of Arhatship. Verily, the same fire of spirit, the same monad is aflame in woman as in man; the psychic apparatus of woman is more subtle than that of man. That is why in ancient Egypt the high priestesses of Isis transmitted the orders of the Goddess to the Hierophants, but never vice-versa.

2. All the present and coming miseries and cosmic cataclysms to a great degree result from the subjugation and abasement of woman. The dreadful decline of morality, the diseases and degeneration of some nations, are also the results of the slavish dependence of women. Woman is deprived of the greatest human privilege—complete participation in creative thought and constructive work. She is deprived not only of equal rights but, in many countries, of equal education with man. She is not allowed to express her abilities in the building of social and government life, of which, by Cosmic Law and Right, she is a full-fledged member. But a woman slave can give to the world slaves only. The proverb "great mother, great son" has a cosmic, scientific foundation. As sons mostly take after their mothers, and daughters after fathers, great is cosmic justice! By humiliating woman, man humiliates himself! This explains today the paucity of man's genius.

3. New Age writings present various other ideas for women today. Woman is the one who should know and proclaim the power of culture developed from spirit because she was chosen to link the two worlds, visible and invisible. Woman possesses the power of the sacred life energy. The coming epoch brings knowledge about this great omnipresent energy, which is manifested in all immortal creations of human genius.

4. Woman must defend not only her own rights but the right of free thought for the whole of humanity!

The goal of Agni Yoga—*yoga* means "union" (as does *yoke* in the Bible: "Take my yoke upon you")—is to provide a new comprehension of the nature of reality of humanity and the universe, stirring aspiration in the hearts and minds of humanity. Agni emphasizes the natural laws of the cosmos by advocating appropriate interaction of masculine and feminine energies and by teaching that misuse and abuse of either gender brings imbalance to the laws of nature.

Today's women—awakening to this stirring of the divine feminine—must be alert to the danger of repeating the pattern of swinging from one extreme to the other, seeking revenge for errors suffered, or devaluing men in retaliation. Wise ones who recognize the universality of spiritual teachings demand dignity for all. Recalling the rules of high consciousness, they must assist the lesser-aware to respect every being. The seven great "world-old" Hermetic Laws, from *The Kybalion,* published by The Yogi Publications Society in 1940, teach:

1. The Principle of Mentalism: All is mind, for everything flows from the mind of the Creator, i.e., Father-Mother God.

2. The Principle of Correspondence: Everything relates—the laws and all planes of matter, the ethers, and energy, of being and life. *As above, so below.*

3. The Principle of Vibration: Everything is in motion, reverberating, never at rest.

4. The Principle of Polarity: Everything has its opposite aspect, differing only in degree.

5. The Principle of Rhythm: The pendulum swing manifests in everything. Just as the tide ebbs and flows, matriarchy and patriarchy rise and fall.

6. The Principle of Cause and Effect: Everything happens according to law; "chance" is just a name for law unrecognized.

7. The Principle of Gender: Everything is feminine and masculine. *Gender,* meaning "to generate," manifests on every plane.

As the pendulum returns to the feminine, may the Inner Knower within each speak strongly and clearly, with balance and forethought.

Woodeene Koenig-Bricker is the author of *365 Saints, 365 Mary,* and *Prayers of the Saints.* A freelance writer for such magazines as *McCalls* and *Catholic Digest* and editor of *Catholic Parent* magazine, her writing interests lie in integrating traditional Christian theology and belief with contemporary spiritual needs. She believes that while life is serious business, to take one's self too seriously is one of life's cardinal sins.

The Age of the Spirit

We peer into the Millennium like tourists on the rim of the Grand Canyon. Never mind that the date may be off a few years because of improper calculation of the birth of Christ or squabbles over whether we should actually count 2001 as the first year of the third millennium. Intuitively we understand we are standing on the brink of a psychological new age. Just as January 1, all too often a drab, grey, inauspicious winter day, gives a us chance to wipe away the tears and trials of our past year, so too the year 2000 presents us with an opportunity to start over, leaving not just the pain of the past year, the pain of the past decade, the pain of the past century, but the pain of our collective past behind.

For me, this communal sense of a new beginning heralds entry into an era of deep, profound, and world-changing spirituality—the Age of the Spirit. In my religious tradition, God is seen in a triune expression: God the Father, God the Son, and God the Holy Spirit; one divinity, with three separate and distinct faces.

The first thousand years after the physical life of Jesus quite naturally focused on the face presented by Christ, God made man. The teachings of Jesus spread throughout the world, revolutionizing all of Western civilization. Yet, because Jesus was himself male, our cultural image of God remained strongly masculine.

The next thousand years concentrated more on the face of God as Father. Western society in particular became much more structured, regimented, and regulated. It's no wonder a patriarchal, highly masculinized vision of Divinity with an emphasis on rules and orders emerged.

The two millennia before us attempted, and largely succeeded, in putting a profoundly masculine face on God. While my religious tradition would never refer to God as Mother, I came to realize how very masculine my own image of God was when I considered what response to prayer I would expect from God as my Father as opposed to God as my Mother. Whereas God as my Father would grant "yes" with a benevolent bestowing of favor and say "no" to me for my own good and self-development, God as my Mother would sing her "yes" and cry her "no." God as my Mother would move heaven and earth for me. God as my Father would tell me to offer it up. Because of years of indoctrination, I realized I envisioned God, who is neither Father nor Mother, but both Father and Mother, as almost exclusively masculine. I know from the shared experiences of other women who struggle with their God concepts that I am not alone.

But that is about to change. Today, I believe, we are preparing to enter into a third age, the Age of the Spirit. Whereas in the past we saw God made man (and I use that word deliberately) in the person of Jesus and God the Father with a strongly masculine demeanor, we are now hungering to view God not with the limitation of culturally imposed gender divisions, but as an all-encompassing entity in which Spirit balances those masculine qualities which have been theologically refined over the past 2,000 years with the highest and best qualities we traditionally have viewed as feminine.

Because God, who does not have gender, has been so thoroughly masculinized by our culture, thinking of the Holy Spirit not as female, but as engendering the feminine qualities of God, is a radical departure for many.

Yet it need not be. The very first verse of Genesis says that "The Spirit of God was brooding over the face of the waters." The word *brooding* carries with it the image of a mother bird, caressing her eggs under her wings, warming and urging them into life. And a few verses later, in talking of the creation of humanity, it says, "God created man in his image; in the divine image he created him; male and female he created them." God could not have created male and female in the divine image if the divine did not encompass both masculine and feminine.

This is not the only place Spirit is addressed in feminine terms. Holy Wisdom, another facet of the Spirit, derives from the Hebrew word *Hokhma* which is translated into Greek as "Sophia" and into Latin as "Sapientia." All three of these words are feminine, as the book of Proverbs so clearly demonstrates: "Wisdom cries aloud in the street, in the open squares she raises her voice; Say to Wisdom, 'You are my sister!'"

Even the word *Spirit* itself has a feminine root. In Hebrew, it is the feminine "Ruach," which is translated into Greek as the feminine "Pneuma." It is only when the word shifts into Latin as the masculine "Espiritus" and then into modern languages as "Spirit" that the migration to male gender is made.

Indeed, Spirit is genderless, being one part of a triune, genderless God. However, calling Spirit "he" feels like betrayal and using "it" renders an impersonality which is the antithesis of Spirit, so I, knowing full well that my choice runs contrary to traditional Christian theology, choose to refer to Spirit as "she."

Spirit, the often overlooked and forgotten third member of the triune God, represents the passionate, uncontrolled, and uncontrollable nature of creativity and growth. She, who is truly and rightly called "holy," embodies and makes manifest those qualities which have been traditionally associated with the feminine: nurturing, creativity, cooperation, gratitude, mindfulness, calmness, authenticity, honesty, delight, joy, comfort, counsel, encouragement, passion, peace. She broods over the waters of creation, warming the Earth to life; she sweeps into our lives, not like a dignified ambassador on an important mission of spiritual diplomacy, but rather like an eccentric, whimsical, and somewhat embarrassing aunt who insists on dancing the tango in the kitchen.

Perhaps the clearest evidence of Spirit's nature is shown in the story of Jesus' followers. After his Crucifixion his apostles were cowering, cringing, and waiting in an upper room. Then, without warning Spirit arrives on winds of promise and flames of change. Suddenly the apostles were speaking to crowds, traveling the world, preaching the message of Jesus. They had believed, but could not act on their belief until Spirit entered their lives and made them into "spiritual" creations.

Today, despite 2,000 years of inculcation into the masculine aspect of God, I sense within our collective soul a profound longing to restore balance by resurrecting a more complete image of God, one which is neither male or female, but both masculine and feminine. However, in order to do that, we must now in the new Millennium begin to recognize and appreciate the feminine nature of God as embodied by the Holy Spirit.

It won't be easy. Spirit cannot be regulated, put in a cubicle, made to work nine to five. She doesn't fit the patterns, follow the rules, flow into the molds. She is the fire which does not burn, the wind that blows through closed doors. She is life itself.

Spirit is crying out to us to become expressions of the gifts she offers in all we do and are. She is calling us to profound, radical, lasting change.

So what are we to do? How then are we to live in the Age of Spirit?

I believe the first step is to pay attention to the shimmers.

Let me explain. My son got me hooked on a computer game which consisted of numerous labyrinth-like puzzles. At one point I was utterly stymied. I had reached a dead-end where nothing I tried worked. When my son saw what I was doing, he pointed out a block that ever-so-slightly shimmered now and then. "Push there," he said. When I did, the wall opened and I was able to pass into the next level. I had seen the block shimmer, but had not paid attention to it. I had decided the shimmer was not worth investigating; that it was unimportant. Thus, I was frustrated in my attempts to reach another level. Once I followed the shimmer, I became aware not only of many more shimmering blocks, but the fact that I had made the game much more difficult than its creator had intended. The passageways had always been there. My decision to ignore the shimmers that indicated their presence kept me from opening them.

In his classic work *The Power of Myth*, Joseph Campbell says that when we follow our bliss, doors will open for us where no doors existed before. I firmly believe that. I believe Spirit is constantly pointing out new ideas, new paths, new doors, but we must be willing to acknowledge the shimmer which indicates the way.

Wouldn't it be much easier if Spirit just laid things out plainly for us? Yes, and no. It would be easier in the short term, but much of the joy of life lies in personal discovery. Spirit is not so much trying to trick us by hiding the way, but rather to encourage us to break out of our narrow views to see the limitless possibilities. For Spirit to help us, we must be willing to consider that a shimmering block is not just an accident, but a call to action.

It isn't easy to believe in a shimmer for it often seems so inconsequential. We rationalize our reasons for not paying attention. How could this be the way, we ask ourselves? We look for a neon sign when in reality all we usually get is a shimmer.

It's like the computer game. Once I knew what a shimmering block meant, I began to watch for their presence. Likewise, once we have stepped into life's shimmers and felt the awesome power and love of Spirit, we understand neon signs are not necessary. In fact, neon would be overkill.

The first step, then, to a new life in the Spirit is to be watchful for the shimmers, for therein lie all possibility.

The next step, I believe, is to examine the ways we limit the work of Spirit in our lives. Spirit can do anything, but we block the flow of Spirit and prevent miracles from occurring.

We do this in many individual ways, of course, but one of the major ways we block Spirit is by concentrating on our lack. When we operate out of a sense of scarcity, we become selfish and miserly. We begin to believe that someone else's good fortune directly impinges on our own. We begin to believe Spirit hands out only so many blessings and if someone else gets the ones we had our hearts set on, we're out of luck. When someone wins the lottery (literally or figuratively), we act as if the prize belonged to us and the other person has stolen our rightful possession.

That's not how it works. Spirit does not allocate blessings by taking from one of her children to give to another. When we can finally believe that someone else's abundance has absolutely nothing to do with ours, then Spirit will be free to give us the blessings that have been ours from eternity.

Unfortunately, we have been inculcated to believe blessings are to be hoarded. A dear friend of mine, who has shared many of his sorrows with me, was loath to share a sudden and profound change for the best in his life. When I finally confronted him with my pain and bewilderment at his withdrawal, he said he hadn't wanted to appear to gloat over his good fortune when I did not have a similar blessing in my life. He said he had remained silent because he hadn't wanted to hurt me by flaunting his abundance in the face of my lack.

I understood, but I also grieved. How could he have thought I would only want to share his sorrow? How could his joy hurt me, unless I saw Spirit as limited and believed joy is a scarce commodity? When I believe there is only so much to go around, then I have to get mine, no matter what. But if I trust Spirit has more than enough for all, then I am no longer in competition for a finite number of blessings. Rather I realize I have my own share of abundant blessing. In fact, I can begin to see another's blessing not as a dead-end wall, but as a shimmer which beckons me to realize my friend's joy is no more my sorrow than his bounty is my lack. His joy truly *is* my joy.

Once we begin to live and breathe this fact, we reach a place where we can both rejoice in the blessings of others as well as share their sorrows. At this point, Spirit can work through us to bless others and can bless us through others. We ourselves become shimmers of grace.

But focusing on scarcity isn't the only way we block Spirit. We also block the action of Spirit by a lack of gratitude. It is a timeless spiritual law that gratitude begets blessing. By giving thanks in all things we open the way to blessing.

Gratitude begins by accepting the fact we truly have what we need at this point in our lives. *At this point in our lives* is the key. We may not have enough savings to send our children to college, but if they are still in elementary school, there is no need yet. We may not have the house of our dreams, but we have a house that protects us from the elements and allows us to nurture our families. We have not what we want, but what we need.

One way to see how our needs are met and to learn to give daily thanks is to adopt a gratitude journal. Many writers have suggested keeping a notebook in which we write down five or more blessings we experience every day. Such a journal is profoundly revealing. As I have concentrated on what I have been given, I have begun to see how much I truly have to be grateful for. It is true for all who have developed this spiritual practice, for, as another spiritual law states: like attracts like. When we focus on our blessings, we begin to attract and experience increased blessing. When we focus on our shortage, we begin to attract wants and desires, all of which block the ability of Spirit to give. In fact, if we don't have what we genuinely *need*, then perhaps we are blocking Spirit's ability to provide both by our focus on our lack as well as our absence of gratitude. Spirit waits with plenty, but we must do our part to be able to receive.

Another way we block Spirit is through fear. I can't explain how fear barricades Spirit any more than I can explain how gratitude frees her, but both are true. Fear creates physical, emotional, and spiritual changes which prevent Spirit from opening new doors. It's not that Spirit can't act; it's that I do not allow her to. I like to think of it being somewhat akin to the old question—Can God make a stone so heavy God can't lift it? Such a question is unanswerable because the creation of such a stone would be outside the purpose and nature of God. In like fashion, fear is so outside the purpose and nature of Spirit that its presence renders her action impossible.

When I fear, rather than empowering Spirit to help me, I actually empower my fear. The more I am gripped by fear, the less attention I pay to the shimmer and the more I experience increased fear.

Which brings me to the final step (or is it actually the first step?) we must take to enter into the third millennium ruled by Spirit. We must not only recognize and invite Spirit into our lives by expressing gratitude, but we must release fear by trusting that Spirit has a purpose and plan for our lives. Moreover, we must trust that her purpose and plan are for our eternal good.

Taking that leap of trust is frightening because we tend to judge Spirit on secondhand information. We see pictures of the starving in a famine-ridden desert and conclude that Spirit isn't to be trusted. After all, if she were trustworthy, wouldn't she have answered those people's prayers?

But the only way to judge Spirit's trustworthiness is from the evidence of our own lives. We seldom know what another has prayed in the secret recesses of his or her heart.

My aunt was dying of cancer. She told family and friends she was praying to live and when she suddenly took a turn for the worst and died, many felt her prayers were unanswered. However, my mother finally told me that the night before my aunt died, she told my mother that she was really praying for it to be over. Her prayer, her *real* prayer, was answered. In like fashion, we can imagine what we would have prayed had we been starving, but we cannot know what those in the famine asked of Spirit or even *if* they called upon her. Thus we cannot know if their prayers were answered for we cannot know what transpired in that mysterious exchange between Spirit and her children.

Asking Spirit to enter our lives requires nothing more complicated than a heartfelt outreach and desire for connection, but sometimes it's difficult to know where to begin. That's where a more formal ritual can be helpful. To begin a conversation with Spirit, I would urge you to find a quiet place where you can be alone for fifteen to thirty minutes. Make yourself comfortable. Light a candle. Relax your muscles and release your cares.

You can then ask Spirit to be with you by using your own words or, if you prefer, you might want to say the following prayer which has been adapted from a traditional prayer of Pentecost, the Christian feast that commemorates the coming of Spirit to Jesus' apostles:

Come, Holy Spirit, love of God, light of my heart, giver of gifts, my comforter and encourager, my refreshment, my defense, my most welcome guest.

Wash me from my inmost fear, heal the wounds of all my failings; water the spirit within me that is dry, free my stubborn, fickle will, soften my sometimes too-hard heart, warm me with your love; guide me, lest I lose myself. Amen.

Once you've invited Spirit, just wait with open mind and open heart. Trust that Spirit will be with you, even if you don't feel anything. Rest in the quiet, letting thoughts and feelings ebb and flow. Ask Spirit to give you what you need right now, this day. Believe that it will be given to you and give thanks in advance.

When it's time for you to leave the quiet, thank Spirit for being with you and ask that you will be mindful of Spirit's presence throughout the rest of your day. Then rise and live in the peace that passes all understanding.

To allow Spirit to enfold us in a relationship so intimate that we are willing to risk trust is difficult. People, even those we love the most, often let us down. To trust Spirit is to turn the prism of life so as to see events from an entirely different perspective. It is to realize the way to fulfillment is not up and over like a military obstacle course, but rather in and through—into life and through to eternity. It is to take a deep breath and choose to believe that Spirit who animates, creates, and invigorates all life will lead us to the self-knowledge we require to live fully in her new age.

Perhaps trust is the real brink we intuitive sense as we peer into the Millennium.

Dare we trust that we have seen a shimmer?

Dare we not?

China Galland is the author of *The Bond Between Women: A Journey to Fierce Compassion; Longing for Darkness: Tara and the Black Madonna; Women in the Wilderness,* and other works of nonfiction. She won first prize from both the California State Arts Council and the Marin Arts Council for her fiction. She is also a Research Associate at the Center for Women and Religion at the Graduate Theological Union (GTU) in Berkeley, the founder and director of the Images of Divinity Research Project, and Associate Faculty at Starr King School of Theology at the GTU. In addition to writing and teaching, she lectures widely on the subject of the politics and spirituality, and periodically leads pilgrimage/social action journeys and wilderness retreats.

The Black Madonna and the Limits of Light: Looking Underneath Christianity, A Teaching for Our Time

> *"...as black*
> *as the black Madonna,*
> *who answers all prayers from the heart..."*
>
> —Kathleen Norris, "A Letter to Paul Carroll"

The Black Madonna is surfacing in the awareness of many Euroamericans, swimming up through dreams, poetry, narratives, academic research in anthropology, archaeology, the history of cultures, world religions, the history of art, through science, psychology, mythology, and the arts. Woven into the fabric of the European Catholic tradition, some say since as far back as the eighth century and earlier, only in the last decade have we in the United States begun to see much attention paid to this figure who has so long been venerated in Europe.

Once I began to search for the Black Madonna, I found her in country after country. From the Black Madonna at Einsiedeln, Switzerland, I discovered the Black Madonna of Poland at Czestochowa; the Black Madonna of Spain at Monteserrat; the Black Madonna of Sicily at Tindari; the Black Madonna of Italy at Loreto, all patrons of European nations, with centuries-old traditions of pilgrimage to venerate them.

According to Leonard W. Moss and Stephen C. Cappannari in "In Quest of the Black Virgin" in James Preston's *Mother Worship,* of the multitude of Black Madonnas in Europe, anthropologists have determined that at least thirty were intended to be dark or black. They were not blackened by smoke, or painted with pigments that turned dark, or made of wood that darkened. Italy, Spain, and France have numerous Dark or Black Madonnas, especially southern France, where the tradition of the Black Madonna intertwines with that of the Magdalene and Isis. And in the Camargue, in southern France, where the Rhone River pours out into the Mediterranean in a delta famous for its flamingos, wild horses, and bulls, is one of the most interesting statues of all: Saint Sarah, the patron Queen of the Gypsies, also known as Sarah–Kali. She stands alone, nearly life-sized and fully dressed, in the crypt of the church at Les Saintes les Maries de la Mer. There, Gypsies come year round and pay homage to her, bring her their joys, their troubles, and embrace her as though she is their beloved.

Les Saintes les Maries de la Mer is reportedly also a site of a former temple to the Egyptian sun god, Ra. The convergence of ancient cultures that gave rise to this site in the Camargue—European, Egyptian-African, and Indian—indicates a multiplicity of sources for the Black Madonnas. (The Gypsies left India by roughly the tenth century C.E., appearing in Europe around 1500.) There is no single source or one explanation for their appearance. The reasons for their darkness are site-specific and must be considered in that context. Though not a Madonna herself, Sarah–Kali functions as the patron saint, similar to a Madonna, within Gypsy culture, protecting them, healing them, granting boons and miracles. The countryside of southern France and Spain that surrounds her is scattered with sites sacred to lesser-known Black Madonnas: Rocamadour, Le Puy, and Clermont-Ferrand, among others.

Some European Black Madonna sites correlate with sites dedicated to pre-Christian goddesses of Greece and Rome, such as the Black Artemis, Demeter, and Cybele. Isis is another likely source for many European Black

Madonnas, an African source, given the widespread devotion to the African-Egyptian goddess Isis throughout the Roman Empire. Black meteorite stones are also possible sources, as is the indigenous pre-Indo-European worship of a black Earth Mother in what is now considered Europe. Could not the Hindu Kali be explored as another source, given the Gypsy migrations?

The subject of Black and Dark Madonnas is a quickly expanding field of study, still unfolding, and much too broad to cover in a short article. (To learn more, see my books *Bond Between Women: A Journey to Fierce Compassion* and *Longing for Darkness: Tara and the Black Madonna*. See also the Resource Guide at the end of this book for further information.) Consider this article a brief introduction to a much larger subject that needs to be explored from a variety of disciplines, both academic and religious, as well as through the arts. Crosscultural parallels found in other mainstream traditions, including indigenous, Earth-based traditions, lend rise to provocative conclusions, some of which are included herein. In sum, the Dark Mother is a figure found in culture after culture, including Caucasian.

In Europe, despite large Caucasian populations, these Black Madonnas reign in magnificent centuries-old monasteries as Queens and Patrons. The Black Madonnas command fervent devotion. In the north, the great Cathedral at Chartres has its own Black Madonna (as seen in Bill Moyers' series with Joseph Campbell, "The Power of Myth"). In addition, as of this writing, I know of Black or Dark Madonnas in Belgium, Austria, Czechoslovakia, Germany, Russia, Finland, and the former Yugoslavia.

In the 1980s, more and more people began to notice this ancient image and be struck by the fact that the deep devotion she inspires is part and parcel of European Catholicism for millions. Some of the Black or Dark Madonnas come out of the Byzantine icon tradition and are not actually black in color, but "cosmic red," such as the Polish Madonna. The Black Madonnas of northern Europe make it obvious that devotion to her is not a matter of ethnicity alone. Black Madonnas are considered especially powerful and efficacious. Known as healers and miracle workers, they inspire thousands and thousands of faithful in pilgrimages to them each year over matters of healing, love, fertility, and liberation.

I know of the European devotion firsthand. I walked the nearly 200 miles in Poland from Warsaw to the Pauline Order's fabled Shrine of the Black Madonna at Czestochowa with over a million Poles in 1987. At the time the

Solidarity Movement, which would later topple the military regime and set off the nonviolent "Velvet Revolution" in Eastern Europe, was still outlawed. I discovered that the Black Madonna was the unofficial Patron of the Solidarity Movement. Even the circulation of a copy of the icon of the Black Madonna from village to village was outlawed. The painting was placed under "house arrest" because it incited so much solidarity amongst the people for liberation. That was only one pilgrimage in one European country alone. Pilgrimages take place throughout the year in many European countries.

I walked the old "Pilgrim's Way" in Switzerland, hiking up from Pffaffikon on Lake Zurich, over Mt. Etzel, past the home of the medieval alchemist Paracelsus, to the enormous Benedictine monastery and Shrine of the Madonna at Einsiedeln. Perhaps one of the reasons that the Black Madonnas are so little known in the United States is that she is a Madonna of the people, beloved by her followers, her darkness largely ignored by a clergy who assured me at two major European shrines that "she is black for no reason." Others maintain that she has been rendered dark by candlesmoke. That the candlesmoke that darkened Mary somehow left all the other saints and figures in the church white defies reason and firsthand observation.

In contrast, when I began to explore the Dark and Black Madonnas in Latin America when I visited Brazil in 1995, Archbishop Dom Aloysius Lorscheider told me that *Aparecida*, the Black Madonna who is the Patron of Brazil, is black because she is the Mother of All. *Aparecida* (the Appeared) is also entitled "The Mother of the Excluded." I tell her story and the story of my visit to her in *The Bond Between Women,* excerpted here:

> According to legend, in October 1717, a poor fisherman, João Alves, and two companions had been unable to catch any fish in the Paraíba River of Brazil. On the last cast of the day, the fishermen pulled up a net empty but for the broken body of a statue of a Black Virgin Mary. On the next cast, they pulled up her head. They named the statue "Aparecida," which means "Appeared." They rejoiced in finding the Virgin and resolved to keep her, and thereafter their nets were filled with fish. This was the first miracle attributed to this Madonna.
>
> This small statue of the Virgin, little more than two feet high, also known as Our Lady of the Immaculate Conception, was passed from house to house in procession after this event. More miracles were reported, especially among the

poor, and the fame of this Black Virgin began to spread. Popular devotion to her became so strong that she was declared the Patron of all Brazil.

How a statue of Our Lady of the Immaculate Conception came to be at the bottom of the Paraíba River is the subject of many stories. One of the best-known legends is that she was thrown there to chase away a water serpent that was terrorizing the people. The serpent fled, the Virgin protected her people.

Ivone Gebara, the indomitable Brazilian feminist theologian of liberation, whom the Vatican silenced for two years; professor of theology, philosophy, and anthropology, and Augustinian nun who lived with the poor in Recife in northeast Brazil, writes of this story, noting that the Virgin that the people threw into the river was white, like the Portuguese colonizers who brought her. Legend holds that the river turned the Virgin black. In the river she lay broken, on the bottom, like the people whom the Portuguese enslaved and colonized, until the fishermen found her and made her their own.

Aparecida became beloved by those shackled by poverty and slavery for the miracles she performed for them. An eighteenth-century story credited with helping spread her devotion in Brazil follows:

One day a slave was traveling with his master near the small shrine that had been constructed for Aparecida. The man entreated his master to stop the wagons and let him pray at the small door of the shrine. As soon as he knelt down in the doorway, the heavy chains he wore fell off his hands and feet and the wide iron collar around his neck broke apart. His master declared him free: the Virgin herself seemed to command it. Word of this event spread rapidly. Though it did not end slavery, the telling and retelling of the story gained this Virgin a strong following as a symbol of liberation among the disenfranchised and the poor. (Slavery was abolished in Brazil in 1888.)

In the twentieth century, Aparecida became the patron of the Black intellectual movement in Brazil. Bishop-poet Pedro Casaldáliga and composer-musician Milton Nasciemento sing of the struggle of black Brazilians in their "Praise to Mariama" in the Mass of the Quilombos (Quilombos are the settlements formed by runaway and freed slaves in Brazil). Gebara points out that an *ama* to black Brazilians means a "wet nurse." Thus "Mari-ama" is also the black woman who nurses and cares for not only her own children but also the whites, she is mother to all. She does not discriminate. When Brazilians sing this song from Mary's Magnificat in the Gospel of Luke from the New Testament, they are addressing Mariama when they say,

Sing on the mountaintop your prophecy
That overthrows the rich and powerful, O Mary,
Raise up those held down, mark the renegades,
Dance the samba in the joy of many feet.

. . . .

Give strength to our shouts,
Raise our sights,
Gather the slaves in the new Palmares,
Come down once more to the nets of life
of your black people, black Aparecida.

(Palmares, a city of 20,000 people in the mountains, was the largest of the *Quilombos,* communities of runaway and free slaves. Hence, Palmares is like Zion, the Promised Land where all are free.)

It is October 12, 1995, the Feast Day of Our Lady of *Aparecida*, the Patron of Brazil. The whir of hundreds of doves taking flight echoes in the cavernous basilica of *Aparecida*, Brazil's national shrine. The basilica is reported to be larger than St. Peter's in Rome, larger even than the Cathedral of St. John the Divine in New York. Handbells ring out from the altar while the thick smoke of incense rises in the air. There is a great stir. I rise up with 70,000 people rising to their feet, waving tiny green Brazilian flags and shouting, *"Viva Aparecida! Viva Aparecida! Viva Aparecida!"* The refrain rolls through the basilica like thunder, filling the air. A priest lifts the small black statue of Our Lady of *Aparecida* high in the air, turning from side to side for all to see.

This feast of *Aparecida* is the culmination of nine days of prayer, rosaries, and masses in her honor. Hundreds of buses from all over Brazil sit in the oversize parking lots outside. For many, the open baggage compartments of the buses provide their only shelter. For some, this is a pilgrimage made every year; for others, like myself, it is the first time. I meet no other Northerner in the crowds over the days I spend here at the Canisian Sisters Retreat House near the shrine. Only last October I was in India, taking part in another nine-day feast, that of Durga, the Hindu warrior goddess, whose victory over the forces of destruction is celebrated and reenacted all over India and Nepal.

An enormous white banner hangs across one of the four naves that open onto the main octagonal altar. The Portuguese words emblazoned high in the air across the western nave in bold black letters are *Aparecida Mae dos Excluidos do Brasil,* "Mother of the Excluded of Brazil."

This Dark One who champions all that is left out also symbolizes what must be included now. Standing in this basilica amidst the shouts for *Aparecida*, I remember the statue in Banaras, India that I was told was Kali. It was a peaceful, serene Kali, unlike any that I had seen and it set me off to find this mysterious darkness in my own tradition, this path to find the Black Madonnas. Over the years hence, I have found a positive, dynamic, powerful Dark Mother in culture after culture. She weaves a bond that reaches beyond cultures, across time, a bond that gives us back our history with one another. She provides a way across cultures, a bridge. She gives us back not only the connection between the sacred and the world of nature and the body, but also gives us the ground of being, the world's body *in* which we live with all creatures. She gives us earth, water, air, and fire. Creation. Then goes beyond. She helps us cross over. She is the other side, the river and the shore.

Whoever this Dark One is, whether she appears as Virgin, Mother, Goddess, Crone, or Queen, she is found underneath tradition after tradition: she is also the Aztec Goddess Tonantzin at whose site Our Lady of Guadalupe, the Patron of All the Americas, appeared in Mexico; *La Pachamama*, the source of all life beloved by the people of the Andes; the African Goddess Isis of Egypt whose worship spread throughout Europe up until the second and third centuries C.E.; the Hindu Kali carried from India by the Gypsies on their migrations; the Orishas brought from Africa to Brazil; the indigenous black Caucasian goddess of regeneration and fertility, the ancient Earth Mother who was worshiped in pre-Indo-European Europe when the color black symbolized life and white meant death—she is the ground, she is both the earth itself and the root below. She gives us our depth, the darkness we need to grow. The taller the tree, the deeper the root system. She is also the Tree of Life, this little dark one, *la morenita*, our mother. And I too, as a white woman, can claim her in the form of the ancient dark Earth Mother of Old Europe. We need only examine our own traditions, look under our feet. She has been there all along.

Venerated for centuries in great cathedrals around the globe, the Black Madonnas have long been proclaimed to be especially powerful miracle workers and healers. Yet few have commented on the darkness of her face. Some say it was because she survived fires that destroyed all but her, others say it was candle-smoke. I say that she is dark because she has entered lives on fire, because she has absorbed so much suffering.

Some say that she is black for no reason, that her darkness means nothing. Others call her a symbol, an archetype, psyche's shadow. I say that she is all these things and more, that hers is a multivalent darkness and that she is also a black woman—a woman of color—a brown woman, a red woman, and more. She is not white. She includes all colors and she is dark because we as human beings come in so many colors, hues, and shades, and no one, no one, is to be left out.

Like a river, her darkness comes from a multiplicity of streams. She is not only the Earth Mother. She surfaces in European and Near Eastern sites where black meteorite stones fell out of the sky and were then venerated. She rises by healing waters, streams, rivers, and deltas and is often associated with water. In some places she is associated with storms, lightning, and thunder. Her waters are fed by streams of a tradition where black symbolized Wisdom. The Womb of God. The world of medieval mystics. The Womb of Enlightenment from the East. From Asia. From Africa. The Root. Wisdom herself. She is rising to remind us that what we call darkness is also invisible light. Modern physics tells us that 90 percent of what is, is invisible, outside the range of the human eye. Darkness matters, is to be valued, treasured.

The image of the Black Madonna, the Dark Mother, is arising in the human psyche now because we need her. Images of the sacred are vessels, containers. They function as portals, doorways, porous membranes through which the unseen world can pour, because part of the information that we need now is an awareness of the indivisibility of our relationship with each other—peoples of all races, nationalities, ethnicities, and classes—*and* with the Earth and all her creatures. We suckle and feed upon this planet we share. We are completely dependent upon such relationships, and this is what we are dying to leave out, our relatedness—with the Earth and with each other.

The shouts for *Aparecida* reach a new crescendo. The priest is taking her from the altar and elevating her again for the crowd to see this little Dark One, this Black Mary. Suddenly I remember the angel Gabriel in the New Testament and Mary's question to him as to how she would conceive the child he asked her to bear.

"The Holy Spirit will come upon you, and the power of the Most High will cover you with its shadow. And so the child will be holy and will be called Son of God," he answered (Luke I:35).

The Black Madonna is also Mary at the moment of conception, impregnation, when she was shadowed by God. It was God's shadow that made the child holy, his Darkness. The Black Madonna, this Dark One, shows us what it looks like to be covered by God.

The crowd goes wild as the priest holds *Aparecida* aloft again, turning slowly in all four directions, then plunges down the red-carpeted steps for the long walk to the end of the eastern nave of the basilica. The priest slowly makes his way down the long aisle with the Virgin, holding her up for people to see and touch, those who are lucky.

The faithful strain against heavy velvet ropes, their hands outstretched to touch the statue as it passes by. People hold up babies, rosaries, little statues of *Aparecida*, bottles of holy water, slips of paper with thanks or requests for miracles. Whatever they have brought they wave high in the air for *Aparecida* to bless. The priest turns when he reaches the end of the red carpet and slowly makes his way back up the aisle to return her to the altar.

Is there an upstart in the crowd? A young woman in cream-white pants and top with a pale purple scarf around her neck follows the priest to the altar, takes the microphone, and begins to walk around, speaking passionately to the enormous crowds on all four sides of the altar. She speaks with her whole body pacing back and forth across the altar of "the Excluded" to whom *Aparecida* is the Mother. And as she speaks, an old dark woman in a gray skirt, black slippers, and a scarf over her head begins the long walk down the aisle to join her on the altar. Just behind the old woman, thirty feet or so, is a slender, attractive, well-made-up woman in skin-tight black pants, with a bright red sequined body-hugging top and spiked black high heels. Behind her is a tall young girl in a blue jumper, at least eight months pregnant, holding her stomach. I don't know why they are doing this. Next in this surprising procession is a man in the striped suit of a convict, followed by a man in a hospital gown, holding up a bottle of IV fluid for the tube that runs into his arm. As they walk slowly single-file down the nave of the basilica to the altar, they stop every few steps to hold up their hands and cross their wrists as though they are in chains.

Once they reach the altar, they climb up the steps and turn away from each other, each finding a place to stand alone with their backs to one another on the octagonal altar, creating a vivid tableau of the Excluded, the forgotten, and the rejected. The convict comes forward as the woman in the purple scarf narrates. She tells us that he is a man trying to start his life over, that he is unable to find work, no one will give him a chance. The woman in red now steps forward. She represents the women and young girls, the children who are forced into prostitution to merely survive. Next the hospital patient who represents the people ravaged by AIDS whom no one will touch or acknowledge. All the members of the tableau move away from him with gestures of fear of contagion. The young pregnant woman represents the young mothers with babies, left to fend for themselves, abandoned by society. The old woman stands for the elderly women who are left out and ignored, discarded. I am spellbound. This is a liturgy such as I've never seen. The entire basilica of 70,000 people is hushed, the truth of what is being depicted on the altar so fully recognized.

A young man in a white robe, representing Christ, approaches and embraces each person in a simple liturgical dance. He draws the Excluded around him into a circle and then gives the old woman the statue of *Aparecida*. The mood of the tableau shifts dramatically. The sorrow of the Excluded is suddenly transformed. The old woman holding the Madonna becomes the center of the circle. She turns and turns, radiant and laughing on the altar, holding the Black Madonna high in the air as Christ and the circle of the Excluded move counterclockwise dancing around her. The congregation explodes into applause.

It is fitting that it is the old woman who holds the Madonna aloft. The wisdom of her devotion shines in her face as she dances before thousands and thousands of people. My heart leaps at this sight of this old woman dancing in a circle of a love that excludes no one. She turns and dips, and waves the Virgin. *"Viva Aparecida!"* we all shout, rising to our feet, hands in the air, flags waving, shouting louder and louder, *"Viva Aparecida! Viva Apareciiiiiiiiid AAA!"*

I think of the older women I've seen in churches around the world, praying before the altar of the Madonna. Many times there might be no one in the church but the old women. They care for the altar, bring the fresh flowers, trim the candles, embroider the vestments and the altar cloth. As I watch this old woman dancing it occurs to me that these women may have been doing something important for everyone. Through their prayers and devotion, through their practice of the rosary—telling the story of Mary's life with Christ, over and over—they have been keeping Mary alive, they have been honoring her—Wisdom itself, they have been upholding the feminine face of God.

Yet before the day's celebration comes to an end outside the basilica with singing and dancing, the priests are exhorting people to "Be more like Mary ... be obedient, reasonable, serene." Above all *obedient*. Once again I see how the devotion to Mary is full of ambiguity and is also used by the Church to control people, especially women.

Does anyone praise Mary for her fierce side? It exists. Consider the Mary who praised God for bringing down the mighty in the Gospel of Luke, the Mary of liberation, the Mary who agreed to bear a child under circumstances which she could not explain, for which she could have been stoned or ostracized, the Mary who was a refugee, who rose in the night, took up her child to flee to Egypt with only Joseph and his dream. Consider the Mary who entered the bastion of the Temple, the one who spoke publicly, who chided her son, held him accountable. The Mary who raised a rabble-rouser. The Mary who watched her son be beaten, humiliated, nailed to a cross, who watched him die and who kept standing, who bore witness, powerful witness, who withstood the pain and then kept going. The Mary who went on, some say, to lead the Apostles. This is a woman of towering strength. Mary as the Black Madonna, this the Dark One, carries an earthy, fiery energy. She cannot be bridled, restrained, or denied.

Seeing the old woman dancing at the center of the altar, holding up the Black Madonna, as the crowd shouts, "*Viva Aparecida!*" touches something in me, taps an energy, inspires me. The dark, old, peasant woman with the Black Madonna is prophetic and victorious.

Underneath the basilica are the miracle rooms, so called. I make my way to see what are said to be the famous broken chains of a man saved from slavery by *Aparecida*. They are displayed in one of the several "miracle rooms" beneath the shrine. These rooms are covered from floor to ceiling with photographs, paintings, uniforms, musical instruments, wedding dresses, model ships, medals, trophies, and wax body parts, *milagros:* ears, stomachs, intestines, legs, hearts, lungs, heads, whole bodies, hands, feet. All these objects have one purpose: to show the miracles brought through the intervention of Our Lady of *Aparecida*. Leaving a *milagro* allows a person to tell their story symbolically and have it be witnessed by the community. There are always crowds of people circulating through the rooms, gazing at the photos, the smiling faces, the notes detailing accidents or illnesses survived.

Many people I spoke with came to fulfill a *promesa* to the Virgin, a physical thank you note for blessings received, an acknowledgment of her action in their lives. She had answered their prayers, so they came to pay homage and praise her.

In these folk practices I find a deeper wisdom, a way of making community, of having coherence in one's life, and keeping culture alive. Though I would have scoffed at all this earlier in life, I see that the miracle rooms provide a time and a physical and emotional space to acknowledge life's difficulties, joys, and sorrows in community.

I am reminded of the first time I walked into the Cathedral of Our Lady of Guadalupe in Dallas, Texas. Off to the right of the front door is a small room, lit only by candles. Dark and warm from the burning candles, the room was silent with the intensity of people deep in prayer. Whatever tears I had in that moment surfaced and had a place among the prayers and sorrows of others. I was not alone. Wordlessly, the others gave me courage, said that I could go on and that I should ask for help from the Virgin and that she would give it to me, and she has. My rational, Anglo-educated self does not want to admit these things. Somehow it is more acceptable to acknowledge a devotion to the Tibetan female Buddha Tara than to Mary.

I ask now how much longer we will whitewash the fact that the woman who appeared to Juan Diego on December 9, 1531, was dark-skinned, like Juan Diego; that she spoke in Nahuatl, the Aztec tongue; that she appeared at the site of the temple to Tonantzin, the Aztec Earth Mother; and that she was dressed traditional Indian style? Tonantzin—the name means "mother"—had the crescent moon and the maguey or century plant as her sign. Tonantzin clad herself in snakes, and hearts, and hands.

It was the Catholic bishop Zumarraga who decided that this apparition of Juan Diego's was Guadalupe, the Dark Madonna from Estremadura, Spain, Eduardo Galleano tells us in *Memory of Fire.* Galleano tells us that Zumarraga was the same bishop who had the Aztec Codices set on fire, who tore down the temples, who destroyed their idols—twenty thousand of them. Zumarraga, the Indian's protector, the Church's shepherd, who kept the branding iron that stamped the Indian's faces with the names of their proprietors.

Guadalupe, one of the many Dark or Black Madonnas in our own hemisphere, is the Madonna that Pope Pius X declared to be the Patroness of All the Americas—North, Central, and South. Guadalupe in Spain is a Dark Madonna. A Dark Mary from the Moorish part of Spain—does this Estremadura Mary go back to Isis, to Egyptian Africa, to Philae in southern Egypt, in what was the Kush, now Sudan? Tonantzin, the Dark Mother of the indigenous people, is covered with hearts and snakes, like the fierce form of the fourteenth Tibetan Buddha Tara; wears hands, like the Hindu Kali.

Guadalupe is a true *mestizo* and she is the Patron of the American peoples. When will we claim her? When will we acknowledge and honor the terrible history that goes with her?

The Black Madonna is the fierce form of Mary, the powerful boon giver, protector, and miracle worker, like Kali is the fierce form of Durga, like Tara, with her fierce forms. The fierce form of Mary is the Mary of liberation theology, the Mary of the people, the grassroots, the Christian base communities. Ivone Gebara calls Mary's Prayer of the Magnificat in Luke's Gospel her "War Chant" and "God's Battle Cry" for the liberation of the poor.

She is coming to us now because she is the Earth's own Wisdom showing us what we need now—right relationship with the Earth and all her creatures. That means sustainable economies and communities that live in acknowledgement and celebration of our complete dependence upon this living system we call the Earth. We are as dependent upon it for air, water, and food as any infant is on its mother for food and milk, for life itself. And it is this dependence, this childlike position that we are actually in, that flies in the face of our out-of-control, independent, twenty-four-hours-a-day, seven-days-a-week, consumer-oriented, disposable, growth-driven economies and multinationals who now command treasuries larger than many developing countries and who have no loyalties—that is, dependencies, ties, responsibilities, or systems of reciprocity—to anything or anyone but the nameless, faceless, and silent bottom line.

What can one practically do? As the Solidarity Movement in Poland showed, if we want the future to be different, then we have to act differently in our daily lives. There is no one solution. I offer three ways that I have found to continue to deepen, transform, and refresh my own life knowing that change begins, first of all, within. The path of the Black Madonna is the path of the heart. My own must be examined, mended, repaired, and purified. Often. My motives examined.

First, a daily practice of prayer, meditation, spiritual reading, and self-examination, listening, to consider the places where I may be wrong or need to change. I cannot control others, but I can be responsible for my own behavior.

Second, the practice of rejoicing and celebration. I belong to a small group that comes together to be in silence and to build altars using images of what is held most sacred. It might be an image of a Madonna, or of Christ, or a Hebrew letter, a river stone, a tree branch, a persimmon, a Sufi poem, a Hindu deity, a Buddha Tara, a Shanti deity from West Africa, or the beads of an Orisha. We share our spiritual journeys in this small, nondenominational, pluralistically-minded community. We educate ourselves about other people's cultural and spiritual beliefs. We reach out. We want to know people from different cultures and faith traditions. We respect other's beliefs. And we make mistakes. We always have a period of silence for prayer or meditation, we share meals together. We pray for those who are not well. We honor confidentiality. We use Christina Baldwin's book *Calling the Circle* and her *Peer Spirit Guide to Circles* to fall back on, when our process goes astray or becomes confused.

Third, I go out into nature daily if at all possible. I am blessed to live beneath a mountain and most days I walk its flanks and along the creeks. I take part in an anonymous community project that no one in particular originated that I call "the spirit house."

A spirit house is a small trailside structure of stones that have been placed in a circle with a person in mind and a prayer for their well-being. They are like Navajo or Tibetan sand paintings. I end with this passage from my journal:

I took a walk to the spirit house and found that it had been knocked down again, every single stone kicked off the mountain, sent flying, the spot now bare and dusty where it stood, all six inches high and one foot in diameter of it, off the trail, at the edge of a drop down into the chapparel covered canyon. I started to give up and hike past, thinking I'd find some hidden place where I could build one and no one would find it, but I realized that if I did that, I would be building it alone.

The power of the spirit house is that it is being built by a community, a community that I belong to, though I don't know who is in it and I can't see them; there is an invisible community of kindred spirits who feed me. If I want that wonderful feeling of delight when I rise to the crest of the ridge where we build the spirit house and find it not only intact, but added to—taller, more stones, flowers left, a tiny roof of twigs put on—then I have to accept the disappointment, I have to feel it in the pit of my stomach. I have to accept my lack of understanding at why someone would kick it down, and, most importantly, I have to start over. I have to be humble, I have to be willing to not know. I have to be willing to not give up—no matter how many times it gets knocked over—if I want to be a contributing member of the community, if I want to surprise another soul with delight as mine is when I see it, if I want to raise our spirits.

And so, once again this morning, despite my discouragement, I remember the mountain's teaching: whether I can see it or not, whether it is shrouded in clouds, whether I'm aware of it, the mountain is there, abiding, being. Do not trust appearances, the mountain tells me. The world is not as it seems nor is it otherwise.

I have to keep making that choice, against all odds, for love. Choose beauty, choose goodness. This is the way of the mountain. This morning the blue mountain is talking to me, teaching me. The wind-blown cedar that I greet each morning on this path; is it the cedar that I hear whispering?

I make my bows to the four directions—may I serve you well. I send my prayers out onto the wind and clap my hands to raise the mountain spirit. Then I begin again to collect small stones from this rock-strewn path, kneel down by the bare spot and build a new foundation. First, a stone for each one of my children, my husband, and my family, my beloved friends, my prayer circle, the list is endless. With each stone I see that person's face, send them a prayer. And now the hardest part—the prayers and good wishes for those whom I might want to call my enemies. This is the most difficult lesson: "Love thine enemies," the Christian teaching says; "Treasure the enemy as your teacher—they give us the occasion for our spiritual growth," the Buddhist teaching says. First, I pray for the person who destroyed the spirit house and wish them happiness and joy. Then, if needed, I pray for each person with whom I might be struggling or angry, just as I do for my loved ones and my friends.

Love is a choice, not only a feeling. Choose love, the mountain says; choose love, the cedar whispers. For even nature knows that this is the purpose of Being.

Choose love.

Flor Fernandez is a transpersonal psychotherapist in private practice in Seattle. Born in Cuba, she is a ritualist, artist, and writer as well as a member of Los Noteños, a Latino group of writers dedicated to the promotion of cultural awareness through storytelling and theater. She is presently working on a collection of essays about her spiritual journey as a Cuban exile.

The Birth of a New Dawn

When I was a young child growing up in Cuba, oftentimes I heard the elders of my family talk about the end of the millennium. It was during the hot summer nights, when the balmy and sweet breeze of the tropical island would draw us out to the porch of our home. There we sat in a circle ready for the stories.

At that time, the end of the millennium sounded so obscure to me, so unreal. It was something on the far horizon, as nebulous and distant as the planets and the galaxies. And yet, when the subject came into the conversation, a big knot grew inside my stomach as I heard them say, "The world is going to end," or, as my Grandmother Patricia would say, "Volcanoes all over the world are going to erupt. Earthquakes will sink huge masses of land. Our tiny island itself is going to disappear in the depths of the ocean."

Throughout my life, I have read about the numerous millennial prophecies with their apocalyptic visions of the destruction of the world. The Hopi, Mayan people, Christians, and others spoke of the coming time when earthquakes, volcanoes, and floods will come and shake, burn, or drown us forever.

There is, of course, the promise of "salvation" and with it the guarantee of a better place, with light and abundance in the reins of our savior. That is, if we follow the rules of some god. These Big Endings seem to hold the mystery of a curse or a blessing.

On the one hand, if we adopt the attitude that all will be ending, then why should we bother? Let's enjoy life. Let's rape the land, cut down the forests, pollute the air, trash the oceans and rivers without any concern for other species or future generations. We become voracious ants devouring the flesh, blood, and bones of our Mother Earth.

On the other hand, there are those who hold on to the promise of paradise. These people are blinded by the myths of pure light, harmony, and happiness. They deny the dark forces innate to our beings. The New Age philosophies of life, healing, and wholeness are an example of this denial. Sure enough, we all want a harmonious existence, but "thinking positive" at the price of ignoring what I call the shadow flow of energies into our lives can be equally conducive to destruction.

New Age thinking, with its unsubtle implications that we create our own cancers and misery, has left many of us with a deep sense of failure and shame. The message is that a truly enlightened individual is healthy with no afflictions of any sort. He or she has managed in some miraculous way to become fully balanced and whole, almost godlike or guru-like. In this model, health, light, higher chakras, love, harmony, the masculine, and so on, are valued and preferred to the dark side of life, such us the passages of illness and dying, the lower energy centers of the body and their corresponding primal emotions such as sex, anger, hunger, envy, and even hatred; to confusion, pain, the unknown, the feminine, and to all the destructive forces.

Any time I hear the word "enlightened" used by people in spiritual workshops, lectures, and retreats, I can't help but to think about our ignorance. Why put so much emphasis on the "light"? How come we make so little reference to the "dark"? To that side of life, not so benign in appearance, which is also a very important part of us. What if I were to say I have been "endarkened" when in the midst of a deep depression, or after the painful loss of a loved one, or when feeling powerless, insecure, and helpless?

I believe the light-based ideas are well-intentioned, but unfortunately our society seems to suffer from a collective syndrome I call Darkness Phobia. The roots of this phenomenon go back to the beginning of patriarchy and its obsession with the Sun God and Penis God. Freud was, to his credit, the first one to admit this idolization of the God Penis. Both men and women are guilty of propagating the disease. This resistance to letting go of our unhealthy patterns is related to the cultural hypnosis we all suffer to some degree. For example, I have not been surprised to discover how the many predictions and visions about the end of the millennium are dominated by male mythology and symbols. Despite our educated minds and hundreds of years of therapy, shamanic journeys, and so on, both genders continue reenacting in their lives different elements of the negative Father archetype.

A few days ago I went to see the movie *Titanic*. I was moved by my own fascination for this giant. To me, the legend of the *Titanic* has been a source of mystery, horror, teachings, and inspiration. The *Titanic* deeply touches the inner fibers of our personal and collective psyches at a time in our evolution when transformation calls to us. It made me ponder the body of myths that have lived with us for the last few centuries.

The *Titanic* is an example of how the omnipotent way of thinking of patriarchy had infused us with a false sense of immunity from destruction. Any signs of death and disruption are denied and ignored in order to protect ourselves from feeling vulnerable. Even as the *Titanic* is about to sink in the freezing waters of the ocean, the passengers behave as if it's not going to happen. They hold on to their material wealth and personal possessions with a disregard of the tragic reality awaiting them. After all, this man-made giant is indestructible.

The captain, an experienced seaman, falls prey to his own Freudian complex. As Keri Shaw, a friend who saw the movie with me, said, "I know now why the *Titanic* holds such a fascination for people. The *Titanic*, the biggest penis ever built at the time, was not going to be devoured by the dark vagina of the ocean. It was not going to lose its erection and succumb to the mysteries of the waters."

The builders of the *Titanic* had such confidence in their masterpiece that they didn't think it was necessary to equip the ship with enough rescue boats. Thus unconscious, they never anticipated the giant's impotence in the face of the icy goddess. They were consumed by their ego-inflated notion of the invincible-hero mythology.

It is not surprising that as we move closer to the end of the millennium, the *Titanic* comes to remind us of our past mistakes and false assumptions. We are at the verge of drastic and rapid changes and at the mercy of the darkness enveloping our planet and personal lives. We cannot afford to hold on to the old system of values and beliefs that have haunted us for centuries.

And yet, the heroes of our times play over and over their "Quest" mentality. These modern conquistadores, now with more sophisticated toys, are the same ones attempting to rescue the eighty-four-year-old rusted skeleton of the *Titanic* from the dark womb of the Ocean Mother. They bring their computer technology, pressure-proof new penises to unceremoniously penetrate once again the waters of the ocean.

As I watched the TV documentary of the rescue, I couldn't help but feel in my own body, as a woman, the disrespect, the lack of sacredness by the actions of these men and their obsession with power—all this to drag out of the sea womb the reminders of their dead god. But once more, they fail to acknowledge the mystery, and their retrieval attempts are doomed to disaster as they encounter the dark face of the furious Goddess. First, one of the oil bags sinks into the depths of the ocean. Second, a big tower light crashes to the bottom. Not having gotten the message, the heroes are finally challenged by the turbulent waters resulting from a hurricane in the Caribbean. Ropes snap and the once supposedly secure piece of *Titanic* falls back to its resting place. The recovery mission has to be abandoned.

As a therapist in private practice, every day I sit across from people who are experiencing an emergency call to change their lives. They come to my office because their own ships are sinking in the waters of their turbulent existence. They feel a general sense of emptiness and discontent with their lives and relationships, a lack of meaning and purpose. Others are facing terminal illness, chronic fatigue, and allergies to the environment, food, and unknown sources.

These women and men wonder what to do and how to heal. Some of them want to be rescued. They equate therapy and my presence in the room with salvation. So accustomed are they to the "quick fix" mentality of our culture, they want fast cures. Others want to try the miracles of soul retrieval, shamanic journeys, and healing rituals. To their disappointment, they soon discover that there are no magic potions or wands to ease their pain. A visit to the therapist once a week is not going to do the job. Neither will a marathon-like workshop on Native American medicine.

We live in a society where we have learned to avoid commitment and responsibility. The removal of symptoms simply becomes a barrier to the process of healing. It takes away the opportunity to learn and grow from our bodies and psyche. It prevents us from going to the edge of the cliff, from experiencing the void, numbness, loneliness, and fears.

The question I ask them is: Are you willing to take a journey not packaged in a Club Med mentality, but one of wonder, honoring, and blessing the disruptions that you encounter along the way which are your best teachers? Are you willing to feel the hunger and thirst of your body, mind, and spirit? Are you willing to take responsibility for your own healing? Because if you do, then I am willing to commit to being present in your process. I'll be here waiting for you once a week.

In the movie, the big *Titanic* rapidly disappears in the waters, taking under hundreds of people. Out on the deadly ocean, we see the survivors aboard the rescue boats. In silence, they witness their loved ones being swallowed by the cold and dark Goddess. A wave of compassion floods my heart. And I'm reminded of how essential it is for all of us to have compassion for ourselves and others, as the end of the millennium threatens our fragile existence with turmoil, confusion, and death.

Every situation becomes a mirror of our darkness and our light, just as in the legend of Quetzalcoatl from the ancient myth of Mexican-Zapotec origin—The Tree of Life. We are reminded that everything in life had to be in balance. There is a constant fight of good against evil, light against dark. This duality must be honored within and outside ourselves with compassion, in order to continue our growth and healing.

In this myth, we find an abundant source of symbols and images, repeating patterns of human behavior that have led us to destruction as well as creation. The main characters of this drama, which takes place in Tollan where the ancient ruins of Monte Alban reside, are archetypes of the collective energies and their struggle toward balance in times of decadence and renaissance.

As the story of the Mexican-Zapotec people unfolds, Chimalma gives birth to Quetzalcoatl. His name means "the Plumed Serpent," which combines the snake (earth) and the bird (sky), the twin and dual aspect of this lord. It opens to us the mystery of the brothers Ce Acatl (light) and Tezcatlipoca (dark). Ce Acatl, as an emperor, transformed ancient Mexico into a prosperous empire where a good and pure spirit manifested in works of stone, feather, gold, and jade. He pacified his people with Hikuli, a spirit medicine, a source power not to be toyed with, not to be made into a god.

Tezcatlipoca, the evil lord, had not always been bad. He was the Lord of Fire and took over when people began to forget what they had been taught. Hikuli, once used during the Ce Acatl rein as sacred brew, was now used to rule the minds of men. Hikuli became the blinding light. As Ce Acatl walks out of the city, he informs people that Tezcatlipoca is his twin brother. Then he digs a small hole in the earth and places the cactus in it. Hikuli becomes bitter and makes people vomit. No longer a pleasant food, its name now is peyote and it is like an uncontrollable Father, a dark god.

The new people scorned the teachings of Ce Acatl. They became drunk and conceited with power and glory. They brought forth images of their Dark Lord of human sacrifice, Tezcatlipoca, and slowly began to build the nightmare of the future, with war, conquest, and gods. It was said that someday Tezcatlicopa would take off his mask and they would be surprised to learn who he really is.

Unfortunately, even in this origin myth, as in others, definitions of the feminine are flooded with negativity and disdain for darkness. The struggle between opposites is one tainted with the male attitude of war and destruction. Chimalma, the mother of the twins Ce Acatl and Tezcatlipoca, dies giving birth to them, implying that women are only needed for procreation. The drama develops in a similar fashion to the Christian version of Christ and Satan. They become extremes of the light and dark masculine. Both, out of balance, drive their empires to the end.

In this patriarchal definition of change, destruction is the only choice possible. Fear of the dark, of mystery, is dealt with through control and the insatiable hunger for sacrifice and annihilation. No other models of transformation are provided. The uncontrollable Evil and God-Father figures shine with their heroic journeys. So as we reach the end of what the Mayans predicted to be a cycle of hell, it is no surprise that we are prepared with this kind of dark mentality or with a denial of the forces affecting us.

Even for us women, it's almost impossible to remember the gifts and wisdom of a different kind of transformation. We have been exposed to patriarchy for too long. In essence, all our mothers have died at birth, when they willingly made a pact with the men in their lives to idolize them and to give them their power in exchange for a false sense of protection and dependability. Even those women in positions of power have bought into the patriarchal definition of good and evil. We treat ourselves with the same disdain and inferiority and we go about living our lives, adopting and enforcing those same rules that have oppressed us.

What can we do? First, I believe we need to search within us for that blinding light that has enslaved us. Second, we have to be willing to bless the disruption that change creates in our comfortable existence. We cannot pretend to be fully enlightened until we are willing to be endarkened. We must honor the call to tear off the mask of Tezcatlipoca in our personal lives and works. We cannot move forward until we have acknowledged the dark God that resides within each one of us.

We must dig into our graveyards and find other ways to grow and heal, ways not yet defined. Personally, I feel very strongly about us women being able to help in the unfolding of a different mythology based on a balance of all the forces and elements, without discrimination against anything or anyone. As individuals, we must face the blindness affecting all of us. There is no magic cure, but it is in this well of darkness that we can discover the light with its full spectrum of possibilities.

In my personal life and my work, I see people getting this call. The voices are becoming stronger and louder in our dreams and at all levels of existence. There is blessing in the discomforts brought about by this need to change and to examine our choices. The dark reflection of the remains of a dying Mother Earth is dancing in front of our eyes. We can't build anything new above the ruins of the past. At the same time, these ruins are like the roots of a tree that nurtures and sustains us.

In the patriarchal model, the approach would be to sever the roots and to clear them from our sight. That way their ugly stumps won't be there to remind us of our past mistakes and illness. This clear-cutting technique eventually will create more illnesses of the forests, with more silt and debris flowing into the rivers and oceans. Eventually, it will force us to deal with the dark mud obstructing our path or we'll die. This is very much the place we find ourselves today. There is learning to be had from the past, from our mistakes. There is hope if we honor and embrace both the old and the new, the evil and the good, the light and the dark.

Too much emphasis has been placed on the light, on the bird essence of our nature, in the masculine. We cannot turn the wheel of life backwards, but perhaps it is time to incorporate more of the positive and negative aspects of both the feminine and masculine. Remember, Tezcatlipoca was not always a bad lord—he once had been the Lord of Fire.

Both women and men are being challenged to understand and embrace these qualities in themselves in ways never anticipated. As a woman client discovers the uncontrollable and destructive masculine forces within herself, she decides to leave her high-paying executive job and take six months off to figure out how she is going to heal this energy within that is killing her. For the last two years, Belisa, as I'll call her, had struggled with chronic Crohn's disease. Her belly was on fire; it burned constantly as it destroyed the walls of her intestines. Frustrated with Western medicine, she followed her dreams to a sailing class. Puget Sound is more comforting than any of the drugs her doctor has prescribed. Sailing teaches her how to surrender to her own feminine self. Learning how to navigate the winds is the most valuable lesson for Belisa, as she begins to understand the work of the elements in her own body.

Recently, I received a call from a woman, Frances, the director of Richard Hugo House, a sanctuary for writers. She was concerned about the ghostly apparitions in the building. The benign, but nevertheless scary, entities have been spotted by residents, volunteers, and workers.

Frances wanted me to do some sort of cleansing of these energies. She informed me that during the 1900s, the Richard Hugo House had been a mortuary and funeral home. The house was then sold and was used by different groups, most recently a theater company that ran out of financial resources. Frances and her husband Gary were made restless by the ghostly presence in the house. They believed that before they could move on to creating what they envision as an art and literary house, they needed to clear the energies inhabiting the place. This is an example of how the spiritual ruins of the past, in this house, needed to be honored and healed before anything new could be created.

My experience at the Hugo House had implications deeper than my own personal process. I believe that what happened there that day of the cleansing was part of a bigger collective dynamic that is happening at all levels of life. I realized that at this point in the evolution of our planet, we are given the opportunity to move into the shadows of the past and make peace with our ghosts. As we do so with consciousness and integrity, we are then taken into the present with a glimpse of a future that brings with it hope and the freedom to choose.

As agreed, we met at the Hugo House one afternoon in December. To my surprise, forty people showed up for the ritual cleansing. Among them was a Jesuit priest, a psychic, local artists and writers, members and friends of the Hugo House community, and a small group of homeless youngsters who come to the literary sanctuary weekly. We opened with a brief ceremony of prayers to ask for permission and support in the process. We lit black and white candles and then made a procession around the house.

As we moved to the basement, to an area where in the past the bodies of the dead were embalmed, I had a sudden feeling of déjà vu and memories of an unknown source. I was transported to a room inside an ancient temple where a sacred ritual was taking place. The body of a dead man was being dressed in his finest clothes, then wrapped in a cotton blanket and carried by family and friends to an altar. Then, a priestess blessed the body. She poured a potion made of herbs from a crystal chalice into the lips of the dead. This magic formula would help and protect the spirit in his journey to the other world. Gifts and offerings were made and the people sang sad songs, wept, and mourned the dead.

Back at the Richard Hugo House, I realized that as a culture we have forgotten the sacred rituals of death. My vision in the temple came as a reminder of the importance of the proper and respectful ways to treat the dead. Whether the "dead" is a beloved one, an aspect of the self, a part of our lives, or the last cycle of the millennium, the releasing is to be done with compassion and with all the ceremonial elements required to honor their essence, gifts, and contributions.

As if in sync with my thoughts, a man in the group expressed his newly received vision of the need to create an altar in this area of the Hugo House. A woman writer said she had been told by one of the spirits in the house to open the large and wide door to the east side. As we did, the room was equally divided by a beam of sun that created a demarcation between light and dark. It was suggested we stand on both sides and that we say blessings to that line between the worlds of life and death.

After four hours of intense work, the healing ceremony came to an end. We had embraced the ghosts of the Richard Hugo House. The making of peace through compassionate and honest dialogue had opened new possibilities for creation. The restless entities had been reassured in their roles in the project of building an artistic community. The end result of our journey was the successful negotiation between the old and the new energies inhabiting the house.

As the millennium closes its doors to the old, it is essential for all of us to take the time to visit the dark and terrifying embalming basements of our existence. We must do so, not with the intention to get rid of dead bodies and the wandering "bad" entities, but to embody them and make them part of our creative endeavors. This is the time to look into the smoky mirrors and to own the greedy, envious, evil, power-hungry, destructive, abusive, and other shadow aspects of our psyches and personalities.

Recently, a female client I'll call Aurora shared with me a frightening dream that had awakened her from her sleep the night before our session. In the nightmare, a man with a butcher knife is chasing Aurora. She runs and runs, but the man catches up with her. Aurora fights for her life. After much struggle, she manages to wrestle the man down. At that moment, the killer shrinks into a tiny and ugly creature that she clasps firmly in her arms.

For more than a year, Aurora has suffered from severe colitis. As we worked on her dream, she made the connection between the "killer" and her painful illness. With tears in her eyes, she said: "For years, I had lived in fear of my own rage. I have kept this killer inside my gut." Aurora realized it was time for her to face her own dark and destructive nature. She stopped taking the medications that numb her from feeling and she began an intensive dialogue with this "killer" through her journal writing.

Every day, I'm reminded by the many life stories of clients like Aurora of the importance to pay attention to the blinding lights or Hikuli. Too much light can be as harmful as too much dark. With misuse and excess, what is nurturing and healthy can turn bitter and intoxicating. Therefore, the call is for us to implement balance and to take responsibility for our own messy basements. For example, it is not right for us to blame the loggers for the rapid disappearance of our ancient forests. We must look inside and acknowledge the "logger" who resides in the shadowy lands of our greed and consumerism.

This destructive instinct is human and therefore should be confronted and transformed into creative forces for the healing of the individual and the planet. One only needs to look around to see the signs of the renewal of which nature is capable. And despite the pollution and rape nature has suffered, grass still grows out the cracks of the concrete in the cities. Her body, covered by carbon from automobile exhaust, is still alive. She breathes under the layers of heavy trash. Even in her death, there is hope, because, like Chimalma, mother of the twins, she gives birth to the new dawn.

As we dig out the bones of the dead from our graveyards, we have the choice to learn from our past mistakes. The *Titanic* and its salt-corroded fragments is a smoky mirror of patriarchy with its idolization for man-power, and its denial of the Goddess Kali and Tezcatlipoca. This is a god culture out of balance where the feminine is desecrated, reigned over by a bloodthirsty lord, warriors, lies, sacrifice, horror, rape, control, murders, a God Sun that has forgotten the moon and her dark temperament. Her voice, though, is still there; she lives in the body of the ill and the crazy. She struggles to bring to the surface her wisdom as we face life-challenging situations of any nature: physical, emotional, and spiritual.

One myth that attempts to be inclusive and that I have found useful in my personal life as well as in my work is the Navajo myth of Changing Woman. Here the different roles women play in the creation of a new world are presented in their Beauty Way Chants. The cultural richness of the Navajo people, based on matriarchy, presents us with five major models of feminine wisdom: First Woman, Salt Woman, Snake Woman, Spider Woman, and finally Changing Woman.

In this myth, dark and light are equally important in the processes of birth, death, and rebirth. Transformation is a journey where we experience the cycles of time, seasons, development, and the moon. Creativity is seen as a dance that requires the thoughtful interaction and collaboration of these five archetypes. It is the spiral dance of the feminine constantly moving us from unconsciousness to awareness.

The first lesson in the journey comes from First Woman. She is creator—primal, nurturing, and passionate. She teaches us to feel comfortable with our bodies, feelings, wants, desires, even our envies and hurts. Daily, in my practice, I see men and women, but more often women, who have become disconnected from their bodies, from the earthy aspect of their lives. They develop sexual and eating disorders. Suffering from numbness, they torture and mistreat their bodies.

Before we can move forward in the journey, I believe we must heal the conceptions and perceptions that have defined us and limited us from having a better relationship to our physical temple. The medical model has been one that tells us about symptoms and nothing about causes. First Woman, on the other hand, teaches us that our sickness, anger, pain, and mistakes are part of our nature. Therefore, honor them! And learn to nurture yourself, to embrace the pleasures of life, whether eating, sex, sensuality, etc. The body is precious, with its curves and voluptuousness. It is a wise teacher.

Many women lose themselves in the nurturing business of the family, and others, like men, become slaves of their jobs. There is no balance between work and pleasure. Our lives are driven by the compulsion to be out there doing, making. It is in this area that the wisdom of introspection and quietness, offered to us by Salt Woman can be of help. She teaches us about the importance of going away to remove ourselves from stress and pressures. Solitude and time to rest is what we need most as our lives spin faster into the end of the millennium.

Most of us wait to retreat only when forced by a crisis. Salt Woman withdraws to get in touch with her changeless core. She chooses solitude as a means of gaining distance from the frenzy, to evaluate her needs and wants. I see many of my clients and friends creating space in their busy schedules to meditate, rest, play, and to be alone. These are the people who are making conscious choices to be healthy and balanced.

Snake Woman, as a form of feminine wisdom, becomes our guide and dance partner when we begin to honor the disruptions encountered in our path. She leads the way from passivity to choice, from above to below, from female dependency to Medicine Woman. She is the force that motivates us to take responsibility for our own healing. With her dance, she helps us move from the place of the victim to self-empowerment. More people these days have grown disappointed with Western medicine. They have turned to alternative healing such as naturopathic remedies, massage, acupuncture, herbs, etc.

As we learn to trust the inner healer, we are able to move away from the dependency encouraged by traditional doctors. Getting to know Snake Woman means developing a better relationship with the underworld of our bodies and emotions. Illness is seen in a positive light because it is an invitation to descend into the darkness of depression, anxiety, abuse, hysterectomies, chronic fatigue, allergies, and so on, to face and to let go of the patterns of behaviors and attitudes no longer conducive to growth and health.

Once we have encountered Snake Woman and gone through the process of shedding the old skin, there is an intense and painful space of time where our vulnerable self feels raw, tender, and confused. It is at this point that the compassionate and quiet guidance of Spider Woman becomes a necessity. She, with her delicate but resilient web of threads, becomes the wise grandmother to teach us about safe and flexible structures, as well as how to find within them the silky line of purpose and meaning in our lives.

Finally, Changing Woman and her forever dance of movement comes to lead the way into the new millennium. Her close relationship to the mysteries of birth, death, and rebirth places this form of feminine intelligence at the top of our priorities. Developing an intimate connection with her requires from us the ability to change, to flow with the cycles of time, with the disruptions we find in our path.

The essence of Changing Woman is about embracing the destructive and creative forces of life. People who work with their inner universes, such as those who are faced with health challenges, mystics, writers, therapists, painters, and healers, are continually describing in a variety of ways experiences of renewal, rebirth, and transformation. In order for Changing Woman to be a vibrant force in our lives, we must be willing and committed to the process of developing a deep and honest relationship with the internal dance of our bodies, mind, and spirit.

The end of the millennium presents us with the enormous challenge of how to integrate and balance all the opposites inside and outside us. It is an invitation to face all the ghosts that have inhabited our physical, emotional, and spiritual residences. But unlike the hero's journey, this is not about slaughtering monsters, conquest, and war. It is about embracing, listening, befriending, nurturing, shedding the skin, creating safe and flexible structures, and understanding the transformational forces with clarity, responsibility, compassion, commitment, and a sense of purpose.

M. C. (Mary Caroline) Richards is a poet, potter, painter, teacher, and author of *Centering: In Pottery, Poetry and the Person; The Crossing Point; Towards Wholeness: Rudolf Steiner Education in America; Opening Our Moral Eye;* and *Imagine Inventing Yellow*. She lives with disabled adults in an agricultural working community in Pennsylvania and gives creativity workshops locally and abroad. She has a Ph.D. in English from the University of California, an honorary doctorate in the humanities from King's College, and is a Fellow of the Collegium of American Craftspersons. In recent winters she has been teaching at Matthew Fox's new University of Creation Spirituality in Oakland, California.

Separating and Connecting: The Vessel and the Fire

Wholeness has been my concern since I first formulated it in *Centering*, published in 1964. The image of "gathering opposite elements into a Oneness" came to me from the potter's wheel. I had begun to work in clay in 1952 at Black Mountain College, where I was teaching English. I was turned on to clay by Robert Turner, Peter Voulkos, Dan Rhodes, Warren Mackenzie, and Karen Karnes, all of whom came to teach at BMC.

To "center" the clay is one's first task on the potter's wheel. Immediately, one's imagination is fired with the experience of moving the clay in opposite directions in order to find its balance. Up and down, narrowing and widening, working all the ingredients into an even grain.

And then, opening the ball of clay and raising the wall of a bowl, one grasps the mystery of holding the inside and outside between your fingers. You work the inside and the outside at the same time. One affects the other. Press from the inside and the outside changes. Press from the outside and the inside responds!

This initiation changed my consciousness. I have since come to see in all opposites a potential marriage or fusion. The theme of this essay is the integration of separating and connecting, of war and peace. Both are inherent in life processes. Individuation makes us separate; social and civic intercourse makes us connected. Conflict develops between differences. Peace is longed for. Can we come to a state of awareness in which Peace and War come into center to enrich the forms of our relationships and intentions?

Separating and connecting are polarities in the wholeness of consciousness. They express an ongoing dynamic in the world. How do we bear its stress? How do we create an art of peace which includes the necessity of conflict and its resolution? These are nitty-gritty questions. They live in both the personal and social-political realms.

Now more than ever we struggle to know ourselves and others. We work for justice, mercy, a faithful imagination of love, perception cleansed of prejudice and preconception.

This essay began in a time of acute personal encounter with fear, guilt, and woe. It was a time of inner war between anxious dependency and a resolve to change and grow, between a part of me that was in its death agonies and a part of me willing to be born. It seemed to me that the path to peace was through experiencing the conflict and coming to know the adversaries more compassionately. Perhaps a new relationship would form between them. The sense of an "I" within the *me* was quickening. This proved to be important new ground. A picture of human being as vessel, separable from her life contents, arose. This was a fulcrum, a midpoint: a person who mingles with her life in spiritual dialogue, as a coworker.

Metaphors of separating and connecting are felt vividly in the world scene and in the individual scene. While crossing this threshold in my own life, I could see that it was an objectively real and common threshold—like that of puberty. Except that this one, crossed later, confronts us with precisely that image of ourselves that is most unacceptable to our daily conscious ego: *the shadow*. The shadow stands there, guardian of the threshold. It is more than one can bear. If one steps through, and faithfully tries to develop a living commitment with one's inner enemy, it will be followed by other steps and births, and transformations, on the inner lifeline.

This journey may consist in large part of getting to know one's inner family: for example, the fearful child, the scornful brother, the sorceress, the fanatical seeker, the possessive parent—who stand in the shadow and create difficulties. Through the years I have struggled to know and to embrace the different members who have spoken to me through dreams or introspection. Gradually there have emerged a motley crew. An inner friend has joined them. Perhaps because I have sought a mothering feminine being as well, such a person has recently appeared in my inner world: a womanly friend and teacher, standing in a group of children with her arm around the shoulders of myself, a four-year-old, who is looking up at her with beseeching, anxious eyes. Both speak in me: the hungry child and the steadying affection of a good mother. At last I have hopes for that worried little girl: here is someone now who respects her and loves her as she is, shadow and all, and who spends time with her. She may begin to feel the love in her own heart, to relax, to play, and to grow.

Inner development may be measured by an ability to be peaceably at war, neither victorious nor defeated.

It is apparent, both individually and socially, that even as we say we favor peace, in fact, we wage war. Are we hypocrites? Are we insane? No, I do not think so. Let us trust the facts of life and be guided by them. This paradox may express a wisdom, if we listen to it dispassionately. If we do not, we may continue to murder our way through life in order that good may prevail.

For in this paradox lie two opposites: the need to fight and the need to love, both. The need for antipathy, the need to say *no*; and the need for sympathy, to say *yes*. To separate; to connect. The reservations we may feel in our body as we brace ourselves against the fearful *no* frequently have as their counterpart the reservations we may feel in our body during an intimate *yes*. There appears to be a physical connection between our ability to bear the tension of conflict and the release of surrender.

Nature tells us we are self-directing, self-correcting organisms, who function therefore by a dynamic of polarities: in-breathing and out-breathing, sleeping and waking, expanding and contracting, seeking balance. Our inner development as persons comes about as we are able to bear the wholeness of these opposites, to experience them as mutually completing, as interdependent and interpenetrating, in some sense simultaneous. To see them, in other words, as *alive, moving, and interweaving,* like the distinct and yet interflowing rivers that course through the oceans.

War and peace are both necessities *in what they represent.* Can we have them at the same time? Can we experience conflict and the easing of conflict so that they do not eliminate one another? As soon as we become aware of others, we come into the possibility of external conflict. As soon as we become self-aware, we face inner conflict. We are continuously "at war" with others and with ourselves. But we wish to live "in peace." What's to be done?

Can we imagine a kind of peace that includes the freedom to conflict, a kind of warmth that includes the freedom to withdraw, a kind of union that asks for free and unique individualities, a kind of good that grants the mystery of evil, a kind of life that bears death within it like a seed-force?

Perhaps the following picture will help toward this imagination. I had a dream in which a tremendous fire was burning clear across the full length of the horizon. It was moving toward the house where I lived. A woman neighbor and I packed our suitcases and ran away. One person remained behind, he did not run away. He was a friend, the director of a craft school where I sometimes teach in real life. This friend remained and the fire swept through the landscape, through the house, through the pottery vessels, through the person. I could see it flaming and coursing through everything, but nothing was consumed! After the fire had swept through, I returned, and the director said, "Everything is still here. Only the color is deepened." And it was so. He was intact, and the pots were there, transformed.

The color is deepened!

When color deepens, it adds both darkness and light to itself; it contains more color. Goethe said that color is "the sufferings of light." *The sufferings of light!* That is, what light undergoes, *we* undergo; as vessels, we are deepened by our capacities for darkness and for light. It is an inner light that wakes in the lustrous stone. It is our darkness, our guilt and guile and greed and hopelessness, that, undergone like a fire, may flame through our consciousness, through our sense of ourselves, deepening our capacities, changing into colored light. Though we may feel annihilated in the process, we are intact.

War and peace are dispositions of the will. We cannot move our limbs without an inner will to do so. Whatever we do, we in some sense want to do. Whatever happens is prepared for by the voice of nature in the unconscious. It is only ignorance of this voice that enables us to say, "I didn't want to hurt you." We do not know the forces driving us. If we want to create our life rather than to be its victim, we must inform ourselves about what may be happening on the inside. It is for this reason that self-knowledge is so important. We have to come into life *from the inside.*

Since our will is almost completely unconscious (I am not speaking of willfulness here, but rather of the deep motivations of our behavior), self-knowledge is difficult to attain. We know little about the world that lives in us, what beings and powers weather us. With mixed feelings we may discover that the part we play in Art and Beauty and Love is Lucifer's mask. How hard to relinquish the earnest masks of Professional Success, Technical Refinement, and Contempt for Weakness, should they turn out to be not our own faces, but the Adversary's.

The world is a living organism, visible and invisible, of enormous complexity, deep feeling, overwhelming fertility, will-forces so formidable that they maintain the stars in their orbits and the cells in their relationships and the babyhood of mercy surviving in the human jungle. The nuclear bomb everyone is so impressed with *begins* in every cell in our bodies. We sense intuitively the power we have to oppress whoever gets in the way of our dominant self-image. Whoever gets in the way of our conceit and our ambition, our despair. Whoever is our "enemy." The one whom we have not embraced: the enemy is the one to whom we have not surrendered. It follows us everywhere, sleeping and waking, like a shadow.

How shall we come to the condition where we embrace our wretchedness and guilt and woe? Not approve of it, but *embrace* it? How to fill with warmth our weakness and deformity and need? How to love our foulness, lie down with our leper? When will we be human enough to let the childish demanding self come to the table, to befriend her, patiently to come to understand her soul experiences, to let her be herself, and not to have to carry the burden of our reproaches? When will the loving soul in each of us reach out to comfort the shaky trembling twisted ego? Twisting and turning and telling jokes and shooting 'em up....

Conflict and the easing of conflict is a process through which our human nature may develop. Conflict is a tension between contrary impulses: for instance, the desire to be free and the desire to belong; the desire to be mobile and the desire to be rooted. Guilt is the sensation of an unwillingness to be in conflict; it is the sensation of being accused of being who one is, of being separate and apart and different. And probably unacceptable. We are born innocent of conflict, innocent of individuation yet to come. Therefore, we are born guilty! Childish innocence is unaware of the opposing forces in life. The love it wants leaves no place for the privacies of others. It can be made to feel guilty when an authority requires not only obedience but inner compliance, asking that conflict be repressed rather than celebrated.

Adults tend to feel guilty when they are unwilling to express their strength, which would bring them into conflict with others. They may be unwilling to be at war openly, especially with those they care for. By avoiding conflict, they may think they will be at peace. We may find out different when we abdicate from ourselves to avoid war. We may gain not peace, but duplicity and outbreaks of violence.

Why are we afraid of engaging our strength in the battles of life, the battles *for* life? Afraid of our energy? Afraid of the power that is in us? Perhaps for good reason. For this is not merely a personal fear, it is, as it were, a divine fear. We cannot handle our power. We tend to be overwhelmed by it, misuse it, abuse it, waste it. The gifts of fear, shame, and impotence disarm us. By fighting the inner battles that our fear and guilt bring us we become able to bear the power that is ours—when the natural violence of our self-will surrenders in love with its weeping shadow, the power sweetens and reforms, taking on the quality of Person, of Vessel, of Being, active and attuned. The dark side of life bears the seeds of light. Perhaps this is why we are advised to consent to the evil in ourselves and in others, and at the same time to struggle with it.

"Resist not evil." And yet, "If thine eye offend thee, pluck it out." What is evil but one-sidedness?

The sensation that may feel like guilt, like self-accusation, is the sensation of becoming a separate person, no longer identified with the lover, the parent, the brother and sister, the group of friends, the place, the time, the society. A separate and unique and unknown being into whom our consciousness has barely penetrated, just far enough to feel the cold winds blow. Chill, self-doubt, shame—these are signs that separateness has soon to be acknowledged, and that the conflict, the drama, is about to begin. We may be anxious and bewildered because some part of us may have no wish to be separate, and yet there is someone in us who is moving and growing as if by inner laws. We may have no wish to grow up, to grow old, to become the senior citizens, elders of the tribe, and yet there is this law that bears us forward continuously in time. We have no wish to die, and yet there is this necessity. The "parent" in us afflicts us with guilt as we prepare to take our freedom upon ourselves, as we prepare to "leave home." Perhaps this inner parent too needs to become less possessive of her children?

Conflict and pain are part of the fire of life. They must not be killed. Conflict is an energetic form—it is the way things work. How may we understand this and use it creatively in our lives? We begin by understanding that conflict and pain are not personal, any more than sexuality and old age are personal. What becomes personal is the way we relate to them, how we use them to create our vessel. How we learn from them to deepen our humanity.

When we disentangle our personal emotions from our powers of perception, we see that there is a kind of *play* between inner forces as they struggle in the depths and slowly work their way toward consciousness. There is a *dialogue* between the impulses growing toward independence and those growing toward relationship. There is a questioning and answering, an offering and a resisting. These living processes keep the play alive. We must respect them.

It is not a matter of changing human nature so that it can experience the transformation of its power and the wisdom in its pain. It is a matter of discovering our inner capacities. Voyages of discovery tend to be uncomfortable and perilous and lengthy. We commit ourselves to an unfolding mystery. We may be less ready then to grab at immediate goals. (Mystery may take time, and civilization praises quick results.) And we carefully remember how important we individually can be to each other in such an undertaking.

On a voyage of discovery, we look for possibilities. We cultivate a kind of openness of attitude, a wonder and caution combined. Our patterns of behavior become more flexible, our systems are organic routes. Above all, we cultivate an art of surrender, for we know the new reality must lead us into itself; we do not define it in advance. We look for surprises, knowing we may find our destination very different from what we have supposed.

Surrender is strenuous: *active* surrender. It is an inner activity by which we may enter intimately into the innerness of that which is different from ourselves, from our conscious everyday mind. This is why making love is called surrendering. To come into deep mingling contact with the one who is not us. Not to lose ourselves, but to surrender ourselves. And when we thus make love to life, it flows into our souls as from our beloved. Deepening our color. The flush of the fire.

To enter into the conflict, to feel its spiritual contours from the inside, to be unseparated from it, not to resist. To enter into the resistance, from the inside: not to fake it, not to withhold. To surrender to the whole truth, to become its countenance, not to conceal. For truth will crawl out of all the crevasses, like tiny lichen or blades of grass out of the coldness of stone, and it will with its tiny ray split our foundations apart. The very stuff of existence will bear witness, however diligently we work to stifle its cry. (All the truths we do not tell cry loudly through the halls of our being, and echo into the world through our tone of voice, the expression in our eyes, our choice of dress.)

The act of surrender does not get "good press" in our culture. Perhaps the reason is that we are in the throes of an individuation process that makes surrender seem threatening. Or it may be a regression, since to surrender to something we have to be willing to feel its separateness from us. Witness the symptoms of sexual impotence and frigidity, which are an unwillingness to surrender. Witness the pursuit of the "high," which tends to make surrender a reflex. The pretensions of the loner: touch me not; I believe in half-measures!

The most popular curse is taken from the sexual act which, ideally, is a sacrament of mutual surrender. Like so many other things in our age, it indicates how unconsciously we live by the power principle. F—— you means "I reject you, I reject your power." If we say that a person has been "f——" or "screwed," we mean that she has been humiliated. It is evident that the art of surrendering one's inner being in a transmuting experience with one another that deepens our color, is not part of the popular image of lovemaking. But the truth is that the delirium of the orgasm itself is crude when we know something of inner rapture.

Surrender is actually a concentration of inner power through the process of yielding: yielding in the sense that a plant *yields* seed. The gain of the seed is the loss of the flower, which withers as the ovary develops. Surrender gains an inner substance that cannot leave us. It will invest the future, as the spirit of the plant within the seed does.

Thus sexual commitment may be a deep and powerful and for-keeps kind of experience. For when one's intimate personal being is awakened in a sexual embrace and surrenders to its beloved in trust, a birth takes place in a spiritual realm. There is an alteration in the lifeline. It is bound with the fate of the psyche itself. When one's consciousness lives deep in the tissues like this, deep in the spirit-light of the blood, deep in the will that turns thus to the beloved as lungs turn toward the air, one's commitment is much more than personal.

In fact, this is part of why surrender is so at the heart of the human being. For surrendering to love is more than surrendering to another person of the same natural order as oneself. The human act of love is an expression of deeper surrender—a relation to a being of love, or a power of love, in the world, entrusted to us. It is an awesome trust.

Human beings are inspired by serving a purpose larger than themselves. This is one reason why sexual love works so well to entice us. (As with flowers, which are so beautiful and smell so sweet: to attract bees—a purpose larger than their own existence! Larger than our pleasure in them!) For the period that passion and fascination endure, we feel ourselves supported by a larger purpose, a larger wholeness. Our lives have meaning, we seem to have some function after all, to labor on behalf of the love that has been entrusted to us.

Then the mood changes, and the "show" of love has the opportunity to evolve into conscious relationship, faithful in sickness and in health, for richer or for poorer, in all the ups and downs of moods and conflicts. It is no trick to love when one is "in love," or in a state of innocence—there is no freedom there. One is free to love in the moment when one *falls out*, awakes from the spell, sees the other person nakedly, sees oneself, and reconfirms the union on behalf of the Love whom one serves. It is an initiation into conscious relationship, a necessity that awaits us as our soul's enterprise, just as loving kingship awaits the amorous prince. It is the sacrifice of unconsciousness for separateness. At this moment, devotion becomes possible. And when one reaches this moment, commitment to love is a serious matter indeed, rooted as it is in the very organism of one's spiritual self-awareness. Love of others quickens in the birth of the self. The capacity for loneliness and the capacity for love are counterparts in the human heart.

Peace can be thought of as a fusing of the opposites. It overcomes the onesidedness of violence. Violence is a quality of natural energy when it is seized by its own fire and blind to consequences. (But the energies of violence are glorious and useful. The fires burning in us: our natural drives, our libido, raging in us. Like the great fires in the smelting furnaces or pottery kilns, the glassblower's fire, the forge. The blinding desert storms, the cruel sun, cataracts. The slow stubborn relentless violence of falling snow, inch after inch, foot after foot, covering everything, *everything*.) When we harness and transform it, violence lights up a continent.

In the psyche, violence creates trauma: consciousness breaks down. We lose our memories; we become deaf, dizzy, disoriented, disorganized, nonfunctioning. A violent emotional experience pulverizes us in the same way that an avalanche or flood dissolves the structures of a lively town. But transformed from a ravaging force into a capacity for feeling, it is our warmth. It is our caring. It is the smile and touch that bless. It is our tears. It makes all the difference. And when it blows wildly and yet may be contained, it fills the forms of life with inspiration.

We can feel the energy that is in us. We can feet the violence, the thrust, the passion, and its disregard. It is like a great horse we may learn to ride. To give direction to, to rein in. Yet it can carry us, where otherwise we could never go. It is a part of ourselves that we can understand if we pay attention to it and come into human relation with it. It can serve us if we serve it in a wise way, sensitive to the inner laws of how things work. Willing to listen, willing to be taught, through the inner ear. It is a trustworthy symptom of onesidedness. Violence is self-absorbed and cannot surrender. We cannot surrender our power until we have ceased to identify with it. We can do this by allowing to arise into the inner ear, the voice of its opposite. Rage harkens to pity.

There is another violence than the hot gush that spills where it spills, or the massive withholding. Another violence that neither spills forward nor locks, but regresses, demanding that there be no differences between us. For there is not only the forward movement of evolving consciousness, but a resistance to it. The claim that to get on together we have to be like each other can be found in the columns of literary criticism, politics, art gangs, and personal relationships. At the level of gossip or tourism, differences are charming. In community, they discomfit. This is not a moral issue, it is how the energy works. When persons and experiences begin to differentiate, to separate and become individualized, this movement is felt as anxiety. Anxiety is the labor pain of consciousness.

When a new country begins to assert its own identity, to break away from "the parent," violence breaks out. When a new child moves into the neighborhood, violence breaks out until she is accepted. When we extend ourselves into a new vocation, violence breaks out: we burst into tears, are a prey to doubt, are aggressively confident and talk of nothing but our plans—violence and disregard take many forms. We are going through a deep energy change, a spiritual change, and we are producing symptoms.

It is like when a baby starts to be made. The egg and sperm have been separate. Suddenly they come together—wham! Then the new union begins to differentiate: it divides into two cells, four cells, and the parts of the body begin to develop, the functions, the whole new being begins to be created in the physical plane by operations so extraordinary in their wisdom that we do not yet understand how it all works. It takes nine months for a tiny baby to get ready to come out into the air. Before, it's been all fluid and dark and cozy. Then wham! down the canal, out into the light, the umbilical cord cut—you think there is no violence there? For mother and child alike? Such violence that the tiny baby shrieks and the mother often goes into depression. These are reactions to *division*. To *separation*. Our shrieks bear important messages if we have ears to hear from the inside.

During labor, if we hold our breath we will cut ourselves off. I find that if I exhale into the pain and anxiety and woe, I am able to contain it. To contain it is to honor it, to be its vessel so that it may perform its work. The bearing of pain is part of expanding consciousness, it is an inner discipline and need not lead to self-pity or isolation. It is, actually, like bearing any pure experience: pure sweetness, pure salt, pure air, it's all too much to bear. One exhales and thus is carried into the mystery organically.

We do not need to go with every gust of energy that rises naturally in us. We do not need to follow every lust. We can stay still, containing it. But the violence needs to be felt and handled. Lust is part of nature and can become a resource; it is like changing the form of energy from an erupting volcano to a diamond needle. For are not volcanoes and diamonds the results of different stages in the same fiery process?

The invisible inner world is as specific in its contours as is the outer physical world. As our sense organs are adapted to the physical world, so inner spiritual organs perceive the supersensible world. We cannot know ourselves *from the inside* with machines, I do not think so. Machines do not pick up the feeling tone, nor do machines pick up the sensations themselves. They pick up the patterns, they do not pick up the real thing. We are not patterns, we are living persons. Living vessels.

Is it in the poetic imagination, where conflict is the basis of its truth, that we may find a clue to our new perception—in the altered consciousness and fusion of opposites that poetry achieves? Experience in the spirit is real. The dream of the fire is a real event. Inner experiences of loneliness and of love alter our substance. Little may show on the surface, the forms look much the same, only the color is deepened. The undergoing is richer. The tolerance for pain and ordeal is greater. The ability to undergo violence in the psyche, without discharging it, enables a transformation of behavior to develop. For physical actions have their source in the psyche, in "the voice of nature in the unconscious," which we may make into a human voice.

There is an impulse within the unconscious to seek itself in consciousness. How gladly we would agree to slumber if we could. But we can no more withstand the movements of our psyche and the evolution of our consciousness than we can withstand aging and renewal. Of course, we can stand in the way. We are free to do that. We can take potions to catch some rest from the dread grinding of the divine mills. We can try to hide from the great inner eye. Hide, hide. We can decide to think about all that later. And in this way we can greatly affect what happens—we can imperil our safety and the safety of others. Scriptures and legends tell of the efforts of humankind to deny relationship with spirit, to avoid the drastic contact from which there is no escape. We will gladly betray if only we can be left to play as children, manipulating our bodies and our concepts and our relationships as if they were moves on a chessboard: we call it "playing the game."

Meanwhile, back in the central nervous system, the spiritual powers are going about their business, while the children play in the battlefields. We children know the gods are in there, that there is another level of awareness we are supposed to be preparing to enter when we are grown up enough. The gods call, the children do not obey. We must be free, the children cry, free to disobey. Okay, sigh the gods, we can wait. But of course it gets harder and harder to obey: postponement becomes a way of life. People get to rely on certain kinds of postponements from each other, to save us all from face-to-face encounters, when we let the gods come forward to dance in our faces and our limbs. We may have to sacrifice our lives as we have so far made them for this to happen. Make way, make way for the gods.

If we are not careful to sacrifice our games, we may die in childhood, aging children, undone by our strategy. And the gods weep and cover us with leaves and wait while we withdraw ourselves in death and school ourselves again in the spirit. Perhaps the next time round we will be readier to let the holy voices sound through us.

The divine Oneness has to be dismembered, an ancient wisdom tells us. And then the god has to be reconstituted in the differentiated aspects of consciousness. The unconscious mind grows into multiformity. Multiformity grows into ego strength. Ego evolves as spirit-self. The gift of the inner self mediates the realms of Union and Aloneness, and reveals them to consciousness in a bearable paradox.

We want this. Everywhere the cries arise for the *One* World, the *United* Nations, for the people of the world to *Unite;* and at the same time for independence, autonomy, self-rule. It is precisely because these are not mutually exclusive that people clamor simultaneously for them. The fusion of the opposites is the way forward.

For some, it begins in self-confrontation: courage and fear, wholeness and guilt; in efforts to bring about in the depths, "behind the brain," an intermingling of those poles where energy tends to gather. Consciously we try to bring the terrors into dancing interplay with tenderness. The weeping child into the breast of the gift-giver. Bringing anger and woe into listening and offering. Churning the cosmic milk, as the *Vedas* say. Churning, churning! For the "clarifying of the butter," the transformation of consciousness. The labor, the spiritual strenuousness. Come in, baby, come on in. Inviting ruin and destruction into oneself like a lover. Like a lover. Take me. Take all my beauty and my hope and my innocence; envelop them in your dark, cold, angry embrace, in the embrace of love, where love is transformed by having slept with its ruin, where the ruin is transformed by having slept with its love: where anger and hopelessness and guilt are transformed by having felt the orgasmic trembling surrender of a released power that moves through them in radiating waves. This is what happens, physically, psychically ... the transforming power of the mutual surrender, we feel our Being *move* even as we dwell within it.

We seek to experience ourselves from the inside: as one experiences sunshine or cold or the taste of an apple or a lemon or the pinch of a shoe or the release of a cramp; to experience the Being within our Being, our spirit-self within our unconscious.

How may we practice oneness in a world where differences and oppositions and conflicts are the daily realities? How do we experience conflicts as the dynamic inner law of oneness? How may we wake up, grow up, see where we are, and learn to step aside so that the flow *both ways* through the center can take place? Both ways. One wind, two directions. What a tremendous mystery we live within. It is not enough to be alive, or wise, or willing to fight, or willing to love. These pass through each other like simultaneous impulses pulsing through a center so that what we feel is one throb, but its texture and resonance animate an awareness of many levels of body, soul, and spirit in an organic oneness. It is not like electric circuitry. It is not like multiple screen projections. It is not like watching ourselves have visions. It is like being a living word that is being spoken. *A living word.* The word communicates past all bodily obstruction: even when our senses are blighted, we see and hear in the inner realm.

The dark is all about us. We light our little lights, our candle flames, the sensible flame, the living flame. This brings light into the darkness, shows the darkness to itself, its terror abates, its ecstasy abates, the forms emerge, the dark forms turn into light. As the light moves, new shadows form and how beautiful it is, how stirring and formidable and unheard of. Our consciousness changes. We step carefully. We know where we are going. We have been there before. It is a dark narrow passage to the inner chamber. There is the threshold, obstructed with a thicket of brambles, the narrowest possible passageway, the dark earth obstructing and at the same time opening. Our hearts are so full, so swollen with painful weeping and surrender, perhaps they will not be able to squeeze through the tight spots.

Into the dark chamber at last. The light is the half-light of the underworld, the twilight of the inner realm. Shadowy figures. The dark lady poet and seeker is there, checking to see who is coming through the dark passage. Who is it I am bringing with me? A large soul is following us. Too large, really, for the tight places. He will have to go through the needle's eye. Will his largeness be able to be small as a mouse, or a worm, when the tight spots come? Able to slither through the narrow places? We cannot get everywhere on two legs. Sometimes we need four, or none! Sometimes we are fish out of water, and then we must be birds if we are to be able to swim in air. Strong feet, strong thighs, for the long climbs up and down.

How to come at it, how to come at it … by the serpent's path, indirectly, never straight on. Picking our way through all that befalls us and besets us, all the experiences streaming toward us as well as those we initiate. For in the intricate mesh of our mutual involvement, we befall each other constantly. Weathering each other, by the atmosphere of our invisible being. Invisible as air. As wind. Visible only in its effects. We do not see the wind. We do not see the air. We see the plane mounted upon it. We see the leaves it stirs up: we hear its pressure against surfaces: the wind of the spirit bloweth, bloweth. Befalls us everywhere, through the breathing kingdoms all about us, through the fiery exhalations from the planetary worlds.

How can we contain our own violence so that it does not explode or leak out prematurely? How can we hold it, with firm gentleness, so that the inner processes, the metabolism, can work? How can we bear the heat, the deep shifts in the world within?

It takes a special caring of our inner being. Often we are helped by solitude and silence, to hear our inner voice from the house of self. Certainly we cannot be always busy with something else. Sometimes it seems necessary to fall apart to begin from a new place, the way a seed falls apart to reveal a germinating center. It may well be the growth process that causes our conflicts in the first place. The bud, pushing from within, cracks the outer forms. It is these outer forms that feel the violence. They will be helped to contain their pain if they understand how they are a part of an evolving wholeness. What a vessel we have to be to hold the polarities of our experience together.

By awakening the feminine within our inner life, we may transform power into human being-ness. This is the Mary to Creative Spirit. And we do not bear the Child without Mary. Here is something for us to think deeply about, whether we are men or women. For women may be as estranged from the feminine function in the psyche, as doubtful of its importance, as men may be. The awakened feminine function turns like a tender woman toward the wandering unclaimed features of oneself, turns like a bride to soften the fiery powers of creative spirit.

For creative spirit is incomplete, unwhole, out of phase with life, when it rules alone. A marriage is needed with the feminine, who lovingly receives, nurtures, and maintains. The feminine brings us capacity for relationship, brings spirit into earth. The union happens slowly because body does not wish to give itself up and spirit does not wish to be contained. What a muddle.

How can we come to feel what we do not yet feel? Know what we do not yet know? Perceive what we do not yet perceive? There are, of course, ways of meditation and spiritual discipline taught by initiates through the ages. But there is another idea I would like to suggest, which has to do with a middle ground, with play, and with theater.

Think of a middle ground which has the quality of an actor's art. The actor remains himself, yet he invites emotions not his own to dwell in him. How much feeling other than our own are we capable of? What thoughts inimical to our self-respect can we bear to think? Indeed, are we able to feel any emotion dissimilar to our own? Are we able to entertain seriously an idea that is incompatible with our habits? Do we have the power of fantasy—an imagination that enables us to have an inner experience different from our own lives? Can we receive into consciousness an experience mediated through the body but that does not lodge in the body, is not given authenticity by physical density, but rather by precisely its opposite, by its power to take hold of us, to enthrall as a story does, to possess us and release us—can we be changed through an inner imagination?

The middle ground makes possible a rapprochement between conscious and unconscious realms, between light and dark. It is "a holy distance" between the sensations of our experience and our being that is undergoing them. We feel ourselves *within* to be separate from the whirlwinds and forces and temptations that beset us, separate and distinguishable, in a position to come into a conscious relationship with what besets us, to struggle and work with it, to become freer agents. For it is foolish to speak of freedom so long as we are captivated by our bodies, our feelings, our social attitudes, our accomplishments. These are our riches. Attachment to them is our poverty. In the space between, the lifeline evolves. Conflict can be viewed as artistic process.

Once this inner distance shapes itself in us, we are in a position to explore and search out the meaning of what we are feeling or thinking or doing. Masters in our own house, we may be less fearful of being overwhelmed by unconscious contents. We do not need to take other people's opinion of what is happening. We may discover that when we begin to look thoroughly in the places where we have been warned there is nothing to see, we find realms of great meaning. This is why I speak of pain as I do, and guilt, and anxiety, and violence, and death. Kingdoms, kingdoms—all of them!

So here we are, *free at last*, only to find that if we are to live in peace, we must live in conflict and in pain as well as in the easing of conflict and in joy. Peace can be thought of as a special way of experiencing difficulties, an "art of war." Can we learn to be artists of peace, at home in paradox? And to disarm "conflict" of its onesidedly negative overtones? To see it as part of harmony and goodness? For every path we take is governed by its law: the law of polarities. It is hard to accept the fact that we are in a big league, that we live in the universe and not just on Maple Avenue. But that's the way it is. We do indeed live in the universe and we are potent actors in its future.

It will help us to look in this new way if we reconnect with the dynamic living processes working all around us. The vessel of our being evolves in fire and, once formed, the fire is forever present in it. So it is with our pottery, and our kilns as well. The fire turns clay into stone. Fire in the stone. The fire-tried stone. The fire-filled stone. Fire is changed and body is changed. Life-vessel may be experienced in imagination as a stage of evolving human inner form. It gives off both warmth and containment.

A sense of one's own form may begin to deepen: this, and not that. As our individual being evolves, a new social impulse begins to quicken. Within a full experience of person as unique being of body, soul, and spirit, there exists, as a polarity, a sense of infinity, a sense of otherness, an experience of community within our own form. The question may then rise: how may I manifest this polarity in a wholeness of practice? How may I project both a contemplative integrity and a warm social impulse? To get to this question, we may walk a path of separating and connecting, of war and peace.

Margot Anand has studied with numerous Tantric masters, particularly the mystic Osho in India, and is the creator of a unique transformational course called SkyDancing Tantra, which she teaches in her SkyDancing Institutes. The author of *The Art of Sexual Ecstasy*, *The Art of Sexual Magic*, and *The Art of Everyday Ecstasy*, she has a graduate degree in psychology from the Sorbonne and lives in California.

Beyond Duality: The Path of Tantra

The beauty of Tantra is that it sees everything as an opportunity for awakening. It teaches that when you live your daily life consciously, you can become enlightened. You don't have to retire to the monastery; everyday life is your path. For a long time I thought there was a deep split between living in the world on the one hand, and reaching enlightenment, waking up to our full potential, on the other. Now I see that the task is to bring awakening to more areas of daily life so that we live in a more integrated way. This is, for me, the whole point of being human on this planet.

Until now it was always seemingly either/or—either you chose the "flesh"—everyday life in the world—and in so doing gave up the life of the spirit, or you chose to lead a life of the spirit, but then you had to renounce the world, go live in a monastery, give up sexuality and relationships. Either way required a kind of sacrifice. There was always a duality: you could have one thing but you couldn't have the other.

This notion of duality, of either/or, has pervaded our thinking for the last millennium. First, we had the matriarchy with the goddess religions; then we had the patriarchy, and the goddess religions were replaced by the holy male trinity—God, the Son, and the Holy Spirit. As a consequence, the female aspect of our spirituality was strongly repressed, and we lost our images of the divine feminine as whole and integrated. We found ourselves in an either/or situation, which Riane Eisler has described as the "dominator model." But many people don't understand that this model is still being reinforced even in "new" visions of spirituality that present one extreme to replace another.

One new vision of spirituality talks about returning to the goddess, re-honoring and understanding the feminine aspect of God. Unfortunately, all too often this makes it seem like we all made a big mistake and in order to correct it we have to go back to how it was, to the ecstatic time of the goddess religions, when everything was peaceful and wonderful. But it's not like that. What we need now is not simply to replace the masculine models of spirituality with feminine ones, but to create a true partnership, an integration of the two.

Tantra has much to teach us about this. It is the only path I know of that presents the partnership model—equal partnership between male and female that Riane Eisler suggests will replace the dominator model—is not only something that has to happen on the economic or social level, but also on the spiritual level. An internal partnership is called for as well as an external one.

My whole understanding of how to wake up, which I describe and teach in *The Art of Everyday Ecstasy,* published by Broadway Books, is that it means to fully understand, fully develop, and fully express both the male or animus side of our natures and the female or anima side.

This has huge implications. Women have made great strides toward political and social equality. Yet as long as we think that we need only create the partnership model outside of ourselves, by changing institutions through political activism, we will never achieve true, lasting partnership. It must begin with a very deep mystical quest, a desire to heal the split between the masculine and feminine within each of us.

This quest for integration often begins with what mystics call a "dark night of the soul," when we realize to what degree we are caught in the split between the male and female components of our psyche. The divide between men and women really starts from the split between the inner man and the inner woman in each of us, the dualities of feminine and masculine, sex and spirit, body and soul, energy and consciousness. It separates us from the healing power of ecstasy, because only when the split is healed and integrated can ecstatic consciousness begin to come forth.

So we shouldn't seek just to replace the male deity with a female one but to restore the divine feminine to the world. Then the female aspect of our world—the planet Earth, Gaia, and womenfolk—will have an image, a model, of the divine vision of our ecstatic potential.

Healing the split between the divine masculine and the divine feminine is essential for both men and women. The image of divine masculine, portrayed as the wrathful patriarch, is wounded by the absence of the feminine, just as we have suffered unbearably by that separation. Living only under the image of God the Father, a woman never has a chance to affirm her identity as a reflection of the divine. She doesn't have a sense of the wholeness that comes from realizing her divinity in her female as well as in her male aspect.

Constantly living under a one-sided image of the divine, we all suffer a spiritual lack. After all, we are born from father *and* mother, and as long as we don't reintegrate these archetypes in ourselves and feel our connection both to the nurturing of the mother and the spiritual dimension of the father, we are not whole and cannot manifest wholeness in our lives. Instead, we project this split in our relationships with our partners.

In order to heal the split, we need to understand the roles we play in our relationships and in society, which are reflections of the inner man and the inner woman in our psyche. Ultimately, if we become acquainted with our inner man and woman and really manifest them fully, we can reach an ecstatic state where gender has been transcended. But it cannot be transcended until both its male and female aspects have been fully lived and explored.

I often start a conference or class by ringing a wonderful sacred bell from a Tibetan temple. There is a long, powerful, subsiding sound that totally enchants the mind and draws away all thoughts into a place of emptiness. In fact, in Tibetan Tantric tradition the bell symbolizes emptiness: the true nature of consciousness, which reflects everything yet holds nothing in itself. So I ring the bell and after a period of silence, I ask people, "Now, who was doing the listening? Was it a man or was it a woman? Are you aware in a difference in your consciousness, of a gender awareness when you listen to such a sound?" Invariably people say, "No, it's absolutely irrelevant whether I'm a man or a woman; I am beyond that place. It's a place of emptiness and ecstasy."

In general, we can't just go to that place of emptiness where we realize our wisdom mind. In order to go there, we have to concretely understand what it means to fully live our inner woman and inner man. Living your inner woman means being comfortable in your receptivity and feeling that you deserve to receive the best because you're an expression of the goddess. Living your inner woman means allowing yourself to meet experiences openly in a non-goal-oriented, trusting, intuitive, and receptive way. Allow the flow of your energy, connected by your feelings and guided by your intuitive wisdom, to transport you into the reality of your life moment to moment. Honor your emotions and your capacity to be in your loving heart and to be a healing presence to others.

When a woman is fully aware of the potential of her female energy, everything falls into place around her. She can then nurture the world and nurture her vision into the world. This inner potential is not just limited to gender—when a man is in touch with his inner woman he too can have the attitude of approaching life in a non-goal-oriented way. I recently taught a workshop on this topic, and the male participants said that they had gained a totally different perception of their sexuality when they approached it in a non-goal-oriented way—not focused on orgasm, not focused on performance, not focused on achievement or technique, but just on being there and allowing whatever happens to happen.

Fully living your inner man means meeting your experience directly and confidently, acting from power, with natural authority—again regardless of gender. It also means allowing yourself to be guided by clarity—you have a clear vision of where you're going that is connected with your destiny. Living your inner man means you can cut through obstacles, that you are aware of what you need and can express those needs, and that you can create situations which empower other people, as they empower you, to have a goal and clear direction.

When the inner man and woman act in harmony, there is balance between not having a goal and flowing with what is, while at the same time knowing where you're going and what you want, and being able to express it. You can boldly move toward what you want and yet not be attached to the outcome because you've incorporated both the forceful masculine and the fluid feminine. You are able to change course naturally as the movement of life opens you up to change. Through this integration, both aspects of yourself can manifest in every moment of your life, and you will experience wholeness.

This will affect all aspects of your life. Many women—*The Hite Report* says 75 percent—say they don't experience full orgasm with a partner. Many women say, "I get off better when I do it myself." But if a woman has fully integrated both her male and female aspects, she knows how to guide her partner to give her maximum pleasure. She is totally clear that she deserves to have an orgasm; she knows her own body—she knows she has a G spot and a clitoris—and she's willing to show her orgasmic pleasure to her partner. This directness reflects her inner man. If her partner doesn't like to be told what to do, a woman can go more into the female aspect—which is seductive, patient, waiting to find the angle and the moment where she can step in and guide without seeming to guide. This is the strength of the female in the sexual arena.

The integrated woman is willing to value her pleasure until she gets it the way she wants it. But she can ask for it in a graceful, elegant, and feminine way. She can seduce. So all at the same time she guides and attracts and teaches and inspires and initiates.

Integrating the inner male and female isn't just good for your sex life. Once you've understood how to be an orgasmic woman and value the art of being pleasured and appreciated, your masculine side is empowered also.

I receive feedback about this from the women who come to my trainings all the time. A client of mine, a successful businesswoman, recently told me that during a Love and Ecstacy Training, through some sessions of internal pelvic massage work she had healed the negative painful places in her *yoni* (vagina) and was able to experience powerful orgasms from the place of the G spot with the help of her partner. As a result, she felt she could take on million-dollar accounts at work, something she never allowed herself to do before because she didn't believe that she could handle it. So, in a way, her empowerment as a woman sexually has had huge repercussions for her career and her company, which has tripled its sales! This woman now runs her company more "orgasmically"—she knows how to weave the male and female energies in herself and her clients, she has developed a greater sense of humor and doesn't take problems so seriously—and as a result she has become much more successful.

When our inner woman is out of balance, when she's not supported by the power of her inner man, we tend to become overwhelmed by our problems. We lose ourselves in our relationships, in our mate or in an idea; we surrender our identity to another. We see many sides, yet we don't have a central, directing, anchoring perspective and thus we lose sight of our main goal. Paralyzed by confusion, we have difficulty making decisions and choices. So we give over our authority to someone else and then feel vulnerable emotionally, psychically, or physically.

When men are not in touch with their inner woman, they tend to rely exclusively on power and ignore the heart. Imbalance in a man is usually caused by a split between the power chakra and the heart chakra. A man is able to open his heart when he feels strong and empowered; confident in his power chakra, he can open his feminine side, his heart and his feelings. Most men try to compensate for the fact that they don't really sense their own power by covering up for it, so they never dare open their heart fully because vulnerability is too much of a threat. Out-of-balance men try to dominate people and situations; focus solely on progress and results, rather than the process itself; and ignore the subtle feelings that make life pleasant or painful as well as the warning signs that they might be off-track. They want to seem very sure of themselves, and easily become angry, rigid, or judgmental when their infallibility is questioned.

Our task, then, on the path of becoming fully aware, is to understand how we manifest these various energies and begin to play the roles—masculine and feminine—consciously with one another. We must avoid getting stuck in the one-sided ways of being male or female that society presents to us.

EMBRACING ECSTASY

To create a healthy, strong relationship between our inner male and female, we must be willing to embrace ecstasy. Ecstasy is the connection between energy and awareness, and this is at the root of Tantric teaching. When you bring awareness to the way you cultivate, generate, and manifest energy, then you begin to understand how to transcend blocks and other stuck situations, and you see that what connects the two is *flow*.

Flow happens when the chakras are open. When we feel flow, we feel excitement. When we're excited or aroused, our heart expands, and when the heart expands, our spirit sparkles and we have a taste of enlightenment. When we know how to be relaxed and pleasured in our bodies, energy can flows through us. It can move into our hearts and if our hearts are open and trusting, we can experience the energy of loving ourselves. Then we can consciously channel the energy from our hearts into our minds, where we can begin to make the distinction between the traffic of everyday thinking, which can diffuse our energy and cut us off from ourselves, and a peaceful mind that knows the state of receptive emptiness. This then allows the flow of energy to move into the spiritual dimension, in which we understand that we are first and foremost energy beings.

If we begin to see all of life in terms of energy and consciousness, we actually understand the marriage between the inner woman and the inner man. From the Tantric perspective, Shakti, the archetype of the goddess, is the embodiment of pure energy, and Shiva, the god, the divine masculine is the embodiment of pure spirit. When the two meet, their joining creates the fusion of energy and consciousness. This union is, in a way, reenacted every time a man and woman join with each other; potentially every couple reenacts this tremendous union between Shiva and Shakti, between energy and consciousness.

LIFE AS TEACHER

The Tantric approach recognizes that everything in life—every moment, experience, or situation—is a dance between energy and consciousness. And every moment is also an opportunity for further awakening. If you come to life from a closed, ready-made way of interpreting it you will merely be creating your own movie of what is and will be. But if you come to each moment from an open place of not-knowing, you will be ready to receive the deeper, invisible level of teaching.

The sacred is invisible, it's not evident. It is something you bring to a situation from your spirit, and it requires a willingness to come from a place of emptiness—from what Zen masters call "an empty cup." If you are willing to live in the place of not-knowing, then you will be able to receive the teaching when it occurs and will have an opportunity for further awakening.

This point of view makes all of life a matrix for learning, healing, and growth. Even when things are difficult, you can change your experience by changing your perspective of it. For instance, until recently I thought that happiness was dependent on changing my outer circumstances, specifically where I live. I thought that I'd be happier if I lived in Bali or someplace else. But as we wake up, we realize that internal awareness, the way we apprehend reality, is really at the root of whether we can be happy or not—geography has nothing to do with it. True happiness is based on making choices, in each moment, by engaging your inner man and inner woman to approach any particular situation.

The practice of Tantra is to apply this awareness to every moment of your life. The bank teller, your secretary or employee, your partner, anybody around you can and may be a teacher. As the great Tibetan teachers say, we are already perfect, we are already enlightened, but we just work very hard at getting in our own way. We all have moments when enlightenment sparkles through, and it is up to us to value those moments and find ways to cultivate them.

With the Tantric perspective, we see that the most intensely difficult situations are giving us the highest teachings we can receive, because they provide great opportunities for awakening. So often when people talk about ecstatic experiences they've had, they also reveal the incredible changes, transformations, or suffering they've endured—something was pulled from under them or they lost a loved one or their fortune—then all of a sudden, they wake up and their values and whole worldview change.

If we begin to look at life from the perspective that everything is an opportunity for awakening, it becomes very interesting. We don't want to manipulate it as much and we actually become more receptive; we hear better. We are open to dancing with the energies that flow around us and to the life that lives *through* us.

When we begin to see life as a flow of energy and consciousness, we become aware that in every moment of our lives we have to choose between what to take in and what not to take in. Which telephone call do I accept? Which date? Which event? Which project? Which friend? Which book do I read? What food do I eat? It's a conscious decision to choose what is pro-life, pro-ecstatic, and pro-expansive, as opposed to what is destructive. And this is a tremendous challenge; it's not easy. Do I say something or not? When I say something prematurely, I'm having what I call a "premature ejaculation"—I waste energy and affect my whole environment negatively.

THE CHAKRA CONSULTATION

As we move toward wholeness and begin to see everything that happens to us as a teaching, how do we make decisions and move forward in our lives? If we want to truly hear both our inner woman and inner man, what should we do to make sure we are not merely following old, deeply ingrained habits, but are allowing both the male and female energies to flow appropriately?

I have a very simple way of approaching this which has been very helpful, especially when I have to make important choices or discover what's right in a given situation. I call it the Chakra Consultation. Essentially, what you do is check in with every part of yourself to see what's true for you in that moment.

Before you make a move, take stock of the situation. Exactly what are the parameters of the situation? Are you about to be audited by the IRS and are trying to decide which lawyer should represent you? Have you found out that your mate is having an affair and you are not sure what to do? Are you trying to buy a new house or make an important decision in your job?

Sit in meditation, quiet your mind, and connect with what I call the inner witness, that peaceful part of yourself that just observes without having any preestablished agenda or fixed attitude. Start to imagine that you're in the situation you are wondering about—feel the energy of the situation, visualize the people involved, make it as real as possible.

Just sit in the situation for awhile, and then start traveling through each of the chakras. Go to the first chakra, which I call the root of creation, the sexual chakra located in the groin area. Go to that part of your body, lay your hand on it or focus your hand on it in your mind, and ask yourself, "Does this situation (or choice) turn me on? If I choose it, will it turn me on? Does this feel safe? If I decide X, am I going to get what I need?"

Continue visualizing the situation, moving your awareness to your second chakra, at the level of your navel, your belly. I call this chakra the "flowing stream" because it's our gravity center, the center of strength and movement. Here you ask, "What is my gut feeling about this? Does this feel comfortable? Do I feel in balance or off balance in this choice or in this decision?"

Then move to the chakra located at the level of the solar plexus—which I call "the radiant sun"—and again, visualizing yourself in the situation, focus your hand on the solar plexus and ask yourself, "Do I respect myself here? Am I gaining or losing power in this situation? How do I stand my ground here?"

Move to the heart—the "pulse of life"—and ask yourself, "Is this person or project attractive or desirable to me? Do I feel a 'yes' from the heart?" Then ask, "Am I taking care of myself?" Too often in such situations we are overly concerned about the others involved and we forget about ourselves. "Is this good for me? Is this good for others? Is this a loving kind of situation, is there fun, is there love, is there connection?"

Then move to the throat, what I call "the song of the soul," which is concerned with communication and creative solutions. Touch your throat with your hand, again connect with the situation, and ask yourself, "Is this the creative solution? Is this the truth? Am I in my truth and are the other people in their truths? Am I being authentic and speaking my true feelings and are they being authentic and speaking their true feelings?"

Then move your hand to your third eye, which I call "the full moon." This chakra has to do with insight, intuitive guidance, and the ability to envision. Here ask yourself, "Do I know where this is leading? Is this clear for me, do I really understand? Am I getting the whole picture? What does my inner guidance say?"

Finally, focus on your crown chakra, which I call "the open sky." Ask yourself, "Is this furthering my spiritual evolution? Is this helping others? Is it helping the world? Does this situation open me to light and spirit? What does my higher self have to say in the matter?"

By taking the time to consult with our chakras, we can make decisions from a place of wholeness, with the combined wisdom of our inner man and woman. The more we are able to do this, the more the ecstatic energy of the divine will be able to flow through us, and the more we will be able to trust in the benign protection of the higher forces, our "unseen friends," as some people call them. Even in the chaos of these times there is an incredible opportunity for us all to wake up. And the more we wake up within ourselves, the more we can all join in a positive way in the remaking of the world.

Cheri Huber has been a student and teacher of Zen for over twenty years. She teaches at the Zen Monastery Practice Center in Murphys, California, and travels throughout the country and beyond holding workshops and retreats. She is the author of, among other books, *That Which You Are Seeking Is Causing You to Seek* and *There Is Nothing Wrong with You.*

There Is Nothing Wrong with Us

If the ways we have been trying to affect change were going to work, they would have by now. If "changing" and "doing" and "improving" worked, we would be a world of perfected beings living in Utopia, and the idea of publishing a book like this would never have occurred to the folks at Conari Press. But that is clearly not our experience of ourselves and the world. The great majority of us are still struggling to become who and what we believe we should be.

Are we really determined to do things differently in the next millennium, or are we going to continue the same tired old ineffective processes, changing only the content to fool ourselves into thinking we are doing something different? Will we continue to try to fix ourselves and the world, or will we find the willingness to sit down and be still long enough to see through the illusion—yes, it is an illusion—that anything needs to be fixed? Will we accept that our beliefs, not the world as it is, is causing our suffering?

In my experience, there is much to be sad about. But I am well aware that something that makes me sad might thrill someone else. What I see as the senseless death and destruction of war, another sees as just and righteous retaliation. If I believe my view is the correct one, and that those who do not agree are wrong. I am perpetuating the violence just as surely as if I held a gun.

Centuries ago, Zen Master Bunan said, "Die while you are alive and be absolutely dead, then do whatever you want; it's all good." He was talking about dying to our beliefs and assumptions, letting go of our better ideas about how the universe needs to be, and getting really clear that compassionate action comes only from being in the present moment, unencumbered by the dictates of conditioned mind.

With these things in mind, I offer the following for your consideration.

We already are that which we are seeking. Every spiritual path tells us this: "That which you are seeking is causing you to seek." "We are God manifest in time and eternity." "For behold, the Kingdom of God is within you." But why is this so hard for us to know? To me, it is because the social conditioning we receive as children teaches us there is something wrong with us, and that to be loved and accepted we must improve ourselves. We start out just how we are, and then we are changed, fixed, punished, and altered until we become someone who is "appropriate" and "acceptable." Then we are able to fit into a family and a society. Miss Manners(!) said, "We are all born charming, fresh, and spontaneous and must be civilized before we are fit to participate in society."

Unless you were raised by wolves, you probably heard at least a few of the following as you were growing up: "Don't do that.... Why don't you ever listen?... Wipe that look off your face.... You shouldn't feel that way.... You should have known better.... You should be ashamed of yourself.... I can't believe you did that.... It serves you right.... What were you thinking of?... The nurses must have dropped you on your head.... I had great hopes for you.... Don't talk back to me.... Do as you are told.... Don't you ever think about anyone else?" Somewhere along the line we conclude there is something wrong with us. What else could we conclude? If there were nothing wrong with us, people would not say those things, would they?

Being intelligent creatures, we soon take over the job of punishing ourselves, punishment being the way to improve so that we can be who and how we should be. We learn the self-improvement process as quickly as possible so we can fix ourselves before anyone else notices we need fixing. As a result, most people grow up with an unshakable belief that the primary reason they are "good" is that they punish themselves when they are "bad." The very thought of not punishing ourselves when we make mistakes, say and do stupid things, feel inappropriate feelings, or act "bad," makes us nervous: If I don't punish myself when I do something wrong, what will keep me from doing it again? I might do even worse things!

To this I would say that one process does not lead to another. Punishment does not make us good, punishment makes us punishing. Hating and rejecting ourselves in this moment is not good practice for loving and accepting ourselves in another. Goodness is our inherent nature and punishment is what keeps us from knowing that. We are never going to improve ourselves until we become who we "should" be. If self-improvement worked, it would have by now. Punishment is what keeps us from seeing that there is no one who needs to be punished. It is a learned response, it will never work, and we can let go of it if we are willing.

"But, Cheri, how can I do that?" you might ask. "It's so deep and automatic, and it feels like the 'good person' thing to do. I say or do or feel something wrong, I beat myself up to ensure I don't do it again. Swift and sure. It's scary to consider not doing it ... but I guess that's part of the conditioning, too, isn't it?"

Yes, it is. Self-improvement, punishment, and self-hate are survival mechanisms and feel like "good person" things to do. Isn't that ironic? Isn't that sad? Yet when we beat ourselves up to improve, we are doing the same thing our parents did to us in childhood (and their parents did to them, and so on down the line—no blame here). Again, it didn't work then to make you the person you believe you should be, and it won't work now. This "Build A Better World Through Hatred" school of thought is doomed to failure from the start.

How can we turn this around? How can we realize that our True Nature is goodness, and that when we stop doing everything else, goodness is what's there? How can we find compassion for all aspects of ourselves? Is there a process that is not just another stab at self-improvement?

In my experience there is a process, the basis of which is meditation. There are other helpful practices and concepts, but meditation brings it all together. Much of the rest of this article describes the process I am talking about, but before going too deeply into that, I want to give some examples of how, as adults, our lack of self-acceptance plays out.

THE BIND WE ARE CAUGHT IN

Little in social conditioning and child-raising teaches self-acceptance. We have few models for how to be generous with ourselves—in fact, quite the opposite. "Inappropriate" needs, wants, impulses, emotions, attitudes, and beliefs are systematically stripped from us and replaced by whatever the people responsible for our survival believe is best (if we are raised by someone who cares). Even if this is done in gentle ways, we conclude that we are flawed, that our natural responses are wrong and bad. We internalize this search-out-and-destroy survival system so that we can monitor ourselves and stop inappropriate behavior before it goes too far. As adults we unconsciously carry this around with us, and it is still running our lives. We no longer express "inappropriate needs." We no longer require another person to point out what we are doing wrong; we do that for ourselves. When we do not meet certain standards, we punish, blame, berate, discipline, and abuse ourselves until we are who we "should" be. And if we do not, we feel guilty. We spend our lives either resigned to the fact that there is something wrong with us, feeling hopeless and inadequate, or we spend our lives trying to "fix" ourselves, never quite knowing what is wrong or how to fix it but feeling compelled to keep trying. I call this punishing, blaming process "self-hate."

Two places where many can see how lack of self-acceptance controls their lives are "going on a diet" and "getting regular exercise." Both are often begun as self-hate's response to what it sees in the mirror. And while it might be true that shedding a few pounds and exercising regularly would be a wonderful thing to do for ourselves, beginning a program with self-hate at the helm cannot succeed. Self-hate's *job* is to hate you; self-rejection's *job* is to reject you; self-improvement's *job* is to judge you. We cannot use conditioning to release ourselves from conditioning! You could starve until nearly dead (some have), you could exercise until unable to walk (many have), and still not like what you see in the mirror. With self-hate in control, you will never hear the words, "Good job, goal achieved." It is relentless, and it has us right where it wants us.

Self-hate will talk you into dieting and exercising, complain when the going gets hard, dupe you into quitting, and beat you up for having quit. Not pretty, but highly effective at keeping you trapped in its illusion. What is its illusion? The illusion is that it is on your side, that it is the voice of reason and common sense, and that to succeed at life you must listen to it.

The bind we are caught in is trying to end self-hate with self-hate, trying to find self-acceptance through self-rejection, trying to become who we believe we should be by destroying who we are. The really good news is we cannot destroy who we inherently are. The miracle of existence gives us the opportunity to find out who that is.

THE HOW-TO OF SELF-ACCEPTANCE

First of all, what is self-acceptance? My answer to this is quite simple though often not easy to realize in our lives. Self-acceptance is allowing ourselves to be exactly as we are without needing to change anything.

"But, Cheri," you might say, "I really, really want to change some things about myself. Are you saying I should just accept those things and not try to make my life any different?"

When I suggest we accept ourselves as we are, people get upset. The belief is that if we just accept, if we don't struggle to change, we will never be different and evil will win out over good. I further suggest that struggle perpetuates the "problem," and that it is really rather arrogant of us to presume that we can control something by not accepting it. Let's say I lock my keys in the car. Now, I can stomp around and curse, kick the door, and call myself names. I can do all sorts of things, but if I don't accept that my keys are indeed locked in the car, I'm not going anywhere. Acceptance doesn't mean I have to like it or approve of it or anything else. In fact, I don't have to have any relationship with it at all. I simply must accept that my keys are locked in the car. Yes, this is the reality, where do I go from here? From this place of acceptance, many possibilities become available to me that might never have done so had I persisted in my conditioned responses.

We need to allow ourselves to be as we are long enough to see who we are. Underneath the conditioning, who are we? Don't you agree that we could risk dropping the hate, judgment, and rejection long enough to experience that? Wouldn't that be worth the risk of running amok?

Here is where meditation practice, or awareness practice, is essential in learning self-acceptance.

MEDITATION

Zen meditation is the practice of sitting still in the present moment, holding on to nothing, pushing nothing away. As we sit, we make ourselves available to whatever arises. Thoughts and feelings come and go. Sometimes our thoughts wander, and we wake up to find our attention has been a million miles away. When this happens, we gently bring the attention back into the present, back into the body, back to the breath, and begin again.

There are three things I always encourage meditators to do: (1) Pay attention. (2) Believe nothing. (3) Don't take any of it personally. I will explain these further because to me they are the basis of a meditation practice.

Pay attention. Pay attention to everything. Develop what I call "passive awareness." I like to use the example of solar heating to clarify what I mean by passive awareness: The sun warms some type of collector—tiles, stones, barrels of water—and the collector stores the heat. The sun is not trying to heat the collector, and the collector is not trying to store the heat, but together they create solar heating. Each is present, and the transformation happens.

In the same way, if I am practicing passive awareness, I am simply here, aware and present. If, on the other hand, I am busy trying to know what is right or wrong, to be a good meditator, to have deep insights, I have missed the point completely. So if I am practicing passive awareness, I am not trying to accomplish anything. I am simply aware and present, noticing everything that happens—not judging, not solving problems, not making plans to improve.

Here is an example of how passive awareness might work. I hope you apply it to whatever "fault" you are on a self-improvement campaign about. It could be something like cutting back on coffee, engaging in fewer mind-numbing entertainments, eating less, being on time, keeping your temper, meditating more—we all have those pet areas of self-torture being perpetuated under the guise of being a better person.

The example: I hate to do the dishes. I put it off for as long as I can, and let everything stack up until it becomes moldy and disgusting. I feel ashamed, guilty, and embarrassed. I know this is a sign of some deep flaw, but life is hard and I don't want to do one more hard thing!

Each time I go into the kitchen the anxiety builds. I decide to bite the bullet and wash those dishes. The voices begin, "Not now. You're too tired. It's been a long day. You deserve to relax. Why are you so compulsive? You can do the dishes later. All you do is work. Go see what's on TV and just relax." Later, as I'm brushing my teeth, a little voice says, "You didn't do the dishes. Again. You know you said you were going to. Now they're going to be awful tomorrow and you won't do them then either." I look myself in the eye in the mirror and say, "No! I'm sick of this. I am going in there right now and do those dishes." On the way to the kitchen I remember I promised to call my sister. "Is it too late? No, I'll only talk for a minute." A half-hour later I'm getting into bed and the little voice says, "You forgot to do the dishes." My heart sinks, I plunge into despair. "Oh, it's okay," comforts the little voice, "you can do them tomorrow."

After having exasperating scenes like this play out over and over with a variety of subjects, I begin to suspect there is more to this than meets the eye. I want to know experientially, not intellectually, what is going on here. I begin to practice compassionate, passive awareness, paying attention, believing nothing, and taking none of it personally.

So, with passive awareness added to the mix, I eat a meal and watch very closely how I avoid washing the dishes afterward. "I'm too tired. It would ruin the meal to have to clean up right now. I'll do it later." I listen to what the voices tell me as I don't do the dishes. "You really should do them now. You won't do them later. You are a lazy slob and you always will be." I notice how I feel when the voices are talking to me and I'm caught in this "I should do the dishes/I'm not doing the dishes" duality. I begin to feel the toll it takes on me physically, emotionally, spiritually, and mentally. I observe that I feel defeated and depressed.

As I practice, I realize that if this were only a matter of doing the dishes, they could be done in no time. But this is not about doing the dishes. It's about keeping me in prison. All my time, energy, attention, and awareness are locked up in "Will I wash the dishes and be a good person, or will I not and be a bad person?" If doing the dishes *didn't make me a good person*, and not doing the dishes *didn't make me a bad person*, what would I do about the dishes?

This is where spiritual practice, awareness practice, begins. Spiritual practice does not begin until the beatings have stopped. If I become aware of something about myself that I don't like, and I beat myself up for it, I am once again using the old childhood system of conditioning. The missing element is compassionate self-acceptance.

Believe nothing. All thoughts, images, and impressions are filtered through conditioning and are after-the-fact interpretations of events. For example, we have made connections in our minds between certain situations and a set of physical sensations we label "stress." When we encounter these situations and feel these sensations, our automatic response is to believe that, yes, in fact, this is stressful. As we sit in meditation, we begin to notice that when we feel *this* we have *that* thought, and it triggers *that* emotion which in turn leads to *this* action. This is all learned, inauthentic, and devilishly seductive. Do not believe it. Question every sensation-thought-emotion-action sequence that goes through your mind and body. Is anything inherently stressful, or is stress something we add? Do this with literally everything. In the dish-washing example, as you pay attention, you hear the same words but you don't believe they are true about you or about the situation.

"But, Cheri, don't some situations call for certain responses? If a tiger is chasing me, for example, shouldn't I be afraid ?"

No, it is all learned. Examine fear and you will discover nothing more than a set of sensations, thoughts, emotions, and actions, all of which you have learned to associate. But don't believe me, find out for yourself.

Don't take any of it personally. The universe is not personal. For "personal" to exist, there would have to be something separate from all that is, and there is not. The feeling we humans have that we exist apart and separate from everything else is an illusion, a trick of the mind. There is nothing wrong with that, it is just that being caught in the illusion of a separate self makes us feel alone, afraid, and insecure. Believing we are separate (in Christian terms, believing we are out of the presence of God) is the source of our desperate desire to control life. Trying to control life—hold on to this, get rid of that—is the cause of suffering.

As we sit in meditation, we see all kinds of things about ourselves. Some we like; some we do not. The practice is to watch from the "center," our core of wisdom and compassion where nothing is taken personally. If we see something about ourselves we do not like, our attitude is, "Ah, judgment"; if we see something we are proud of, "Ah, pride"; if we become confused, "Ah, confusion." In this way we grow accustomed to watching conditioning instead of identifying with it, which is a giant step toward self-acceptance and freedom. From this greater perspective, we might ask all sorts of questions, such as, Who (which aspect of the personality) makes decisions about what needs to change? Where does that part get its information? Does the part who is being required to change agree? Has trying to change in this way ever worked, and if so, at what cost?

This nonjudgmental questioning allows the parts of us who have felt so threatened feel safer, and they begin to relax a little. We have created a safe place for all the aspects of who we are. Compassion has turned inward, and the joyous work of self-acceptance has begun.

In Zen meditation practice, all that is happening is that we are sitting there facing a blank white wall. We notice all the drama we are capable of acting out with others is being acted out with no one but ourselves and that white wall. Everything we feel, think, and do in all sorts of situations in daily life, we do while sitting there on the cushion. No one else is required for conditioning to be triggered, just ourselves. We just sit there and it all arises ... and begins to fall apart. The mind is a fascinating thing right up until we notice how repetitive it is. Our issues are "real" and "true" right up until we notice how arbitrary they are. The trap we are caught in is inescapable right up until we notice we have the keys.

For meditation to make a difference, we must do it. Reading or listening to someone talk about it will do little if anything to make it real, but, as with diet and exercise, we cannot approach it as a "should." If we do, self-hate will quickly talk us out of our practice. Self-hate's power lies in its covert activities. It requires darkness. When we begin to shine the light of compassionate awareness on our inner workings and begin to see that blindly following conditioning robs us of our lives, self-hate starts to unravel. It does not want to unravel, and it knows it cannot stand up under scrutiny. It is a false overlay keeping us from seeing that we already are everything we seek. So if beginning a meditation practice is another attempt at self-improvement, if it is not our heart's deepest desire (and, often, even if it is), we can expect self-hate to do its worst.

OTHER HELPFUL PRACTICES

In pursuing the work of self-acceptance, there are many helpful practices.

Treat yourself as if you were someone you love. Think of a person or a pet you hold dear. Imagine that this dear one is having a problem and needs your help. How would you respond? Feel the caring and generosity you have for this being. Now give that to yourself. (That voice in your head telling you this is self-indulgent is the voice of self-hate. Don't believe it!)

Focus on your breath. When you become aware of an urgent, judgmental, stressful, fearful, hateful thought or situation, simply bring your attention to your breathing. This practice can very quickly bring us up against a mountain of resistance. Our self-hate—our belief that we are inadequate, that we must control life—goes berserk when we begin to practice dropping whatever urgent, stressful, life-and-death thing has us in its clutches today. "That's crazy! That's just flat-out irresponsible! Everything is going to fall apart around me if I don't keep my mind on what needs to be done." Focusing on the breath brings up our deeply held belief that we make life happen, and that we must be tense in the process. But if we are resolute in the face of this fear, if we maintain the practice of bringing the attention back to the breath even though the voices in our heads are screaming, we begin to see that nothing bad happens. Our lives don't fall apart, no one dies, we don't lose our jobs—nothing happens except the *urgency* of egocentric conditioning begins to be less believable. We begin to be free of the tyrant who runs our lives, the taskmaster who cracks a whip over our heads.

Notice self-hate. People say to me that the term self-hate seems extreme. "But Cheri," they say, "I don't exactly hate myself. Disapprove sometimes, maybe, but not hate." To know that "self-hate" is not an overstatement, attune very closely to how you talk to yourself when you don't meet your standards. Notice the choice of words, the tone of voice, and the undercurrent of judgment. Notice how often you don't meet your standards. Notice how seldom, if ever, you do meet your standards and how short-lived the satisfaction is. Notice how your standards constantly change, how the ante is always upped just before you begin to feel really successful. Do this for a week. The awareness may change your life.

Challenge yourself. Enjoy doing something you currently believe you can't enjoy—not to change, not to improve, but to see through the beliefs and assumptions that control your life. Learn to enjoy doing the dishes, spending time with your mother-in-law, commuting in rush hour traffic, or eating healthy foods. Do this, not because it will make you a better person, but because it will help you be free of the conditioning that says you can't possibly enjoy those things.

Stop watching television. I compare sitting in front of a television to being hooked up to an intravenous infusion of toxic waste. Madison Avenue knows that if it can make us feel inadequate, which it can, it will have us in its back pocket, which it does. The thin, savvy, beautiful people have the world by the tail. Are you one of them? No? Buy this product, act this way, do this thing, feel this feeling, and you will be. The obvious message is that how you are now could be improved. The not so obvious message is being thin, savvy, etc. makes you right, and being anything else makes you wrong.

Watch your projections. "Projection" is the notion that everything mirrors who we are. We always see ourselves when we look out at the world and other people. It is not possible to see something that is not a part of ourselves.

When sitting in meditation and facing a blank white wall, it is relatively easy to see projection at work. As stated earlier, everything we do in our lives we do while just sitting there. With no one else participating, it becomes clear that we are seeing ourselves. In daily life, recognizing projection is not as easy, there are so many distractions, but it is no less revealing than seeing it in meditation. Accepting that what we see is who we are is, to me, the most powerful tool for awareness practice.

Discover your "identities." A helpful construct to consider in developing self-awareness is that of "identities." Identities are the various parts of ourselves, the different roles we play as we go through the day. The terms *roles, personae,* and *subpersonalities* are often used to point to the same thing.

In Zen it is said that we live in the *world of duality*. Simply put, this means that everything has an opposite. Up/down, good/bad, right/wrong are examples of pairs of opposites. One cannot exist without the other. Most identities also exist in inseparable pairs. Examples of pairs of identities are miser/spendthrift; athlete/couch potato; devoted spouse-parent-family member/desperate individualist. Sometimes we are identified with one side of a pair, sometimes with the other. Our conditioned belief that we must be consistent is challenged by this. This is confusing, a problem to be solved, an improvement to be made. "I can't be changing my mind like this all the time. I have to make a decision and stick with it. That's how strong, capable people operate." Conditioning, self-hate, self-improvement kicks in and goes on its campaign to get rid of the side it judges to be the wrong one. You can see the futility of this.

The practice of noticing our identities, and how we move back and forth between them, gives us enormous freedom. Not identifying with either side—in fact, *disidentifying*—and observing from a larger perspective, brings us to an awareness of how the world of duality works. Once we see that of course we are inconsistent, and that we will never hate one side out of existence, we can relax and stop trying to improve. Accepting that we are sometimes this, sometimes that, is the only change we need.

Learn to disidentify. Disidentification is the action of "stepping back" from whatever identity we are in and viewing ourselves from a larger perspective. Almost all of us know the experience of suddenly realizing we are no longer caught up in the drama of a situation but are observing it and ourselves from a place that feels "outside" or "above" what is going on. With practice we can learn to do this at will. Why? Disidentification enables us to begin to see the universality of experience. When we see that we are one of six billion people, that we all have our "stuff," and that we are all trying to get the best deal for ourselves (in Zen, "seeking better accommodation"), we can begin to take our own stuff less personally. We see ourselves caught in the illusion of separation, struggling and suffering, and we can have compassion.

Write it all down. Write down every judgment, of yourself or anyone else, you hear go through your head. Get them outside of you. Expose them to the light of day. Many people tell me they are afraid doing this will make the "horrible things" they judge themselves for more powerful and real. I tell them no, the power of these judgments lies in their covert operations. They whisper a self-hating thought in your ear just beneath the level of conscious awareness, stir an emotional response, and you are caught in the illusion once again. It never occurs to us to question this conditioning. So when we practice writing down *everything it says, every time it says it,* we begin to take back the power it has had since we were children. We discover its repetitious nature is rather boring. We begin to take it less personally.

There is nothing wrong with us. We are the loved and loving beings we seek to be. But don't take my word for it; don't believe it because I say so. Begin, or continue, the practice of aware self-acceptance and experience it, know it, for yourself. Meditation and awareness are simple because they don't require fancy techniques or expensive equipment. They are difficult because they require the willingness to challenge a lifetime of conditioning. They are powerful and transforming, changing us through compassionate acceptance of what is.

Formerly a teacher and family therapist, **Sue Bender** is now a ceramic artist, best-selling author, and much sought-after national lecturer. The author of *Plain and Simple: A Woman's Journey to the Amish* and *Everyday Sacred: A Woman's Journey Home,* she holds a B.A. from Simmons College, an M.A. from Harvard University School of Education, and a Master's in Social Work from the University of California, Berkeley. Her ceramics have been shown in museums and galleries nationwide, and she loves making handmade, crooked black-and-white ceramics. She lives in Berkeley, California with her husband Richard, and is the mother of two grown sons.

The Cracked Pot and the Millennium

"The soul thinks in images, " Aristotle said.

"That's what I do," I thought. I trust images.

I want to tell a story about a pot—a cracked ceramic pot that had become sacred to me, sacred with a small *s.* This object has nourished my soul and become my teacher.

What has a cracked pot to do with the millennium?

When Conari Press called and invited me to write something about the millennium for this anthology, I said "No. I'm not an expert." I was quite definite.

The word *millennium* was overwhelming. Exciting and threatening. I began to daydream about the millennium and its significance. A few days later I called back.

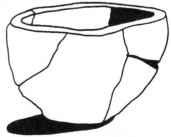

"Yes...."

What changed?

I didn't become an expert overnight. When I thought about the millennium some more and what I could possibly offer at such an important moment for all of us, I thought about what I have been learning in these last years.

When I started to write my second book, *Everyday Sacred*, I was hoping for a miracle, one that would change my life dramatically. What I found instead was far more important.

The power of small things.

Faced with this giant overwhelming marker called the millennium, it's reassuring to know that the really important things are contained in the details of our everyday lives. *How* we do whatever we do—the spirit we bring to our work (whatever it is) is as important as *what* we do.

How we feel about ourselves will always be important.

For as long as I can remember I have been listening to a harsh critical voice inside me, but I lived with it so long I never really noticed the influence it was having on my life. I not only listened, I believed what this harsh judge was saying. No matter what I did or accomplished, something was always missing—and I never knew what that "something" was.

Not everyone has a harsh judge, but many of us have some inner voice that has the power to undercut, to make us doubt ourselves, and leaves us wondering why we aren't more content. That demon of perfection—the judge—keeps us from honoring ourselves. I have come to trust that it is not selfish to think about oneself.

To be truly generous toward others, we must start with ourselves.

Back to the story of the cracked pot and how it become my teacher.

My friend Loie has a beautiful bowl, hand-burnished with a patina that takes a great deal of time and attention to achieve. Each time I visit Loie, I stop and say hello to this pot. When I look closely, I can see it has been cracked and glued back together.

"That's my friend Kevin's pot. Kevin makes cracked pots."

"Do you think I could meet him?" I asked, excited. I'm a potter who makes simple, handmade crooked black-and-white pots. I was intrigued that someone would crack their own pot.

I went to visit Kevin in his studio. "I had a really strong desire to make pots," Kevin began, "but I would sabotage myself by taking unnecessary risks, and I'd have lots of accidents. I would drop nearly completed pots, blow them up by raising the kiln too fast, and I simply wouldn't finish some pots. I didn't understand what was happening.

"Finally, I saw I had a destructive side.

"Before I acted out unconsciously. Now I make pots and deliberately crack them" Then he added: "Once I gave the saboteur a voice, I noticed I wasn't breaking as many pots." I loved what Kevin was saying.

These pots were a tool for healing.

I signed up for a workshop with Kevin. In the middle of class he asked, "Is anyone interested in cracking pots?" I raised my hand, ran back to the studio and found a bowl I had made that still needed to be glazed. Though I acted "as if" my intention was to really crack the pot, I could feel my body constrict. I could feel myself holding back—unable to let go.

"You'll have to bang harder," Kevin said.

"Let go!" I shouted to myself silently.

"You're acting as if your life depended on keeping the bowl just the way it is, and you say you want to change."

On the fifth try, the bowl cracked.

The effect was visceral. I took a long, deep breath, feeling great relief—a release. Release from what? I didn't know, but the expression "fear cracked open" came to mind. Perhaps my judge was loosening her grip on me.

As I collected the nine pieces to return them to the fire one more time, Kevin came over to me.

"*Save the slivers,*" he said.

Later he showed me how to piece together my broken pot. Like making a jigsaw puzzle, I had to begin by finding two pieces that "fit." Then he showed me how to hold these two pieces together—now joined with shipbuilders' glue, held still in my hands for about five minutes till the glue hardened. I could not have imagined holding two pieces of broken clay together and waiting could be so deeply satisfying.

"All of me" was present.

As each one of the pieces was joined to make the pot whole, that same calm engulfed me. When I finally held my own pieced-together pot in my hands, a circle was completed. I looked at my bowl and saw it was beautiful.

In the past, no matter what I did or accomplished, I had always felt that something was missing. When I put the pieces of my cracked pot together, I saw that *nothing* was missing.

Nothing.

I saw I was WHOLE.

What I saw, really saw, when I held my own pieced-together pot in my hands—is that that is true for each of us. Each one of us is whole. We can focus our energy and thoughts on all our cracks and lumps and bumps—or we can make a shift and see our *imperfections* as a gift, the very qualities that make us unique.

I thought of a strikingly handsome Japanese tea bowl I had seen a long time ago in a museum in Japan. The image of that bowl had made a lasting impression. It had been broken and pieced together. Instead of trying to hide the flaws, the cracks were emphasized—filled with silver. The bowl was even more precious after it had been mended.

Sometimes at a crossroad, a new stage in life, a crisis, a turning point, we feel we may crack, or we do crack. These times can be difficult, frightening.

And, sometimes we deliberately crack our own bowl.

With time and great care and tender patience, we can reexamine the pieces, knowing that when we are ready, a solution will come. We can glue the pieces back together.

My bowl was far more interesting than before it broke. The pieces are the same, but it's a different bowl than when I started.

Kevin's story was a gift to me.

The story of the cracked pot is in *Everyday Sacred*. When I'm invited to give talks across the country, I always tell this story—to groups of every age, social and political status, religion, family background. They always understand the story. Stories have a way of taking care of us.

I not only want to share this story with you, but each time I tell it I feel nourished. I need to be reminded of what I am telling you.

Now, approaching the millennium, we can pause and feel the wonder of this 1000-year marker.

At the same time it's important to stop—and honor how durable our own unique *spirit* is. We can also celebrate knowing there will always be things beyond our control. We have faced many tests—and will face many more. Our challenge is to make peace with our paradox, so our lives can feel whole with the pieces we have.

I now own one of Kevin's pots. And I have the one I cracked myself. Each has a special place in my heart. Each is a talisman—bringing me back, grounding me in some truth I am in danger of forgetting.

To be WHOLE doesn't mean we have to be perfect.

4

THE JOURNEY'S WAY: BRINGING THE FUTURE INTO BEING

"Dare to be naive."

—R. Buckminster Fuller

Here we come to the more practical, day-to-day considerations of how we can prepare ourselves for the future. These essays return us to our daily business with new direction, renewed enthusiasm, and tools better suited to the world that is being born.

We start with Shakti Gawain, who asks us to imagine the future and recognize that this is both an exciting and frightening time. We are in a healing crisis, she maintains, and we need to integrate our shadow side and learn to trust our intuition.

Possibilist thinker Dawna Markova goes a step further, suggesting that we need to liberate our imaginations in order to help create a future we would want to participate in. "We cannot have conversations about co-creating a possible future for the world if we don't have courageous conversations about how we can re-create our own personal destiny," she notes, and offers a powerful tool to help us do just that. Starhawk follows with a process for creating a vision and directing energy toward it, as does Rama Vernon, each from her own unique perspective. Writes Vernon, "Serving the global vision through our personal vision may change thousands if not millions of lives."

Buddhist teacher Sylvia Boorstein reminds us that as we navigate through difficult times, kindness is "the natural compassionate response to understanding how difficult life is for everyone regardless of the external circumstances of particular lives." She urges us to practice mindfulness to see clearly and foster kindness, remembering the key word *practice*. "We don't get it together once and for all. We just keep practicing."

Vimala McClure reminds us of the profound role parents play in creating a better world through healthy, happy children. She offers some Taoist principles for parenting in a more conscious manner.

Several women suggest ways to create communities of support as we go through change. Echoing the wisdom of the Dagara, her people in West

Africa, Sobunfu Somé urges us to reconnect with the ancestors, create community, and renew through ritual if we want the kind of spiritual grounding we need to go happily into the future. "The Ancestors have the ability to see past, present, and future.... The more we stay connected to them, the more we will live our lives wired, connected to our original source." Brooke Medicine Eagle reminds us that "the method you use to transform yourself or the world around you must have the energetic quality of the end you seek." She suggests a number of ways to create community, including a Circle of Seven, people coming together in commitment on a "mutually important issue." Glennifer Gillespie also advocates circles of support and describes those she's been part of in South Africa and the United States since 1975; now she too is a member of a Circle of Seven.

Marianne Williamson and Gloria Steinem go beyond the personal to advocate new forms of political activism, infused with the feminine principle of wholeness. Williamson exhorts us to create a spiritual politics, to use the force of the soul "as a social and political tool.... Learning to love is the highest form of political training." Steinem calls on us to go beyond either/or thinking when it comes to sociopolitical change, urging us to whatever form of activism we individually feel drawn to. "Our part in the next quarter-century depends on the groups, issues, and styles that make us feel supported, angry, inspired, or energized."

And finally, we close with a deep reflection by Nancy Mairs on the notion of charity and how we need to profoundly reexamine our attitudes toward it and those to whom it is "offered" if we as a society are to take better care of those in need. In very different language than others have used in talking about the feminine, she calls for an upheaval "so radical that it exalts every valley and makes the rough places a plain, not along the San Andreas Fault but in the human psyche, which will no longer choose (not desire—it may well still desire—but *choose*) to organize itself and its relationships with others in terms of power and rank."

Shakti Gawain is an internationally renowned speaker/workshop leader in the world consciousness movement who has helped thousands of people learn to develop and act on their own intuition and creativity. A bestselling author, her books include *Creative Visualization, Living in the Light, The Path of Transformation*, and most recently, *Creating True Prosperity* and *The Four Levels of Healing*. She cofounded Whatever Publishing, which later became New World Library. Her imprint there is Nataraj Publishing, whose mission is to bring forth books and tapes that carry important messages for those on the path of personal growth and transformation. She and her husband make their home in Mill Valley, California and Kauai, Hawaii.

Moving Toward the New Millennium

A very amazing kind of moment is upon us—the symbolic shift from one millennium to another. The first thing I'd like to do before I tell you my thoughts about that is to give you a chance to check in a little bit more with your own ideas about the future.

I'd like to ask you to close your eyes for a moment, take a deep breath, and as you exhale let your awareness begin to move inside to a quiet place within you. Think about the future, about your personal future, the future of your life over the next few years, the next few decades. Just allow spontaneously whatever thoughts, images, or feelings come to you when you think about the future, without trying to control them or change them or censor them or do anything with them—just whatever comes, whether it seems positive to you or negative or mixed or you don't understand them—just let your own thoughts, feelings, impressions, ideas, images about your future arise.

And now I'd like you to expand your imagination to begin to think about our collective future, the future of humanity, the future of all beings on this

Earth, the future of the Earth itself. Again, just open up your mind and let whatever thoughts, feelings, images, impressions, ideas come without censoring, controlling, or changing, just being with it. Just notice whatever the thought of the future brings up for you. Then when you're ready you can gently open your eyes and come back here into the present moment.

I've done this exercise with a lot of people all over the world, at different workshops in different places, and there is always a wide range of experience. Some people have wonderful visions and lovely, hopeful feelings about their future and the future of the world. Others have more dark, frightening, or concerned feelings and images. I really think it's very appropriate at this point that we have a very wide range of feelings about the future because, on the one hand, we are probably living in the most frightening time that has ever existed on our planet. Modern life is very complicated. Each of us as individuals has enormous challenges to deal with on a daily basis in terms of our work, our relationships, our health, and finding our true expression. Many of us have a lot of freedom, more freedom than most people have had in the past, but such freedom can be overwhelming. We don't play the same roles we used to. In the past, human beings' lives were more or less mapped out for them and they knew what they were supposed to do. That's no longer true for most of us.

Because of such freedom, there are times when each of us wonders, Is my life going to work out the way I really want it to? Am I going to be able to be able to solve my problems, am I going to really be able to manifest all the potential within me and find real satisfaction in my life? On a individual level, life is scary and difficult and challenging at times. It becomes even more intense when we look at the world situation and hear about all kinds of very real and severe problems, kinds of crises that human beings have never had to face before. Up until now, people had to worry more whether they were going to get enough food to survive or whether their family or their nation was going to be safe, and that sort of thing. But now we're dealing with the very existence of the human species, the existence of other species, and the existence of the Earth itself.

It's truly frightening and we have a right to be afraid. I think it's important that we let ourselves feel those fearful feelings. It's hard to feel them because we don't like to feel helpless, so we distract ourselves by focusing on other things. Yet the only way to solve problems is to confront them and tell the truth about them. It's only when we're willing to tell the truth to ourselves and to one another about what we see, feel, and experience that real inspiration and real problem-solving can take place.

On the other hand, this is the most exciting time that's ever existed on this planet. More and more and more of us do have real opportunities to create our lives much more the way we want them to be—to really delve inside and discover who we are and work on developing and expressing that. Many of us don't have to just be worrying about survival anymore and, therefore, have the opportunity to go deeper and do a lot more. And in doing that, we are discovering so much hope and so many possibilities and so much vision—vision about what's possible for human beings on earth. So, it's also a very fantastic time, and I don't think it's any accident we're all here. I feel that on a soul level, we've probably chosen to be here right at this time precisely because of the challenge and the possibilities that exist.

One of the things that we are here to do is to learn to contain this paradox. Our situation is not black or white—it's both. It's difficult, it's scary, it's challenging, it's confusing, and, at the same time, it's fantastically exciting. All possibilities are open. And we have to really stretch a lot to be able to contain all of that.

There are a lot of well-meaning New Age people who spend time meditating and visualizing for peace—and that's actually a wonderful thing to do, visualization is a very powerful tool. The problem is that so many people who are in spiritual work have gotten so identified with those qualities that we think of as "spiritual," like being loving and giving, kind, considerate, and peaceful, that we think the way to make the world peaceful is to be those qualities. But we don't understand the principle of duality that exists in the world, that you have to always embrace the opposites. You have to always embrace the paradox. That's where peace comes from. It doesn't come from identifying with one side and denying the other side. That's where conflict and war—both inner and outer—comes from. If we try to say, "I'll just be loving all the time and I'll never have any feeling of resentment or frustration," we're out of balance and at war with that other side of ourselves. So real peace comes from embracing both sides, embracing the paradox, embracing the part of us that's peaceful and the part of us that's not peaceful.

So if you want to meditate for peace, that's great; but be sure that you are also equally honoring your inner warrior. That's the part of us that can stand up and act on our own behalf—and this doesn't mean that it has to hurt people or be violent, but it has to be willing to do whatever is required to take care of us and to really live for the truth and what we feel is right. How many of us deny that side of ourselves and then create a big shadow out there in the world? That's how we get people like Saddam Hussein, who are like the warrior in a distorted way. If you own the truth of your inner warrior and embrace the ability to defend yourself and to take care yourself, you'll embrace your power in such a way that you never have to use it because people will feel it energetically. So it's not that you have to act this power out, rather that you must own it internally.

To create peace in this world, we have to make peace inside of ourselves. That has to come from a place of knowing that we are spirit and we are human, and being human includes the whole range of everything human. When we can acknowledge that and say, yeah, I have all that in me and can love myself with it all—that is the true place of integration and peace, and that will begin to be reflected in our world.

A HEALING CRISIS

I believe that the world today is in what I call a "healing crisis," which is very much the same as many of us are going through in our individual lives. A healing crisis in our personal lives is a time when we get really shaken up, usually because of some kind of challenge that comes along in our life, and we have to change in some way. Maybe the loss of a relationship, a financial loss, loss of a job, or a health crisis. When it's happening, you feel like, "Oh, no! Why is this happening? This isn't what I wanted, this isn't what I planned. Why is life doing this to me?" or "What's the matter with me?"

Later, looking back at it, you see that something emerged from that experience that was very important. There was some kind of deepening, learning, growing, or perhaps even a whole change in your direction in life as a result of going through that experience. You can see that in a certain sense you had already outgrown the old form, but it took the crisis to vault you to the new place.

Each one of us individually is in an evolutionary process. That means from the time we're born, we are learning and growing and becoming more and more conscious. Most people don't know that they're in an evolutionary process. Most people don't know that they're on a consciousness journey. But aware of it or not, we're each in such a process that gains momentum as we go along.

So what happens as my consciousness begins to expand? The form that felt so comfortable starts to feel too confining and doesn't work any more. So either the form has to begin to expand and grow along with me, or it starts to crumble. It's as if my energy literally starts pushing outward and the form starts to fall apart and to crumble around me. And that's exactly what happen with the forms in our life: as we grow, the relationships, the job, etc. we're in have to grow too—or they start to fall apart, to die. There is always a time when we have to go through a kind of death. We have to trust that at that moment there's something new already being born inside of us and coming forth, even though we may not see what it is yet.

Humanity as a whole is also in an evolutionary process. It's been going on since the beginning of time. And that evolutionary process is also expanding and gaining momentum and pulling us along with it. We as individuals are pulled along by the momentum of the collective consciousness process, and we're also contributing to it.

Because the consciousness is expanding so fast, the world as a whole is in a healing crisis. The old forms that used to work pretty well—they had their problems but we could live with them—are not working any more and they're crumbling and falling. The governmental systems that we had are not working anymore, and it's kind of scary because nobody knows what else to do. The economic systems that we've had are beginning to fall. The religious institutions we've been living with for at least a couple thousand years or so are beginning to disintegrate as well. Even our relationships, our family systems, the ways we relate to one another, aren't working. We can't do it the old way and we don't know what else to do—we're stumbling around, trying to figure it out.

Because of the crumbling of the old forms, it's easy to feel concerned. And, as I said, it's okay to feel concerned because that's part of the process. But what we also need to do is step back and see it with a bigger perspective and see it as an evolutionary process of death and rebirth.

OWNING THE SHADOW

A healing crisis always requires facing things that we have denied—getting to know parts of ourselves and parts of life that we have been afraid of, and have therefore tried to shove down or get rid of or get over. In crises what we've denied, disowned, and repressed starts coming up in order to be healed, so that we can to begin to embrace it and integrate it into our lives. So if you look at the healing crises in your own life, you find that there's something you had to discover and get to know and make peace with that you weren't at peace with before. Or there may be something that you weren't expressing or bringing through in your life before, which you need to now.

And that's also true in the world today. We have a great big shadow out there—all the things that we have not wanted to look at, all the things we haven't wanted to deal with, and all the things we haven't wanted to face because we were scared and didn't know how to deal with them. We've done the best we could, and a lot of times that's been just to push it aside.

But now it's coming up, the shadow is saying, "No, you can't push me aside anymore, you've got to look at me." All of the problems, all of the pain, all the confusion, all of the powerlessness, and the people in our world that carry those energies. All of that is coming up and we've got to look at it and work with it. We've got to discover how we can create it differently.

OUR CHALLENGE

So how can each one of us most effectively face the challenges in our own personal life, becoming as conscious as we can while also facing the issues in the world at large and have a real effect? The most important part of the answer to that question is through our individual commitment to our own personal growth process. First, by acknowledging that we are here on a journey of consciousness and then making a real commitment to that process in yourself. A commitment to doing whatever you need to do to learn to discover who you are, and express more of who you are. Second, following through on that commitment by being really willing to tune in to your inner guidance, your intuitive sense of what's right for you, and learning to act on that in your life in a very real, practical, moment-by-moment, day-by-day way.

Not only is that the way we can really transform our own lives, it's also the way that we can heal and transform the world we live in. Because there's a level on which we are all one consciousness, deeply connected to the one mass consciousness. That mass consciousness is what's creating the reality in the world today, just like I am creating my personal experience of my reality. So when I grow, when I understand something and become more aware and live in a way that's more in alignment with my own truth, my whole life shifts. I know many of you have had this experience when you recognize that you have a deep pattern that doesn't work too well and you do some healing—you do therapy, perhaps, and you begin to become more aware of a pattern and shift it. As you do, you shift how you feel about yourself, how you look at things and behave, and suddenly life changes. People treat you differently. Doors seem to open where there weren't doors before. So that's how our reality reflects our consciousness in our personal life as we grow.

But what most people aren't sufficiently aware of is the fact that the world—what we're experiencing out there—is also absolutely a reflection of our consciousness. It's a reflection of the mass consciousness and we're all part of that, so therefore it's also a reflection of our own consciousness. What this means is that any step that I take in my life of true healing, of true integration so that I really shift my experience, affects everyone in the world and affects what's happening in the world.

Indeed, every step that we have taken, all the hard work we have put in already into our own process of self-discovery, is what's catalyzing all of the change and chaos in the world right now. It's the very fact that we've been growing as we have that's making everything fall apart. Isn't that lovely? It's true! We need to own that truth and to acknowledge that we have that kind of power, because when it comes to having an effect on the world, most of us feel helpless and powerless. We ask ourselves, Who am I to be able to do anything? Who am I to really make a difference? I am suggesting that it is not so much what you do outwardly that's important, as long as it's coming from a real sense of your inner truth. More important is that you see how you are creating the world and take responsibility for that.

That doesn't mean blaming ourselves. We tend to get "blame" and "responsibility" confused and think, oh, my God, am I to blame for what's happening in the world? It's not that. It's that we have this fantastic feedback mirror we've created in the physical world and we can look into it, see ourselves, and make changes, and then the world changes.

Another thing we can do is to begin to come together in groups. I spend a lot of time in groups, with groups, in front of groups—and I finally realized why that is: because groups are so incredibly powerful. Each one of us as an individual is incredibly powerful, particularly when we are in the process of clearing out whatever blocks and limitations we may presently have. This allows more of the universal creative life-force to flow through us and we're able to create our lives more fully and freely.

Whenever we get together in a relationship with one or more other beings, we intensify that process. That's why our relationships are so wonderful and difficult and challenging, because they always intensify whatever process we're in. And if we work with it, we're able to do that opening and clearing process more quickly and strongly. Just as each one of us is in the process of being able to channel through more of that universal life-force, when we come together in a group we create what I call a "group channel," which brings through more of that power than any of us could do alone.

FOLLOWING INNER GUIDANCE

Ultimately it is up to each one of us. I believe we are here on Earth to integrate and develop all aspects of who we are—spiritual, mental, emotional, and physical—and bring them all together. This means moving beyond the traditional spiritual approach to life. In the past, sages and gurus have followed what I call the path of transcendence, where people are always trying to transcend and rise above what's human, because we see the human state as lesser. We are ready to take another step into what I call the path of transformation, which is where we begin to bring all aspects of who we are together and really learn to enjoy being both body and spirit deeply and fully. Nobody's done that yet.

There's nobody to tell us how to do it because all of the saints and the enlightened masters that we think of as being so spiritually developed are only really developed in the spiritual aspect, in the transcendent plane—there's nobody who's integrated it all and is fully living it in the body on Earth. If there were, we'd all be doing it pretty soon, because we're all part of one consciousness—it's not really possible for anybody to be way out ahead of everybody else.

At this new stage of our evolution that we're entering, there's no authority out there who can tell us, "This is what you must do." We can have teachers and healers and helpers along the way. What we can't do is give our power away to anyone else, because it's time for each of us to tap the deep inner wisdom in ourselves, a deep inner wisdom that is here to guide us through every step of our life. We have a teacher inside of us and that teacher knows what each one of us needs better than anyone else. We hold the power and authority to know what's right for us inside of us. We then must allow ourselves to receive from whatever our inner guidance tells us.

So the most important thing on the path of transformation that we can do is to cultivate the relationship with that inner guidance. When we have that, it will take us step by step through the rest of our lives. It will tell us where we need to go for healing, for learning, for resting, and for nurturing ourselves and all living things.

There are many wonderful resources for beginning to tune into your inner guidance. My book *Living in the Light* is primarily devoted to this topic. There is also a workbook to supplement it, and the book is also available on audiotape (along with other audiotapes *Developing Intuition* and *Contacting Your Inner Guide*, at New World Library, 800-972-6657).

First, remember that when you ask your inner guidance for something—for clarification or direction or support—it doesn't always come right away, and it isn't always immediately apparent. But if on a regular basis you practice going inside and asking, listening, and trusting, and then acting on whatever sense you get of what your inner, deepest truth may be telling you, you start to build a relationship. As that strengthens, you start to get a lot more trust in the process. Like everything else, it takes practice.

Second, be open to help wherever and whenever it comes. You might just find that the next day or a week after asking for guidance, you happen to walk into a bookstore and "just happen" coincidentally to pick up a certain book and read just the paragraph you need to hear. Or you just bump into a friend and they say something to you and—boom!—that's just want you needed to hear right then. Now, you won't necessarily remember that you'd asked inside for that help, but your inner guidance got you into that bookstore or to the street where you bumped into the friend. I've had a lot of people write and tell me that they walked into a bookstore and one of my books fell on their head. I think it's very bizarre—like my books crouch up there on the shelves and just jump on unsuspecting people. Whatever it takes, your inner guidance will make sure you get the message, if you're really asking for it.

Sometimes people say, "I just really can't get in touch with my inner guidance—nothing happens for me." When I meet someone like this, I usually find that the person is expecting some kind of really big event, like God speaking from on high or some profound mystical experience in which he or she sees the rest of their life unfold psychically. Things don't happen very often like that. Once in a while they do, but usually it is a lot more subtle.

Another way to describe inner guidance is to call it "gut feeling." What's your gut feeling about what's true for you? We don't always know. We have a lot of different mixed-up feelings inside of us, so sometimes we're not going to be in touch with them. But just keep trying to really tune into a sense of your gut truth—yes, this feels right, or, no, something doesn't feel right about this. It's that simple. Not some big profound thing about your whole life. It's usually just step by step by step. That's why it's hard, because we want to be in control, we want to know what's going to happen. The process of following your intuitive sense doesn't usually tell you more than about one step at a time. It says, okay, step here. Whoops! Okay, I hope something's going to be there when I get there. But it doesn't tell you to go jumping off buildings because you can fly. You just take the small steps and work with that until you have a sense of being able to trust that relationship in you.

There are many difference voices in us. Trying to discern which is the voice of our true intuitive wisdom, and which is the voice of a part that's afraid or ambivalent does take some practice. You can learn to distinguish the vibration or the specific feeling that your intuitive guidance has, and you can learn to tell the difference between that and the other ones. But just takes practice.

One way to practice is to notice how the guidance comes and then experiment with it: When you act on this, what happens? If you don't act on it, what happens? The important thing to understand is that when you're acting on your deepest sense of truth, you feel more alive; when you don't act on it, you generally feel more dead.

The new millenium promises to be both exciting and tempetuous. The more that you can tune into your intuition as time progresses, the more you will have your own inner compass as to how to proceed when life throws you a curve, and the more you will be the instigator of your own future.

Dawna Markova, Ph.D., is an author, consultant, and organizational mythologist dedicated to helping people think with passion, feel with intelligence, and learn with joy. She is the author of *The Open Mind*, *Art of the Possible*, and *No Enemies Within*, coauthor with Andy Bryner of *An Unused Intelligence* and with Anne Powell of *How Your Child Is Smart* and *Learning Unlimited*, and contributing editor to *Random Acts of Kindness*.

From Rut to River: Co-creating a Possible Future

The O'Hare airport in Chicago is a bridge between There and Here for me. The only way to get home from almost anyplace I go to work is through the neon-arched tunnel between concourses B and C. In my best moments, with only one small rolling bag, I can make it in fifteen minutes without breathing hard. Last March, flying from San Francisco to Vermont, I found myself with only fourteen minutes to make the connection. As I was about to begin my sprint off the inbound plane, I passed a distraught older woman, waiting for an attendant and a wheelchair to take her to the same outbound plane. I reassured her as I raced by, "Don't worry. We Vermonters have to stick together, I'll hold that plane for you." I blurred through the tunnel, arriving at gate C25 dripping, panting, and barely able to speak. The door to the jetway was still open—barely. I tried to explain to the agent about the woman in the wheelchair, but he just looked at the ceiling and shrugged in such a way that I knew arguments were useless. Without saying another word, I rushed down to the end and planted one foot on the edge of the jetway and the other on the plane. The stewardess explained politely through tense, white lips that I would have to get on the plane immediately. The attendant, his hand restless on the jetway controls, explained I would have to get off immediately since he was about to retract it. I just stood there, my legs forming a bridge between what had to be left behind and what I was moving toward. I must have stood frozen in that position for no more than five minutes before the woman in the wheelchair arrived, but it felt remarkably familiar. That posture was an explanation of my whole life.

THRESHOLDS OF THE POSSIBLE

> "This is an age of 'narrative dysfunction.' We have lost track of the story of ourselves, the stories that told us who we are supposed to be and how we are supposed to live."
>
> —C. K. Williams

We are a fulcrum generation. We live, all of us, with one foot in the past and one in the future, in a house built over a fault line. The growing failure of our personal and cultural myths widens a crevice in each one of us. The support beams are giving way, because we have undermined the stories that brought them into proper alignment and bound them together. Those stories told us what it meant to be a woman, a man, a family, a member of a church, an organization, or a nation that would take care of us.

Every fairytale used to begin with the words, "Once upon a time ..." and end with "happily ever after." Before our generation, those stories, and indeed all the cultural myths we lived with, were never questioned. People weren't even aware there were stories. They lived in a world of givens and unquestioned assumptions that mostly directed them. Almost everyone played the game by the same rules—work hard enough and you would progress—and expected the same prize: security. The world was easily divided into Good and Bad, Black Hats and White Hats, Us and Them. We were expected to live in one place, be married to one person, have one job, one parent of each gender, one common destination, and one God. The certainty of misery was definitely preferred to the misery of uncertainty.

These stories were guiding images that required a culture high in continuity and control. In this time of immense flux and chaos, however, people on a large scale are refusing to give their power away to an abstract, be it a company or nation or government, that in the end is only made of human beings. We are coming to accept that no Big Daddy is going to make everything all right, and thus are refusing relationships that involve domination. We are insisting on adult-to-adult interactions. All false boundaries are coming down. We are beginning to recognize that we cannot sustain life if we continue to think in a way that pits ideas against action, actions against feelings, feelings against thinking, and the past against the future.

We who live in the transition time between the twentieth and twenty-first centuries have been largely responsible for the unraveling of the dominator mythology: of power over, of command and control, of walls that separate and ladders that you climb to places you never wanted to go in the first place. As we end this century, we have first been going through disenchantment—trying to hold on to the old stories—by putting new people in the old roles. Disenchantment has decayed into cynicism and finally crumbled into disillusionment—letting go of the old stories altogether.

Disillusionment can feel like dying. What *was* is falling apart in some deep way, as if a shedding were taking place, but what *will be* has not yet emerged. I've been told that as it is about to shed its skin, the eyes of a snake turn milky white, leaving it temporarily blind. The creature then withdraws into the familiar darkness of its burrow, waiting for its new skin. If we are to make it through this time of shedding, we need to be guided by the wisdom of all natural creatures. We need to reclaim our comfort with the unknown.

Disillusionment is not necessarily a bad thing, for imagination begins where development hits a wall. We need to move beyond the fear of our own imagination. We need our imagination to create new images and stories that will unify us. No longer are we inspired by Athena stepping out to do battle with a sword. Instead we must learn, somehow, to step out *without* armor, to participate in transformation through relationship and conversation. We must find transnational ways to define who we are. Our old stories are not big enough for what we have to do now. Through the twilight of the old stories, we, like so many of the characters in them, are lost in a dark wood with only the small flame of our individual hearts to light the way. In losing our feeling of where we belong, we have lost our passion.

Being lost need not be such a terrible thing. It can bring you fully alive, alert to every nuance and shadow as if it were a clue to tell you where you are. It is a time to come to your senses, to notice where you are in acute detail. It is a time to sort out whether the sound you hear is actually a bear or merely your own stomach growling. Being lost can help you become aware of the stories you tell yourself that determine who you think you are, how you connect or don't to the world as a whole, and whether or not you think the universe is a friendly place.

What has never been understood so fully before is that we co-author our future. Life doesn't just happen *to* us: we inhabit a participatory universe, influencing and being influenced on a cellular level by everything that is around us. We know now that we are not simply parts of a machine, and that the greatest gift we can offer is the use of our consciousness to transform our experience. However, we cannot have conversations about co-creating a possible future for the world if we don't each have courageous conversations about how we can re-create our own personal destiny. We need each and every one of us to participate in crafting a trail of stories to guide us collectively to our true home.

THE CRUCIBLE OF THE UNKNOWN

> "You must have a place in your heart, your mind, your house, your day, where you can go and where you do not know what you owe anyone or what anyone owes you."
>
> —Joseph Campbell

This millennium brings us to a time where the most abused and underutilized resource we have available to us is human ingenuity. It is as if we are all born with two arms—our capacity to think in the rational domain and our capacity to imagine and think mythically. But in our linear culture, living with one arm tied behind our backs is considered normal. Most of us have even forgotten that we have thus handicapped ourselves. In order to create a future that we would want to live in, we need to reclaim our imagination as a strategic force from the domination of a media that narcotizes us into conceiving of lives that are too small and fragmented for any of us.

I once visited an eight-year-old girl in her second-grade classroom. The teacher told me that the girl had attention deficit disorder. I knelt down beside her desk as she was staring out the window during a creative writing period. She whispered, "It's just that my imagination keeps getting in the way."

We live in a time when most of us are used to having our imagining done for us. A leadership team in a health care system to which I was consulting complained that it was having difficulty creating a shared vision. When I asked how I could help, the team members explained that I should come up with the vision for them, and then they could react to it. They did not realize that they could not hope to capture the imagination of their organization without recapturing their own.

Current research on learning indicates that we have the capacity to think in many modes—analyzing and organizing, which have been dominant for this century, but also those dormant capacities of relational logic, synthesizing, and mythologizing—which give us the spider-like capacity to weave new stories together from things that historically have had difficulty being held in the same room or same place. The emergence, in the postmodern world, of women who have developed these capacities more fully means that we have more possibility to co-create an all-inclusive mythology of kinship, a synthesis of a multicultural aspiration that is trying to take place through us.

In order to be comfortable in the enormous change and unknown future that presents itself at every corner of the outer world, we must relearn to become comfortable with the inner aspect of ourselves that doesn't know where or who it is. If we are bereft of our relationship with the unknown, we cannot be aware of what stories are trying to be born in us at any given moment. We live on the surface of our lives, losing connection with our miraculous capacity to regenerate ourselves through our imagination.

THE TYRANNY AND GLORY OF THE IMAGINATION

> "Stories are our nearest and dearest way of understanding our lives and finding our way onward."
>
> —Ursula LeGuin

Stories are much more than entertainment. They gather our experience into shapes, in much the same way that a fish tank gives form to the watery reality of a goldfish. Researchers place them at the foundation of memory and learning. Stories provide the meanings that structure our lives, that take the individual moments and place them in a cohesive movement. Whether we tell them publicly to others or murmur them secretly to ourselves, stories fuel the engine of our desire and invoke our actions.

And most of us, like the fish in the water, are not even aware of them. Several years ago I was working with a renowned professor of psychology. Within minutes of entering my office, he lit a carved pipe and began to tell me stories. The conversation went something like this: "Dr. Markova, you must understand that I am not a very creative person. I'm extraordinarily analytic, left-brained, actually…. You, on the other hand, are very imaginative, which I am definitely not. If we are to work on this project together, you're going to have to validate your reasoning in an appropriate manner…."

The facts of this experience were as follows: he came in, shook my hand, sat down, lit his pipe, looked at me, tightened his jaw. I asked him how he knew I was very imaginative. He shrugged, puffed on his pipe and just said he could tell. After much inquiry, his final response was, "You are of Russian ancestry as was my mother. *She* was very creative, so I imagine you are too." When examined from outside the tank, the facts were that his mother and I both had a similar genetic background. Everything else was story. And all of this from a "not very creative" person! Once Dr. Freudenberger became aware of the stories he told himself all the time, he realized how much he was the author of his own existence.

I'd like to invite you to pause for a few moments and discover some of your own personal mythology: Narrate, out loud, the facts of your current reality. For example, you might say, "I'm sitting in a green chair, my legs crossed, reading page 290 of this book." Observe the landscape of your thinking as you speak, as if a part of you were a witness sitting on your shoulder. You'll soon notice the terrain starts to take on a specific shape. For instance, you might notice yourself saying, "I'm sitting in this green chair, reading, and noticing that it's getting late and I'd better make dinner." Imagine the witness asks you, "What story are you telling yourself about that?" Your response, when you pause to notice, might be something like, "I glanced at the clock and told myself that I was lazy sitting here reading for so long, while there were hungry mouths to feed." This brief but potent story reinforces a belief about yourself (lazy if not coerced into action), your purpose (to nurture), and your relationship to the world (as long as you're taking care of the hungry, you belong).

These internal, constantly playing, invisible stories form the strategy of our imagination. They are essential tools of personal identity and community-building since they tell us, individually and collectively, who we are, what our purpose is, and how we connect, or don't, to the whole. As soon as we join the human community, people start shoving stories into us as if they were software disks: "Oh, isn't he cute. He's colicky, isn't he? Probably has a delicate constitution just like his Uncle Sam." Or, "Everyone knows that the human race is basically hostile and aggressive." Like the DNA in our cells, these myths teach us how to be human by shaping and passing on our best and worst qualities.

NOT ALL STORIES ARE CREATED EQUAL

> "When people come to see me, their problem is that they experience life as the same damn thing over and over. If we've been successful, when we're finished with our work together, they perceive it as one damn thing after another."
>
> —Carl Whittaker, M.D.

As with any great force of nature, there is danger and glory in the stories we tell ourselves and each other. Some of these myths rally against understanding, others promote it. Some are toxic and keep our problems festering. Others are tonic, bringing us into healing. Some have the potential to expand possibilities, some to limit them. As in that fish tank, some mythology determines who the good guys are who get to be on the inside, and who the outsiders are. To be in a life of our own definition, we must be able to discover which scenarios we are following and whether they help us grow the forms that offer us the most interesting possibilities.

To do this, we need to differentiate between what I call *rut stories*—the inferences, beliefs, assessments, and assumptions we hold which tranquilize us into passivity, and *river stories*—those that energize us into exploring the current of our lives through all its tributaries. There are four basic categories of rut stories: impossibility ("You can't fight city hall"), invalidation ("I'm just not a sensitive kind of person"), blame ("My family life is shot because the company expects me to work eighty-hour weeks"), and non-accountability ("I'm in accounting. Let HR deal with personnel problems"). Since everything in nature has its balancing counterpart, there are also four categories of river stories: possibility ("I wonder what I could do differently to make this happen?"), validation ("I certainly have learned how to organize my life, I am curious to discover how I could become more aware of people's feelings"), choice ("Even though everyone else works too much, I'm just not going to do it. My family is too important to me"), and accountability ("Even though it's not my job, I know a lot of people in HR. I'll see to it that someone takes care of this problem").

Rut stories tell you. You tell river stories. The easiest way to discern them is to step outside of the tank as often as possible and pay special attention to the inner narratives that leave you feeling numb or zoned out. Since I am habitually addicted to rut stories that blame, one of my favorite practices is to spend one day a week frequently asking myself, as compassionately as possible, "What are you trying to prove?"

A word of warning: a tool can also be a weapon. Do not undertake this practice of awareness unless you are willing to shift your perspective from that of knower to learner. Let's say, for example, that you discover your head is filled with invalidating rut stories about how you really are not very intelligent. If you castigate yourself by telling yourself you *knew* you were a stupid idiot underneath it all, you're just burying one rut story under another, and suffocating any possibility of change. Don't bother going any further. The world has enough suffering.

If, on the other hand, you're willing to engage in this process with curiosity, you might instead write down each story you discover, murmuring to yourself, "Isn't that interesting?" At the very least, you will have added to the mercy in the world, and at the most, you will have taken a significant step in freeing yourself from harmful family and cultural patterns that have limited your growth and giving. The more we all move from rut to river stories, the more we free our imaginations to become partners in creating a possible future.

EVERY FORWARD MOVEMENT IS A STEP ACROSS AN OLD BOUNDARY

> "Identity would seem to be the garment with which one covers the nakedness of the self, in which case, it is best that the garment be loose; a little like the robes of the desert, through which one's nakedness can always be felt, and sometimes, discerned. This trust in one's nakedness is all that gives one the power to change one's robes."
>
> —James Baldwin

Several years ago I was diagnosed with cancer. I discovered the rut stories I heard about the illness were as much an assault from the outside "expertocracy" as the cancer cells were from the inside: "This is your diagnosis. The form of cancer you have is incurable. It will kill you. There's nothing anyone can do." Or "You are responsible for creating your own reality." Each time I sat down to imagine my system healing, those rut stories reinforced the ones I had carried for most of my life: "Who am I to think I could heal from this? No one ever has. I've never been very physical anyway. I'm constitutionally inadequate. If I had expressed my anger, this never would have happened." Be it ever so toxic, there's no place like a rut story. I had been putting myself to bed with them, waking up to them, and playing them as the top-ten tunes on my mental Walkman for most of my life. They were the hand-me-downs and heirlooms of some of my kith and kin. They were killing me. But without them, all I had was my human helplessness and congenital fear of the unknown.

Then two things happened that changed everything. First, I read *Man's Search For Meaning* by psychologist Victor Frankl, written about his experiences while in a concentration camp. In those pages, I learned that no one could take away my personal freedom—the meaning I ascribed to any event that happened to me. If I could learn to be comfortable in the unknown, I could choose which stories I told myself about cancer, what I was and was not capable of doing, and what I was and was not responsible for.

In order to become comfortable in the unknown, I first had to develop awareness of my personal mythology. I began study with Moshe Feldenkrais, the founder of a system of psychophysical re-education. In the first class he had us fold our hands habitually, as we had done all our lives when trying to sit still and be good. Then he asked us to notice *how* we had done that. Were the right fingers in front of the left or the left in front of the right? Next, he asked us to unfold them and reweave our fingers in the opposite, nonhabitual way. We folded and refolded for several minutes, habitual to nonhabitual, while he asked us questions. "Which way feels more comfortable, easier?"

My hands gave me the answer immediately. "Habitually."

"Which way feels safer?"

Again, the answer was obvious. "Habitually."

"Which way are you more aware of the spaces between your fingers, of your bones and the feel of your skin?"

This was interesting. "Nonhabitually."

"And which way are your hands more alive to you?"

I was stunned. "Nonhabitually."

Moshe took us one more step. "Now reconsider which way your hands are safer. Which way could you move more quickly, get out of the way if they were in danger?"

I kept folding and refolding. I couldn't believe it. Obviously, my hands were safer if I was more aware of them, and obviously I was more aware of them if I folded them nonhabitually! But I had spent most of my life finding the easy, comfortable, habitual way, and avoiding what was awkward at any cost, believing somehow that this was making me safe. Instead, it was making me dead.

Living through a crisis in the unknown is awkward. Choosing to discard the stories that make us passively comfortable leaves us vulnerable, helplessly human, but ultimately free to utilize the most undervalued and abused resource available to us—our own imagination.

FROM THE RUT TO THE RIVER

> "Trying fails. Awareness cures."
>
> — Fritz Perls, M.D.

How can we be in conversation with what is hidden in ourselves in such a way that we can be exploring what brings us more alive? How can we create the conditions that maximize the possibility of a ripe future? Actually, transforming a tranquilizing mythology into a energizing one is a natural process. There's no part of creation that does not go through a cycle of growing, falling away, disappearance, and reemergence. Think of a tree. Or the moon. Why should we be the one aspect of life that is exempted from this cycle? Because our old mythology has trained us to think of ourselves as perpetual motion machines, like stair climbers in a gymnasium, our habit when things are slipping away is to believe there is something wrong with us that needs to be fixed. So we run faster and faster, exerting more and more effort, up and up, getting nowhere very quickly.

But what if you thought of yourself like the moon, and had equal faith in what was ready to fade away and what was invisible as you did in what was shining? What if you let go of the known and comfortably habitual ways of thinking about yourself and the world in order to engage with things within that are dormant, in seed form? What if, instead of assuming you were depressed or falling apart, you gave yourself three days a month or three hours a day to allow everything you know about yourself to disappear? Giving yourself this opportunity to be engaged in innocent inquiry with who you are and what you are becoming creates a rich and dark soil for regeneration.

Often, as the rut fills with the current of your present experience, the stories begin to change in and of themselves. This is sometimes called "reframing." Such a story was told by Dr. Milton Erickson, a remarkable being disguised as a clinical hypnotherapist. A young and very innocent woman who had just been married came to see him complaining that her husband was impotent on their wedding night and it must have been because she was unattractive to him. Erickson leaned forward and whispered in the bride's ear, "He was so overwhelmed by your beauty that he froze like a deer in the headlights. Tonight, turn the lights out and murmur sweet nothings in his ear. Give him time to get used to being married to such a stunning woman."

The skill that seems to be the most effective for supporting this transformation is called awareness. In effect, it is a process of widening one's periphery. Scientists know that when we go into a fight or flight response, which is what most rut stories produce in us, we narrow ourselves into "tunnel vision." This affects much more than our vision, however. All of our senses become narrowed. We can only perceive how we are stuck. Think of a day recently when you were "in a crisis." How much of the world around you did you actually notice? Have you ever been in a situation like that, and, for one reason or another, just gone to a beautiful natural setting for a while? Did you discover that as your imaginings fell away, there was a whole world alive and present for you?

You can foster this skill by asking yourself some very wide and wonderfull questions that cannot be answered, such as, "I recognize my work is too small for me. I wonder what I could do so that it would bring me alive?" Or, "I'm just going through the motions with my kids. I wonder what I need to be doing so that I'm actually enjoying them again?"

Then comes the challenging part—do nothing except get very curious and widen your periphery. When we notice what is, without *trying* to change it, fix it, or judge it, we establish a feedback loop with our own experience that enables us to choose the most natural direction in which to change. This is how we learn naturally. It is how a baby learns to walk. It's how you learned the most complex neurological task your system has ever been challenged to accomplish—speech. When, on the other hand, you filter your perceptions through ideas of what is good and bad, right or wrong, it as if you are covering the glass walls of that fish tank with graffiti and, consequently, cannot see clearly. When we try to figure out what went wrong, we overcompensate for our errors and try too hard, producing only more errors the next time around.

Any mind I've ever met hates a void. A very effective way of giving your mind something to fill the ruts with is intriguing it with the data of your current reality. For instance, if you have become aware that you habitually tell yourself the story that you are shy and inarticulate, you might tap your foot every time you notice that ("Isn't that interesting?"), and then widen your periphery by directing your attention to something you see outside that interests you even more—visually: "Those clouds look just like lambs playing tag"; auditorily: "My right foot seems to make a louder sound when it hits the pavement than my left one does"; and kinesthetically: "I can feel my ribs expand and contract as I breathe and my throat seems to be closing. I wonder how I could make it just a bit more closed and then reverse the process and open it?" By intriguing yourself into paying attention to something very simple and very relevant—your own experience—you give your neurological system the chance to learn in the way it has been designed to do most effectively.

A very powerful journal process to help create a bridge of awareness from rut to river is one I call "Who Am I Becoming?" In it, you reflect on the various energies you currently experience in your life. Usually, when someone asks you how you are, you may consider one or two aspects—your physical health, your work, or even your love life. Rarely, do any of us consider the whole spectrum of energies that reflect all of who we are, where we've been, and where we're going. These questions can be a way of perceiving your life as if through a prism, revealing places where rut stories can open into new possibilities of your own design. One by one, in your own rhythm, consider each question:

- In your current life, what are you being a voice for?
- Who or what are you serving?
- What is it too soon for, too late for, and just the right time for?
- What brings beauty into your life now?
- What are you valuing?
- What are you drawn to in others?
- How would you have answered these questions in the past? How would you like to be answering these questions in the future?
- What is currently bringing meaning to your life?
- In what areas of your present reality are you finding security?
- In what areas are you taking risks?
- What aspects of yourself are in hiding or dormant?
- What is trying to be born?

- What are you studying?
- What are you teaching?
- What are you cultivating?
- What is expanding in your life now? What is contracting?
- What would you like to be?
- What is the connective tissue of your life? What used to be? What would you like it to be?
- If your heart could speak right now, what would it whisper to you?
- What are you yearning for, dreaming of?
- What are you standing up for? What would you like to be taking a stand about?
- Who were the authors of the story you have been Living? What kind of story is it—fairytale, mystery, melodrama? If you could co-author this story with anyone, real or imagined, living or dead, who and what would it be?

DEEPER MOMENTS, WIDER HORIZONS

> "Let yourself be silently drawn by the stronger pull of what you really love."
>
> —Rumi

As you shed rut stories, you will find yourself and the world becoming more and more real. You may notice that you no longer feel as if you have to stop the world and hold everyone and everything in it still in order for you to get on and participate. You may start to move along and dance with it. This is the natural flow of the life-force coursing through you. Just as geese have an internal capacity to follow coastlines and the magnetic resonance of the earth to tell them where to go, just as bats can echolocate to find their direction, so you can begin to trust your own inner resources to guide you to new possibilities. These are the tributaries of your own river stories.

You don't have to become an optimist or recite programmed affirmations to find a river story. Become a possibilist. Imagine that which you seek is floating somewhere around you. Every river begins and ends in the ocean. All of your life has been moving toward it. All of evolutionary intelligence is supporting its emergence, because you are unique. Your gift lies in what you love, and the whole human community needs you to bring that gift to it. You will be propelled by that intelligence in the same way as a jellyfish is by the might of the entire ocean.

Your job is to be quiet and alone from time to time, ready to tune into the emergence of a river story. Creating the conditions which allows your river story to emerge entails reestablishing a relationship with your own silence. If you are divorced from this resource, you will have no patience with yourself. You will always judge yourself on the basis of activity rather than presence. But that capacity to be present is what will help you offer yourself to the most interesting possibilities.

The stories that emerge often reveal what I call "the other side of the rug," the history of health and sanity that you have been living all along, but which may have gone unnoticed in a culture so addicted to pathology. You can evoke this in time of need by revivifying times when you successfully met challenges or trusted your own wisdom. For example, if you have dissolved the old story of being shy and inarticulate, you might sit yourself against the trunk of a tall old cedar tree and recall in detailed awareness a time when you found the way to express what had heart and meaning for you. What did you look like? How did you sound? How were you moving? What were the sensations in your body?

There is also an inner resource I call "following in their footsteps." If you cannot access a time when you expressed your authentic truth in a similar situation to the one you are facing, you can imagine how one of the great souls of your life would do it. You might call upon the vivid memory or image of a mentor you respect deeply and notice in great detail how they would look, sound, move, and feel in your circumstance. Similarly, you can also invoke an older, wiser, more authentic, and practiced "you" of five years in the future who has made it. You can then follow, step by step, the path they mark.

EACH OF US CREATES FOR ALL OF US

> "I am convinced that the universe is under the control of a loving purpose and
> that in the struggle for righteousness, [humans] have cosmic companionship.
> Behind the harsh appearance of the world, there are benign powers."
>
> —Martin Luther King, Jr.

All of us have experienced fragmentation that has limited our past and threatens our future. As a result, we have become more convinced of our separation than of our connection. The journey from rut to river increases the porosity of the membranes we believe divide us from each other and the invisible.

As we wonder ourselves forward, we can choose to engage in the kind of inquiry, individually and collectively, that encourages "leaky margins": Who is there that I will not allow myself to learn with? What do I love so much that in the doing of it I find a kind of grace in the world? What are the ways of working and relating that bring me alive? How can I move the pivot of my existence so that I am serving a fine purpose? What is it that if I don't do, I die a little each day? Who are the people and what are the conditions that bring out the best in me ? How do I risk becoming more real and more alive? What will liberate my heart? Questions like these cannot be answered. They become companions that draw you forward, connecting you to your heart. They are allies in the unknown and thresholds to the possible.

We may or may not be able to change the world, but it is within the sphere of influence of every person reading this to choose to create a new personal mythology of active engagement with our present and future. Being between stories, we are leaving behind patterns of thinking that have limited human possibility for generations. We are also at a wonderful beginning, a second innocence, perhaps, where we can use our consciousness to realize the dreams of all those who have nourished, protected, and passed on their life to us.

We are supported, perhaps guided, by an evolutionary intelligence that has carried us from the age of handcrafting through the age of the machine and now—where? The information age? The age of mindcrafting? If we let go of the too-small circles we have drawn around ourselves, if we allow ourselves permeable boundaries, moving from rut to river, we may discover that we are not as alone as we think. We may find we are held and guided by hidden hands.

Author of the bestselling *The Spiral Dance: A Rebirth of the Ancient Religion of the Great Goddess*, **Starhawk** has founded two covens in San Francisco and is a licensed minister of the Covenant of the Goddess. Her other books include *Truth or Dare; The Fifth Sacred Thing*, her vision of a possible future; *Walking to Mercury*, a novel; and her latest, *The Pagan Book of Living and Dying*.

Envisioning the Future

Just about every culture on earth up until modern so-called scientific culture has had the understanding that there are energies that are more subtle than those in the physical realm which are very important in maintaining our health. These energies are part of the structure of life and cannot be ignored. Most cultures have had techniques for shifting and affecting those energies. Witchcraft really is what remains of some of the traditional European knowledge about them.

In this century, we've broken a bit out of our European isolation and encountered other cultures. In the '60s there was much fascination with India and the East. Then in the '70s, when China opened up, people began to be interested again in Chinese medicine. It was as if people were saying, Oh, there's a whole other world here, people who think differently about these things, and they might have something to teach us. We have also become more fascinated with indigenous cultures. I think part of it is a wish for escape from a culture that doesn't feed us and part of it is a genuine realization that unless we get a lot smarter and learn from people who haven't lost their connection with the earth, we're not going to make it.

"Witchcraft" is the old spiritual tradition rooted in the goddess, who is the living Earth. It's based on the understanding that the Earth is a living being that we name sacred. For me, this is the vison and value system we need if we're going to be able to get to the new millennium without throwing the life-support systems of the planet completely out of existence.

Witchcraft can help at this time because it connects us to the sacredness in daily life. When you have a spiritual tradition that names the Earth and nature as sacred; when you celebrate that in ritual; when you make your spiritual practice center on learning about nature and how to live in balance; when you take that into your daily life so it's not just an abstraction or a meditation, but gets down to things like composting your garbage or making sure you turn the lights off when you're not in the room, naming those as spiritual acts—then you begin to develop the kind of integration and the kind of understanding we really need to shift the way we live in this world.

One of the problems with the way we live in this world is that for most people environmental issues, issues of the Earth, aren't very real. They seem to be removed from life, very abstract—unless you actually live in the country or you're living close to nature as a farmer, for instance. It seems as if environmental issues are much less important than day-to-day stuff, like paying the rent, making a profit for your corporation. But of course the reality is that we can't pay the rent and we can't make a profit and we can't survive unless we actually live in harmony with the natural systems that sustain our lives no less now than they did thousands of years ago. It's just that now we're a bit more removed from the process, most of us. Witchcraft helps make those connections less abstract so that we can begin to return into balance with nature.

Witchcraft teaches that everything in nature is cyclical and that opposites are in balance. In the natural world you have opposites, like day and night, but they're not in opposition; they're complements to each other. They're part of one whole, and you have to have both. One isn't "good" and the other "evil." The more that we can start to look at the world in this way again, the more integrated we can be.

This principle operates throughout all of life. Destructive energies are always present, as well as creative, nurturing, life-sustaining energies. However, they are out of balance in the world. Aggression is a human potential and it's not necessarily a negative one. Without a certain amount of aggression, we wouldn't survive—we wouldn't get out there and do new things; we wouldn't create new possibilities; we wouldn't explore. And certainly destruction is part of nature. There's no life without decay. As soon as you start gardening, you realize that everything comes from rot—you've got to have it or you don't have any fertility. But rot is very different from war. War is a certain kind of organizing and valuing of that aggression and those destructive energies in a way that gets very out of balance.

One of the things I ended up thinking in my book *Truth or Dare* is that in some ways the destructive power of war isn't the worst of it—it's the organization of society around war so it becomes a model for every other structure in society. That's when we get in real trouble.

WORKING MAGIC FOR THE FUTURE

In order to get from where we are to a future in which we are more in harmony with nature, we need to work magic. We work magic by creating a vision and then directing energy towards it. We may not know how it's all going to work out, but if we hold the end in mind and begin the motion, then we set the magic in place. We have to figure out what our vision is and work towards it. And we have to resist as much as we can the enormous forces of destruction that are going on around us. We all must be taking both positive, forward-moving action, and at the same time actions that are in resistance to the destruction around us.

In my own life, for example, I've recently been very involved in the Headwaters action, a grass-roots movement to save an old-growth redwood forest in Northern California. Many of us from our community here in the Bay Area have been involved with ongoing actions and support these. My partner and I are also looking at our own land and saying, Well, okay, we have a forest. What do we need to do to learn to really learn how to tend this forest? Can we do sustainable harvesting here? What would that look like? How do we learn what we need to learn to create an alternative to commercial logging? I'm also involved with permaculture, which is a movement around sustainable agriculture and culture. That's again a way of looking at how to create an integrated system where we can live on the land that we've got in a way that creates more diversity and more life, and helps to heal the land instead of destroying it.

It's not necessary that we all have exactly the same vision. How boring, in fact, if we all had the same vision! What we want is not one model of the future but a mosaic of different adaptations to different places and circumstances. In *The Fifth Sacred Thing,* that vision is very much centered in the city, in San Francisco; it's a vision where people have lots of different religions, cultures, and subcultures but they can all come together and work together. It starts with a woman climbing a hill for a ritual and visiting all the different shrines of all these different religions and cultures that are up on the sacred mountain. To me, that symbolizes what I'd like to see. Culture is like a sacred mountain that's big enough for many, many different approaches to spirit.

In the future I envision in *The Fifth Sacred Thing*, everybody speaks two or three different languages and makes a concerted effort to preserve the languages spoken by their ancestors—and in the diverse neighborhoods—because they've come to realize that each language enriches you, enriches the possibility of what you can see and what you can experience. People live in the city, but a city that's become very integrated with the natural world: they grow a lot of their own food, they've torn up the streets and planted gardens, and brought the streams up from the sewers and have them running free again. So there isn't a dichotomy between city life and country life. People can live in the city and learn the lessons from nature that right now you have to be in the country to learn.

When I was writing this book, I was able to jump over the question of how we get from here to there, because of course that's the hardest one. Because I think there isn't one simple way to get from here to there.

However, there are several things we can begin to work on. What I've found in my own life in the last couple years is that most of the groups I've been working with have grown to a point where we actually have to figure out how to organize on a different level than before. For many of us who have been alternative all of our lives, it's a leap—a fearful leap—to do things that feel like we are becoming an institution. And yet, to quote my brother Mark Simos, who does organizational development, if people with alternative values don't figure out how to organize on a larger scale, then it means that the only large-scale organizations are going to be the ones that reflect the status quo.

This organizational drive is not happening just to us, but to a lot of different groups. And there are a lot more of us out there than we realize.

Researcher Paul Ray, in a ten-year analysis of the American population, discovered that one-quarter of the population is composed of what he called Cultural Creatives, people with a cohesive worldview that encompasses environmentalism, feminism, peace, social justice, and spiritual searching. We're larger than we realize and at some point we've got to look at this question—all of us who've gotten so good at empowerment—How do we turn that into actual political power? Because if we are 24 percent of the population, we should be able to make some big changes. Part of the problem is that the major media and the mainstream institutions are very much devoted to maintaining a different worldview and marginalizing this group (although that certainly hasn't stopped it from growing).

One of the keys to being able to organize in a way that's participatory, especially across time, space, and distance, is communication. We have to really start to understand that communication itself is a sacred act. When you send out an e-mail at three o'clock in the morning because you're annoyed and you just shoot off your mouth at somebody in your organization—that has a kind of destructiveness that goes beyond what it means when you have a fight with a friend and say something that you want to take back later. When you say, "I will communicate this to so-and-so" and you don't, when you don't call people back or don't answer your mail—that has an impact. When you're working in a small group and mostly meeting face-to-face, you can get away with sloppy communication. But the larger the organization becomes, the more disciplined you have to be. Think of it as part of your personal spiritual practice to communicate clearly.

We also need to learn to deal with interpersonal problems in a new way. I used to believe that if there was a problem in a group, it was the group's problem and the group had to deal with it. Now I believe that if two people in a group have a problem, it's best if the two parties involved go outside and settle it—don't take up everybody else's time. The more people who get involved in any conflict, the less it will be easily resolved. The dynamics become more complicated, and there's the added factors of losing face and humiliation. This is an increasing issue. It used to be that you have to be in the same room or talk on the telephone to get everyone involved in your problem. But with e-mail, you can send out one message and potentially get hundreds of people involved in your upset—unless those hundreds of people are smart enough to say, "No, thank you." But I think people are getting a bit smarter about that.

We also have to have a new relationship to the whole. I've been thinking lately about how many times people say things like, "I have to take care of myself," or "I have to watch my energy," or "I can't take on too much," or "I don't want to be codependent," and how little people talk about responsibility or use that sort of nasty, pre-New Age word, "duty." Maybe we need to revise that a little bit and say, "We do all have to take care of ourselves, but what's our responsibility to society?" We all want to guard ourselves and take care of our energies, but for me, the most life-changing moments in my life come in those times when I haven't focused on myself, when I've said instead, "This is so important I'm going to push myself to the absolute limit and see what happens." We behave as if we were all wracked with guilt that we have to free ourselves from, when the reality is that most of us don't have that much terrible guilt to begin with. We risk becoming very self-indulgent.

Perhaps the first thing we can do to get over our self-indulgence and connect to a strong vision of the future is for each of us to sit down and ask ourselves, What is sacred to me? What is most important? What do I most deeply value? And when you answer that for yourself, ask, Where are my life energies going? Are they going toward what's sacred to me, or are they going somewhere else? Am I working for somebody else's ends and goals, or am I really leaning towards what I most believe in? And if not, then, What do I need to do? How do I change? How can I do that and still survive?

We need to be talking to young people, too, about these issues instead of saying, "You've got to get a job, you've got to be secure, you've got to do this, you've got to do that." Why aren't we asking instead, "What's most important to you in life? Do that. If I can, I'll get behind you and support you." If we all operated from those values more, we would be helping create a positive future in everything we do.

In *Truth or Dare*, I included what I call The Next Step Meditation, which is designed to help readers tap into a strong vision of the future. I hope it works for you too. Remember, what matters is that you envision it strongly and work toward it diligently—that way the magic can happen.

NEXT STEP MEDITATION

Breathe deep, and follow your breath down to your belly, the belly of Spider Woman. Feel the place within you where she spins the thread of your life. Around you stretch all the roads of possibility, like a great web with you at the center. Look around; see which one shines for you. Which one is the future you want to create?

Take a deep breath; draw power from the earth, and jump! Let yourself float out on the breeze, trailing your thread, jumping far, far into the future, until you land in the world you want to create.

Now look down at your feet. Who are you? Where are you?

Turn and look to the East, the South, the West, the North. Breathe deep and notice what you hear and feel and sense and smell and see.

Now look to the center. What is there for you?

How do you live in this world? Who do you live with? How do you get your food?

Who do you love? How do you raise the children? What is your work? What are your rituals and celebrations?

What knowledge do you have in this world that you need at home? What message, what wisdom, do you have for yourself?

Now say good-bye to this world. Say good-bye and thanks to everyone you've met. Thank the East, the South, the West, the North, the Center. Thank yourself.

Now breathe deep, and begin to walk back along the path. Notice what you feel and hear and sense as time rolls by. Feel the ground beneath your feet and the air on your skin, and continue, until you reach a point halfway to the future.

Now look down at your feet. Who are you? Where are you?

Turn and look to the East, the South, the West, the North. Breathe deep and notice what you hear and feel and sense and smell and see.

Now look to the center. What is there for you?

How do you live in this world? Who do you live with? How do you get your food?

Who do you love? How do you raise the children? What is your work? What are your rituals and celebrations?

What knowledge do you have in this world that you need at home? What message, what wisdom, do you have for yourself?

Now say good-bye to this world. Say good-bye and thanks to everyone you've met. Thank the East, the South, the West, the North. Thank yourself.

Now breathe deep, and begin to walk back along the path. Notice what you feel and hear and sense as time rolls by. Feel the ground beneath your feet and the air on your skin, and continue, until you reach a point that is the very first step into the future you want to create.

Breathe deep, and know what that step is for you. How will you take it? What will you do? What will you change?

Breathe deep again, and step back into the center. You are in the center of the web. Look around you. See the roads, as they stretch in so many directions, beckoning and foreboding, shining and dim. Know that the road you have taken is one future, one possibility. You can choose it, or you can make another choice.

Thank the Spider, who spins time. Breathe deep, and follow your breath up, up from your belly, up to the place where She spins your cord of life, up into the body that remains here in this room. Breathe deep, and bring back with you your memory of the future, as you come fully back, and become fully awake.

Take time to discuss your visions and your next steps. Share feelings and thoughts with others around you. We can bring the future into being.

Rama Vernon is the founder of Women of Vision and Action and President of the Center for International Dialogue, formerly known as the Center for Soviet-American Dialogue. She developed and cultivated a broad range of organizational contacts in the former U.S.S.R. Her success led to expanding the work in the Middle East, Ethiopia, Central America, Africa, and the United States. Ms. Vernon is a writer, educator, and lecturer in Asian philosophy and East-West psychology, which has inspired her unique approach to conflict resolution. She has codesigned a Conflict Resolution and Peace Team Training program, and is the recipient of the Inside Edge Foundation's World Peace Award, the Evart T. Loomis World Peace Award, as well as outstanding achievement awards from South America, India, and the former U.S.S.R.

Manifesting the Vision

Vision is! It is timeless and eternal. We do not create vision, we simply link into a piece of the Universal Vision that already exists as it filters through our own perception. Sometimes we can see the immediate sequence of steps needed to map a plan of action to bring vision into form. Other times, we can only see one step at a time. How do we allow vision to flow through us? How do we manifest it?

Timing is a most important factor in vision manifestation. If we force it or try to fit it into our mental constructs or framework of understandings of "time," we will grow frustrated and fearful if our timelines are not met by the Universal timeframe. If, due to our fears, we rush a vision into "being" before its full gestation period, we rush the embryonic beginnings with high forceps or cesarean delivery. If, instead, we act as patient midwives bringing the fully developed infant into the world after it is complete on the subtle and unseen plane of existence, the vision will fulfill itself far beyond anything our human minds can conceive of. The final result will be transformative for nearly all involved.

This is the difference between a great project and a good product. Both take the same energy output. If we have faith and ride the waves of "universal rhythm," attuning ourselves to the rings of energy that are always flowing within, around and through us, we are carried by the tide of vision as it carries itself into its full manifestation. We are only the vehicle—not the doer.

I have observed many times, with each expanding project, that I do not hold the vision, but the vision seems to hold me. Manifestation requires faith, trust, surrender to a power higher than oneself. As we walk, jump, and sometimes crawl through the intiatory rings of fire in the completion of our "mission," it leads to ever-expanding vistas of understanding and compassion for others.

What is it that keeps us in the "dream" phase, talking about what we are planning to do and yet never getting it done? Where does the plethora of excuses for not stepping out of our comfort zones come from? Rather than complaining about all the things we could have done and ending our lives with remorse and lack of fulfillment, we can trust the process, for we are led from one point to the next, until one day we awaken and realize we are fulfilling our life's purpose.

It is not easy to embark upon the path of bringing vision into action. Sometimes the path is lighted and the way is effortless; other times it asks us to step out in faith, one foot in front of the other with only our own inner light to guide us. "Thank God," I have thought many times, that I was only given one step at a time. If I could have seen where my first steps would have lead, the enormity would have overwhelmed me, causing a retreat into a safe, secure, and comfortable environment. As we fulfill our destiny through the guidance given us at each juncture, windows of opportunity begin to open, leading to doorways and eventually to gateways that clear our path regardless of how difficult our undertakings may seem. As we clarify our vision, we gain greater power in our ability to "hold the vision." As we do this vigilantly, we will see the miraculous play of momentum swirling around us as the Universal energy helps us bring Vision into form. The appropriate people, serendipitous chance meetings and events begin to happen, confirming that we are moving in the "right" direction at the "right" time.

Another area that restricts us from fulfilling the Vision is allowing ourselves to be limited either consciously or subconsciously by our perceived constraints. When this happens, we give from an empty heart, creating fatigue. We don't have to learn to say "No" to preserve our energies if we can let go of our perceptions of limitation and shift our awareness to each moment as if we were seeing and doing things for the first time with joy. If we can do this, we will always have enough energy for whatever is required. After all, our hands are the extension of our hearts.

When others do not feel fulfilled in their own lives, it may be difficult for them to watch others fulfill theirs. This may manifest through envy, which leads to criticism, expressed doubts, and negativity, which is one way to hold someone else back if even in thinker's own mind. It is all right—understand the source of pain, see where this is coming from in the other person, bless them, and go on. It is such a temptation to want to criticize the one who criticizes or to become intolerant of the intolerance of others. Be compassionate without letting others' self-imposed limitations limit you. As we continue, regardless of the obstacles, our "vision quest" leads to ever-growing contentment, unshakable peace, and a rich sense of love and fulfillment that flows like warm lava through the cells of the heart, spreading out to every cell of our being.

Each time we fulfill the "tasks" that cross our path, it becomes easier and easier to activate the required momentum for each wave of manifestation. If we take on a project and do not follow through on our particular task, then the next one takes even more effort to formulate and "lift" off the ground. There is sometimes a rhythm of ebb and flow. If we can keep a sense of "non-doing" or inaction within each of our actions, we will not grow tired or feel the need to withdraw to recuperate. As we combine a sense of ease, of stillness within our activity, we will feel renewed each hour.

The following guidelines have helped me considerably over the years in manifesting vision:

1. Do not identify with your vision or think that *you* are creating it. We are the vehicle through which Vision manifests. I have found over the years that it is important not to identify or "lose" myself in the vision. Especially remember to hold the vision each day until it holds you.

2. Carry through always—even if it seems impossible, even if on a smaller scale than originally planned. This creates momentum for your next action.

3. Do not let money, or the lack of it, influence the fulfillment of your dreams. Money is a scapegoat for fear. Be creative and resourceful. The success

of a project does not depend on funding alone. Money is one resource, but people are another. When there is shared vision, when others join you, there is a collective commitment that is a powerful manifestor. When you begin regardless of funds, if it is an idea that is meant to be, the forces of the Universe will array to help bring forth the Vision into being.

4. When you reach an impasse, pull back ... wait ... meditate, pray for guidance and answers. Ask yourself: Is this *my* work or the work of another? The *Bhagavad Gita*, the sixth Canto of the *Mahabharata*, the great epic of India, says, "One's own work done imperfectly is far better than another's done perfectly." Each time a new idea filters into your consciousness, test the waters to see if it is "your" work.

5. Watch for the universal signs—events, people, a word, a sentence, a book—that confirms and reaffirms your vision and even helps move it toward eventual manifestation. People may suddenly appear around the idea and help lift the vision onto the crest of a wave that has its own momentum. Have the courage to ride it instead of wanting to control it. Our need to control usually comes from our fear of "the unknown." We do not know where it will "take us." This is why so many people today and throughout history have not yet fulfilled their dreams.

Fulfilling Vision, I have found is like surfing. First, we must have the courage to swim out beyond the breakers, leaving the solid, secure beach with all that is familiar behind. On a calm day, we may wait and wait for a big enough wave to arise. We wait for our vision, we grow impatient when it does not appear. Finally a large wave arises, an inspiration, a thought. To catch the wave, we must paddle very fast to align our rhythm with the rhythm of the wave. Once we catch the wave, then we must be discriminating and vigilant in knowing when to stop paddling and surrender effort to let the grace and power of the wave carry us to shore. If we let go in time, we have only to maintain our balance as we ride the crest of the wave.

Our vision begins when the mind is momentarily free of everyday thoughts, worry, fear, expectations, criticisms, etc. When the moments grow between each thought, Vision begins to appear. We may receive it as an idea, an impression, an inspiration. It arises from the field of collective thinking, a gene pool where ideas originate and perhaps even return. Sort through the imprints, watching them like clouds passing through the sky of your mind. Write down a few. If these ideas are retentive and keep persisting, frolic with them, brainstorm with yourself, entertain their possibilities and potentials. Do not speak about them yet. Sharing your vision prematurely with others can create discouragement and in turn dissipation before passion has had a chance to come to maturity.

If after a time, the idea(s) keep forming, gaining greater clarity, excitement, and momentum within you, try them out on a trusted and supportive friend, a confidant. Watch and observe reactions and then wait and watch for a "sign"—a call, a letter, a conversation, a person who crosses your path confirming the pulse and clarity of your vision. Watch for the signs that carry messages parallel or in alignment to "your" idea(s) and see if you feel deep within that this is your piece of the Universal imprint. Then hold the vision with clarity and purpose, asking your own inner guidance to reveal why you are being called to bring it forth. What is its purpose in service to humanity? When the time is right, you will be shown the first steps if not more. Have the courage to trust the inspiration pouring or even trickling through at this time.

Take the first steps toward manifestation. Succeeding steps will be shown progressively—not always at once. Sometimes a veil will lift, revealing the future in its entirety. When this happens you will feel a deep sense of joy, gratitude, and overwhelming love. There is no fear, even though we may be shown how our path grows increasingly steep and narrow, with less margin for error and fewer cul de sacs for momentary detours from our mission. These are the moments of clarity that carry us through the times when the veil once more drops and only darkness lies on the path ahead. We commit our feet to the path in these moments where everything seems open and become as clear as a cloudless blue sky. When the veil drops, covering the future once more, it may momentarily feel like "the dark night of the soul," as we begin the process of the next phase of our own inner evolution in the service of humanity.

Serving the global vision through our personal vision may change thousands if not millions of lives, and in turn change our world. However, it serves nothing if we ourselves are not transformed in the process with a growing sense of fulfillment rather than an empty feeling of resentment of having given too much. The importance of the work is not so much in changing our world, but in transforming ourselves in the process.

Fulfillment of vision is an inner process that teaches greater love, compassion, and caring for all life's species, if we can meet the labyrinth of challenges along the way with joy and a heart lightened by our own inner faith. You are not alone, even though there will be times it will feel as if you are. These are the times that strengthen our fortitude, faith, and commitment. There is a "higher" power guiding us even in moments of greatest distress. These are the blessings given to us to smooth our sharp edges and sensitize our conscience to feel another as ourself. Instead of armoring and layering ourselves with defenses because of past hurts, we can open ourselves even more and experience a renewed sense of joy and fulfillment never dreamed possible.

It is up to each of us. As we move into the twenty-first century let us align with one another to bring our highest vision into manifestation. We can make personal and collective dreams a living reality. Let us work together. We are the architects of our own destiny.

Sylvia Boorstein is a cofounding teacher at Spirit Rock Meditation Center in Woodacre, California, and a senior teacher at the Insight Meditation Society in Barre, Massachusetts. She is the author of *It's Easier Than You Think: The Buddhist Way to Happiness; Don't Just Do Something, Sit There;* and *That's Funny You Don't Look Buddhist: On Being a Faithful Jew and a Passionate Buddhist.*

About Practice, Clear Seeing, and Keeping Faith

I saw a cartoon recently in which the father of a desert clan traveling astride their camels is chiding his children (riding behind him on baby camels) saying, "Stop asking 'Are we there yet?' We're *nomads*, for crying out loud." I am a Jew and I teach the mindfulness practice that the Buddha taught, and more and more these days I hear myself talking about faith in (and for) the journey rather than imagined destinations. What I am most sure of about spiritual practice is that it isn't about arriving somewhere new, or learning something different. I trust that it is about discovering the deep pleasure, part of our inheritance as humans, of feeling loved and of expressing compassion. And I trust our capacity to calm down and forgive ourselves and everyone else for being who they are and life itself for being whatever it is. Discovering is hard and remembering is sometimes hard. We are, after all, mammals with self-preservation nervous systems and memory likely encoded in our genes. We startle easily and, confused by fear, we perpetuate pain. But we also have elaborate emotional systems and reflexive, self-conscious potential. We tell stories, write poetry, make music, love with partiality, and so suffer broken-heartedness. We could be kinder.

Mindfulness practice—the balanced, alert awareness of the truth of the present, always-changing moment—finds it expression in kindness. When we are confused by lusts, or anger, or fatigue, we are self-serving. When we are relaxed and at ease we are kind. We are kind, not because it's *nice* or *proper* or *commendable*, but because it's the natural compassionate response to understanding how difficult life is for everyone regardless of the external circumstances of particular lives. Kindness is natural, but it is not easy. We lapse into self-serving, and/or we lose confidence in our ability to serve. I think about practice as being the *balance* that keeps us in our camel saddles so that we survive the trip. Since the trip is all of life, practice never ends.

The biggest challenge to equanimity is discomfort. When unpleasant feelings fill the mind, the mind grumbles. It grumbles at anything in its path. It continues to grumble even after it knows better. I learned that lesson swimming in Jerusalem.

The pool where I swim in Sonoma County, California, is very orderly. People swim back and forth; they know about lane lines and about swimming laps. When I arrive to swim, I can insinuate myself easily into any one of those lanes. I pick out a line of swimmers that seems to be moving at my speed and get in. Then we all swim in long circles, forward and back. Everyone knows the convention, and everyone respects it.

Whenever I visit Jerusalem, I swim at the YMCA. The scene is familiar now, but I remember the surprise I felt on my first visit when I found the pool full of very large women in shower caps, zigging and zagging in all different directions. I recall getting in gingerly and attempting to swim back and forth. Almost immediately I ran into somebody. She got mad. I apologized, but I didn't speak Hebrew very well. She called the attention of the lifeguard, pointing me out to him with angry gestures. I felt humiliated. I decided I would swim with my face out of the water so I could see where I was going and avoid hitting people. But even when people saw me coming, they didn't move. They had conversations in the middle of the pool!

For several weeks I swam daily, but I swam grimly, churning up irritable thoughts like, "They should put in lane lines," "They should give protocol instructions," "If these women want to talk they should get out of the pool." I swam back and forth fueled by righteous indignation. It wasn't pleasant. I wasn't happy.

One day after swimming, while changing in the dressing room, I relaxed my internal diatribe long enough to listen to the women talking to each other. They spoke a combination of Russian, Yiddish, and a little Hebrew—they were recent Russian immigrants. I looked at their faces and bodies—older, more tired, more worn out than mine. Lots of varicose veins. They had lived through fifty years of the Soviet regime and through the war before that. I suddenly thought, "I am in a shower room full of naked Jewish women, and we are *safe.*" I was very happy that they were alive and well and swimming in the pool at the Y and that I was there with them.

I was also very happy and *relieved* by my change of heart. "Whew," I thought, "now I'll be all finished with my irritable thoughts about these women, and I'll be able to swim peacefully in the pool with them." I told my husband my revelation. "Now I have my values straight," I said. "I love these women. They can swim however they want."

The next time I swam, the women zigged and zagged, and the irritable thoughts came back. When present circumstances are disappointing, aversion arises. That's just the way it is. We don't get it together once and for all. We just keep practicing.

I am somewhat reassured these days to discover that (at least sometimes) my periods of confusion are brief. I take heart in thinking that my practice must be working. I had a fatigue-inspired loss of faith attack yesterday. I finished teaching a seventeen-day mindfulness meditation retreat and drove away feeling—as I often do after long retreats—emotionally drained. Wobbly. The retreatants had left feeling—as they often do—buoyant, encouraged, grateful. They'd had seventeen days of confronting the truths of their lives, grieving their losses, recognizing that life is always disappointing as long as we are wanting something (and we are mostly always wanting something), and they'd survived. More than that, they'd forgiven themselves *and* their lives. Most people had left feeling hopeful, even inspired. They were ahead of me. I was tired, overwhelmed with the intensity of everyone's struggle, stunned by the mind's infinite capacity to create suffering. I drove through heavy rain thinking, "The Buddha was right. Endless rounds of suffering. The mind in constant karma-fed combat tying itself in gratuitous knots! Why do we bother?"

Had conditions been different, I might have recognized, "This is Doubt. I'm tired. My attention is slippery. This will pass." But I didn't. The radio newscaster confirmed my despair and dismaying thoughts by announcing that meteorologists are suggesting that El Niño, the unusually warm sea current producing this year's extra-heavy rains and floods, is probably caused by the hole in the ozone layer that we humans have created with our unwitting overuse of hydrocarbon fuel.

"Once again," I thought, "greed has led to suffering. Greed that we didn't even *know* would lead to suffering. And all the *worse* that we were ignorant," I rumbled on, "because we are *always* ignorant. No one *purposely* wants to make a mess of things. Suffering is limitless." I drove into the parking lot of the All Saints Lutheran Church of Novato two minutes before the scheduled start of the winter recital of Miss Bonnie Rassmussen's Suzuki violin students, in which Leah Boorstein, daughter of my son Peter and his wife Patricia Fernandez, was to begin the program with "Twinkle, Twinkle Little Star" and "Joy to the World."

Leah is beautiful. She has Peter's oval face and almond-shaped eyes and Trish's caramel Latina coloring. Each of her two dozen long braids was tied at the end with a jingle bell, and she wore her red iridescent Dorothy-in-Oz shoes. *All* the young violinists were washed and braided and combed and were solemn and serious as they played, one after another, more or less in tune, as their parents looked pleased. Ten novice musicians. Ten sets of family. Warm lighting. An altar decorated with evergreen branches and a church that smelled like Christmas. A table with Gingerbread Bear cookies against the back wall for the post-recital party. I felt my mind relax and balance itself in appreciation.

"Human beings are amazing," I thought. "Here we are, with minds and bodies and relationships which, notwithstanding constant maintenance, will decay and die, and still we braid hair, and practice violins, and decorate churches and bake cookies."

"But wait a minute," my suffering-awareness voice insisted, trying to tighten its grasp on my mind, "there is *so much pain.* Here people are making music, but so many others are making war. These people are warm and clean and well-fed, but so many others live in crushing poverty produced and maintained by the force of greed."

"True—and open to change," said my sympathetic joy voice, delighted enough by Peter and Trish's pleasure and everyone else's pleasure to have energy to wish that all beings be warm and washed and well-fed. And to feel inspired to work to end suffering. Mindfulness *is* about seeing suffering clearly, but also about seeing *everything* clearly, including human tenderness and sentiment and compassion. Suffering *is* limitless and so too, I trust, is our capacity to respond.

I am consoled, and inspired, when I discover that my confusions are briefer. I think about cellist Pablo Casals, at age eighty-five, practicing for three hours every day. Responding to his students' questions about *why* (at his age) and why so *diligently* (given his proficiency), he is reported to have said, "I think I am making progress." I think I am too. I think we all are.

Miss Bonnie's students each performed individually and then ended with an ensemble rendition of "O Come All Ye Faithful." Indeed. Perhaps what we most need to do when we, any of us, see clearly the possibility of living with kindness and compassion in spite of (*and* because of) the great challenges of life, is to deputize each other to remind us of what we know when our own strength and vision fail. Let's be keepers of each *other's* faith.

Sobonfu Somé was born and raised in the traditional context of her tribe in Burkina Faso, West Africa. She teaches the wisdom of the Dagara, her people, in the United States, Canada, and in Europe. She is the author of *The Spirit of Intimacy: Ancient Teachings in the Ways of Relationships.*

Is There Hope for a Better Future?

M ost people know what is wrong in the world. But in order for things to change, you have to consciously take in the energy around you and try to see what exactly it is that has been wrong and begin to take steps toward changing it. Instead, people pretend that all is well and continue as if nothing ever happened. In that state of denial, people continue to hope that things are going to get better without them actually doing a thing.

Change can never take place if we don't get out of our comfort zones and our old patterns. Change requires that we move out of whatever place we are in and let what is obsolete in us die in order for rebirth to take place. We have to learn to stretch ourselves beyond our limited prospective and to look at our definition of truth with a brand-new eye. Truth, as most of us understand it, is often too harsh for us to take in, and so we cultivate a great deal of denial and hypocrisy around us and we continue to live our life in a zombie manner. Of course there are those of us who have reach a dead end with denial and are now having to deal with these problems and can't seem to stop. The crucial question is: Can one survive the pain, the feeling of being overwhelmed, burdened, and surrounded by cruelty, and actually take steps in a direction that will bring about healing? Having been clobbered for so long by these problems, we often think that somewhere there is a quick-fix remedy that's going to wipe from the world every form of ill so we can be at peace. The quick-fix mindset wants you to become a hero and tackle the problem in military, take-over fashion. That way, everybody can continue about their way without getting involved. But if we stop for one second and remind ourselves that things did not simply happen overnight but took a long time to get to the place they are at now, we will see that the quick solution is not an option.

However, if we can begin to look at ourselves as the eyes and voices of the Ancestors, we will see ourselves as the people who have been picked not only to do the garbage-cleaning job but also to start the healing work. One that requires our whole being present and able to take things in. This is not a place from which we can jump to quick conclusions, but one that allows our wisdom to come through as we inhale and feel the anatomy of the problem. Only then we will be able to change our relationship to the problems and to one another. And having the blessing of the Ancestors, we can begin to tackle the problem knowing we are not alone and that each one of us holds a piece of the puzzle that when put together gives us the big picture. For change does not always come loaded in a truck; it might be in the form of a baby step—it is the knowing that someone else is out there working with us that makes the difference.

We must have hope. Not the passive hope of "Oh, I just hope things will get better." But a real sense of hope that gives us the strength to do our small part. One of the reasons we lose track of the big picture is that we don't feel the work that's happening around the world. We don't feel the presence of spirit and the Ancestors. It's like trying to dig through a mountain. If you don't know that there are other people on the other side doing the same thing, it seems like what you're doing is meaningless and hopeless. But our commitment to doing the work and the deep sense of working with other and the Ancestors will keep us going, because true change will not happen from outside in, but from inward to outward.

RECONNECTION TO THE ANCESTORS

I have peacefulness because I know absolutely that the Ancestors are here and they are supporting what I am doing. Even though what I am doing might look like a very tiny grain of sand in the whole pile, knowing that I am connected to the Ancestors makes me feel like each time I stay true to my purpose and do my share of the work, I pick up more grains of sand. Someday I hope to fill a cup.

People often feel hopeless because there are disconnected from the Ancestors, and as long as we stay disconnected from the Ancestors, as long as we ignore them, things will be harder for us. We will never be able to see the big picture in such a way that it makes us feel, "Yes, we can do this." The Ancestors have the ability to see past, present, and future. They have a bird's-eye view of the world and know what the problems are, and which wire in our system is wrong and needs to be recallibrated. So the more we stay connected to them, the more we will live our lives wired, connected to our original source. They will help us create the kind of bond we need between the human and the spirit worlds.

Reconnecting with the Ancestors is an important step people in the West should take right now to be able to move forward—especially in these changing times. But in order to fully connected with the Ancestors, many people have to go through the grief of not having been connected with them in the past, either because they do not know them or because of things they have done in the past they do not relate to. The Ancestors come in various forms—trees, creek, animal, and mountain, as well as foremothers and forefathers. We cannot run from or reject our lineage Ancestors. When the relationship between the living and the Ancestors is in crisis, the living suffer a great deal. So the grieving process is the beginning of healing those wounded places in our relationship with the Ancestors.

Many of us believe that grief is a waste of energy, but we cannot have genuine happiness unless we feel and act on all the emotion inside grief—sadness, unresolved issues, etc.—because grief and happiness walk hand-in-hand. It's like having a nose and a mouth. If you lack one, you might still be able to survive with the other but it won't be as effective as if you had both of them to work with. And so it's important that we look at happiness and grief not as "good" and "bad" but as "right" and "left." We need both for balance. That's why I never see a way for me to be happy without going through my grief. I am not advocating living in an endless grieving state, but I strongly believe in the importance of being able to grieve and in the healing power of grief. (I must make the distinction here between true grieving and whining. The first one allows our spirit to be reborn. It cleanses our soul, body, and spirit. It is also a sacred act. The second one is intended to manipulate people, it keeps the whiner and everybody around in a debilitating state, and is extremely irritating.)

Dagara people believe strongly in the concept of healing the Ancestors, because until we are at peace with the Ancestors, we can never truly feel at peace with ourselves. This is why when somebody passes away in the tribe, we have what we call the grief ritual. It is a process that allows us to not only grieve for the loss of that person, but also allows us to deal with all the unresolved issues we have had with the person who just passed away. It is an opportunity to bring all your unresolved issues and emotions out into the open to be healed. The grief ritual isn't about one person sitting in their own house and grieving; it is the whole village grieving together to acknowledge the loss and pointing out those places in us that were hurt by this person or in general so we can heal together and let go.

A lot of people in the West would rather be disconnected from their Ancestors than to be connected because they have had an unhappy history and they know in order to heal they are going to have to feel anger for all the person has done to hurt them or betray them or fail to give them what they needed. Because grief work is solitary in the West, most people realize that to open the door to grief is like opening a faucet without a way to turn it off. Without the support of the community in helping you get grief and anger out in a sacred container, the feeling that you are going to get squashed by the weight of your feelings is immense. Yet, it is important to grieve and to let go.

Letting go is so hard because we have held the object of our grief for so long that we become one with that object. It's like a mask you wear. After awhile, it is sewn on so well that you don't know the difference between the mask and the true self. So when you talk about letting go, what people hear is death. They feel that "If I let go of this, I'm letting go of myself, and I am going to die." In a way this is true. In order to let go, we must let the old self or the part of ourselves that is not useful to us anymore die. This is a normal process, but it feels really strange, as though the whole world is tumbling down. Yet you have to be able to see that your problems are not you and you are not your problems. You have to be able to see your problems as things you are to get strength from, to work with, and to extract the gifts out of.

Maybe this will click for people in the West when they see how people in other parts of the world are able to let go of their differences, acknowledge what has happened, and take steps toward reconciliation. This is what is happening in South Africa. They are saying, "Yes, I acknowledge this happened, and I take strength from it—I take strength from my mistake or take strength from my woundedness and grow from that. I can learn from it and come forward with something new, something positive."

Such healing is deep, necessary, and important, though difficult, work. Unless we do it, we cannot feel the connection to the Ancestors we need to move forward, knowing we are supported by them.

CREATE COMMUNITY

Another important thing we need to be doing is beginning to create community. A true community will acknowledge the importance of their Ancestors and the need to keep a strong connection with them. Without the strength of the Ancestors behind a community or a person, letting go will be particularly difficult because their wounds are the only way they know to identify themselves as individuals. This process of victimization and clinging to wounds is a symptom of the isolation people feel in the West. In a true community, the Ancestors and the people in the community are there to reinforce who you are, to encourage you to move along with them so you can let go. Most importantly, in community you don't have to hold your pain alone and "babyfy" it.

There have been attempts to creating community in the West—for instance in churches, in workplaces, or when people stand for something together. But such communities do not necessarily take into account where the individual is at on a daily basis or care about the need to have a connection to or the blessings of the Ancestors. Often there is not the kind of deep knowing and support that takes place in true community. In a true community, the slightest sign that a person is not feeling well is noticed right away, without the person having to say so.

To be useful, the term *community* itself has to be redefined since the old sense of community has been battered for so long that it is now vague and empty. The new definition of community need not be geographical, but one that offers a new sense of home in each member of the community's heart and soul. Community is a place where the individual is seen, witnessed, acknowledged, where your soul can lay bare without fear and your gifts are valued.

If I know that you are a part of my community and I am a part of yours, we don't necessarily need to be in the same place. I know I can count on you no matter what. I know that you know me inside out, and so I don't have to wonder if somebody really knows who I am.

What happens when you start to define community solely as a geographic place is that there are certain neighbors that you never meet, no matter how much you chase them. They aren't interested in knowing you. You can also run into the problem of some people wanting to control you because they want you to buy into their ideas of how things should be.

That's why to create community you need to start anywhere where you can be true to your soul and spirit. Because when we are in a community, naturally we start to send an energy capable of attracting others who feel the same and slowly the small pieces of the puzzle came together without us having to work too hard on it.

The huge barrier to community life in the West is the lack of a sense of an underlying connection that is stronger than what each individual wants. I believe that the exaggerated desire for privacy in the West is actually a desire for something bigger in disguise. We all want to connect to something sacred, powerful, and positive, and to be seen, yet the fear of being seen is so immense that we need our private space. The irony is that I have felt more privacy in community than alone in my house in Oakland, California.

Living in a community back home where there is supposed to be no privacy, I feel a sense of wholeness that allows me to be my true self. I know I will not go unnoticed. If I am feeling bad, somebody is going to ask me, "What is going on with you right now?" There is a way of noticing a person that does not require an expensive microscope or a laboratory. The simple way of being attuned to someone's energy and using all our senses is probably the best way to notice one another. As a child and even now, when I leave home and am doing something I know I am not supposed to do, I know somebody will notice me and point it out, just as they will validate the gifts that I am here to bring to the world. Because what I do affects not only me but the whole community and the entire cosmos.

This is a system of checks and balances, where I'm constantly being helped to notice that it's not my own little world, that what I as an individual do affects positively or negatively the whole village. This piece needs to be taken into account when talking about community, since community is not a place where you masquerade as someone else. Not dealing with your shadow is opening a doorway for many more shadows to come in to destroy you. If you only look at one side of the coin and refuse to see both sides, what happens is that the part that is not seen can easily overwhelm what is seen. In community, we are encouraged to face our shadow and bring it into the light.

Until we really start to unattach ourselves from our privacy and our unwillingness to show people all of who we are, it is very hard to start to a community. In our village, everybody's trouble is everybody's business. In fact, when you have trouble you are not bringing to the whole community, people will notice and wonder what is so good about this particular trouble that you are not willing to share it. That's because everyone wants what's in everybody's best interest; they won't look at the issue and think that you are a bad person. They will see it as a community problem and deal with it communally and not let the weight sit on you alone.

Being in community requires thinking about conflict in a different way. People in the West think of conflict as bad, but we believe that conflict serves as a notice that our spiritual energy is being stopped and needs to move. In our tradition, we believe that we all have energy: when we work with one another, our energies may not necessarily work in the same direction, and when they rub up against one another it will bring tension. We look at this tension as a gift that spirit is bringing to us and so we must therefore notice this gift and work with it. When unnoticed, conflict grows bigger. But when you notice it and work with it, it allows you to give birth to a new energy.

It is impossible to have everything be nice all the time. Think of community as a journey with a precise destination. If you want the spirit of the community to be constantly regenerated, you are going to run into many dead ends. You can't just say, "There is a dead end here, let's stop here or go back." What about the original intention to reach the destination together? People are not taught how to look at conflict as an opportunity to grow stronger, so when there is a conflict, they think it's not good, or it means that it is time to split.

In the village, if you have a conflict and don't bring it to the people, they will hold it more against you than if you bring it forward. They will take it as a sign that you don't want them in your world and they will have a conflict session with you. It is impossible for us to get to a place of peace if we don't look at all those little conflicts and work with them.

RENEW THROUGH RITUALS

We also need to renew ourselves through ritual. Ritual is a way of working with spirit, the Ancestors, and our soul. Ritual provides us with a way of connecting to our soul, our purpose, and to spirit. Ritual helps us see all our broken or loose wires that need to be tightened up. Ritual help us heal at the soul level, because problems do not manifest themselves on the physical level unless they have been experienced at the soul level. The sacred container of ritual makes us shine like a beacon.

Ritual also allows spirit and the Ancestors to bring us their gifts, without their having to be in a human form, and to remove obstacles in our path so that we can have a clearer vision of our destination. Without ritual, our village would have tumbled down a long time ago.

Ritual helps people to truly connect at the soul level and to be able to see each other's spirit. It takes away judgment and righteousness. Our daily life should organize itself around ritual so we can look at our problems ritualistically in order to see the kind of energy are we dealing with and apply the appropriate ritual to it.

Unlike modern medicine, a ritual cannot be proscribed. For a ritual to work, it has to take into account the space, the problem at hand and its specifics, the people involved, and the material we have to work with. There are many rituals in Africa that won't work in the West if transplanted as is. Each participant in the ritual has a unique gift, an energy to contribute to the ritual. That's why a ritual can never be repeated.

When you are given recipes, formulas, for rituals, it's like being spoon-fed—you really never learn how to feed yourself properly. Ritual requires our full participation, our imagination, and the collaboration of our spirits so we all blossom together. If we can think of our contribution to the ritual as our gift that's important to the ritual, then everybody's contribution will provide all the spices and other ingredients for the making of the meal.

It's very important that people don't try to re-create ritual word-for-word the way somebody described it, because my way of doing it is not necessarily your way of doing it. Just as if when I cook a meal, what I might use may not be what you might use. What tastes good to me might be repulsive to someone else. You have to be able to bring your own soup stock, your own visionary thought, into a ritual.

The key is to be able to have the intention clear with spirit, telling spirit where you want to go. Don't hesitate to say that you don't know how to get there. There are elders in the village who have been doing rituals for years and years, and each time they are to start a ritual, they always say, "I don't know how to do this, but spirit, I expect you to come and sit in the driver's seat and make sure that we reach our destination and come back safely." This is not to put yourself down; it is a humble way of asking for help, the kind of help you need.

There's nothing wrong in not knowing. Actually, spirit loves to know that you don't know, because they do know and they will take it as an invitation to do what they have to do. Spirit is always there waiting. Just say the magical words "I need help" and help is there. The Ancestors love to be able to help us. Just like what we do helps them, they love to help us, so that we can be of help to each other. So it is important that we are able to say, "I don't know" or "I need help," and see it not as a failure but as a way of letting spirit take over and help us.

In a community where you are known and believe that people value who you are and what you have to offer, you don't have a lack of self-esteem. You don't have to pretend you know everything or be a failure if you admit you don't. Not being willing to admit you don't know makes it unsafe for people to bring their creativity out. It also prevents people from taking the initiative and being responsible. This kind of mind-set makes people in need of healing say to someone else, "I want to be healed but don't ask me to do any work. All I want from you is to fix everything so things will be right from now on." But healing is impossible without the person herself taking certain steps, bringing certain pieces.

This element of spiritual creativity is crucial for our survival. Unfortunately, most Westerners are often cut off from their spiritual creativity and imagination. This the result of the lack of community and continuous regenerative rituals. This is very dangerous because a culture that does not see the importance of keeping imagination alive is spiritually dead and will not survive. For the sake of our children let's not continue on this deadly path. We could avoid lot of therapy sessions if we avoid putting the pressure of failing onto our children. It would take a lot of stress away; then their creativity could blossom even more. Let's let our lives be fluid with the power of creativity so that we can continuously change for a better tomorrow.

Vimala McClure is a writer and award-winning fabric artist living in Boulder, Colorado. Her books include *Infant Massage: A Handbook for Loving Parents; The Tao of Motherhood; A Woman's Guide to Tantra Yoga; The Path of Parenting: Twelve Principles to Guide Your Journey;* and *Bangladesh: Rivers in a Crowded Land.*

Parenting in the New Millennium: Using Taoist Principles to Guide Your Mission

It is the end of the year, nearly the end of the millennium, and as usual I am reviewing my personal mission statement, thinking deeply about my life as I try to envision the coming time. I have found that each year my mission statement is shorter, simpler, and more deeply felt, and I hope this is because it is working its magic on my soul, bringing me closer to alignment with my true purpose.

What I know without any doubt in my own life is that bringing every gift I came here with, every iota of strength and wisdom, every drop of love and loyalty, everything I have, to the task, the mission, and the gift of bringing up two souls to live their own lives and destinies is the most important thing I have ever done or ever will do. I don't expect this singularity of purpose from others, but because of it I have been able to pay attention more closely to the dynamics, the secrets, the lessons of real parenthood—much more so, I believe, than many so-called educated experts who observe interactions in made-up environments and offer made-up theories on what is healthy or correct, in manuals with formulas that rarely work.

What I am attempting here, rather, is to go deeper with the idea that parenthood is a mission, however large or small a part it takes on for you personally. From that perspective, everything you think about it changes. No longer are you solving problems, because there are no problems. Just as pregnancy is not a disease, parenthood is not a puzzle, nor is it, as many would have you believe, a long series of equations to be solved for X.

If there is one thing I wish to do with this piece, it is to help you, encourage you, and empower you to remember that if you are a parent, you have chosen this as an important aspect of your purpose on this earth. So rather than always trying to find the right thing to *do* as a parent, you will be successful in that mission as far as you can discover the right thing to *be*. Contrary to most articles on raising children, this one will, therefore, focus on you, the parent. My assumption is that if you feel fulfilled, purposeful, aligned with your integrity and satisfied with your role as a parent, your children will "turn out" just fine. You don't need much in the way of how-to advice; each child is different, times change, and your family configuration and values will likely change with time too. What you do need is a firm understanding of the timeless nature of your soul's commitment to your child, and how that commitment plays out in your personal life, so that, when the time comes for you to review your life, you can feel proud of who you are to your children and of what you have learned by being a parent.

The new millennium brings with it an entirely different picture of "family." No longer are most of the paradigms we have developed over the last millennium viable. Because our family structures, our values, and our experience of "family" will continue to change at lightning speed, it is particularly important for us to understand now that being a good parent and raising healthy, responsible children requires a grounding in the deeper meaning of the role of parent. We need an ability to change beyond what may now seem possible to us, and the only way to achieve that is to develop a firm rooting in the spiritual dimension of parenthood.

Approaching the new millennium, we need both the long-term, philosophical view and short-term practical solutions. So I will try to provide both, with an emphasis on the former. That doesn't, however, mean an overcomplication of the subject of "parenting as mission." Rather, it is a way to continually bring ourselves back to the simple Truths that make the universe work and therefore can be counted upon to make our own little microcosm run smoothly.

The biological urge, the psychological need, to bear children rarely helps us look beyond pregnancy and birth. We may fantasize about what our baby will be like. We may form some opinions about home or hospital birth, breast- or bottle-feeding, even about if or when we will put our children in day care. But few parents take the time to discover and define how being a parent fits into his or her lifelong mission. Few of us look ahead to how this new person will change our lives.

It's hard to imagine a new baby as a gap-toothed eight-year-old, a gangly, belligerent thirteen-year-old, a high school senior with expensive tastes, a college student experimenting with alternative lifestyles, an adult with financial problems. We leap into parenthood, not realizing it is only the beginning of an ever-increasing expansion of our responsibilities. This new being will bring a long series of others into our lives: babysitters, doctors, friends, teachers, boyfriends and girlfriends, pets, spouses, in-laws, and grandchildren. How we handle all of these relationships will have a profound effect on our children's lives, on their relationships, and on how they in turn relate to their own children. Perhaps if we really thought about all of this, none of us would take that leap!

When I was researching ancient Taoist teachings in preparation for writing *The Tao of Motherhood*, I was struck by the depth of the principles upon which these teachings are based. I also researched and began learning the martial art of Tai Chi, which has its genesis in Taoism. Tai Chi could also be called Taoist yoga. Like its counterpart in India, Tai Chi is a practice which quiets and focuses the mind with the goal of self-realization or union (yoga) with the Tao (pronounced *dow*; supreme consciousness or God).

A symbol often associated with Tai Chi is the "yin-yang." The black area represents "yin"—passive, soft, open, yielding. The white area represents "yang"—active, hard, tight, assertive. The curved line is the synthesis or synergy of these two aspects of consciousness. The black-and-white dots indicate that each contains its opposite. It is not possible, therefore, to separate them. Like two sides of a sheet of paper, both are intrinsic aspects of the Tao. The balance of these is the goal of Tai Chi practice. Striving for this balance is also the key to good parenting.

RELAX

"Relax," from the Taoist perspective, is the principle upon which everything depends. For us in the West, relaxation is something we do on our day off, when we get a massage or do yoga. To us, relaxation implies limpness, flaccidity, emptiness. But to Taoists, relaxation implies fullness. As a practice, it can take years to master and it is respected as a difficult discipline. No problem. When you have children, years of mastering difficult disciplines comes with the territory. Tai Chi master Ron Sieh advises students to "let everything you have—mind and body, thoughts and reactions, plans and avoidance of plans— sink with gravity into your feet to beneath the earth. Relax your intention. Put everything underground where it can support you. Strewn anxiously through your body, it can only distract you." Relaxation is a state of openness, allowing space for listening and receptivity. Taoists consider it a discipline because it takes a conscious intention to learn and practice it. We must decide we want to relax, and we must know if relaxed is truly what we wish to be.

The word *yield* is often used to signify this principle. Again, it has a very different meaning to Taoists than it does in the West. When we consider the word "yield" as more than just a traffic sign, we picture surrendering to a stronger force—which in the West we often consider failure. Yielding is done reluctantly, when there are no other options. To Tai Chi practitioners, however, yielding is the finest quality we can have. It means flexibility, clarity, and faith. It gets the maximum positive result from the minimum effort, and thus it is efficient, a much sought-after value in the West.

Taoists like water. They say that water is the most yielding of all things, yet it can overwhelm that which is most hard—rock. When an individual dipper of water is placed into the ocean, it merges with the ocean as if separation never existed. Studying the qualities of water can give us important clues as to how to relax and yield in the Taoist way. The three aspects of water most useful to us as parents are those most closely identified with the Tao: First, water nourishes without needing to be nourished. Like water, good parents give selflessly to their children. They provide for their children's physical welfare, intellectual growth, emotional security, and spiritual connection, without expecting anything in return. They are willing to sacrifice, if necessary, so their children may grow and prosper. The "martyr" parent is the opposite paradigm, exacting payment in guilt for every sacrifice. Remembering that every principle contains its polarity in seed form, we can catch ourselves before fatigue or frustration goads us to shame our children for requiring so much of us.

Ideally, marriage prepares us for the bigger sacrifices required when children come along. We have the opportunity to practice selfless giving, to test and stretch ourselves, and to explore our programming. We may consider ourselves giving people, but sometimes when confronted by the stress of another's need we discover how limited our patience can be. We may find ourselves doing and saying things that echo precisely the voices of our parents. But how do we then think and act to correct our course? It is exactly at those moments when we are most un-God-like that we have the opportunity to choose to grow toward oneness rather than separation. So, the idea is not to suddenly be the perfect parent; rather, it is the excitement of a journey upon which we have real opportunities to become what we wish to be.

So where do we get all this strength, if we are to endlessly give and provide? Again, water is our model. There is an ocean of consciousness from which all things are created. Some call it God or Goddess; Tai Chi practitioners call it the Tao or the Way. Yielding like a cup of water yields to the ocean, we merge our consciousness into the great, eternal consciousness which creates and maintains all things; it merges with the ocean as if separation never existed. Thus our strength is omnipotent; our well never runs dry. That's why wise parents take time for personal spiritual renewal so that the strength upon which we rest is that of the infinite source of our being.

Second, water flows into places where there seemingly is no room. Rigid things can't do this. Only that which is relaxed, yielding, and fluid can go into seemingly full places and be effective there. I have discovered this principle over and over again in my mission as a mother. To discover what my child needed, a deep, yielding receptivity was vital. The temptation is to become more and more rigid, but the more you do, the less you understand. When faced with a child who is testing your resolve, relax and yield in the manner of water. Absorb the child's energy without moving. Sink your power into the earth with the relaxing breath. Allow the child to bounce off your energy, discovering without harm the nature of your power.

As a parent, the frustration of not knowing how to fill a need that cannot be articulated can be overwhelming. Often we direct the rage that stems from that frustration toward the child, which serves to distance us even further, making it impossible for the child to open up to us. To get to this type of receptivity, a practice of conscious relaxation is a must. To know how to belly-breathe, to relax each muscle group, and to sink your mind into your heart is the way to go from rigid to fluid; to be able to flow into the cracks and crevices of a child's hurts and anger, to soothe, to heal, to allow the child to find whole-ness again, and best of all, to claim the finding of it for him or herself.

The type of strength we need as parents is that of water, not rock, for the challenges we face are numerous, repetitive, and long-term. We need the kind of strength that flows over obstacles rather than that of the sledge-hammer. If our strength is rigid—authoritarian—there is no space for our children to develop their own strength. Rather than exercising their mental and emo-tional muscles, their will is broken and the result is failure. Children with no inner strength either become passive victims of others or they lash out at authority in a desperate attempt to reclaim their sense of self. Some people spend their lives alternating between the two, tortured, never feeling the sense of security that comes from a solid sense of one's power. The only way to give that security to our children is to be flexibly strong, like water. Chil-dren need to know that nothing they say or do will break us, make us "snap." And the only way they discover this is to test us. When they know our strength, they relax into it, and they develop that kind of strength for themselves. Respect for us arises out of their confidence in our strength; eventually, they want to be like us.

The third aspect of the Tao which we can learn about and use is its immutable nature. While all things animate and inanimate are "made" of Tao, it is impossible to truly separate it from itself. Therefore, there is an aspect of being that is unchangeable and is not separate—between you and your child, the dog or cat, the rocks in your driveway. All is one. The ability to sink into this awareness on a conscious level is empathy. The occasions for this aware-ness are innumerable, and the more you practice it, the more you feel the lim-itlessness of your own being. So rather than contracting into a hard, little "I"-ness that has no common ground with, say, a teenager with green hair and piercings (or whatever the passing show of seeming separation requires for costume at the time), we expand into an awareness of oneness that includes all of it. We learn to acknowledge the game of hide and seek the Tao is playing with itself. How different can it be? How many pieces can we break into and test this knowing that all is one?

This is why holidays like Halloween can be such fun. We play God, creating ever new and interesting creatures, dancing and singing and doing naughty things in these disguises. We pretend, and we help others pretend, that these disguises are real. But the knowing is there; it need not be spoken. Some Halloween enthusiasts are so good at it, they can fool their own mothers. But that does not alter the truth, the bottom line of who they really are. At the end of the day, the costumes fall away and here we are, who we have been all along. Recognizing that we are one, and bringing that recognition to consciousness during times of conflict, things which seem important within a consciousness of separateness are no longer as critical; we find it easier not to "sweat the small stuff" and to recognize the small stuff when we see it.

THE OPPOSITE

Often, to deeply understand a concept like this it is helpful to examine its opposite. In Tai Chi this is essential, because everything contains its opposite within it; we must understand its opposite in order to truly understand anything.

Where there is pain there is tension, and that tension creates more pain. Therefore, tension is the opposite of relaxation. When we apply relaxation to pain, it diminishes. Underneath tension is its root—fear. Now we get to the key, the essence of the discipline of yielding: the release of fear.

Fears and worries assail us at every point along the path of parenting. If you are beginning on that path, let me tell you the truth:

IT NEVER ENDS!

Until the day you die, your children will be producing, in a never-ending stream, triggers for anxiety in you. Some of these fears and worries are justified. Stuff happens. You can't predict your children's lives or destinies, and if you love them you will always be there for them. Because life is fraught with dangers for your children no matter what you do, you will be a better parent, a healthier role model, and a happier person if you learn how to relax.

Fear hardens us as we try to hold on to the familiar. If we are fearful, we want to stop the flow of time and change. But cessation of change is called *death*. Acting out of fear, our inner "juice" slowly dries up and, like a dead tree, we are easily broken. Relaxation—yielding to the flow of change—is essential for life. If we wish to continue to be full of life, we must learn to relax and yield, to flow. Like the young tree, we can be flexible and strong, ever-growing, with abundant youthful energy. But if we cannot relax, we cannot listen and truly hear our children. Thus we miss their messages to us, misinterpret their needs and wishes, and lose touch with who they are.

DISCIPLINE

Children sooner or later let us know that they arrived in the world with agendas of their own. While we have a tremendous influence over the way they express and live out their agendas, we do not mold and control them. They have as much to teach us as we want to teach them, and the wise parent realizes this early on. Because of this give-and-take dance, we sometimes feel out of step with our children and conflict arises. We may try to teach at a moment when we should be receptive. Our children may not be able to listen to us because they have not been heard. Therefore, the dynamic of opposition is always arising in these relationships. Tai Chi can help us learn how to dance with this flow of energy.

In Tai Chi, the goal is not to defeat an opponent. Rather, the Tai Chi practitioner learns to flow with the energy of opposition, assisting its movement toward its natural conclusion, which is exhaustion. The opponent then is defeated by his own momentum rather than by stiff resistance. Ultimately the practitioner's goal—peace and harmony—is reached without overt violence or force.

The principles of Tai Chi are based upon eternal truths: Tao is the immutable Being, the oneness toward which all beings are moving. Harmony prevails when we find harmony with the eternal flow of Tao. Strength is in the persistent, gentle flow of the life-force. Water is often used as a symbol of the kind of strength Tai Chi develops; the gentle drip of water on a rock eventually carves that rock as no brute force can. A river made the Grand Canyon; no bulldozer could create such a phenomenon.

In Tai Chi, you learn how to flow with the life force of the universe. You do not oppose an attacker's force, you step aside and permit the attacker's life energy to pass. As he is flying by, you give him a nudge to assist him to get where he is going more quickly. Similarly, the Tai Chi practitioner learns to ground her energy into the earth in such a way as to have all the strength of the earth within her body. When she has mastered this practice, she is unshakable. The strongest person cannot move her.

I once saw a tiny, elderly Tai Chi master standing calmly in a pose. Several large men were asked, one at a time, to shove him off balance—even an inch would do. The young men were all over six feet tall, very athletic and robust. One by one they threw themselves at him, pushing for all they were worth, and he didn't budge even an inch. Finally, all five of them simultaneously lined up, pushing one upon the other. The combined force of five men did not move him even a fraction, and his face and body remained relaxed, calm, and serene. The men grunted, red-faced, straining against his upraised arm.

The wise parent learns to discover the life-force within and move with it to guide her children. When met with opposition, she grounds herself in the eternal and allows opposition to exhaust itself naturally. She remains calm, providing an immutable base for her children's growth. In this way, she teaches them how the universe works, she provides a model of healthy parenting, and she gains their trust and respect in the process.

Children need the same things in different ways at each stage of their development: respect, acceptance, encouragement, boundaries, assistance, understanding, affection, and above all unconditional love. Parents who know how to observe and learn can provide their children with the right kinds of each.

YOUR MISSION AS A PARENT

Before putting Taoist (or any other) principles to work, it is important to know what you are trying to achieve. Stephen Covey, author of *The Seven Habits of Highly Effective People*, says, "Begin with the end in mind." Everything we do begins in the mind. First we create a mental picture, then physical manifestation follows. The more clearly we can define our goal, the more quickly and accurately we can reach it. We are often caught up in the busy hustle of everyday life, reacting to everything that comes our way. We react automatically, based on what we have internalized—the "blueprint" of information we have from our life experiences. New mothers are often surprised to hear themselves sounding exactly like their own mothers. These internalized scripts are usually ineffective, sometimes outright destructive. Many people just go along reacting to everything in this way, not bothering to examine their blueprints and create something new for themselves, and then they wonder why their children are disrespectful, sullen, and rebellious. In the new millennium, the speed of change around us will make it impossible to rely on old social scripts to raise our children. Our only hope is to live our lives according to timeless principles and base our parenting on deep values, taught with love.

We all have the power to change the scripts we have been given, to alter them so that they reflect accurately our values and the principles we decide to consciously embrace. The operative word here is *consciously*—it requires a deep desire and daily practice to change. We must examine our values with regard to our families, and to engage with our values as passionately as we can. Only then will we have the requisite spiritual fortitude to communicate those values appropriately to our children. Covey says, "If you want to raise responsible, self-disciplined children, you have to keep that end clearly in mind as you interact with your children on a daily basis. You can't behave toward them in ways that undermine their self-discipline or self-esteem."

Children are experts at detecting hypocrisy. They know, even if it is at a subconscious level, when you are parroting sermons rather than communicating what you deeply feel and believe. They also know if you respect them. In my twenty years of working with infants and mothers, it became very clear to me that even babies know if their mothers respect them or not. Babies invariably become fussy and irritable when their caregivers are *doing* the right things but their minds are a million miles away. Nobody likes to be treated like an object.

Becoming conscious of our deeply held values and committing ourselves to living congruently with them is the means by which we realize our mission as parents. "Mission" may sound very big. But what is bigger than being a parent? What job or role is more important? What has a direct and intimate impact on more people, leaving behind us a legacy for generations to come? Thinking in terms of "mission" we can begin to give this part of our lives the respect it deserves.

For good or ill (and probably a bit of both), you learned most about being a parent from your own parents' example. Bringing both positive and negative sides of these experiences out into the open can help you clarify what you want and what you do not want. Sometimes we need to start with what we do not want, and this will show us the way to what we want. Being congruent with what we deeply want is the best insurance for happiness and success. *Being* what we admire in others engenders high self-esteem, perseverance through hard times, and joy, all important qualities to model for our children.

THE VALUE OF A MISSION STATEMENT

A mission statement shouldn't be just a collection of idealistic phrases. It is a compass, a way to keep yourself on course as you handle all the variables of daily life. When you read your mission statement, it should make you smile and feel inspired about the future and energized today.

The following exercise will help you clarify what aspects of your mission as a parent are most important to you. Set aside an hour to complete it and commit yourself to total honesty. When you are finished, you will have a mission statement that can help you as you parent in the future. I have included, with permission, the responses of a friend who graciously completed the exercise for me.

Some people develop lengthy mission statements; others need only a sentence or even a few words. Take time with this project, digging deeply into your soul to find your true purpose as a parent. Revise and rewrite portions as you learn more about yourself.

1. Were there times in your childhood or adolescence when you thought, "I will never treat my children that way!"? If so, write about these experiences. What aspects of your mother's and/or father's parenting style do you think were counterproductive?

Example:

My mother worked very hard as a nurse, a single mother of five children. Her day off was spent cleaning the house and doing laundry. She was always very grouchy that day, and she often yelled at me and sometimes hit me with a belt when I didn't do what she told me to in the right way. I felt unfairly persecuted and vowed never to be like her. Now I understand how much stress she was dealing with, and why she sometimes "snapped."

It was counterproductive for her to hold all that stress inside until it exploded on her children. Hitting may have relieved her immediate stress but ultimately it created deep resentment in me, and she must have felt guilty which stressed her even more. It would have been more productive for her to sit down with me and tell me how she was feeling, why she needed my help, and request the kind of cooperation she needed. It also would have helped me feel more responsible and closer to her if she apologized after losing her temper instead of blaming me.

Now try to distill these into several words or phrases (try to keep it less than ten)

Example:
honesty
respect
humility (apologizing and making amends for mistakes)
responsibility for own behavior
cooperative spirit
sacrifice

2. Think of the times you felt close to your parents, or when you felt admiration for them, and write about these experiences.

Example:
I admired my mother for her sense of responsibility and her ability to sacrifice for her children. She always made sure that holidays were celebrated with all the magic she could muster, regardless of how little money we had. I felt close to her when she spent time one-on-one with me, during our annual shopping day for school clothes. She took me out to lunch at a fancy restaurant, and I felt very special. I also felt good when she gave me good feedback about myself, noticed when I did something well, and attended functions that were important to me.

Now try to distill these into several words or phrases.

Example:
responsibility
sacrifice
unconditional love
encouragement
quality time one-on-one

3. List all of your words or phrases, and sit with your list for a while. Is anything missing? Think of other people you admire as parents. What do you admire most about them? If you were able to have anything you wanted, what do you wish you had as a child? If you come up with tangibles such as more physical affection or a room of your own or a pet, think about what these represent to you (love, respect, trust).

Example:

I wish I'd had more one-on-one time with my mother. I wish she had helped me more, especially when I was a teenager, to learn how to be an adult. For example, I wish she had helped me learn how to balance a checkbook and take care of a car. I wish she had been more open about her own experiences growing up and that we could have conversations about issues like sexuality and politics, rather than one-way lectures. I wish she had shown me more physical affection. I wish my mother had been able to request and elicit cooperation rather than obedience. The families I admire most talk a lot with each other, and they joke and tease a lot; there is laughter in the house and a feeling of warmth and welcome. My house growing up, because of our financial situation and other problems, was pretty tense. I wouldn't want that for my children.

4. Imagine that your children are grown, and they have become famous. They are interviewed for television and asked, "How did your parents contribute to your success and happiness?" What do you want them to say?

Example:

I would want my children to say that their parents supported them in every way. I'd want them to say I taught them values of integrity and responsibility, that they were loved unconditionally and that their parents' values and sacrifices made it possible for them to succeed. I would want them to smile when they think of me. I would want to see their love and respect for me shining in their eyes.

5. Back to your list of words or phrases which represent your values and the qualities you want to have as parents. Add concepts you came up with in the last two questions. If what you have is basically the same as some of the original ten words, underline them.

Example:

honesty
responsibility
respect
humility
sacrifice
cooperation

encouragement
unconditional love
quality time

6. Now write a paragraph in first-person present tense, incorporating the values you defined into a Parenting Mission Statement.

Example:

I love my children unconditionally and I demonstrate that love to them every day in my words and actions. I tell them I love them every day, and let them know I love them even when I am angry or disappointed or disagree with them. I respect my children and demonstrate that respect in my words and actions. I allow them freedom of choice and respect their choices even when they are different from what I would choose. I am honest and open with my children, appropriately sharing with them my struggles and requesting their understanding and help when I need it. I continually seek out information about healthy parenting skills and improve myself as a parent as much as possible. I admit my errors and make amends, and I allow my children to make mistakes and learn how to apologize and correct themselves. I find peaceable ways to discipline my children, never resorting to physical or verbal violence. I listen carefully to my children and treat their concerns with the same respect I want for myself. I spend time with each child and encourage each child appropriately according to his or her needs. I take care of myself and my own needs so that I have positive energy to give to my children. I try always to demonstrate the values I teach, knowing that my children learn primarily by my example. I provide my children with deep roots in home and family, and wings to fly away into new experiences, knowing that love will always bring them home again.

I wish you joy on the incredible journey of parenthood. It began with an act of love. With consciousness and some deep internal work, you can create a beautiful family whose love continues in forever-expanding circles, touching our communities and thus healing the world.

Brooke Medicine Eagle, an American native healer, teacher, singer, ceremonial leader, sacred ecologist, and author of *Buffalo Woman Comes Singing*, is creating "Spirit Dances" and "Wakantia: Flowering Earth" trainings in response to the millennial issues we face. This chapter is adapted from her forthcoming book about visioning and creating a renewed Earth, *The Last Ghost Dance*.

Creating a Path of Beauty

The first thing to understand as we look toward creating a beautiful path into this new time is that we are beginning to receive an enormous wave of Light, brought to us on the cycles of time. Everyone from ancient native prophets of the Americas and Vedic seers to modern scientists tell us of this. Whether it is called the photon belt, the pillar of celestial fire, or *wakantia*, there is a tremendous amount of vital life-energy cresting and rolling our way. It will eventually bring a golden time to Lady Gaia.

Because this is true we might assume that the energy which is coming is all *good*, harmonious, immediately beneficial energy. It is not. It is simply energy—titanic waves of energy. What it becomes as we call it into manifestation on Earth is up to us. It is just like money—you can use it to buy a hungry child a meal or to trade cocaine on school grounds. Or like electricity: it can burn up a careless person or light an entire city.

Our response to this incoming flow of power is determined by the dedication of our energy and the Intent we hold for the future: *whatever we are and feel and imagine and believe and call forth will be magnified exponentially.* Implications of this lie in many personal and global directions, and the one I wish to now address here is our method of proceeding as we come into the new millennium.

THE MEANS ARE THE END

The most important lesson in the entire process is *that the method you use to transform yourself or the world around you must have the energetic quality of the end you seek.* To elucidate, you can't dash wildly about to create peace in your life, although we have all tried that: "If I can just get this and this and this and this done, then I can sit down and have some quiet time." And you know as well as I do that it doesn't work that way. Instead, try stopping for a moment, taking a few deep breaths, and intoning softly to yourself: "I am a peaceful woman with abundant time and energy to do all that I need and want to do with grace and ease." Write that out beautifully on a piece of paper and put it up in the bathroom and the kitchen. Repeat it often. Feel the relaxation that hits your shoulders as you move into *that* energy. Then go back to your life with that energy. This will create much more peace in the long run than hurrying to complete all your tasks. What we wish to accomplish is to create peace in the process, even though it is also the end product.

We must also break the fearful cycle that pushes us to try to make things OK. We live with a tremendous distrust in the unfoldment of things because we have cut ourselves off from the natural world around us. If the basic "vibration" we carry is one of fear and distrust, we will bring ourselves the results of that energy. If, instead, we can rest back in the arms of the Mother in whose womb we live our days and in the arms of the Father who gives us aliveness, we can approach life as an adventure, not a disaster. Emmanuel says something through channel Pat Rodegast that has been most helpful to me: "Fear says, 'Come to me and I will make you safe.' Love says, 'You *are* safe.'"

A good exercise is to examine any moment in your life and get down to what is motivating you. Simply notice how much you base your every decision in some fear, logical as it may seem: "I need to go to work, because I'm afraid I'll lose my job if I don't. If I lose my job, I'm afraid I won't get another easily—good jobs are hard to find. If I can't find another job, how will I take care of my family? I hear stories everyday of middle-class people who have lost their homes and end up living in their cars...." On and on it goes.

Even if you can't suddenly leave your job and find your "true calling," then change the way you think about your job. Question the fear motivations and practice transforming them in the moment: "I'm going to work because I like to support my family. I can make a difference right where I am. As I bring my knowledge and skills and truth more fully into my everyday life, it is moving toward more and more appropriate work. Opportunities to do what I would most like to do are opening up each day. I intend to have a fabulous day today—to feel good and to do something good for others."

Is that kind of thinking too much of a stretch? It's certainly a different way to approach your day, isn't it? This is an example of making the difference in your life right now, rather than waiting until "someday" when everything is finally just right externally and then you can be just right within yourself. *The news is that the inner experience comes first, and eventually creates what happens externally.*

SILENCE

The basic skill is that of silencing the mind. If there is any one thing I would recommend for you, it is to find a practice which assists you in this. This will not only help you receive information, it will help you receive information that is *individual* to you. Although everyone is going through this process, each of us has our own needs and our own path. Listening deeply is our personal responsibility. It will serve us profoundly.

One of the important aspects of the silencing is to stop the inner chatter through which we continually create our world. We do our thinking and keep concepts together through language: we do our thinking in words, and we most often experience a large part of our emotional experience through words. Seldom do we have pure bodily emotion or a kind of thinking that goes beyond languaging. So our internal dialogue is how we put our world together and how we create the images through which we determine our reality. In order for the new to become available to us, we must stop this languaging. This quieting of our internal dialogue helps us to still our usual emotional patterns and modes of thought. Since thinking and old emotional patterns tie up a large majority of our energy, this quieting is profoundly useful in freeing up your power to do the magic which is possible.

Here's the silencing technique I use. It is based in the southern seer's ways, and works because it is grounded in our physiology. The focus is on your physical ears, specifically the openings of your ears, so we begin with awakening that part of your body. Turning your hands backward, place your palms over your ears. Do this is such way that you create by gentle pressure a "vacuum seal" so that when you speak you hear it from inside your head, not outside. Now you have effectively sealed your ears. Keeping this gentle pressure, massage your ears and ear canals by rotating your hands around in circles, forward and back. The next step may take a little practice so that you can accomplish it and keep the seal on your ears. Putting your middle finger over your index finger, pull it off with a snapping motion. Try this on your knees if you need to—notice that you can give whatever is under your fingers a good strong tap that way. Once you have this down, then go back to the position with your hands sealed over your ears and tap the back of your head using this method eighteen times. When you take your palms down from your ears, you may notice a sense of more acute physical hearing. The idea of this is to wake up the actual sensing of your physical ears and ear canals—create more awareness there—because this is where your attention must be for the actual silencing part of it. I even lower and stretch my jaw dramatically to open the area around my inner ear from the inside.

Now, I suggest closing your eyes as you begin your practice of this, because it cuts down on the distraction. Sitting up where you can breath fully and easily, begin drawing in full natural breaths through your nose, and as your release your breath, imagine that you can send the air out through your ears! Place the tip of your tongue gently on the roof of your mouth behind your teeth, and keep it there for the entire process. The final step is to put *all* of your attention on the openings of your ears, listening intently. Remember that you want to be able to really feel your ears and ear canals, so if you can't, it might be helpful to actually put your little fingers into your ears and give a little massage there to get more in touch with exactly where to put your attention. When you are focusing your attention there, you *will not be hearing words* inside your head. If you are hearing words, you are not focused on your ears, so return to focusing on them. Put all your attention there. Let any word which comes up be a signal to draw your focus back to your ears.

Practice of this technique, even in conjunction with other meditation practice, can be very useful. In time, you can open your eyes and look around you, yet still not be naming and talking to yourself about what you see. Eventually, the idea is to move about through your day without constantly naming and categorizing things in your old ways. As one of my teachers Dawn Boy exhorted me, "Leave space for the Great Mystery to offer something new and wonderful!" Everything is unfolding in beauty; we need only stop holding on to the historically and personally familiar.

Once you find that you can maintain the inner silence, then another step is possible. To best understand this, you must understand that *our vibratory intent is what determines how the potent energy of the Invisible manifests in our world.* In other words, what we hold up in front of that energy as it comes into physical reality is like a mold or a cut-out pattern for the light to come through. Everything that we are and everything that we are running inside our minds is what creates the pattern. When we come to true silence, what comes through is what Creator is sending through, unrestricted, and is of very high quality. As a matter of fact, the definition of Christ-energy is one who allows the energy of creation to move through the heart, unrestricted. It means letting go of our control and manipulation to a large extent.

Yet part of our function is to co-create this experience, so when we become clear about something that we choose to manifest, touching into the Silence is potent. When there is nothing else in the pattern, when the "space" is open and clear of all our usual images and beliefs, then we can manifest exactly what we throw up into the empty place. In that instance, what we place into the silence is singular and *gets all the energy* that is coming through, and in this way, manifests immediately! There is an enormous amount of energy available, which we normally have tied up in many other ways. This is what the great masters are doing when they literally manifest things like magic! They place something into the silence which has the total energy available to become real. Nothing clouds the picture—no old ideas, no limitations, no past history, no negativity. It truly is *magic*, and that is the science of it!

What we are doing is stepping into shaman's time, stepping into the invisible just "across the line" where our energy impacts the incoming energy most profoundly. If we were able to focus our intent far out in the invisible, in the most subtle realms of the infinitesimal, it would still have to "travel" a long way before it became manifest, and many things could influence or change it on the way. Contrastingly, if we act on the manifest side—in the world as we usually know it—the density there requires tremendous amounts of our human energy. The latter method is what we have been trying throughout most of our history. We have been attempting to make a difference in our world by pushing and shoving around material things. That has drained not only our personal vitality, but the resources of our Earth. The only way that we will truly make a difference at this point is working in a spiritual way; it is our challenge to ourselves to learn this new, magical, graceful, easy way of doing things—by *being* in a different way. And the key—the basic skill—is *silence*. By freeing up the gift of energy Creator gives us each day, we can become conscious co-creators of a beautiful, whole, and holy life for us and All Our Relations.

LIGHTENING UP!

Creator has given us an especially wonderful tool to use in clearing ourselves of old patterns, which most of us have forgotten to use. In the Lakota way, it is said that there are four Great Powers: the first is the power which created all that is; the second Great Power is the power or spirit that lives in everything; the third Great Power is a mysterious power in the west which has to do with awareness; and the fourth Great Power is *heyoka*, the power of laughter and humor. The magic and mystery of laughter is an amazing capacity which Creator placed within our own bodies as two-leggeds, available at a moment's notice. Laughter is Creator's way of helping us lighten up and release the old—a vital aspect of our everyday life, and ultimately important as we approach these new times.

This fourth Great Power is one that we can use and practice with wonderful results, because it is Creator's gift of clearing. Remember a time when you were totally consumed by laughter, and realize that there were no thoughts, no images, nothing except the bubbling mirth of true laughter in your mind. *Laughter's function is to cast loose all our moorings to the past and open our minds totally.* In the few moments after we have laughed like this, we are able to program our consciousness with new information which goes deep and hooks up powerfully. It is a bodily metaphor for our own personal power which resides within our bodies in the everyday world. Perhaps you and your friends can make a game of creating really deep, joyful laughter—then the first words you speak will be those of what you are wishing to create in your life.

One of the most useful attitudes is that of humor and of being able to spin ourselves out of depression and frustration by creating laughter. Sometimes we need our friends to help us with this. I have a set of warm, witty, humorous stories by Garrison Keillor from the Prairie Home Companion series on Minnesota Public Radio, titled "News From Lake Wobegon" (available through the Wireless catalog, 800-669-9999) which lighten my spirits immensely. You may have a favorite funny movie. It's great to keep these things on hand for emergency upliftment!

In the midst of all our focused "work" upon ourselves, it is refreshing to know that Creator has given us a happy way of doing the clearing we want, and of creating an energy which is one we would like to have magnified. It is a constant challenge for us to "lighten up" in the midst of the process of lightening up! We often get terribly serious about the process and forget that we must continue to create the energetic quality we wish to have in the end. *Letting go of what we don't want is only one side of the process; creating what we do want is just as important.* So find ways to spend time laughing, and remember to bring images of beauty and radiance and a golden world into your mind after that good belly-laugh!

NATURE AND SOLITUDE

Mother Nature can be helpful partner in our process, too. Although we two-leggeds have interfered with and influenced much of what surrounds us, there is still a web of Being moving all of life forward, beyond that which we can control or manipulate. That numinous web is evident to our deeper awareness whenever we take time to quiet ourselves in nature. By quieting ourselves, I don't mean just not talking, I refer to that inner stillness mentioned above which allows us to really see and hear what is happening around us.

An image I often use when I am in nature is that of a spider web. Although its fibers are tremendously strong, it is very delicate. The slightest breath of breeze or the movement of a tiny insect caught in its elastic fibers communicates information to the spider resting upon it. So let your mind be as open and flexible as a delicate web in the sunlight. Then the subtle, the simple, and the magical can play upon its fibers like the strings of a harp. I learned this from a spider who had made her web very near the head of my bed, weaving together some special objects there. In order to call my attention to them in a different way, she danced on the web in such way that my still mind heard an actual tune, a vibrating of the strings. It was a tremendous gift.

I like John O'Donohue's way of speaking of nature on his *Aman Cara: Wisdom of the Celtic World* tapes: "The great divinity called nature is not matter, but a luminous and numinous presence which has depth and possibility and beauty within it."

Taking time for solitude in the natural world is a vitally important practice for we as humans. In that solitude, we seldom find isolation or outward silence. Instead we find a great, buzzing family of life all around us. The wind whispers, the trees dance in the breeze, the birds fly by or sit to sing a song of beauty, insects busy themselves in every nook and cranny, flowers nod and turn toward the sun, and the rain blesses it all. In such a setting, it is easier for us to understand ourselves as part of a numinous kinship which offers gifts of wisdom at every turn. When we come to a sense of outer belonging and the rightness of all the unity, then it may be easier to come to a sense of inner belonging—to accept all aspects of ourselves as parts of an evolving wholeness. In this way, both inner and outer solitude can bring us to a sense of the holy in all things.

GRATEFULNESS

The final thing I would have you remember to practice is gratitude. When you are focusing on things you are grateful for, you are investing your energy in what you would like to see more of in your life. Be grateful for the gift of life you receive every day; be grateful for the opportunity to be alive in this amazing time; give thanks for the difficult issues that are in your face, for soon you will be clear of them and moving toward the light more smoothly. Be grateful for friends, for Grace, for the great Light which Creator is sending our way to uplift us into a time of exquisite beauty on Lady Gaia. Give joyful thanks that we are on our way Home!

TOGETHER WE FLY

The most intensely burning edge of spirituality which we face today concerns our relationships. They are, in a word, bad—at almost every level I can perceive. In order to awake ourselves fully, to *embody* spirit at the level of which will serve us, we must shift this aspect of our lives, and shift it radically. This we won't do by "resolving all the issues we have with each other"—we will more likely do it by relegating them to the level of non-issues and simply letting most of them go. Many of our challenges in this line are manufactured problems—not real issues of spirit. The real challenge here is to get large enough that our petty issues are dropped, so that we can see more clearly what really needs to be addressed.

We need to touch each other—literally and deeply. The communion, the oneness on this Earth plane we seek, will not be found in separation. Our own connection with Source through our personal and silent time, yes, but not the fullness of our daily lives: that must be found in common union—community. I believe that much of the actual healing we need will occur as we place our hands upon each other and ask Creator to bring oneness, and thus healing, wholeness, and in the end holiness into our bodies and our lives (the words *health, heal, whole,* and *holy* all come from the same Latin root, and have a similar sense of the inclusion of All). The medicine we need will never lie in getting smaller or more exclusive; it lies in the direction of unity, expansion, and inclusiveness.

When White Buffalo Calf Woman came among us bringing the Sacred Pipe which represents wholeness and holiness—the respectful honoring of our unity with all things—she reminded us of its importance for the continuance of Life itself. Ken Carey in *Return of the Bird Tribes* brings us her words: "Creation does not take place where there is a scattering and dissipation of energies," she explained, "Creation requires a gathering together and focusing of your power within a circle of commitment—like a seed, an egg, a womb or a marriage. If you would create and not destroy, you must remember always the Sacred Hoop. Consider wisely the ways in which you would use your power and then around those ways draw the sacred circle of commitment. In the warm atmosphere of that circle, the power of love builds and builds like a storm above the wet summer prairie until the circle can hold no more and explodes in the conception of the new." Our holy Elder Sister encourages us to enlarge our lives to include all levels of life. "You here live in all possible worlds, but you are conscious only of one, the physical, the external."

White Buffalo Woman calls us, over and over again, to awaken ourselves into the fullness of who we truly are—the richness of our total being, inclusive of and yet far greater than the simply physical. In this way, her call is the same clarion call which has come to us down through the ages, and for which we now receive enormously supportive light and energy.

In sharing the lighting and smoking of the Sacred Pipe, she tells us, "This, your individual human life, like the single flame that burns this twig, is sufficient to light a great fire. As long as the love that burns within you is turned toward self-centered pursuits, it will remain tiny like this flame. Remaining tiny, it will bring you no joy. Eventually, in the swirling winds of spirit, it will be extinguished. But when you in harmony with the Great Spirit, your flame of love is fanned by those same spirit winds. You are in love with the very purpose of life! You light the fire of love in all you meet. You know the purpose of your walk through this world, and you know why the Great One gave you a life flame: not so that you could keep your tiny flame to yourself, loving what you need only, but so that you could give it away, and with the fire of your love, bring consciousness to earth."

Too often these days, we find numerous and sufficient reasons not to share our love and thus bring more consciousness into our daily lives. Whether it be race or color or tribe or class or locale—we find ourselves excluding others. The cycle of victimization and violence has become too much a part of us—having been victimized, we in turn seek to victimize others. And running through it all is devilish Judgment—we foolishly feel wise enough to judge others. We use our small-minded standards, and haughtily decide the worth or goodness of another person or group. How very foolish! What heavy and unnecessary burdens we are shouldering by doing this.

The great teachings of all time tell us that whatever we put out, we are receiving back at the very same time. We make war on others through conflict, anger, judgment, negative energy, exclusion, yet think we will find peace even though we are living in a war zone of our own making. Such a strange way to proceed! How harshly judgment comes back upon us when we presume to judge others.

The energy we extend is immediately perceived, even though on levels that may be less than conscious. Our angry, harsh energy sent to someone who does something foolish or pushy in traffic may be just enough to send them over the breaking edge in their life. We cannot know what events and forces have shaped their life and their day; what challenges and traumas are weighing upon them. Rather than the barbs of anger that we usually sling, we might just say, "Oops, that didn't work very well. That person must need some love and light in his life—to feel better, be more functional, be more courteous, be more awake to what is happening around him. I'll just send him a little good energy. And thanks, Great Spirit, for the opportunity to extend and grow my love." Standing in a committed circle of Love, the love bounces right back to you, making your day better. And it is certainly received by that one to whom you sent it. Perhaps, instead of tipping over the breaking edge, you might help trigger a lifting of mood and spirit that makes a real and positive difference in that other person's life. Which would you rather do? Which way would you rather be treated?

Carolyn Myss in her "Energy Anatomy" teachings tells a story of a woman who is stopped in heavy rush-hour traffic by an accident. Ahead of her several cars, an injured woman is lying on a stretcher beside the road. Rather than be angry that she will be late home from work, the driver has compassion for this woman, and sends the most loving energy she can send to her. On the other end of the exchange, the injured woman is "unconscious," and through an out-of-body experience she literally sees the warm golden energy come to her from within the car down the line. In her altered state, she is able to see the license plate and the loving face of the woman behind the wheel. It takes her months to recover her health, but she has brought through into consciousness the license number of that one woman, of all the drivers honking and yelling and cursing the stupidity of those involved in the wreck, who sent her love and light. Looking up the kind woman's address, she one day rings the doorbell to present her with a bouquet of flowers!

The energy we put out *is* perceived. More even that the flowers after the fact, the kind woman was gifted in the very moment of her sending love, with a heart full of love. What a wonderful gift to give oneself!

STANDING TOGETHER

An important understanding is one from our recent history. As we awakened in the '60s and early '70s, we were beginning to form an invincible force for unity, peace—for taking care of each other and our Mother Earth. People from all walks of life, all races, all countries—our unity was incredibly powerful. We understood our power at some small level; but those who stay in power by creating fear and division and unconsciousness knew it even more fully. Big international cartels and powerful monied interests saw us more clearly than we saw ourselves, and began a campaign of divisiveness. After directly confronting us at Kent State and Wounded Knee and other places which received very negative press and actually *helped* our cause, they realized that tactic was not the right one. We would obviously not buckle their direct pressure.

So they got very smart. They went underground, if you will, and began planting seeds of anger, judgment, division, prejudice, and hatred among us. We were not ready to recognize them for what they were. Too many bought into the conflict game, and our power was splintered. I felt it most in the anger and scathing attacks which came toward "rainbow" and half-breed teachers who worked across the lines of race and tribe to create awakening. Those in other areas of the country and other walks of life felt it in a backlash of fundamental "Christians." Foresters and ecologists threw injurious words and actions back and forth. Wherever its ugly head arose, the quick judgment and negativity which followed it shattered the power we were building. Some forgot that peace was the objective and began to play the games of conflict again. Sad, but very true. Disillusionment naturally followed.

Now is time to awaken from those games. Like children fighting and scratching over a toy who then drop it and become friends when each is offered an ice cream, we must literally drop our conflict, our *attitude* of conflict. Yes, there are things to work out among us. Yes, our learning in the area of good relationship is very lacking. And yes, we can work all this out by practicing unity and peace *in the process*.

My friend Lynne Dusenberry Crow shares the way of keeping humor in our lives by understanding that we are all so very human, that we all have our Achille's heel, and that no matter what we might do, we are still part of the family. Someone might say,"Uh-oh, there goes Barbara again, moving one more time, spending her energy on packing boxes. I wonder if she will ever get rooted in one place and stop asking us to help her move that darn heavy stuff!" and then laughter ensues, because the speaker recognizes that she herself is just getting divorced for the third time—her own Achille's heel. And John is being angry and hateful again, his Achille's heel, and Pete is wanting to run things and have power over everybody—his weakness. More laughter. Aren't we a deal? Aren't we crazy? And aren't we all so very human—we are obviously here to learn and grow. And isn't it true that we can grow past these things in a loving circle which stills our fears and lays to rest our need to separate ourselves? Even when a child in a native home is sent out of the circle as a punishment, he is not sent outside the circle of love. That love still holds him, saying, "The most loving thing I can do for you is to let you know now that violence and hurting others is not acceptable. You think about how it feels to be outside of things, and then let's find other ways for you to get what you need and want. You are very much loved."

Inclusiveness, nonjudgment, yes. Discernment, for sure. But meanness, conflict, threats, injury, denial—no, no, no. We are a family. White Buffalo Woman reminds us that we are more than family; we are one with each other.

"Whatever you do to any other thing or being in the circle of life," she exhorts us, "you do to yourself, for you are One." Lifting ourselves to the level of spirit and wholeness, we come to our conflicts and challenges with a much different energy. And in the meantime, we practice peace, moment to moment.

There has been a terrible history among we two-leggeds, certainly in the last few hundred years on this continent. Yet if any of us are to live well, we must listen with all our hearts to Ken Carey's words from White Buffalo Calf Pipe Woman:

> Remember always to treat every creature as a sacred being: the people that live beyond the mountains, the winged ones of the air, the four-footed, the fishes that hide beneath the cool rock in silver streams and lakes, all of these are your sisters and your brothers. All are sacred parts of the body of the Great Spirit. Each one is holy.
>
> The most difficult part ... may be to extend this respect to the people of your neighboring tribes. Remember, like you, they are sacred people, given a specific task to do in the great Being of Wakan Tanka. Their work is not your own, their tasks differ from yours, but the purpose you serve is the same. The sun that shines upon you does not see you as being so very different. In peace you must live side by side with those of a different shade of the color red.
>
> For a people are coming soon who do not share the color of your skin, but are white like the snow that falls in the winter months. With them will also come those of black skin. And those of yellow skin. And those of colors in between.
>
> ... The colors [must] blend together in rainbows that arch across the prairie when the storm has passed.... Through peaceful blending with your neighboring tribes, be an inspiration to the wandering peoples. Help lead all races into the harmony of the rainbow.

The good news is that the rainbow is arching across all our people again. We are finding the power and the sweetness of unity and cooperation, of sharing and honoring.

CIRCLES OF POWER

It is vitally important for us to come together in circles of power to create the life we envision for ourselves and seven generations of our children. Here are several of the ways I see to do that:

1. Circles of Seven

The Dawn Star, who native peoples know as the Christ-light in the Americas, tells us that a new pattern has been set in the etheric realms of Earth. That pattern is one of seven people coming together in a circle of commitment on a mutually important issue. Rather than working on it from the usual viewpoint of the physical and manifest realm, using the normal tools of intellect and emotion, the members of this circle are asked to clear themselves of personal and interpersonal concerns enough to lift themselves into another level of functioning. This new, unified level is the Spirit or unmanifest level—the shimmering invisible where energy is yet unformed. Out of the awareness and understanding they find there, a mutual intent can be formed and placed into the Silence, magnified exponentially by the power of seven. When a circle gathers together with this Intent to upliftment, the Dawn Star indicates that He will create a corresponding pull from above, especially as we visualize His energy as a star slightly above the center of the circle. This configuration puts into practice the scientific magic of Intent, Silence, and Unity. And whatever is placed into the Silence will manifest powerfully in the world, helping us deal with real issues and crises on Earth in a new way. James Redfield gives a teaching story about this kind of action in *The Tenth Insight*, based on principles of unity he brought through in *The Celestine Prophecy*. It's useful to review these as you gather your circle of seven.

To help you understand this a bit better, I will illustrate the principle through an example that my friend Pam Montgomery uses in her teaching and expounds in her book, *Partner Earth*. Let's say a group of researchers wanted to create something that was light, unbreakable, easy to form in many shapes, and waterproof. They came up with something we call plastic. It, indeed, met the criteria which they had set out, but in the end has caused great challenges ecologically and otherwise through the toxicity of its manufacturing process and its very indestructibility. Thus, a small problem was solved, yet it brought about larger problems for All Our Relations. Then picture of different scenario: these researchers set out their criteria, and then added one more thing—that it work for All Our Relations down through the generations. They might have gathered together and meditated to lift their energy into Spirit, where all answers are given from oneness and harmony. The product that would have come from that larger collaboration would have met the initial criteria, and as well, been in resonance with the larger life, harmonizing in a good way with the ongoing flow of things without damage, destruction, or harm.

This is how the circles of seven can proceed. The most challenging work is to eliminate the urge to control, manipulate, force, push against, exclude, and move from fear or judgment. The next step is to image the highest possible outcome and add the prayer for All Our Relations. Then, Silence, and putting that Intent forward. After that the work is done and the seven are free to go. They will naturally scatter into other circles of seven, drawn by other issues and the people vitally concerned. This is a new way of leadership, without hierarchy—fluid and incredibly powerful.

2. Dedication Dances

Another way of coming together which I have taught for years is the Dedication Dance. This is the coming together of an entire community of people, hopefully on a regular basis, to create a beneficial outcome.

To illustrate, let me use a native American community as an example. In this community, people come together for pow-wows. These are cultural events where everyone wears their finest traditional clothing and dances for prizes. I have suggested to them that instead of only gathering in this way and for this reason, that they come together in their high school gym once a month. During the previous weeks, a group of interested persons would meet to decide the theme for the month—perhaps it would center around issues concerning the children, the elders, the school system, nuclear waste dumping on the reservation, or the need for rain during a parched summer. When the basic issue was decided, then a clear image of the outcome desired would be formed, so that all people who came for the dance could hold a similar vision, one in harmony with All Our Relations.

Beginning with a prayer or dedication to that vision and All Our Relations, the evening would be spent dancing in one's finest outfit for the outcome that had been set. Every step, every conversation, every exchange, every bit of energy that is put forward in any way for the entire evening would be dedicated. Then as a completion, all would enter into the Silence and send forth the vision.

Very likely, a pot-luck meal would have been brought, and the evening could conclude with a feast and celebration. What a good feeling to go home knowing you had put your best energy forward for something important for your people! And besides, you would have had a wonderful visit with friends—an enjoyable time for all.

3. Spirit Dances

I am being asked to bring together large groups of people to do ceremony and dance to uplift our energy. These gatherings will very likely have seven teachers to help participants deepen their learning about the Four Directions, Mother Earth, Father Spirit, and the heartbeat drum at our Center (whether our own beating heart or a great community drum). Each group will be asked to create an honoring for the aspect they are working with, and all will gather together to present a pageant of these honorings. There will be drumming, music, dance, and a high intention for what we can create in our world as we put our energies together. In the music and in our relationships we will practice harmony, and have a wonderful time doing so.

These "dances" will be an opportunity to come together to find unity and joy and high purpose in being together again. What have we had for a decade or two that calls us to this kind of aliveness and joy? Very little, in my estimation. Through these large gatherings, we will energize a whole city, an entire region, to live at a different level of wholeness and Intent for the world. We will awaken again our hope and our hearts, something of which we are very much in need.

There is another thing to consider as we think about these dances. I have spoken of the vibration we carry as being very important. Another vibration that is of utmost importance is the speed of our lives. Mother Earth's frequency is somewhere around eight megahertz, yet we spend more time at the 120 megahertz level of electricity. Our lives are more like intense screeching and pounding on a tin drum, jumping wildly about, than they are listening to the soft beats of a hide drum and dancing rhythmically in a circle. Mother Earth feels our energy and the quality of our steps on her face.

It is time for us to dance in soothing circles upon her, stepping lightly with joy and a beautiful vision in our hearts. It is also time to dance wildly, with spirited aliveness, ready to make a positive difference with our energy. It is time to truly "Dance Awake the Dream," a theme I began with the Harmonic Convergence gathering in 1987.

In your community, these gatherings would likely be simple to create. Nonprofit events are easily publicized, and often the places for them are donated. Those who care deeply about the focal issue, as well as those who simply wish to put forth some positive energy and enjoy the gathering, will be called together.

It's time for us to practice these ways again. Primary peoples of the past understood that this was how they created their lives—through gathering in circles of commitment and power to dance awake their dreams—whether it's the Sun Dance among the northern plains tribes or the Pueblos' Corn Dance. We will come to know again the power and joy of this way of co-creating our world. We will vision and walk a path of beauty into a radiant future.

4. Wakantia: Flowering Earth Trainings

I also want to share with you another new level of work I have recently been given in vision; this is the description:

> *Wakantia*
> *Flowering Earth Trainings*
> Come join us in places of beauty and sacredness.
> The purpose of this work is to awaken and challenge
> you to the next level of being human on this sweet earth.
> It is to tune and tone you, cleanse and clarify you,
> so that new ways of being will become available.
> It is to support you and en-courage you
> so you have the heart and skill
> to leap into the unknown.
> We seek beauty and Magic Leading to Miracles !!
> Come along!
> Ho!

These trainings are meant to create groups of dedicated people who work together toward the next level of being human. As I find those individuals who are willing to commit deeply to the process, we will delve into the truth which lives within us and rise high on the currents of Love and Light which come toward us. We will explore music and magic—becoming minstrels of a new way of playing the human game. My sense is that new ways of teaching, sharing, and dancing our aliveness (rather than making a living) may ensue. Coming together in new configurations of community may arise from our mutual endeavors.

Long after I was given the idea of the Flowering Earth Trainings, I was given the name *Wakantia*. Although I sensed that it was a Lakota word, I did not know its meaning. What I learned from the elders is that it is a feminine word meaning "keepers of the sacred house," or in the old concepts, "dog-soldiers of the sacred lodge." This could mean as well "caretakers of the sacred home," which led me to a deeper understanding of the work of this group. It is to be an elite (meaning light pouring forth) corps of individuals dedicated to caring for our home, this sweet Earth, and All Our Relations upon her, through exploring and sharing ways of bringing light to our new level of being. It seems a tall order, yet I know that working together in star configurations of seven, setting our Intent for the highest and finest, supporting each other, and lifting into Spirit will be an unstoppable combination. We will mount up on the wings of eagles, and from that uplifted place, create a flowering of life, all life, on our Lady Gaia.

I am happy to be included in this book, which is a beautiful model of putting our wisdom together to make a better world. I am proud to be one feather in the magnificent bird which is a great nation of women who care enough to fly in front of the V on this transformative journey, making the way easier for all who follow.

For All My Relations—I have spoken.

Glennifer Gillespie lives and works in the United States and South Africa. She has lived in an intentional community for sixteen years and has at various times in her life worked as a teacher, journalist, film and theater critic, and at improving the quality of education in the disadvantaged communities of South Africa. She currently earns her living as an organizational development practitioner while continuing to explore and practice a lifelong interest in the evolution of human consciousness and women's ways of being.

Ringing Out into the World: The Transforming Power of Women's Circles

Even here in the desert of New Mexico, thousands of miles away and years later, all I have to do is imagine for a moment, and my feet remember the way to our meeting room. I can feel the uneven brickwork and smell the Yesterday-Today-and-Tomorrow bush, evoke the interior world of my life in Cape Town in the '70s and '80s. I am immediately back in South Africa, walking the narrow path across the garden to sit in a circle with the women of my community.

At times I went eagerly, knowing that there was joy and friendship ahead or that we would be exploring something I was really interested in; sometimes I dragged my feet, afraid that I might have to reveal something of myself that I was ashamed of, or aware that I had to speak the truth publicly about a difficult matter and that few would agree with me.

Some of the women who sat with me in those circles in South Africa from 1975 onward lived in intentional spiritual community together; others formed part of an extended community that gathered regularly for work, worship, and fellowship. Many of us are only now beginning to see something of what we were doing when we obeyed the impulse to gather in this way, and can reflect on and harvest what we rather awkwardly learned then. Many of us have moved on to sit in other circles or live in other communities, taking with us the understanding of women's ways of being and knowing which unfolded as we worked together in the circle.

As we struggled with what to do and what to talk about, we discovered that in the process we were healing and blessing and challenging ourselves and each other. We often chose a topic that was important to us to talk about. We also listened to music and made music and sang together. We danced and talked and read poetry and gave gifts to each other. We created ceremonies and rituals to celebrate daughters' passages into womanhood.

We talked about men, about our own bodies, about the changing cycles of our lives. We speculated about the millennium and Earth changes. We read articles about sun flares and celebrated the solstices. We wondered about the appearance of crop circles in England, and devoured videos about ancient mother goddess practices in Europe. We determinedly held the vision of an integrated and just social order for our beloved South Africa. We supported and blessed both F. W. de Klerk and Nelson Mandela, and we wrestled, aghast, with our own and one another's prejudices. Against the prevailing political climate, we struggled to include women of all races in our circles. And we ran public workshops and seminars for the wider community of women to share our stories, insights, and experiences about the archetypal stages which unfolded in women's lives.

We were willing to be bored together, to sit and wait until something happened. We each took responsibility when it was our turn to lead, follow, organize, or set up the space, and we always came to circle meetings. We came when we didn't feel like coming, when we were afraid to come, when we could easily have been doing something "more interesting." We stuck it out when our husbands and partners complained, and some of us drove for hours to be together for just an afternoon. The deliberate commitment to something larger than ourselves, which at the same time was something unnameable which nourished each individual, was a critical part of the process we were engaged in. This process was partly conscious and deliberate, and partly unconscious in the sense that we were creating as we went along. These circles established a foundation of friendship and exploration that continues to this day.

Because most of us came from a spiritual tradition that was nonconflictual and which held agreement as a core value, we struggled in the circle with whether and how to disagree. Underlying the need for consonance (which I have come across in many spiritually oriented communities, particularly young ones which have not yet developed processes for surfacing and articulating divergent viewpoints) was the fear that differences would fragment rather than strengthen the circle. And behind that fear lay the old inherited behaviors and coping mechanisms of women, developed because submission and obedience have been required of us. These behaviors sprang from experience that taught us that our only power lies in solidarity; that to stand up and challenge existing rules as individuals is dangerous and could bring punishment; that there are safer, indirect ways to get around things; and ultimately, that conflict brings violence and that we as women will likely be the losers. So learning to disagree directly with one another while at the same time avoiding voting, taking sides, or ganging up was one of the challenges that faced us, especially in the early days.

There was another important piece of the emerging picture of our women's circle at that time. From about 1986 onwards, many of us who sat in the circle meetings also became involved in women's outdoor programs of all kinds, from one-day group excursions into the mountains to six-day wilderness intensives. Encountering the Earth in this way deepened our relationships profoundly and took us into our wilder selves and the rhythms underlying everyday experiences.

Vivid in my memory is one occasion when sixteen of us, including two women in their sixties, one in her seventies, one in her fifties who had never hiked before, and several remarkably unfit women in their forties, took off on an expedition into the mountains. We wanted to visit a mountain pool and waterfall where the Cape Red Disa, a rare local flower, grew. We arrived back at the base camp at the end of the day just before dark, the younger women almost carrying some of those who had found the trip challenging. If someone had looked down on us from above, they would have seen something resembling a slow-moving caterpillar inching its way across the mountainside, with all the parts draped over one another in various ways for support! Experiences like these deepened the spirit of the circle and connected us to our internal wildness.

CIRCLES OF SUPPORT AND MEANING

While what we were creating was new in the late '70s, everywhere I go nowadays I notice the phenomenon of women's circles. They are emerging in many places around the world as part of a movement to explore, reinvent, and reintroduce women's ways of knowing and leading as an alternative to the prevailing cultural modes. They are also part of a larger pattern of psychospiritual development which is not confined to women, but is being undertaken by both women and men for their own growth, for the greater good, and to influence human consciousness. Circles both provide support for the participants and encourage them to explore new models and processes for relating to one another. These new ways of being together allow people to feel their way into the future.

Some of the practices in this field include the work of Dialogue, the revival and development of indigenous Tribal Council processes, old Quaker practices, storytelling circles, and sacred ritual work of all kinds. The culture of the circle is egalitarian, inclusive, truthful, loving, respectful, community-oriented, and diverse, and one of its greatest gifts is its capacity to hold and sustain ritual space for a variety of purposes.

Women's circles have always been present in indigenous communities, usually relating to traditional customs and the observance of rites of passage of various kinds. In these communities, women's circles have been essentially conservative in nature, with the overt intention of maintaining the status quo of the culture or tradition of which they are a part.

One of the main differences between the new circles and those of tribal communities is that they seem to be radical in their purpose, at least with respect to the larger culture of which they are a part. They are definitely not conservative. They are in many ways a revolt against the accepted ways of behaving, and certainly against the norms and values of current Western social practice, in particular the prevailing American philosophy of competitive rugged individualism.

A foundational premise of the circle is the idea that collaborative social interaction can help create a different way of doing things. These circles are providing a container for women in which to think, to experiment with new practices, and to risk in a safe space knowing that they will be seen, heard, and respected for what they are trying to do. Doing all this outside the company of men, or with other women who have similar values, means that women can grow and strengthen new ways of doing and being in a friendly environment where the odds are not against them and they are not constantly challenged to provide rational proof for what they are engaged in. They can work with others who value intuition as a useful premise for moving forward.

I think that circle gatherings are one of the places where the transformation of consciousness is being intensified. What this means will of course be different for each circle, depending on where the participants are in their own growth cycles and what their expressed or tacit needs may be. In some circles, women simply tell their stories. I was invited to a one-time-only women's circle in England two years ago, in which everyone had a chance to tell their stories. For some, this was the first time they had been listened to, or had listened to others, in this way, and they found that the experience stirred the deeper recesses of their beings in touching and unfamiliar ways.

In other circles, women work a particular field together. A good example of this kind of grouping is a dedicated circle of seven musicians I know of who use music to work with the dying and who meet regularly to develop their art. Still other circles exist so that women can learn from one another using their everyday life as a learning lab. The members of one I am aware of in Michigan are part of a church congregation and they join with a sister circle in the same town to celebrate the solstices. I have sat in an annual International Women's Dialogue circle for a number of years, the purpose of which is simply to enter into dialogue together and to bring our whole selves to the experience. A circle I know of in Stellenbosch, just outside Cape Town, consisting of about twenty members, meets every two weeks with the purpose of encouraging women to tell their life stories into a deep listening field.

THE WISE WOUND: LIFE PASSAGES

In 1988, our women's circle came across a book by Penelope Shuttle and Peter Redgrave, *The Wise Wound*, which is a powerful psychospiritual exploration into the territory of menstruation. At the time it was written, it was a courageous venture into an undiscussible field. After a few of us had read the book, we decided that we would draw together a circle of about twenty-five women to delve into the subject of menstruation and its meaning for us. We were deeply into making sense and meaning of our life experiences as women, and this seemed a worthy new area that was ripe for exploration.

The winter of 1988 was especially wet and dark, and it felt as though those of us who chose to commit to this particular circle project were going into womb-space together. We found ourselves embarking on a journey which profoundly changed our lives, the lives of our daughters, and those of the other young women for whom we felt responsible. We met every Wednesday evening during that winter, with the rain beating relentlessly on the tin roof, the notorious Cape Town wind howling outside, and the woefully inadequate South African heaters struggling to warm the room in which we gathered.

As we thought about how to begin, we realized that menstruation was only one of a series of critical significant stages in a woman's life, some of which were social and some of which were biological. This led us to trying to identify what seemed to us to be the most important and powerful life stages or transitions common to all women everywhere, whether they lived in New Guinea or New York City. These we agreed were

birth
the onset of menses
the first significant relationship and/or induction into sexual practice
marriage or committed partnership
mothering
the cessation of menses
aging and dying

We realized that not all women necessarily experienced all stages, but that they were at least possible for most. We also knew that none of us had made the transitions between these stages either fully consciously or completely successfully. For some of us, they had been messy and unsupported. For most, they had been relatively unconscious experiences during which we were only dimly aware of what was happening.

We had all ages represented in the circle. The eldest women were in their late sixties and early seventies, the youngest in their twenties. Most of us were in our thirties and hungry to hear what lay ahead for us from those who had already walked the sections of the path we had not yet reached. I was thirty-nine at the time—just touching into midlife, restless and uncomfortable without knowing why.

As we told our stories, the enormity of what we were undertaking began to reveal itself. It became clear that each of us was really telling the story of her life as marked by the significant stages, and that we were learning to know each other in ways we had never touched before. Many of us had been friends for ten years or more, and some had lived intimately together in community. Yet we began to see ourselves and each other anew and, as we spoke our lives into the ritual space created by the circle, we found that we were reconstructing and recreating—even changing—our past. It was the power of the circle to change what had been, if people were willing to speak the unspoken and be witnessed doing so, that awoke us to the potential of this work.

A woman in her seventies spoke about how she had gone into her wedding night totally unprepared for what to expect. Another told of the trauma of her first sexual experience as a teenager. No one had been adequately prepared for the onset of their menses, although we knew that our parents had done the best they could. We listened in amazement to a woman who had been slapped in the face by her mother when her periods began, as part of the tradition she was raised in. Some of us had at best been ignored at that time, and at worst had ended up feeling ashamed, embarrassed, confused, or "cursed." The only induction many of us had received was that we were furtively given a packet of pads, and then been the recipient of comments from our fathers such as, "I hear you're a woman now." Some of us had had the fear of God put into us because now we were able to "fall" pregnant, it seemed with astonishing ease, by associating with boys. The boys we had always known suddenly became strangely attractive potential enemies of whose intentions we had to be suspicious.

A tough subject to talk about for the older women was the experience of menopause, which at that time was even more undiscussible than menstruation. Those of us who were younger had heard alarming tales about vaginal atrophy, loss of libido, osteoporosis, and insomnia as some of the accompanying characteristics of menopause. Most of us were determined, though, not to go the route of hormone replacement therapy. Our values led us to believe that we could negotiate this passage "naturally" and emerge wise women. To our amazement, we heard from the older women of our community a whole range of stories. One was on HRT, another had sailed through perimenopause without even noticing until one day her periods simply stopped. Yet another was still bleeding in her sixties. We were fascinated. Our mothers, many of whom had had hysterectomies, never spoke about these matters. At that time, there seemed to be no meaningful or reliable books on the subject. We remembered our grandmothers, victims of hot flashes, turning red and fanning themselves vigorously (mine used to say "*O, ek kry benoud!*—I'm claustrophobic!") but never speaking about what was happening to them.

By speaking about what had been missing in our life passages, by remembering our pain and bewilderment at those times, and by being witnessed in the circle, we began to heal and affirm ourselves and each other. We also saw the difference it might have made in our lives if these stages had been marked and celebrated significantly. We began to feel some pride in our womanhood and a sense of wonderment in reclaiming our birthright.

WHAT ABOUT OUR DAUGHTERS?

With new awareness born out of storytelling and reflecting on how transitions in our life-passages had been handled, we knew that we would never want the young women we were responsible for to have the unconscious or painful experiences to which we had been subjected. So we began thinking about what we could do as a community for our daughters.

Together we created a Rites of Passage program for our fourteen- to sixteen-year-olds that involved all the women in the community. This program took the young women through a structured process over a period of three to six months, depending on what felt right for each girl. The program was based on the seven stages of women's lives which we had worked through during the previous winter, and the idea was that at the end of the process, the young woman would be formally and ceremonially received into the community of women who had initiated her.

The backbone of the program we created, and which is still operating, is that small groups of three or four women are responsible for taking each girl through one stage of life, basing their session on their own insight and life experience. The session is tailored to suit the girl; for example, one young woman from a single-parent family required specific open discussion about divorce. A girl whose mother was in a same-sex partnership needed uniquely different information and conversation around the themes of marriage and partnering. Some girls are quite innocent and need a gentle introduction to their own sexuality. Others are more worldly-wise, and must be met differently if they are to break open and experience themselves anew. It is very important that the young woman wants to engage in the program, and that she chooses the circle of women with whom she would like to be directly involved. To initiate the process, the community women's circle meets to honor the girl's unique spirit and her life thus far, and to establish a container or holding space for the transition process she is about to undergo.

An important aspect of the program is the way in which parents release their daughters into womanhood. The first Rites of Passage session is attended only by mother and daughter; after that, the girl is in the hands of the other women of the circle. In this initial session, the mother tells her daughter the story of her conception and birth. For me as a mother, this was a touching and powerful experience.

In preparation for the session, and aware that every detail mattered, I chose my clothes carefully. I decided to wear red as a symbol of the womb, blood, and birth. My daughter Kelly got ready in her own room, and I left before her to create the ritual space to receive her into. When she arrived at the meeting place, she, too, coincidentally, was wearing red. Kelly is now a young woman of twenty-two. Here are some of her thoughts from her journal about that time:

> I have just had my first Rites of Passage experience. Ruth picked me up at 3:50 and dropped me off at Ros' house. I was greeted at the door by Dorothy, who welcomed me and showed me into the lounge, where Mom was sitting. There were beautiful flower arrangements, including a single red rose on the coffee table and a paraffin candle. Dorothy brought us tea and scones and then left Mom and me alone in the house. I felt embarrassed because I don't feel very comfortable being alone with Mom anymore. But after a while, I began to see her in a totally new light.... I know that it is hard for a person to tell someone else, especially if the person is a lot younger, about a very special part of her life, and as I listened to my mother sharing with me about my conception, birth, and childhood, I realized how deeply I respect and appreciate her.... When I left, Mom gave me the rosebud, I blew out the candle, and I felt within me an absolute desire to be a beautiful and creative woman.

Today, Kelly comments, "A sweet and naive entry, but I can still remember the breathless beauty that clothed that first meeting. I still know the jolt that awoke my fourteen-year-old consciousness to the realization that this was to be no ordinary process, and that what my mother was giving me was to be of great importance in my life.

"What followed were six other meetings—in homes, on the mountainside, at garden picnics—which always involved a profound amount of care and preparation on the part of different women from the community. At one meeting, I was given something particularly special—a letter and a silver locket from my father. The letter explained how significant and exciting it was for him to share in the difficult process of releasing me into a life stage requiring him to let go of the control and protection he had previously provided in my life. This letting go, with care and concern, was what characterized my Rites of Passage process and enabled me to step with power and certainty into a new dimension of myself."

As parents, my husband Gary and I both experienced the relief of releasing Kelly, who at fourteen, was showing all the usual signs of adolescent rebellion, into a larger community space. She needed to spread her wings and our nuclear family alone was no longer enough for her. We wanted her to be mentored and held by a body of adults whom we could trust.

The Rites of Passage for Young Women has been enormously successful in our community. There is far more to it than what I have described here, but the point I am making is that it sprang from a dedicated women's circle. This circle created the space for tremendous psychospiritual growth for those who were part of it, as well as for the young women we were privileged to serve and mentor. It is an excellent example of what can spring from sustained ritual space in which life serves life for the greater blessing of all. It also illustrates that women's ways of knowing and leading throughout the entire process, from idea through conceptualization and planning to execution, were essentially egalitarian, participative, and collaborative.

This circle emphasized listening and affirming, creating, and birthing a new approach together, gathering into our midst the resources we needed and sharing them, and creating an atmosphere of mutual love and respect which was never broken. We deliberately nurtured each other, and our intention was to explore, heal, and understand the meaning of our own past experience. We wished for our daughters a conscious experience of the common passages they would be entering as their lives unfolded, while acknowledging that each girl would be different and would have a unique destiny. We took steps to ensure that the next generation of women in our care would, to the best of our ability, be given the foundation which was the fruit of our own healing, so that as they matured, they could move on from the finest that we had to offer, into territory that our generation would probably never know.

THE CIRCLE OF SEVEN

Many years later, as I approach fifty, I find myself part of another circle—a circle of seven women of whom the eldest is seventy-three and the youngest thirty-six. It is a dedicated circle, which means that it is voluntary, meets regularly, retains the same membership, and that we are all committed to one another and the emergent work we are doing together. It also means that it is a virtual circle in that we remain closely in touch with one another's lives when we are not together, and at all times hold the space of the circle.

We have been meeting for three years and gather approximately every three months for four days at different places in North America, since the members come from New Mexico, New York, California, Colorado, and British Columbia. We travel as cheaply as possible, stay for the most part in one another's homes, and divide up the expenses among us. Whoever is hosting buys the food and plans the menu, and we all take turns preparing the meals and share the housekeeping. We schedule circle meetings one year at a time, and they are priorities in our lives in spite of many family and professional demands on our time.

The Circle of Seven began with a specific idea in mind—that we would meet to create a Rites of Passage Program for women, so that those who were going through a life transition could enter ritualized liminal space to mark the passage they were entering and be consciously held through it by other women. Six of us met for the first time in Santa Fe in June 1995. We pushed ourselves hard to create a women's program, but it didn't take long before we realized that this was not the real reason why we had called the circle into being. It was really for us.

As we all spoke in the circle for the first time, letting every voice be heard at the beginning of our time together, it became clear that we were all in transition ourselves. Two of our number were moving out of the intentional communities they had been part of for much of their lives. One was in the process of leaving behind a home and a marriage that had sustained and nourished her for over twenty years. Another had moved from her home country, changed careers, and separated from her husband. Yet another had experienced a painful separation from a partner of thirteen years and had just entered a new and challenging relationship. The last one was facing a life-challenging illness in her husband of fifty-two years. All except two of us were experiencing homelessness and dislocation because we did not know where we were going next and had lost many of our external landmarks and moorings. We later discovered that several of us were in menopause.

After we realized that we had called the circle into being for a purpose that was not yet clear, and were comfortable with not knowing what that purpose was, we began experimenting. We somehow knew that the only place we could start from was ourselves. So we began to speak our lives as they were then, sometimes by describing what was happening to us, sometimes by talking about our inner landscapes, sometimes by telling the circle about a particularly uncomfortable or difficult situation. One woman spoke touchingly about her small grandchild who had begun having seizures and of her deep desire to support her daughter, who was a single parent and short of money. Another told of the love she had for two men, one young and the other older, and of her inability to resolve these two important relationships in her life. As each person spoke, the tears began to flow—not just for the speaker, but for all of us. We began to accept weeping as a necessary part of the circle.

As we shared our lives in this way, though, it became clear that we each had "stuck" areas which were inhibiting us, and which we needed to release for the sake of ourselves, our circle-psyche, and for those in our immediate worlds. And so began the ritual of witnessing each other as we worked our lives and worlds.

PUTTING A LIFE BACK TOGETHER

The story that follows is an example of what ritual and ceremony can do. We have found over and over again that what we create together in the Circle of Seven manifests in the larger world of our lives. Our experience is that the power of imagination and symbol, expressed into a field of love, can change our worlds in remarkable ways.

Jane had for some years been moving around a lot and was experiencing her life as fragmented. She felt burnt out, her friends and family were scattered all over the country and it felt as though pieces of her being were scattered about with them. She was looking for a way to integrate herself and her life, and had a sense that if she could somehow draw together her past and the relationships that had meaning for her, she could feel whole again.

Liz, who is particularly good at designing in-the-moment processes, suggested that Jane choose symbols from around the room to represent the scattered elements of her life, and that the rest of us witness her as she, like Humpty-Dumpty, put the pieces of her life back together in a way that felt right to her now.

The two women sat in the middle of the circle. Jane chose a few symbols such as a picture and a rock, and, to howls of laughter from the rest of us, a bowl of chocolate-covered raisins to represent her friends and family. Liz invited her to speak her heart, telling one by one the stories of the people she loved, where they lived, what knowing them meant to her. She also asked Jane to place each person, represented by a raisin, in the position that felt right in her life now—to create a mandala of right relationship. As she re-created her world on the floor of the circle, Jane cried for what she had lost and for the desolation and loneliness she was experiencing.

After around two hours, when the process she was engaged in ended naturally, Jane sat back, exhausted but clear and clean in herself. She had worked hard to symbolically reconstitute her life in the presence of attentive witnesses, and she knew that something in her internal landscape had changed. Prompted by gentle probes and suggestions from Liz, she had opened up and done some profound inner work. Those of us who had been engaged as witnesses had also been deeply moved and had experienced change in ourselves, because Jane's difficulty was not just hers. We all had some experience of fragmentation and loneliness, and had been touched and healed by her courageous vulnerability and tenacity in tackling this issue so directly.

Two months later, I received a call from Liz. She told me that Jane had begun a journey around the country to visit some of the people she had spoken about during her circle process. She was gathering together the threads of her life and her history, and planned to finish the journey on the East Coast in her parents' home. There she would rest and stay for a while until the next step revealed itself. She had realized only after she had begun the journey that she was living out the symbolic process we had all witnessed in the circle.

TRUTH-TELLING

One of the most profound technologies we have discovered in the Circle of Seven is truth-telling. When the atmosphere of love is solidly present, it is possible to engage in this powerful practice. Truth-telling has two parts to it. The first is that each person tells the truth about herself and her life, and releases this into the circle. The second is that we all undertake to speak the truth of what we see in one another, and to do this without judgment and with the desire to serve. The result has been that each of us has been strengthened by being given the opportunity to release her defensiveness and to test her view of herself against how others perceive her. The action of expressing different perspectives in charged space can profoundly change a situation and rearrange stuck patterns, both in an individual and in the larger field.

None of us emerge from a circle meeting unchanged. We have become increasingly open and vulnerable to one another and to the truth of what is blocking our expression. We have been building the capacity to engage in truth-telling over the last three years, and are now able to be quite direct with each other. As individuals, I would say that we have developed the ability to take things extremely personally in an impersonal way, to weep and rejoice openly without making a big deal of it, and to look embarrassment and shame in the eye. Once you realize that the things you are especially ashamed of, and have been carefully hiding for a long time, are in reality easily seen by others, it makes little sense to continue to pretend that they are invisible.

Truth-telling in the context of unconditional love gives rise to a powerful sense of freedom and an enlarged capacity for creativity. It encourages us to continue to open up and risk, and to reveal ourselves ever more deeply in the circle. This, together with the magic of ritual space, charges the atmosphere in a tangible way, so that after a while, we find that we have opened up a field of creativity and power which is more than just the sum of ourselves. It has taken the willingness to risk, to endure pain and discomfort, and to make our personal substance with its vulnerability and maturity available to the circle. What has emerged for us as we have continued to do this is an increasing awareness of individual and collective purpose, expanding perceptiveness and sensitivity, and a sense of becoming more available as an instrument of life.

THE GIFT OF TIME

Two members of the Circle of Seven met recently with a women's circle in Cape Town which gathers about once a month for an evening together. One of the topics we discussed was the difference it could make in the quality of their circle experience if the Cape Town women met less frequently for longer periods. One of the greatest gifts we can give ourselves and one another in this rushed and harried world is the gift of unstructured time. *Chronos* (measured, mechanical time) is the common experience for most people; *chiros* (unbounded, natural, or cyclical time) is what is missing in most of our lives. What can happen in *chiros* is that life can take its course according to rhythms that we cannot control and which have their own inherent seasons of completion. In *chiros*, outworkings which are governed by unknown psychic forces can unfold and find fulfillment in their own time.

A good example of *chiros* is the rhythm of a grief cycle, which varies from person to person depending on all sorts of factors which are impossible to know. Grieving simply takes time. You cannot say to someone, "In six months you'll be over it," nor can you expect to predict the waves of grief which appear, sometimes triggered by associative events, sometimes seeming to come out of nowhere. Yet when the cycle is done, the person will wake up one morning and know that she is over the worst of her pain.

Having the combination of unstructured, uninterrupted time and quiet space in which to sit in circle together has in my view been the single greatest contributor to the success of our Circle of Seven. We let the rhythms of community be present in and around the circle, and we let them organize themselves. The work of sitting in circle is punctuated by the rhythms of eating, sleeping, and exercising; of engaging in social time and solitude; of being indoors and surrounded by the natural world.

CREATING RITUAL SPACE

A popular metaphor, which has often been used by chaos theorists to demonstrate the interconnectedness of all things, describes how the movement of a butterfly's wing in Brazil can bring about a cyclone in Japan. We began to see quite early on in our Circle of Seven meetings that what we did in the world of the circle influenced our lives and activated events in the outside world in synchronous and unexpected ways—for example, my earlier description of what played out in the story of Jane putting her life back together again. It is hard to know where her psyche ended and the larger world began.

Our present way of making sense of this lies in our circle's belief that everything is interconnected, that we are all part of one great unified whole. The circle is only one aspect of the larger "field" of our lives. Another way of describing this might be that the circle is embedded in various other overlapping circles, which are all in their turn part of the immense, vibrational "circle-of-the-whole." As we set intentions, "charge" and "hold" the space, or work a stuck or uncomfortable area in our lives, two things happen. One, an intensification in the frequency of the immediate circle field occurs. It is our belief that this sets up a kind of high-pressure pattern which, in turn, influences the larger field in which it is embedded. Two, a field of interrelated reactions is activated—the butterfly's wing initiates the cyclone.

Because the Circle of Seven is connected to the circle-of-the-whole, changes that occur in our smaller circle influence the larger picture, sometimes in ways we can see and track intuitively (though they may be hard to justify rationally), and sometimes in ways we cannot know. The intensification of the frequency of the field is another way of describing the creation of ritual space, which in turn allows for increasingly deeper penetration of individual and collective psyche-fields. The more the collective atmosphere becomes charged, the more you can "see" and "do" in it, and the more the implicate order can emerge and take form. The term "implicate order" was coined by physicist David Bohm, the father of modern-day Dialogue, to describe the invisible patterning which underlies the physical world. In this way, the participative world we live in and belong to responds to and engages with what we are doing in a great dialogue of creation and meaning.

By trial and error and borrowing, we have developed various practices for creating and "charging" the circle space. One of our members is a pipe-carrier in a Native American clan, so she often initiates our time together by calling in the four directions. Some times we start with prayer; at other times with a period of silence. Each day, we begin in a deliberate way by bringing ourselves fully into the circle. We use music and poetry a lot. We sing together sometimes. But we always make sure that everyone has a chance to "check in."

On the first day, our check-in is often quite extensive. Even though we are regularly in touch with one another, each woman is usually working with or thinking about something new—a theme which is preoccupying her, a half-formed awareness, an experience which needs to be shared, a puzzling question, a change in an important relationship. We give each other generous time to speak ourselves into full presence—there is no time limit, only a sense of each one taking her rightful share of the circle's time. From this first sharing of what is in our minds and hearts, come the seeds for what will grow and bear fruit during the course of the next four days.

There is a sense of gathering in, of drawing together, both in terms of individual consciousness and other resources. These resources—books, ideas, art materials, metaphors, music, our own bodies—provide the raw materials which will be acted upon by our collective consciousness and reshaped into new experience and awareness. Once we went out into our environment (first an art store, then the nearby beach) to gather up whatever raw materials spoke to each of us to make a wall hanging for one of our number who was moving into a new home. This is a substantial symbol of what we usually do together—weave and create something out of whatever is at hand, and make new meaning out of it.

It is this sense of gathering in—together with our unspoken commitment to be aware, listen, and pay attention—that begins to create the charged space in which we can experience more intensely than usual. Engaging in regular rituals, such as check-ins, prayer, or silence, further intensifies the atmosphere that is present and enables a deepening of consciousness to occur.

PRESENCE AND PRESENCING

I have found that the greatest builder of charged ritual space is Presence. By this I mean the deliberate attentiveness, conscious engagement, and sustained participation of every woman—but not just that. The natural capacity to Presence yourself flows out of a deep spiritual connectedness to your own being and the ability to bring this into the immediate world. It also requires you to be sufficiently aware to both engage with what is happening and, at the same time, observe yourself and others engage. You are acutely conscious of atmosphere, of potential—and you are intensely alive. This sustained act of Presencing also sensitizes you to that which is emerging from the implicate order—what is about to be born. You are in fact holding the tension between being both in liminal space and being fully present at the same time.

There comes a point in each circle meeting, though, when we are no longer focusing on building the ritual space. It continues to build itself through the intentional work we are doing together in the circle, enabling us to do more and go deeper. What is required from us, though, is an understanding or what it takes to maintain this intensified atmosphere in the circle and through the more "ordinary" times, such as meals or breaks, so that it can continue to build throughout the days we are together. It can dissipate quite easily, often through unconscious behavior, and then must be recreated. Sustaining full presence, what Buddhists call "paying attention," is the best way I know to continue to hold the ritual space.

We have learned much of this through our individual spiritual practices and by reflecting on our experiences and experiments in the circle. It is certainly not necessary to know all this when you begin a circle. You will no doubt create your own rituals and discover ways of charging the space through trial and error. The important thing is to feel free to experiment and to use your intuition to test whether what you are trying out is working, whether it simply requires more patience, or whether you should abandon it and try something else. A great tip to remember is that often something that has worked for a long time suddenly stops working for no apparent reason. I have found over the years that ways to God that have been sure methods for me no longer work—a particular combination of words that evoke communion or a specific place for meditation—and I have to find other paths.

BEING OPEN TO METAPHOR AND SYMBOL AS SIGNPOSTS

When we began the Circle of Seven, there were only six of us. However, we noticed that for the entire duration of our first meeting, there was one empty place in the circle. We had set out what we thought of as enough seating for six people, yet there was always a space for a seventh. By the second meeting, it had become clear that we should include another member who, by virtue of her age, essence, and being, obviously belonged. So we became seven. We have found that noticing and speaking what shows up as symbolic meaning is a vital piece in our circle work. The imaginal psyche has its own logic.

A powerful example of this logic occurred during our first circle meeting in Santa Fe. We designed a process for women which included the components we felt were critical for an initiation. These included, among others, immersion in water (as symbolic of the waters of birth), and a descent into darkness (to recreate the experience of the dark side of the creative process). After we had been hard at work for a couple of days, we decided to treat ourselves to a hot tub at a local spa where you could book a private tub for six. We immersed ourselves in water together under the great New Mexican sky for an evening. The next day, we were invited by a local man and his partner to spend time with them in a magnificent sacred kiva just outside Santa Fe. They had been involved with others in an initiation program through the creation of a collection of resources called "The Box," which they presented us with as a gift to bless and honor the work we were undertaking. As we entered the small opening of the kiva and sat together in the sacred space underground, we became aware of the symbolic experiences we had called into being for this first circle meeting—immersion in water and descent into darkness.

Each Circle of Seven meeting has called forth a very specific theme which has manifested physically during our time together. On one occasion we walked the labyrinth in Grace Cathedral in San Francisco, as a symbol of iterative processes unfolding in our lives; on another, articles and poetry by D. H. Lawrence charged our encounter with the desert landscape of New Mexico, and we further intensified this experience of sensuality and seeing with new eyes by spending a powerful and evocative time together experiencing a collection of Georgia O'Keeffe's paintings.

For me, the inexorable logic of the imagination, which will assert itself if it is given space in consciousness, is an indication of the oneness of all things and the relationship between the living psyche and what appears as the outer world. It is becoming increasingly difficult for us to tell where the collective psyche of the Circle of Seven begins and ends, and how to differentiate between our inner and outer worlds. They have become one stream of awareness. In some way, the fact that we are all women has something to do with this stream. We seem to be immersed in a sea of life substance together which is already present, but is also somehow called into being by the way in which we dwell and act together in the circle. Our experience is that we are learning some of the principles of magic and the dynamics of creating for the greater good.

CIRCLE SHADOWS

Circle experience is not all sweetness and light by any means. I have mentioned that we struggled in my first circle with the fear of conflict, and this is quite common in women's circles, especially if people have notions that peace and harmony are essential characteristics of spirituality, and that spiritual growth and transformation involves only the light end of the light-dark spectrum. "Making nice" is another regular shadow behavior in women's circles. I have a nose for "niceness" and find that if people in a group I am part of are "nice" to each other for too long, I will feel the compulsion to be thoroughly rude or obnoxious to break the pattern. Women's circles, in my experience, tend to confuse niceness with love. Love is muscular and can encompass all kinds of behavior, including conflict. Niceness has more to do with playing safe and pleasing others—something women have learned over many generations to be very good at, and which they use to collude with one another to keep the atmosphere smooth and to hide differences which might cause discomfort.

In the Circle of Seven, we have encountered some interpersonal challenges that have been very uncomfortable. By facing them, we have strengthened ourselves and the circle. On one occasion, one of our members did not attend a session because she missed her plane. She had, in any case, been considering not coming to the meeting, but had not shared this with the rest of us. Some members were feeling angry about it, so on a phone conference with her at the end of our four days without her, we raised the matter of commitment and asked her whether the Circle was a priority in her life—whether, in other words, she was in or out. She told us later that she had felt very alone during the conversation—like a little girl being excluded from a group of friends—and that this had evoked in her some painful memories.

We spent some time during the following circle meeting addressing what had occurred, particularly by being honest about our judgments of her. It took one of our number a couple of one-on-one conversations with her over a month or two before the matter came to rest. This experience served the circle because it helped us intensify our commitment and address a potential interpersonal issue directly.

A shadow we have encountered in other women friends and acquaintances is envy of what the Circle of Seven has together. They dislike what they perceive as the circle's exclusivity. Some feel hurt because they have not been asked to join, or were not included at the beginning. It is, however, a deliberately dedicated circle, and therein lies its power. Envy and exclusivity often have to be addressed at the outset though, from the standpoint of both the circle members themselves and those who are not included. Women friends often have to make a special effort to be generous and to learn to be mature enough to celebrate the joys and successes of others. Circle members have to watch out for smugness, unnecessary secretiveness, or a subtle sense of exclusivity and superiority in their attitude.

There are ways to turn dark shadows into golden shadows by proactively changing the group's behavior and therefore its impact on others. The envy of others can be addressed through generous sharing of the circle experience in a way that can include and enrich them, without breaking confidentiality. We have sometimes invited a woman friend to join the circle for part of a day, especially if she wants to work on something specific in her life, or birth something new which is close to the surface but hard to get at. It is a real joy to give a friend the gift of mature ritual space and assist with inventing a process that will bless and serve her. For one such woman, the greatest gift we could offer was to listen to her, enfold her in our love, and witness her weeping as she struggled with the inner changes brought on by menopause, which were making her working life untenable.

Another shadow that often shows up is the stereotyping of men as insensitive, paternalistic, chauvinistic, and generally incapable of working in emotional territory. This is a leftover pattern from the gender wars and often appears as an unspoken collusive attitude which might show up indirectly through wisecracking ("Well, what did you expect—he's a man!"), or more directly through blaming or scapegoating men in general.

The underlying frame here has to do with the idea that women are more suited to the kinds of understanding and behavior required at this time in history, and that in general, the attributes of circle culture—collaboration, the valuing of diversity, community-building, loving, respectful listening, and so forth—come more naturally to women than to men.

It is my belief that the emergent transformational cultural field is being evoked by both men and women, and that one of the characteristics of the present era is that the stereotypical polarization of male and female behavior is changing radically. I see circle culture appearing in both women's and men's groupings. The receding prevailing Western culture has handicapped both women and men in different ways—men in the sense that they have been actively discouraged from developing emotionally. But this does not mean that we should continue to reinforce this handicap in men by stereotyping them, especially when so many are seeking to express both their strength and their tenderness.

CREATING ALTERNATIVE CULTURE AND COMMUNITY

Sitting in circles is also part of the impulse to re-create and re-member community. Many women have little opportunity to engage in a rich and fulfilling common life with others, and most have, like the rest of humanity, lost "the shelter of each other." We need support and feedback from others as we explore, act, and create in our lives, and most of us have found doing all this alone singularly alienating and often downright lonely.

There also seems to be a compulsion for many women to learn about, share and understand "natural rhythms" and cycles, whether this relates to our own bodies, the seasons, the growing cycles of young people, the rhythms in relationships, or the larger cycles working out in life. Often women I talk to feel that these awarenesses are natural to their psyches and paying attention will help revive that sensitivity. They feel that the revival, articulation, and mainstreaming of this knowledge is an important part of re-creating what it means to be a woman now. While this general area has perhaps always been the socially allocated province of women, there is a strong movement to make it an arena of empowerment and credibility rather than just the soft underbelly of the utilitarian world.

In the Circle of Seven, we are working on developing new social, cultural, and psychospiritual technologies that may help us better understand ourselves, our immediate worlds, and make sense of and influence the larger, complex world we are part of. We are eager to make our learning and insight available to others, but are at the same time aware that what has been of profound meaning and usefulness to us may be of little interest beyond ourselves. We wish, though, to test and apply what we have been doing beyond our own circle, and to learn from the technologies others have been developing. We have often discussed meeting with another women's circle, and want very much to work also with a men's group to integrate their discoveries with ours. At our next gathering, we plan to invite several women into the circle as guests, although we have no idea at this stage how to integrate them or what we will do together. Experience has shown us, though, that we will know when the time comes, and we are content to wait.

If I have anything to say to people who are considering starting a circle, it is this: Do it! In my experience, it doesn't matter what the circle's apparent purpose is to begin with: it will become what it is meant to be. The real purpose emerges as you stay alert, patient, and courageous enough to let what is percolating just below the surface become conscious. It will be the women who sit in the circle with you, together with an unnameable presence which will appear if you let it, whose openness, goodwill, and creativity will renew the present and transform the common world to which you are connected.

Marianne Williamson is a well-known author, teacher, and speaker whose bestselling books include *A Return to Love*, *A Woman's Worth*, and *Illuminata*. She is also the author of a children's book, *Emma and Mommy Talk to God*. This essay is adapted from an interview conducted by Mary Nurrie Stearns in *Personal Transformation* about her most recent book, *The Healing of America*.

Spiritual Politics

If each of us would ask, "How might I best use my time, energies, and talents to serve the larger world?" we would transform this society and transform the planet. It is not for me or anyone else to tell people what to do. It is up to each of us to do those things that we know in our hearts we should do. For some people, it's getting sober. For some, it's forgiving someone. For others, it is giving service. For others, it's something else.

For all of us, becoming more aware and involved in the social and political issues of our day bears directly on what will happen in this world over the next twenty years. We have allowed ourselves to fall in line behind the gross delusion that economic principles are more important than humanitarian principles. We allow those in power to make balancing the budget more important than balancing the universe. We have witnessed the terrible social disruption that results from placing money before love on such a mass scale. We have allowed this to happen, and it is our responsibility to change it. It's not enough to whine. It's definitely not enough to just tune out and throw up our hands.

Over the last thirty years, opportunity—particularly economic opportunity—has tilted in the direction of the already privileged. The main form of drifting is economic injustice. We give gargantuan subsidies—$265 billion dollars over the next five years—to wealthy corporations, while our inner cities are filled with millions of people, primarily African Americans, living under social and economic conditions as desperate as those during the worst days of the Great Depression. This country is in major denial regarding critical violations of our own first principles, not to mention the love of God.

Martin Luther King, Jr., said that when we give money to the poor, people call it a handout; but when we give money to the rich, we call it a subsidy. Why should we be subsidizing our richest companies rather than America's own children? We must repudiate the notion that the market alone fuels social good. It doesn't. And neither does government, by the way. Love does. Americans need to wake up to the fact that seriously disabled children, children who are undereducated, children who receive inadequate care of whatever kind—when cut off from societal compassion—become our main prison population in following years. Our public policies, which perpetuate the disadvantaged state of so many millions of children, are among the root causes of crime and social dysfunction in this country. This is criminally insane, in my opinion.

It's not just that these policies are driven by economic principle; they are driven by short-term, old paradigm, spiritually bankrupt economic principles. For those of us who embrace new paradigm thinking, it ultimately makes no economic sense to spend more money on the military than on educating our children. The growing rage and despair in our children is the greatest threat to our future security.

We spend 22 percent of our federal budget on the military and 5 percent on education. We'll build a B-2 bomber—which the Pentagon doesn't even want, by the way, for $1.5 billion—when that money would pay for the annual salaries of 56,000 elementary school teachers, or 125,000 childcare workers. Public schools throughout the country ask private schools if they can borrow paper. Schools throughout the country not only don't have enough paper to write on; many schools in the inner cities don't even have working toilets. It would cost $112 billion to make the public schools of the United States come up to minimum building standards. The Democrats suggested $5 million seed money to begin the process; the Republicans cut it to zero. Clearly, the political system, as it now exists, fails to acknowledge that taking care of our children should be our top priority. According to the laws of metaphysics, this isn't a matter of opinion. There is one principle that rules the universe: Cause and Effect, or Karma. What goes around comes around. From a spiritual perspective, no society as wealthy as ours, that has as many underprivileged children as we have, has any basis for long-term economic optimism.

We must return to the principles upon which the United States was based. Our founders, as children of enlightenment, believed that there is a spirit of goodness within each person and that from that goodness we can derive the wisdom and intelligence to govern our own affairs. Democracy demands an aware mind. Democracy demands depth of intelligence, soul, and participation. It's not enough that Jefferson said brilliant things or that King said brilliant things or that Lincoln said brilliant things. If the things they said don't live in our hearts, and the things they said don't spur us to action, then one of the greatest miracles in world history will turn into mere memory.

President Roosevelt said that to some generations much is given, and from some generations much is expected. He said that his generation had a rendezvous with destiny. Our generation is one to whom much has been given and one from whom much is now expected. We also have a rendezvous with destiny. The question is whether we're going to sleep through the date. When we watch too much television, we're asleep. When we choose to remain ignorant of social and political issues that affect our lives and the lives of our children on a daily basis, we're choosing to remain asleep. When we take anti-depressants before trying serious spiritual, psychological, and emotional work as an antidote to our despair, we're choosing to sleep. Once you tune in to what is true, once you tune in to what is real, once you tune in to your authentic knowing and your deeper connection to your purpose in the world, you find easily enough what you should do. Until we tune in, we're too disconnected from our own knowing to have any idea what to do next.

That's why the social revolution of our times—and we do need a mass social revolution—cannot be organized. It must be initiated by passion. It must be led, as Gandhi said that the Indian Independence Movement was led, by the "small, still voice within." The power residing within the individual aligns with the basic tenets of democracy. To retrieve democracy, we have to start practicing democracy. We can't blame others for taking it away, if we, ourselves, abdicate all social responsibility because we are too busy tending our own gardens.

Dr. Martin Luther King, Jr., said that we must have tough minds and tender hearts. Most Americans fall in one of two categories: tough minds that lack tender hearts, or tender hearts that lack strong critical thinking. Many people with tough minds need to soften their hearts, but many people with tender hearts need to read a book or two. We must have both and be both if we're serious about changing the world.

SOUL FORCE

The tenets of higher consciousness can aid us in working for this transformation. Everything we do is infused with the energy with which we do it. The first higher consciousness principle to consider is that who we *are* is as important as what we *do*. I asked the Dalai Lama, "If enough people meditate, will that save the world?" He answered, "If we wish to save the world, we must have a plan. But unless we meditate, no plan will work." From a higher consciousness perspective, our spiritual work increases our personal power and thus our effectiveness in the world. Gandhi and King claimed that soul force is more powerful than brute force. Our current dominant political structure defines power in terms of brute force. We have the opportunity, if we're serious about it, to usher in an era in which power derives from soul force. Soul force is neither cheap nor easy to obtain. Many people give lip service to soul force while avoiding its use as a social and political tool. It's easier to talk about than to practice. In fact, there is a temptation to use spiritual seeking as escapism, an easy opportunity to avoid looking at, dealing with, or seeking to transform the suffering of the world. It's an insidious game that the mind plays. We can't resurrect a world whose crucifixion we've ignored.

We must be as committed to our spiritual goals as we are to our political goals. We marry the two by being awake. When you read that 95,000 children are being cut off from disability payments, saving something like $5 billion, but then read that fifty times more than that is going to corporate welfare, you call your congressperson. You write a letter to your local paper. You write a letter to your senator. We need a helathy sense of moral outrage. Public pressure makes the world go around, and that's how it should be, particularly in a democracy. Thomas Jefferson said it is our responsibility to keep the spirit of rebellion alive. Too many of us who have passionate feelings don't turn those feelings into action; we don't turn our energy into social force. Our idea of activism is to yell at the television set.

Taking the energy in our hearts and transforming it into constructive social action is the next step toward our personal and political maturity. That's the essence of democracy, and it's the essence of the spiritual power inherent in a democracy. Democracy means that this country will go in whatever direction the people choose for it to go. Right now our democratic rights are being unraveled for no other reason than that we're not protesting. We act more like the royalists in the days of the colonies than like our own revolutionary forebears. We are not being attacked directly by the power structure, by taxes and other burdens such as George III imposed on the colonies. Our oppression is not through pain, but through pleasure. The system provides us with so much pleasure—things to buy and toys to play with—that we're on the brink of being consumed by our own consumerism. It has become like a morphine drip; we are literally stoned on our lovely lifestyles.

Learning to love is the highest form of political training. Our love for people, particularly children on the other side of town, must become a passionate commitment if we're to save this world. The children are bearing the weight of our insanity. But we must not allow anger to obstruct our effectiveness. It's our own fault that we have allowed this radical deterioration of social integrity. We must take personal responsibility for this, and assert ourselves now. As Gandhi and King made clear, the only way to eradicate institutionalized forms of injustice is by awakening the conscience of mankind. We must not attack the power structure; we must speak to its conscience. Dr. King used this image: the rich and the poor of America are all on the same boat, and if a hole forms underneath the seat of the poor, we will all go down. If we don't redress the terrible economic inequalities in this country, within five to ten years we're all going to be living in gated communities, shopping in privately guarded entertainment complexes, and traveling in police-protected caravans. We already employ in the United States more private police than public police. People in other countries find that horrifying, and we should too.

None of this is to say that I'm cynical or pessimistic about the United States, because I'm not. I'm as much of a champion about what's right in this country as anyone is, and I'm as blessed by what's right in this country as anyone is. I just want all of America's children to have the same minimum level of opportunity that I had. We must seek to make opportunity universally accessible here, or this house will fall. In his inaugural address President Kennedy said, "The free society that doesn't take care of its many who are poor will not be able to save its few who are rich."

We should set morally outstanding goals, such as having the best-educated children. We are supposedly a government of the people, by the people, and for the people. We should have the best educated children in the world. Period. Notice that if we make enough money in America, we send our kids to private schools. It didn't used to be that way. Our public education system should reflect our genius, not our shame.

We need possibility thinking, not just in our private lives but in our public life as well. Balancing the budget is important, but balancing our hearts and actions with the laws of God is more important. Love should come before money. I don't believe that God is asking us to balance the budget on the backs of poor children.

MAKING CULTURAL AMENDS

In order to heal, I believe we must also make cultural amends, to atone for our violations against others, particularly for our legacy of slavery. Social change occurs most powerfully where conscience has been aroused. An apology for slavery carries with it the potential to shift the national consciousness by touching the national conscience. We need external remedies as well as internal ones, of course, but an apology is a beginning.

There are many ways such a ritual could be performed. If we wanted to do it, we could come up with a way. When representative Tony Hall of Ohio submitted a bill in the House of Representatives suggesting that Congress apologize for slavery, there was such an outcry the bill didn't have a chance of going forward. Newt Gingrich called a congressional apology for slavery mere "emotional symbolism." He asked if it would teach one child to read. I say that yes, it would, because it would remove some heavy blocks to our awareness of love and awaken a lot of Americans to the twisted nature of our national priorities. The government recently spent $25 million dollars on a study of adolescents that proved love is by far the most potent positive force in the lives of young people. The word *love* was actually used in a headline in the *Washington Post.* The world is changing and it doesn't matter what the old order thinks. One day our commitment to love will be reflected in our social and political policies. Children will receive more support than the Pentagon, and ways to wage peace will receive as much attention as ways to wage war.

HOLISTIC POLITICS

Once ideas are put on the table, something starts to happen. We have to ask, "What is real political power?" I speak in my book *The Healing of America* about holistic politics. We need to create in politics what we have created in medicine. The holistic model has revolutionized mainstream medicine because it has revolutionized our mentality. Whereas we used to think that what the doctor said and the medicine he gave us was the core of healing, we now know that a patient's mental, spiritual, and emotional involvement is critical to the healing process. We still look at politicians the way we used to look at doctors, and we look at legislation the way we used to look at medicine. What's going on inside the mind and the heart of the average citizen are significant factors in correcting, healing, and revitalizing society. Without that, democracy is a sham.

The word politics, which comes from the Greek root *polis*, does not mean of the *government;* it means of the *citizen*. The ancient Greeks thought of politics as something more than the purview of governmental leaders and the actions they took. Politics has to do with every individual's involvement with a larger community, and the issues that affect us all. When a congressman suggests that we apologize for slavery and Congress strikes it down, that doesn't mean the political power behind the idea is completely lost. Political power is generated if a critical mass of people sees the idea as a good one. It will turn into specific action when the intellectual and emotional soil is fertile. Nothing is more powerful than an idea whose time has come. Our job is to promote the ideas we care about.

Most congresspeople receive fewer than a hundred calls on any particular issue. When you read an article about injustice, or whatever bothers you, call the main switchboard at the Capitol in Washington, D.C.: (202) 224-3121. Ask for your congressperson's office and tell them what you think. That's a constituent call. One call doesn't make that much difference, but a hundred calls make a lot of difference.

When you make that call, an amazing thing happens: you feel more powerful. You feel more powerful because you expressed your power. Receiving such calls is not a joke to a congressperson. These people do run for election. Unfortunately, in America most people are either turned off to what's happening and are politically resigned, or they merely accept and complain rather than exercise their own rights and power.

We should feel that we're part of a broad-based social movement. We should feel absolutely sure, when we learn that 95,000 severely disabled children are being dropped off government assistance rolls—while at least ten times more than that is being given to wealthy corporations—that not only are we on the phone calling our congresspeople, but that everybody of like mind is making the same call.

I've started an organization called the American Renaissance Alliance, in the hopes that it will contribute to that process. Its phone number is (202) 544-1219. Its principles and rules are as follows:

RENAISSANCE POLITICAL PRINCIPLES

1. The power within us *is* greater than any power outside us.

2. Government should concern itself not only with how to allocate our external resources, but with how to harness our internal ones, as well.

3. The source of wealth is our capacity for genius. Creation of wealth through the stimulation of creative thinking is thus the primary source of economic recovery and stimulation.

4. The highest political dialogue is not adversarial, but rather a synergistic conversation between high-minded liberal visions for the country and high-minded conservative ones.

5. The politics of hate is a branch that does not bear fruit. That is why another branch is starting to grow. Love is a more powerful political and social tool than hatred.

6. We will not move forward as a nation without repenting for our lack of righteousness toward other Americans in the past and present, and all other nations of the world.

7. We must acknowledge the power of the inner life, the wisdom found in silence, and the primacy of the voice of conscience. Otherwise, the American experiment will end. It shall have failed.

RULES OF RENAISSANCE

1. It is always our prerogative, as individuals and as nations, to choose again: to say *no* to a direction we've been moving in and *yes* to a new one. Our greatest power is our capacity to change our minds.

2. Alignment with higher principle is always supported by invisible forces.

3. If an energy is not in alignment with divine truth, it is ultimately temporary. It will not last forever, and is more vulnerable than it appears. In the words of Dr. King, "Even though the arc of the moral universe is long, it bends toward justice."

4. The universe is impersonally invested in evolving toward goodness and uses any available conduit for the purposes of doing so. Willingness to be so used activates the conduit. You're as good for the job as anyone else, and your past is totally irrelevant.

5. Don't expect the old order to like you.

6. A life of love and effort on behalf of the collective good promises the satisfaction of knowing that you are doing what you were born to do. You are not, however, promised specific results as you might define them.

7. Your happiness regarding the reality that's coming is a more potent method of social conversion than is your anger regarding the reality now.

Thomas Jefferson said that the forces of tyranny must be put on notice that we are a free and sovereign people and plan to remain so. Social injustice occurs in America mainly because its agents know that we won't complain. They know we're asleep, and they count on our remaining asleep.

We retrieve democracy by exercising it. Democracy isn't a static mechanism. To have a democracy, we must use the tools of democracy. As it is now, out of 163 democracies in the world the United States ranks somewhere around 140 in democratic participation. In our last congressional elections, only 40 percent of those eligible even voted.

The solution isn't overwhelming—that's what's so incredible. We need to act on spiritual principles—have faith, forgive, and act with love. People think there is a more complicated job to perform than there actually is. That's why the story of David and Goliath is so significant. Goliath is much bigger than David, and physically stronger than David, and better armed than David, but David struck him in his third eye. There is one place where the old Goliath order—the giant in our midst—has no defense. We must bring love into the process and bring faith to bear upon it. Once we touch the conscience of the giant, the giant is transformed.

Gloria Steinem is an award-winning author and political organizer and is consulting editor for *Ms. Magazine,* which she cofounded in 1972. Her books include *Revolution from Within, Moving Beyond Words,* and *Outrageous Acts and Everyday Rebellions.* Among the organizations she helped found are the Women's Action Alliance, the National Women's Political Caucus, and the Ms. Foundation for Women. She has won many awards, including the Ceres Medal from the United Nations and a number of honorary degrees. In 1995 she was selected by *Parenting* magazine for its Lifetime Achievement Award for her work in promoting girls' self-esteem. This piece was originally written for the twenty-fifth anniversary issue of *Ms. Magazine.*

Revving Up for the Next Twenty-five Years

> "We who like the children of Israel have been wandering in the wilderness of prejudice and ridicule ... feel a peculiar tenderness for the young women on whose shoulders we are about to leave our burdens.... They will have more courage to take the rights which belong to them."
>
> —Elizabeth Cady Stanton

Feminism isn't called the longest revolution for nothing. I hope this more realistic perspective is something the second wave has gained in the last twenty-five years, because we certainly didn't begin with it. We had come out of various movement stages that were focused on immediate goals: the anti-Vietnam War movement to stop the body-bags arriving home every day; the reenergized and more militant civil rights movement's efforts to desegregate and fight for voting rights; and a male-led intellectual Left that sometimes practiced what Robin Morgan humorously called "ejaculatory politics"—*revolution tomorrow, or I'm going home to my father's business.*

We also lacked women's studies, black studies—all the courses that might better be called remedial studies—to teach us that suffragists and abolitionists had struggled for more than a century to gain a *legal identity* for women of all races and men of color, so we had better be prepared for at least a century of struggle to gain a legal and social *equality.* (Not to mention the newer demand for reproductive freedom, a human right, which attacks the very foundation of patriarchy, taking control of women's bodies and reproduction away from family, church, and state, and putting in the hands of each woman.)

I don't regret one moment of those early firecracker days when explosions of consciousness lit up the sky. Somewhere, women go through them again every day as they discover how much of female experience is political, not inevitable. Even we golden oldies reexperience this excitement again whenever new perceptions and issues arise. But bursts of light tend to flatten out the subtlety of differences between and among women, and a movement fueled only by adrenaline will burn out its members—as many of us can testify.

On the other hand, younger women and newer activists checked into a world that already had a degree of feminist consciousness. They have higher expectations and an acute awareness of the backlash against the growing power of women. These young activists generate a steadier light that exposes the tangled patterns of race, class, sexuality, and physical ability in women's lives. Where my generation externalized almost everything and used its energy to confront injustice, younger and later activists admit how much of that injustice has been internalized, and use this energy to dig deeper into individual psyches and family patterns. Where we risked repeating the same behavior because we didn't dig out its personal and family roots, they risk re-creating a social pattern because they neglect its power politics.

Thanks to feminist parents as well as to women's studies and a popular culture that occasionally pays tribute to a feminist worldview, this new generation has a better idea of the complexity involved in making lasting change. But now, that's also countered by a sound-bite culture, and the resistance to equality that is ever-ready with terms like "postfeminism," (which makes no more sense than "postdemocracy").

Moreover, without the excitement and mutual support of early, small-group feminism, I fear this and future generations won't have the personal rewards and fireworks that hooked us for a lifetime. On the other hand, without large organizations to turn out the vote and raise money to keep generations of struggle going, suffragists and abolitionists couldn't have won—and we can't either.

That's why, old or young, experienced or brand-new, we have to achieve balance in the next quarter-century: between present and future, external and internal, spontaneity and long-term planning. We have to get beyond *either/or* to *and*; beyond ranking to linking; beyond such ridiculous labels as "equality feminists" versus "difference feminists," and into a full circle of tactics that surround the goal instead of approaching it from one direction. We need *both* excitement and steadiness, *both* small feminist support groups and national organizations, *both* bursts of new consciousness that are rewards in themselves and the satisfaction of repeating what has been planned and perfected.

We're going to need crazy women marching in the street who make women working inside seem reasonable *and* inside negotiators who turn street demands into practical alternatives; radical feminists who confront the roots of injustice *and* liberal feminists who make reforms that are radical in the long term; feminists who focus on the shared origins of sexism, racism, and homophobia, *and* feminists who work in intimate depth within their own communities; feminist economists who take on the System of National Accounts plus the structural readjustment of poorer nations' debt *and* women who heal their own childhood sexual abuse in order to end abusive cycles that have made generations of women think, "I'm good for nothing else."

For each of us, our part in this next quarter-century depends on the groups, issues, and styles that make us feel supported, angry, inspired, or energized. I'll briefly list some new or neglected ideas here—each one of which demands balance and deserves a bibliography of its own. My hope is that one or more might incite, invite, enrage, and tantalize readers into becoming a long-distance runners.

MAKING MEN EQUAL

In the last twenty-five years, we've convinced ourselves and a majority of the country that women can do what men can do. Now, we have to convince the majority of the country that men can do what women can do. If we don't, the double burden of working inside and outside the home—always a reality for poor women, and now one for middle-class women, too—will continue to be a problem most shared by most American women nationwide. Let's face it: until men are fully equal inside the home, women can never be equal outside it.

This humanization of men has even more importance in the long term. Children who grow up seeing nurturing men (and women) as well as achieving women (and men) will no longer have to divide their human qualities into "masculine" or "feminine." Gender will no longer be the dominant/passive model that is then followed by race and class.

This journey can start with women who make the presence of nurturing men a condition for bearing children—whether the men are biological fathers, friends and relatives, or workers in child-care centers. It can start with boys who are *raised* to raise children, and with young men who are taught to ask the same question that young women do: "How can I combine career and family?" We have begun this journey with the demands for parental leave and shorter workdays or workweeks, but other structural changes are needed to make both work and parenthood possible—for both men and women.

We'll know we're getting there when an essay like this tries to convince readers that women were once more responsible for child care and family than men were, and younger readers say skeptically, "How could that be?"

DAUGHTER OF "THE PERSONAL IS POLITICAL"

In the last twenty-five years, we've learned that patriarchy and racism politicize almost every facet of life, from who does the dishes to the definition of a war crime. Now, we must begin rescuing whole areas of human experience from being devalued by association with women—to the detriment of everyone. The personal/private sphere has been divided from the political/public sphere; the "feminine" from the "masculine." As a result, the importance of the first has been lost, and its impact on the second has been ignored.

Nowhere is this more disastrous than in the failure to link child-rearing methods to political outcomes; to connect democracy (or the lack of it) in the family to democracy (or the lack of it) in the nation. Except for works like Alice Miller's *For Your Own Good: Hidden Cruelty in Child-Rearing and the Roots of Violence*, or Philip Greven's *Spare the Child: The Religious Roots of Punishment and the Psychological Impact of Physical Abuse*, there have been almost no studies of, say, German child-rearing methods as a reason for its past tolerance of authoritarian leaders, or the link between child abuse in the

United States and the apocalyptic-thinking fundamentalists and militias.

We need political science courses that include child-rearing changes in their study of the decline of totalitarianism in the former Soviet Union, and include the absence of abusive child-rearing methods in many indigenous cultures to their ability to govern by reciprocity and consensus. So far, we rarely even have psychology courses that routinely explore the link between the intertwining of abuse and love in child-rearing and traditions of sado-masochism that so disastrously intertwine pain and pleasure. We need to deepen and widen our understanding that the personal is political.

BEYOND REPRODUCTIVE FREEDOM

Opposition to women's control of reproduction isn't going to end in the next quarter-century. Patriarchal, racist, class-bound, and other birth-based hierarchies exert control over women's bodies as the most basic means of production—the means of reproduction—in order to perpetuate themselves. This control is the deepest reason for women's oppression.

But while we fight for reproductive freedom, we can expand this demand into the larger right of bodily integrity for women and men, a principle that includes freedom from involuntary testing, unwanted medical treatments, unchosen life-prolonging methods, capital punishment, pressures to provide organs, eggs, sperm, blood, other body products, and much more. Not only will we gain new allies for reproductive freedom, but we will all eventually benefit from a new legal principle: the power of the state stops at our skin.

HOW WE USE OUR MONEY

For the last twenty-five years, we've fought for equal and comparable pay, pensions, and benefits—to equalize the amount of money we earn—all of which must continue. For the next twenty-five years, however, we need to add a focus on how we spend.

Think about other liberation movements, from the Gandhian refusal to buy British-made products to the African American efforts to support black-owned businesses. There have been a few similar efforts in the women's movement—boycotting states that failed to ratify the ERA, the Nestle's boycott, directories of women-owned businesses, and more—but in general, we've assumed that having more money to spend was progress in itself.

In fact, the question should not only be "How much can we spend?" but "How do we spend it?" Are we spending more on our outsides (clothing and appearance) than our insides (health and learning)? More on Hollywood movies than feminist political candidates? More on instant satisfaction than long-term security? Are we tithing to patriarchal religions and not to feminist groups? Are we seeking out women-owned businesses and companies with fair hiring and environmental policies? Are we saving for our own independence and paying attention to equity, not just salary? In other words, are we using our dollars as consciously as we would our votes?

WELFARE THAT DESERVES THE NAME

I'm proud of the women's movement for opposing two welfare reform bills that were even more punishing than the current one. I'm proud of the National Organization for Women for staging a hunger strike outside the White House in a vain attempt to get President Clinton to veto the third and successful one that is now causing suffering. But many people on welfare didn't support the original national system *or* the punishing state-based one that has succeeded it. You can't beat something with nothing. We didn't have a positive alternative, and we need one.

How about legislation that attaches a minimum income to every child? It would establish the amounts necessary for a child's shelter, nutrition, and health care—and then provide it. We know that investment in childhood saves money later. We also know that a floor income for every child would end the cruel and crazy inequities that now exist: for example, foster care payments that are higher than welfare payments—thus punishing kids who remain with their biological parents—and welfare that provides health care that employed single mothers can rarely afford.

Yes, such a bill would require a broad coalition to create as well as to pass, but similar models in Europe could keep us from reinventing the wheel. Yes, it would require a national mobilization, but the political climate is more open to aiding kids than single mothers, and definitely more open to providing health care for children than for adults. At a minimum, we would have a positive goal to support instead of a danger to oppose. At a maximum, we would have a New Deal for children, and the beginning of a welfare that deserves the name.

ECONOMICS—WITH VALUES ADDED

Once we understand that economics is only a system of values, we begin to ask questions: Why don't we attribute value to the roughly 50 percent of productive labor in this country that is done in the home? Some economists predict that the gross national product would go up by about 26 percent if homemakers' labor were included at only its replacement cost. There are also many areas of economic planning that are rendered impossible by keeping this huge segment of the economy invisible.

Why don't we attribute value to the environment? If a tree has no value when it's standing there giving us oxygen—not to mention serving as a home for many species—and only acquires a value when it is cut down, then the entire force of economic motive is on the side of environmental destruction.

From the work of Vandana Shiva in India to Marilyn Waring in New Zealand and Hazel Henderson in the United States, feminists are asking these questions, demystifying national and international systems, and attacking such pillars of the patriarchy as the Census (which decides what is visible) and the System of National Accounts (which decides what is valuable). Having learned how to play the game, we will also change the rules.

There are many more magnets to draw us into the future. I hope to be there, too—dreaming, fighting, planning, laughing, and transforming all the way. But as Elizabeth Cady Stanton understood at seventy-two, when she had no chance of living to see victory of the first wave: If any of us make it, we all will.

Nancy Mairs' most recent book is *Waist High in the World*, her perspective on living in a wheelchair. Her previous titles include *Ordinary Time: Cycles in Marriage; Faith and Renewal; Plaintext; Remembering the Bone House;* and *Carnal Acts*. She lives in Arizona.

From My House to Mary's House

"Charity" is a tricky concept. At its root, which it shares with "cherish," the word suggests no ordinary, indiscriminate affection but the love of something precious (costly, dear). Why then has it come to imply condescension? As with so many other ideas pertaining to relationships, our vast cultural passion for hierarchy must be at work. And where did that come from, I often wonder: out of the forest primeval, where if I perched in a tree while you skulked on the ground, I could more readily make you my lunch than you could make me yours? But that was quite a while ago. My mouth no longer waters when I glimpse you, even at lunchtime. As we approach a new century and a new millennium, isn't it time we dismantled a structure that so poorly organizes human interactions? Not that this would be an easy task. Our language, and the consciousness it shapes, is permeated with figures of domination and subordination so thoroughly that if we tried to extricate them, the whole fabric might unravel and leave us gibbering, unable to construct a single coherent thought.

It's a risk we'll have to take, I think, if we are to survive as recognizably human beings in a world of finite resources. Of course, nothing guarantees that we *are* to survive, and a good bit of recent evidence suggests that we aren't, but I think we ought to give survival a shot. I'm not talking about "hanging in there," I'm not talking about a few minor adjustments, or even a lot of major adjustments. I'm not talking about a new world order that permits Iraqi women and children to be bombed at the command of rich white men, just as Vietnamese women and children were under the old world order, only more efficiently and with wider approval. I am talking about an upheaval so radical that it exalts every valley and makes the rough places a plain, not along the San Andreas Fault but in the human psyche, which will no longer choose (not desire—it may well still desire—but *choose*) to organize itself and its relationships with others in terms of power and rank.

We might begin where all things begin: with God. We need to revise the language we use to conceptualize God in relation to ourselves. No more "Lord" and "Master." No more "thrones" or "principalities." No more oracular pronouncements "from on high." God with (in, among, beside, around, not over and above) us. This is one of the reasons that I've trained myself (and I balked badly at first) to refer to God with the feminine pronoun. I don't think God is a woman, any more than I think she's a man, but we're stuck with a gendered language: God has got to be he, she, or it. As a woman, I now feel most comfortable with "she" because traditionally in my culture women have not occupied positions of political dominance, associations with which might corrupt my experience of the holy, and because I identify with her, thus becoming aware of her presence in me, more readily when I use the same pronoun generally used for me. For a long time I considered changing "God," trying out "Goddess," "Holy One," "Yahweh," and the like, but they always felt contrived. Sometimes repeating "God" instead of using any pronoun is effective, but frequent repetitions at short intervals, by calling attention to themselves, distract me. The shift to the feminine pronoun seems to do the trick.

The purpose in finding a comfortable mode of address is to become aware of God drawn "down" into the midst of us, by whatever means will work. If she abides there, then the love we feel both for her and for one another as we embody her moves laterally, not hierarchically, and charity can never be tainted by condescension. When I use the word, I never intend it to suggest the act of a "do-gooder" who gives a "handout" or a "hand-me-down" to someone "less fortunate" than himself; no matter what decency and good-will both donor and recipient may feel, that "less" in the consciousness of one or both ineluctably skews their relationship. Charity is not a matter of degree. It is never *nice*. It wells up out of a sense of abundance, spilling indiscriminately outward. True, your abundance may complement someone else's lack, which you are moved to fill, but since your lacks are being similarly filled, perhaps by the same person, perhaps by another, reciprocity rather than domination frames the interchanges. Some people may be "more" fortunate and some "less," by whatever standard you choose. But absolutely everybody has abundances.

Of course, an abundance may not take a form you much like. I recall stopping one blazing afternoon several years ago at the Time Market for a carton of milk. Outside, I was approached by a man wearing few clothes and fewer teeth and a lot of sweat (life on the street in Tucson in midsummer is grueling), who asked me for a dollar. In those days, I didn't give money to people on the street because I knew they'd spend it on booze and I felt guilty assisting their addiction. Later, I was persuaded by the example of my beloved mentor Jerry Robinett that my task was to give what I was asked for, leaving responsibility for the use of my gift to its recipient. But on this day I still thought of myself as a moral guardian, so I shook my head. Inside, as was my habit when I'd been panhandled, I bought in addition to my milk a large apple and a granola bar (oh, the smugness of us virtuous types—why the hell not a red Popsicle and a Twinkie?).

When I offered these to the man outside, he snarled and turned his back. He'd been joined by a friend, who said to him quietly, "You *know* her. From the Casa. Go on and take them." He just shook his head, so I extended them to the friend, who took them and smiled. There was genuine grace in his gesture, his reluctance to hurt the feelings of a woman he'd seen at the soup kitchen, and I welcomed that gift from his abundance. But the other had an abundance, too—an abundance of resentment—from which he'd given just as freely. I was chastened by the gift, by his refusal to say "Thank you, kind lady," accepting my stupid health food when all he really wanted was a cold six-pack. If he'd done that, I'd never have found out that I'd offered him the wrong thing. I might have gone on believing that poor people were obliged to take what I gave them, consider themselves lucky to get it, and probably thank me politely in the bargain. I never said you had to like getting your lacks filled. I just said that someone, out of his abundance, would take care of the job.

Under ordinary circumstances, our abundances need letting off, like steam, and the family model chosen by contemporary middle-class society, wherein the whole huge human family is fragmented into clusters of only a few members each—which are packed separately and antiseptically, like cans of peas or jars of pickles, into houses and apartments and minivans—lacks adequate amplitude and ventilation. Accumulated, hoarded, our abundances build up an excruciating pressure that we seek to relieve in material acquisition, but the relief this measure brings is always only temporary, and eventually we find ourselves stopped up and sick with things.

I'm not preaching from a lofty perch here, looking down in pity on the rest of you poor fools gagging on your glut. I'm gasping claustrophobically under the weight of my own heap of possessions. Look! Down here! Under the three pairs of boots and the second television set! Admittedly, the boots are different colors to complement different articles in my wardrobe, and the television is a black-and-white portable with a five-inch screen: I'm a practical accumulator. But maybe color-coordination is not a laudable end or even a reasonable goal; and no one except my sports-crazy stepfather attempts to watch more than one television at a time. What am I really doing with all this stuff?

I know what I should do with it. I accept Jesus' admonition to the rich young man: "If you would be perfect, go, sell what you possess and give to the poor, and you will have treasure in heaven; and come, follow me" (Matthew 19:21). 1 know that such actions can be carried out, because I have friends who have done so. And I like to think I have developed to the point that, if only I were healthy and vigorous, I could do the same. If only.... Here's where I get stuck. I am too debilitated now to hold a job or even to care fully for myself. My husband has metastatic melanoma. When he dies, the modest resources we've accumulated may not even provide for my shelter and custodial care. If I were to give them away, then I'd become a public burden, worse than useless even to the poor I sought to serve. Conserving them seems less like greed than like social responsibility. And so I get off lightly. I can indulge in the fantasy that under different circumstances, I would be "perfect" without ever having to put myself to the test: a saint *manqué*.

Well, what I would do if I could we'll never know. I must do what I can. Carrying out the injunction that closes every Mass, to "go in peace to love and serve God and our neighbor," takes the form of the works of mercy, seven of which are "corporal": (1) to feed the hungry, (2) to give drink to the thirsty, (3) to clothe the naked, (4) to visit the imprisoned, (5) to shelter the homeless, (6) to visit the sick, and (7) to bury the dead. Another seven are "spiritual": (1) to admonish the sinner, (2) to instruct the ignorant, (3) to counsel the doubtful, (4) to comfort the sorrowful, (5) to bear wrongs patiently, (6) to forgive all injuries, and (7) to pray for the living and the dead. "As far as I can tell, I'm supposed to do all of these," I say to George, "but some of the spiritual ones make me uneasy. They seem so presumptuous." He nods as I go on: "I'd rather just clothe the sinner"—we burst out laughing and say together—"and admonish the naked."

Seriously, at the risk of spiritual dereliction, I think I'll leave admonishment to someone with more of a flair for it and stick with bodies, their shelter and nurture and dispatch, for which a quarter of a century of mothering all creatures great and small has better fitted me. Let me feed the hungry. Let me clothe the naked (and sinners too). I won't do it well or often enough, I know from experience, but charity isn't a competition to be judged by the Big Examiner in the Sky, who'll knock off seven years of purgatory for every sack of groceries you drop off at the Community Food Bank. Nobody's looking. It's more like a game in which everyone gets a turn, or a dance for which everyone can choreograph a few steps. Even a woman too crippled to tie her own boots or drive a car can, at least if she has a partner who shares her sense of plenty, find a place in the vast web of transactions that binds and sustains the human family.

In such exchanges, no matter how equitable, the power of the giver to dispense or withhold some good is subtly privileged over the right of the receiver to accept or reject the offering by the fact of possession: you've got what I need. Even though I've long understood this distinction, only in recent years have I felt its force. What I need—repetitively, interminably—is help in performing even the most elementary tasks. I can't butter my own bread. Before long I may not even be able to use the toilet by myself. My dependency, in resembling that of a very young child, makes me feel demeaned, diminished, humiliated. This is a horrible situation, one that wracks me with grief and fury for which no socially acceptable outlet exists. What am I going to do if you offer to button my coat, after all—bite your fingers and then freeze to death? Of course not. I'm going to permit you to clothe the naked.

Horrible situations have their uses, however. Mine, in depriving me of the status associated with personal control, has forced humility upon me. I cannot patronize the poor. I am one of the poor. Currently my poverty isn't economic, though it may one day be that as well, but its effects are similar. I must be not only the agent but the object of the works of mercy. I must discipline myself to accept and welcome others' care. I wish I could tell you that I'm doing a terrific job of it, that I'm just the sweetest, humblest little woman you've ever met, but I can't. All I can say is that, in learning to give care whenever I can and receive care whenever I must, I've grown more attentive to the personal dimension of the works of mercy.

So accustomed are most of us to thinking of human neediness not in personal but in economic terms that, asked for a charitable donation, we reflexively whip out our checkbooks and pens. Writing a check to a charity is not on the list of the works of mercy, however. It's a generous act, one that ought to be performed as frequently as the budget will bear, but it can't substitute spiritually for direct engagement with people in need. "Poverty" and "affliction" and "oppression" are abstractions whose remedy might seem to lie in the intangible transfer of a monetary amount from one account to another. Poor and afflicted and oppressed people have faces, and we are required to look squarely into them. We can't love what we won't experience. For this reason, George and I have always sought to make our charity concrete.

Although our most sustained and intimate charitable relationships have grown out of taking people into our home, not everyone has the physical plant or the emotional resources to make room for one more, and currently that includes us. Over the years, however, we've discovered other ways of developing caring relationships, making us, I suppose, one of those "thousand points of light" upon which conservative politicians have wished like stars in recent years. What speech writer, I wonder, came up with an estimate so small in a country so vast, evoking brave scattered flickers of individual endeavor in the very heart of darkness?

Beneath such a metaphor lies a shift from public to private torch-bearing which suggests that the government can just excuse itself from tending to messy human needs and get on with protecting oil supplies and national security and the "American" flag (as though ours were the only one) and capital gains and other things that matter. In this model, even when human beings enter the government's purview, they tend to do so as things, not people. The unborn child—as yet untouched, invisible—must have the government's protection, but the embraceable infant, demanding breastmilk and then a warm snowsuit and later textbooks and finally a steady job, gets thrust into the arms of one of us blinking lights. Unless by acting up she converts herself back into a thing—goes on a murderous shooting spree and has to be put to death, say, or fails to pay her taxes—the government will scarcely concern itself with her again.

This model has served us badly, and will continue to serve us badly, because it draws a false distinction between private and public concerns and between personal and governmental responsibility for coping with them. No things matter, either publicly or privately, except as they preserve and enhance the intricate process that I would call God's creation. All actions, both public and private, have equal impact, for good or ill, on that process. And no one, not even a dim bulb like George Bush, is excused from equal participation in it. We all lead lives of public service, and at last count, there should have been about 250 million points of light in the United States alone, plenty for a conflagration.

Individually and collectively, we must take on the tasks at hand, imbuing them with the reciprocity that arises out of our various abilities and diverse requirements. Until a few years ago, for instance, I refused to hire help around the house because I couldn't stand the thought of making someone my "servant." Eventually, with George teaching in two programs and my physical condition deteriorating, I was forced to find a weekly housekeeper or suffocate under a drift of grease, desert dust, and Corgi hair. At this point, the mistress/servant model no longer represented my reality. Because the need my housekeeper has for the money I pay her is no greater than my need for assistance, our dependence is mutual.

And our relative authority must be balanced accordingly. Since I cannot clean my own house, it has become to some extent no longer my own house. It has slipped from my control, a very good thing, since Celia takes far better care of it than I would have done even in the days when my arms and legs still worked. She cleans between all the buttons on the antiquated push-button stove so that our fingers no longer stick and release with a schloop every time we want to go from hot to warm. She keeps the sliding-glass door so clean that after my daughter walked through and shattered it, we had to paste a hedgehog decal onto the new one to ward off future incursions. But she does not know where things "belong," like the fish-shaped soup tureen on the sideboard; although this "should" be placed sideways, she invariably points its pouty face out into the room. At first I'd turn it back after she left; later, when I got too weak, I'd simply look at it and fret; at length, insight struck: Oh, wait a minute! Whose fish is this anyway? It's mine, I know. When my friend Mollie left Tucson, she gave it to me to hold until her return, but she liked Seattle better and I've got the fish by default. But it's Celia's fish, too, she's the one who takes care of it, and apparently it "should" stare out at us broodily, even though I think it looks dopey that way.

To relinquish not merely control but the claim to control, permitting someone to do what she does best in the way she chooses to do it and viewing the outcome as collaborative rather than "right" or "wrong," balances a relationship that might otherwise be skewed by issues of ownership or prerogative. Celia and I have a hollow, cream-colored stoneware fish. If you want to help us with its upkeep, you may have it, too. If no one drops it, it will outlast both Celia and me. One day, however, it's bound to be smashed, and then no one will have it anymore. Things come to us, and we cherish them for a while, and then they or we are gone. When Jesus says, "You cannot serve both God and mammon," it is not the thingness of our possessions he repudiates but our relationship to them: the way that, instead of simply tending them and putting them to use, we grasp them with knuckles turned white, clasp them against our chests, invest them with the power to represent our worth. Perhaps for this reason the early Christians held their goods in common: so that they wouldn't be tempted into controlling one another through commodities.

As valuable as personal relationships like mine with Celia are in transforming abstract works of mercy into concrete expressions of love, in the end you cannot know every person you serve. Lacks are too great; energies are too limited; and anyway, just as some donors prefer to remain anonymous, so do some recipients. To serve such needs on a large scale requires a whole charitable community like Casa Maria, which runs Our Lady of Guadalupe Chapel and Free Kitchen. At the core of this community, which occupies several small houses on Tucson's south side, are Brian Flagg, voluble and hyperkinetic, and George Petit, softspoken but equally fierce in his commitment, his wife Debbie and their baby Catie, together with several veterans of life on the streets: Lonnie, Lowell, Andy, Bill. These now form our family, too. With them we celebrate marriages and baptisms and birthdays, attend rallies and marches and vigils, and get arrested for civil disobedience, to the consternation of some of our less radical relatives.

Although, in order to avoid the NIMBY syndrome that has closed down similar projects around town, Casa Maria is a consecrated chapel, where Mass is said every Monday morning, and one is required to pray for her or his supper. Holding fast to the thousand-points-of-light principle, the federal government no longer contributes surplus goods like cheese, and operating expenses have soared to about $7,000 a month. The program subsists on donations of money, food, and time from all over Tucson and even beyond: The last time I was there I met several Mennonite grandmothers from the Midwest who spend three months in Tucson every winter; while they make and bag sandwiches, their husbands do home repairs for poor people. Established some years ago for the explicit purpose of performing works of mercy, Casa Maria initially served one meal a day—soup, a couple of sandwiches, fruit, a sweet, coffee, and milk when available for the children—to a couple hundred people. On a recent Saturday the number was thirteen hundred. Although the number of single men has stayed stable for several years, more and more families have come, as the realities of Reagan-Bush-*Clinton* economics have taken hold even here in the supposedly recession-proof Southwest.

"All those people want is a free ride," a woman at an adult education conference told me over dinner a couple of years ago when I mentioned my involvement with Casa Maria. "I have to drive by that soup kitchen on my way to work, and I've seen them lined up three times a day waiting for their handouts."

"Odd," I said. "The soup kitchen serves only lunch."

"Well, whatever. I see them there, just hanging around. They don't even want to find work."

"That's true," I said. "Some of them don't. And some are too sick to work. But some of them do. They're all different. Why don't you stop on your way to work one day and ask them?" The question was rhetorical. I couldn't imagine why this woman drove by the soup kitchen, which is not on a main thoroughfare, but I could imagine how: locked tight in her car, as fast as she could get away with in a neighborhood heavily patrolled by the police and La Migra (the U.S. Immigration and Naturalization Service). And who could blame her? Families there come and leave quickly. Most of the people hanging around the kitchen are men who, now that the old SRO (single room occupancy) hotels have been torn down to make room for luxury condominiums and motorways, live on the street. Unwashed, unshaven, in wardrobes chosen from the boxes of donated clothing Lonnie supervises, they look bad. (They can also smell bad, which is not a problem for this woman with her windows rolled up tight, but is for me, afflicted with a hypersensitive nose, when I'm among them.) They tend to be grumpy, as you probably would be too if you sought your night's rest under the Murphy Overpass. A woman alone might well choose not to mingle in such company.

Her loss. I must sound supercilious, but I'm not. I mean she really has cheated herself of experience in the way we all do when we whiz past the world with the air conditioner pumping full blast and the *Goldberg Variations* trilling from the tapedeck. She has lost the opportunity to know a little more about the world: "know," that is, not in the way she "knows" that the people queued up outside the soup kitchen are freeloaders but in the way she "knows" Paris, say, having spent a summer there between her junior and senior years in college. We know the world, as God knows the world, only by entering it. Photos in *Newsweek* or *National Geographic* won't do. Editorials in *The Nation* or *The New Republic* won't do. Sixty-second clips on the nightly news about unemployment, homelessness, substance abuse, mental illness, and serial murderers won't do. You gotta be there.

And if you're there with even half an eye open, you see that nothing so simple as freeloading is going on. To begin with, nothing's being given out that would seduce you away from a regular paycheck. Except maybe the soup, which is generally excellent, hot, and highly spiced. The sandwiches are most likely orange cheese-like food or peanut butter mixed with fruit cocktail on day-old bread. The apples and bananas are bruised. There might be a stale Ding Dong or a Snickers bar, but if your teeth have rotted to stumps, these furnish more pain than pleasure. You can squat on the ground and eat this stuff if you can fend off the damned pigeons long enough. If you need to take a crap, there are a couple of portable toilets in one corner of the yard. If the soles of your boots have holes, Lonnie might be able to find a pair not quite as worn and more or less your size.

The lap of luxury doesn't draw these people, then. Some are temporarily down-and-out, but many are chronically hungry and/or homeless. The family bags usually go to people in the neighborhood who can afford either rent or food but not both. Of the people on the street, most are men, a disproportionate number of them Vietnam vets. A lot have fevers, wracking coughs, ulcerated legs and feet, abscessed teeth. Some drink, smoke marijuana, do heroin or cocaine. A few are crazy as bedbugs, "freed" from state institutions in the early '70s to be turned over to a community-based mental health system that nobody ever got around to establishing. No amount of exhortation will make these people "better," to use the standard of my dinner companion, or "different," to use a less loaded word. Am I to say to the man who asks for a cigarette and when I give it to him (a dubious charity, I'll admit), showers me with kisses and calls down the blessing of Cristo upon me: "Good God, man, pull up your socks and get right down to the Department of Economic Security for a job interview!?" Who the hell would want him around? I've had him around for at least five minutes now and I don't want him, I assure you. At Casa Maria one learns, sooner or later depending upon one's resistances, that in spite of all our charitable efforts, some of the poor we will always have with us, just as Jesus warned, and our care for them can never cease.

I'm no defeatist. In the decade George taught adult education, we saw person after person on public assistance earn a GED, attend community college, find a job, and become (a point of pride) a taxpayer; and if the government would hand us *illuminati* out here more funds, instead of blowing them on bomb tests and the bad debts of persons in high places, such successes could mount exponentially. But there will always be a Frances, wearing my white wool tam-o'-shanter at a jaunty angle and leading on leashes her two pet chickens, invisible to the naked eye, around the encampment of homeless people at the county courthouse on Christmas Eve. Frances can't depend on herself; she can't even depend on the damned chickens, who disappear unpredictably even from her view. At the least, she ought to be able to depend on me.

Wholehearted commitment to people who are poor, afflicted, or oppressed, although it inevitably necessitates political choices and leads to shared political action, must first be rooted in personal conversion, described by the liberation theologist Leonardo Boff as follows: "The conversion demanded by Jesus is more than a mere change of conviction—a change in theory. It is also, and mainly, a change of attitudes change bearing directly on practice. Nor is it a change only within a person—a change of heart. It is also a change in that person's living, functioning network of relationships." Not by chance, I think, was Dorothy Day, the founder of the Catholic Worker movement, a convert to Roman Catholicism. Every Frances necessitates a new and conscious conversion, a turning again to enter communion at each fresh encounter—for which Dorothy showed an extraordinary gift. One needn't be a Catholic, or even a Christian, in order to undergo such a change or carry out such action, of course, but one must by some means learn the habit of turning toward and taking in.

The charity that begins at home cannot rest there but draws one inexorably over the threshold and off the porch and down the street and so out and out and out and out into the world that becomes the home wherein charity begins until it becomes possible, in theory at least, to love the whole of creation with the same patience, affection, and amusement one first practiced, in between the pouts and tantrums, with parents, siblings, spouse, and children. Relationship: connection: kinship: family: love: the movement from an abstract and emotionless awareness that there are needy people out there to the give-and-take—tender, quarrelsome, jokey, impassioned—of siblings crowded together under the roof of Mary's House. The choice to name Casa Maria for La Virgen de Guadalupe is especially apt, not only because she is the patron saint of Mexico, only seventy miles from Tucson, but because she appeared to a poor man of questionable mental stability: the Queen of Heaven placed a rose in the hands of a bemused peasant. In charity distances dissolve. As a response to the gratuitous outpouring of God's love, charity demands that one turn one's face toward the face of another and confront there both oneself and God.

5

HELP ALONG THE WAY:
A RESOURCE GUIDE

Educational Programs

SkyDancing Institute USA
28 Laurel Avenue
San Anselmo, CA 94960
phone: (415) 456-7310
fax: (415) 456-9599
email: Register@skydancing.com
Website: www.skydancing.com

Margot Anand's SkyDancing Institute teaches a unique process that can open the door to your creative inspiration in love as well as in work. SkyDancing Tantra integrates the ancient spirit of Tantra with the latest discoveries in clinical sexology and the therapeutic methods of humanistic and transpersonal psychology. The philosophy of SkyDancing Tantra and the educational opportunities available through the Institute provide a gateway into the Tantric way of life. Ecstasy, joy, well-being, and intimacy can happen where body, heart, and spirit are joined.

Sue Bender
WARRIORS OF THE SPIRIT
phone: (510) 524-4896
fax: (510) 524-1466

"It takes courage to know who we are and what we want." Sue Bender

A much sought-after lecturer worldwide, Sue Bender's struggle is one keenly felt in today's time-starved world. Speaking simply with an emotional wallop she will share lessons learned—revealing how each step along life's journey can be a miraculous opportunity to learn.

Bender will explore how quieting the harsh inner critic, honoring yourself as you are, and approaching each day with "fresh eyes" can allow for extraordinary things to come your way.

Using drawing, writing, and clay, where suitable, the image of an empty begging bowl as a metaphor for ourselves, will guide us. The workshop will explore what we need and want in our bowl for the nourishment in our lives. We will discover that we can seek the sacred everywhere—in our homes, in our daily activities and, hardest to see, in ourselves.

Institute of Noetic Sciences (IONS)
475 Gate 5 Road, Suite 300
Sausalito, CA 94965
phone: (415) 331-5650
fax: (415) 331-5673
membership: (800) 383-1394
Website: http://www.noetic.org

A research foundation, educational institution, and membership organization committed to developing human consciousness through scientific inquiry, spiritual understanding, and psychological well-being. IONS offers grants for innovative research projects; international membership opportunities with conferences, meetings, events, community groups, and a travel-study program; a journal, *Noetic Sciences Review*, a magazine, *Connections*, and program-related books. IONS also underwrites New Dimensions Radio, a weekly interview program with leading thinkers and innovators, and is affiliated with the Thinking Allowed television program and the Hartley Film Foundation. Basic membership ($35 per year) includes a subscription to the quarterly journal and magazine.

The Esalen Institute
Highway 1
Big Sur, CA 93920
phone: (408) 667-3000

Founded in 1962, the Esalen Institute is a learning center committed to the exploration of humanities and sciences that promote the highest human values and potentials. Its programs and research projects focus on the areas of environmental design, transformative practices, and theoretical development of emerging paradigms. Esalen sponsors public seminars, residential work-study programs, invitational conferences, research, and semi-autonomous projects.

The Fetzer Institute
9292 West KL Avenue
Kalamazoo, MI 49009-9398
phone: (616) 375-2000

A nonprofit educational organization that promotes research on health care methods that utilize the principles of mind-body interaction. The Institute's work is guided by the belief that the study of the mind's influence on the body and the relationship of body, mind, and spirit can provide the basis for developing scientifically sound approaches to health care and expanding the scope of medical science to give individuals greater control over their own well-being.

Jean Houston & The Mystery School
P.O. Box 3300
Pomona, NY 10970
(914) 354-4965

Jean Houston began the Mystery School to teach people to expand their inner potential by experiencing a synthesis of history, music, theatre, world cultures, science, philosophy, theology, comedy, and laughter. The Mystery School is a year-long program of two-and-a-half day workshops over nine weekends. Exercises range from creative arts to altered states of consciousness. Call or write for a free brochure about the Mystery School or a schedule of Jean Houston's seminars and workshops at various learning centers around the country.

University of Creation Spirituality
2141 Broadway
Oakland, CA 94612
phone: (510) 835-4827
fax: (510) 835-0564
email: ucs@csnet.org
Website: http://www.netser.com/ucs

A gathering place for the Creation Spirituality movement, honoring all forms of life and diverse spiritual traditions. Awaken to the artist, mystic, and prophet within through a creative learning process integrating body and spirit, imagination and ideas, contemplation and action. The faculty includes artists, scientists, theologians, and activists committed to personal, cultural, and planetary transformation as well as social and ecological justice.

Foundation for Conscious Evolution
Barbara Marx Hubbard, President
P.O. Box 6397
San Rafael, CA 94903-0397
phone: (415) 454-8191
fax: (415) 454-8805
email: fce@peaceroom.org
Website: http://www.cocreation.org

The Foundation for Conscious Evolution has arisen in response to the unprecedented potential of humanity to either destroy this world or co-create a future of immeasurable possibilities. President Barbara Marx Hubbard says, "When you begin to seriously notice all the things that are working, then your mind changes from the negative to the positive, and you also see there are far more possibilities than ever imagined." (See also listing for the Co-Creation Website under Online Resources.)

California Insitute of Integral Studies
9 Peter Yorke Way
San Francisco, CA 94109
(415) 674-5500
Website: http://www.ciis.edu

An accredited institution of higher learning and research that strives to embody spirit, intellect, and wisdom. The Institute's original emphasis on Asian studies has evolved to include comparative and crosscultural studies in philosophy, religion, psychology, counseling, social and cultural anthropology, drama therapy, organizational studies, health studies, and the arts. Call ext. 241 to request a brochure of public lectures and workshops.

Graduate School for Holistic Studies
John F. Kennedy University
12 Altarinda Road
Orinda, CA 94563
(510) 254-0105
Website: http://www.jfku.edu

A community of educators, practitioners, and students who share a holistic vision of personal and societal transformation. Supports students who are striving for fuller integration of body, mind, and spirit in their personal and professional lives. Programs are designed to provide a balance between academic learning and experiential understanding. Evening and weekend classes allow students to integrate their studies with family, work, and social responsibilities.

Omega Institute
Rhinebeck, NY
(800) 944-1001
Website: http://www.omega-inst.org

The nation's largest adult alternative learning and retreat center offers a combination of education and relaxation. Relax, rejuvenate, and feel at home amid the beauty of gardens, a lake, rolling hills, and a community of sincere, caring people. The faculty is an extraordinary group of innovative thinkers and practitioners from a wide variety of fields.

Sancta Sophia Seminary
11 Summit Ridge Drive
Tahlequah, OK 74464-9211
phone: (918) 456-3421
information: (800) 386-7161
fax: (918) 458-5501
email: lccc@sanctasophia.org
Website: http://sanctasophia.org

Live and breathe the ageless esoteric teachings with serious students of like mind as we strive to discover the parts we are to play in this era of transition. Meditation, dream study, astrology, Kabalah, Agni Yoga, many healing modes, death and dying, leadership, and much more. Enroll in one of several structured programs or attend classes and workshops at your leisure. Graduate program, ordination, or certification as a practitioner or teacher of esoteric philosophies. Individual advising, home study, and residency combine to make this an exceptional program, available to anyone searching for a contemporary path to higher consciousness. Chartered study centers and churches located throughout the U.S.; call for one near you.

Nine Gates Mystery School
Gay Luce, Director
Noetic Sciences Travel Program
475 Gate Five Road, Suite 216
Sausalito, CA 94965
phone: (415) 332-0682
email: ccj@wenet.net

A spellbinding adventure into ancient traditions and sources of wisdom. Presented in a beautiful retreat setting over two nine-day periods, this program is an opportunity to be in the presence of world masters for a transformative, educational experience in a small group setting. Includes initiations, esoteric practices, ceremonies, art, music, and theater from some of the world's most powerful disciplines. Tap into the vast natural intelligence of the nine energy centers or "gates" of the body, drawing strength from the universe, and transforming your ability to communicate deeply and to manifest more personal power. Recommended for seekers of self-knowledge or people in spiritual transition.

The Focusing Institute
34 East Lane
Spring Valley, NY 10977
phone & fax: (914) 362-5222
email: info@focusing.org
Website: http://www.focusing.org/

Focusing is a kind of inward bodily attention, a "felt sense" of how you are in a particular life situation. The Institute brings focusing to the public and the international scholarly community through teaching, research, and written materials. Trained Focusing teachers around the world give workshops and individual sessions. Join the Institute to stay connected with the community and the latest developments and ideas on Focusing. $50 yearly membership entitles you to journal subscription, membership directory, periodic newsletters, mailings, and 10 percent discount on all Institute-sponsored workshops.

The Naropa Institute
2130 Arapahoe Ave.
Boulder, CO 80302
phone: (303) 546-3572
Continuing Education: (303) 546-3578
email: admissions@naropa.edu
Website: http://www.naropa.edu

The Naropa Institute is a private, nonsectarian, accredited liberal arts college offering disciplines in the humanities, social sciences, and the arts. While its learning philosophy of Contemplative Education is rooted in the Buddhist tradition, the majority of students, faculty, and staff are not Buddhist. Contemplative Education balances the study of specific academic and artistic fields with the traditional practices for training in mindfulness and awareness. The Naropa Institute offers graduate and undergraduate studies, and the School of Continuing Education has a diverse selection of seminars and classes for people who are not pursuing a degree.

The LearningWay Company (TLC)
A Tribe of Two Press
Paula Underwood, Director
Post Office Box 216
San Anselmo, CA 94979
phone: (800) 995-3320
fax: (415) 457-6543
Website:
http://members.aol.com/toTPress

A nationwide network of certified trainers in education, corporate strategies, and health services. Enables sharing from a Native American tradition focused on learning and on a system of thought that never neglects wholeness. The Learning Way was recognized immediately by educators and was designated an "Exemplary Educational Program" by the U.S. Department of Education in 1986. It is used in schools and universities across the nation, and increasingly by corporations working to become effective learning organizations. A Tribe of Two Press publishes learning stories, methodologies, oral histories, and other materials developed out of this tradition.

The Women's Spirituality Forum
Z Budapest
P.O. Box 11363
Oakland CA 94611

Call Z for mentoring, soul readings, advice at 1-900-737-4637. The Women's Spirituality Forum organizes biannual festivals called *Goddess 2000*.

Caroline Myss
7144 North Harlem Avenue, #1305
Chicago, IL 60631
phone: 312-409-3071

Throughout the year, Caroline Myss offers workshops and seminars on intuition, creativity, the power of archetypes, and on *Why People Don't Heal and How They Can*. In Janurary 1999, she'll lead a Healing Pilgrimage to Ancient Egypt (call Power Places Tours at 800-234-8687 for further details). For intuition training, Caroline Myss also recommends:

Intuition Training with
    Dr. Norm Shealy
5607 South 222nd Road
Fair Grove, MO 65648
phone: 417-267-2900

CornerStone Consulting Associates
2761 Stiegler Road
Valley City, OH 44280
phone: 800-773-8017
fax: 330-725-2728
Website: http://www.ourfuture.com
John and Connie Dicus
email: cca@ourfuture.com

A consulting organization that provides experiences in teamwork, systems thinking and stewardship. People engage their whole being as they experience new concepts and practice new ways of working together. Hope and awareness are strong internal drives for change. People seek new ways to organize after they experience how future organizations can perform and as they gain deeper insight into the systemic nature of human/business systems. Experimental Learning simulations are incorporated into all sessions providing lifelike learning experiences capable of duplicating real-world effects. Accommodating group sizes to 500, Open Space Facilitation brings the whole system together for comprehensive dialogue, learning and collaboration. Also host Experiences in Stewardship, in-person explorations into the concepts of stewardship, and an open Internet conversation on Stewardship.

Rudolf Steiner Institute
Carol Petrash
P.O. Box 207
Kensington, MD 20895-0207
phone & fax: (301) 946-2099
email: steinerinstitute@erols.com

Now in its 25th year, the Rudolf Steiner Institute offers a summer program of one- and three -week college-level courses for anyone interested in deepening their experience of the arts, sciences, and humanities. Courses take place each year in July. All courses relate to *Anthroposophy*, the philosophy by Rudolf Steiner (1861-1925), which connects individual spirituality with the spirituality at work in the universe.

Rudolf Steiner College
9200 Fair Oaks Boulevard
Fair Oaks, CA 95628
phone: (916) 961-8727
fax: (916) 961-8731
email: rsc@steinercollege.org
Website: http://www.steinercollege.org

Offers Waldorf teacher training programs and Waldorf enrichment programs for public school teachers; foundation courses in anthroposophy and courses in arts, biodynamic gardening, and Goethean studies. Extensive summer programs.

Schumacher College
Hilary Nicholson
The Old Postern
Dartington, Totnes
Devon TQ9 6EA
England
fax: 44-(0)1803-866899
email: schumcoll@gn.apc.org

An international center for ecological studies offering two- and four-week workshops.

PeerSpirit ... In Service to the Circle
P.O. Box 550
Langley, WA 98260
phone and fax: 360-331-3580
voicemail: 360-321-8404
cofounders: Christina Baldwin &
Ann Linnea

PeerSpirit offers seminars, wilderness adventures, consulting and training based on the books of the cofounders: Christina's ground-breaking work in circle methodology, *Calling the Circle: The First and Future Culture,* and Ann's memoir of circumnavigating Lake Superior by sea-kayak, *Deep Water Passage: A Spiritual Journey at Midlife.* The two women, and a cadre of teaching colleagues, offer a practical structure to the art of the circle, inviting people into community-based meetings in their homes, businesses, churches and organizations. All of Peer Spirit's work is dedicated to the belief that by rotating leadership, sharing responsibility and attending to Spirit, people may align their lives with their own dreams, social awareness and spiritual values in order to respond to the pressing needs of the Earth, its people and creatures.

Retreat Centers

Mount Madonna Center for the Creative Arts and Sciences
445 Summit Road
Watsonville, CA 95076
phone: (408) 847-0406
fax: (408) 847-2683

A community designed to nurture the creative arts and health sciences within a context of spiritual growth. Located on 355 mountaintop acres of redwood forest and grassland overlooking the Monterey Bay (near Santa Cruz), the Center offers a supportive community atmosphere for personal and group retreats and a variety of learning experiences. The Center is inspired by Baba Hari Dass, and is sponsored by the Hanuman Fellowship, a group that is unified by the common practice of yoga.

Blue Mountain Center of Meditation
P.O. Box 256
Tomales, CA 94971
phone: (800) 475-2369
fax: (707) 878-2375
email: info@nilgiri.org
Website: http://www.nilgiri.org

The Blue Mountain Center of Meditation offers instruction and guidance in meditation and allied living skills, following the method of Eknath Easwaran. Nondenominational, nonsectarian approach that can be used within your own cultural and religious background to relieve stress, heal relationships, release deeper resources, and realize your highest spiritual potential. The Center publishes books under the Nilgiri Press imprint, and a newsletter with articles by Eknath Easwaran, activities and programs, and news of friends. Weekend and day programs in meditation and a practical Eight-Point Program of spiritual living. Retreats in northern California and at various sites around the country. Retreats often fill up far in advance, so please enroll early to reserve a place.

The Chopra Center for Well Being
7630 Fay Avenue
La Jolla, CA 92037
phone: (888) 424-6772

Deepak Chopra's mind-body spa offers a full range of natural therapies in an environment of healing and transformation. Learn techniques for personal development and participate in classes on mind/body medicine and healthy living. The Center's mission is to provide guests with a life-changing experience, and then show them how to transform their daily lives by applying the knowledge and insights they have gained.

Sonoma Mountain Zen Center
6367 Sonoma Mountain Road
Santa Rosa, CA 95404
phone: (707) 545-8105

A Soto Zen Buddhist center that offers a one-year resident training program as well as a guest program of retreats, one-day sitting sessions, and introductory workshops throughout the year. Instruction/meditation/ lecture program every Saturday morning for first-timers. Rustic cabins and rooms for guests; meals are taken with the community in the dining room. Call or write for *Zen Dust* catalog.

Heartwood Institute
220-CG Harmony Lane
Garberbille, CA 95542
phone: (707) 923-5004
Website:
http://www.heartwoodinstitute.com

A retreat program designed for people who are taking responsiblity for becoming healthier. Live in a caring and nurturing community in a serene wilderness setting. Experience a wide variety of healing therapies, and relax in our hot tub, wood-fired sauna, and large pool. Simple accommodations, delicious vegetarian meals.

Harbin Hot Springs
Dept. CG, P.O. Box 782
Middletown, CA 95461
phone: (707) 987-2477
Website: http://www.harbin.org

A nonprofit retreat and workshop center located on 1,160 acres of wilderness in the wine region north of Calistoga, California. Hike, soak in natural spring pools, schedule a therapeutic massage, visit our organic garden, general store, bookstore, and café. Free guest events include daily yoga and weekly dances. Weekend workshops, week-long classes, and month-long work-study programs throughout the year. Camping, dorms, private rooms, and cabins

for overnight stays, as well as a full-time residential program.

Wild Woman Retreats International
P.O. Box 4943
Gardena, CA 90249
phone: (310) 516-1463
Website: http://www.wildwomanretreats.com

Join top facilitators for a joyful celebration of the feminine spirit and a conscious connection with the wild woman. Participate in story, myth, music, art, breathing, transformational movement, a sweat lodge, and more. Retreats set in the most beautiful, relaxing, sacred locations in the world.

Rio Caliente Hot Springs Spa
phone: (650) 615-9543
fax: (650) 615-0601
email: RioCal@aol.com

One hour outside Guadalajra, Mexico, this is the perfect retreat located near a beautiful national forest. Offers reflexology, massage, hiking, mineral hot springs, vegetarian meals, and exercise equipment. No phones and plenty of quiet time. Very reasonable rates, all meals included.

Kripalu Center for Yoga and Health
P.O. Box 793
Lenox, MA 01240
phone: (413) 448-3400

Located in a huge, former Jesuit seminary near the Tanglewood Music Festival grounds, the Center offers a variety of rest and renewal courses, daily meditation, yoga, and a three-month Spiritual Lifestyle Training Program. A wide choice of accommodations from dormitory to private rooms with bath. Vegetarian food served in the large dining hall; meals are usually eaten in silence. Hiking trails through the pines and Tanglewood grounds, short walk to a lake with a public beach.

Spirit Rock Meditation Center
P.O. Box 909
Woodacre, CA 94973
phone: (415) 488-0164
Website: http://www.spiritrock.org/

Hosts a full program of ongoing classes and day-long retreats exploring the themes of meditation and its relation to life in modern society. Based on the classical teachings of the Buddha, the teachings stress the central role of mindfulness and awareness in developing a life of wisdom and compassion. The practice of Vipassana, or insight meditation, is at the heart of all activities at Spirit Rock. A collective of over fifteen teachers provides spiritual guidance and leads classes and retreats for beginning and experienced students. Residential facilities are under development.

Namasté Retreat Center
29500 SW Grahams Ferry Road
Wilsonville, OR 97070-9516
phone: (800) 893-1000
or (503) 682-5683
email: namaste@lecworld.org
Website: http://www.lecworld.org

The leading spiritual retreat center in the Northwest, Namasté is located on ninety-five acres of tall fir trees and beautiful landscaped gardens. Offers a series of extraordinary programs and presenters, a wide range of ideas and opportunities, and a spectacular natural setting for personal growth and inner exploration.

Green Gulch Farm Zen Center
1601 Shoreline Highway
Sausalito, CA 94965
(415) 383-3134

Accomodations in a beautiful, handcrafted, Japanese-style guesthouse, delicious vegetarian meals with fresh produce from its showcase farm, sauna, pool, library, teahouse, hiking trails, and a fifteen-minute walk to the beach. An active schedule of retreat programs, workshops, Buddhist studies, daily meditation and service with community, gardening classes, and conference facilities.

Sparrow Hawk Village
11 Summit Ridge Drive
Tahlequah, OK 74464-9211
phone: (918) 456-3421
information: (800) 386-7161
fax: (918) 458-5501
email: lccc@sanctasophia.org
Website: http://sanctasophia.org

This intentional community, located on 400 wooded acres on a mountaintop in the Ozark foothills, is the site designated by spirit to Carol Parrish as a home and campus for Sancta Sophia Seminary. Light of Christ Community Church, The Wellness Center, an office-library building, bookstore, gift shop, fire department, modern water system, and forty-five energy-efficient homes comprise this community. A bimonthly newspaper, *The Villager*, features village and seminary teachings, philosophies, classes, and events (subscription $15/year). Visitors always welcome to the church, seminary, and village. Overnight housing available; call ahead for reservations and directions.

North American Retreats (NAR)
Melane Lohmann
P.O. Box 102
Ovando, MT 59854
phone: (406) 793-5824

Offers guided wilderness, spiritual, and educational retreats in the U.S. and Canada. Dedicated to wilderness protection and conservation, NAR brings people into the beauty and quiet of the natural world. Includes backpacking, horsepack trips and trailrides, canoe trips, conservation resource management, and alternative building technologies. NAR also offers Wilderwomen! retreats for women only.

Insight Meditation Society
1230 Pleasant Street
Barre, MA 01005
phone: (508) 355-4378

A center for Vipassana (insight meditation) retreats, located on eighty acres of secluded land in central Massachusetts. The meditation practice at IMS is an investigation of the mind-body process through focused awareness. Silence is observed at all times, except for teacher interviews and evening discourse. Single and double rooms are spartan, with separate floors for men and women, and community washrooms. All food served is vegetarian. Resident work/study programs available. Retreats run from two days to twelve weeks and are generally fully booked, so plan far ahead.

Elat Chayyim ("Tree of Life")
A Center for Healing and Renewal
99 Mill Hook Road
Accord, NY 12404
phone: (914) 626-0157
or: (800) 398-2630

Rabbi Joann Katz and Rabbi Jeff Roth bring the teachings of Jewish mysticism to the forefront, aiming to develop an authentic and healing Jewish practice for our time. Programs reflect humanism, transpersonal psychology, and openness to other spiritual traditions. Located on thirty-five acres along a quiet, tree-lined country lane, this retreat center and sanctuary celebrates Jewish renewal for people from all branches of Judaism. Gourmet vegetarian meals made with homegrown produce are served. Friday night and Saturday Shabbat services offered year-round, as well as meditation retreats with visiting Buddhist teachers, a men's retreat, a singles' retreat, and a training for spiritual facilitators.

Vision Quests in South Africa
Contact: Judy Bekker and Valerie
    Morris
P.O. Box 245
Constantia 7848
South Africa
phone: (011) 27 21 794 4646
fax: (011) 27 21 794 5088

An eleven-day wilderness experience based on the rites of passage of traditional peoples, including four days of solo time. This is an opportunity to mark a particular cycle in your life, whether it be an ending, transition, or new beginning. The experience includes ceremonies and ritual, singing, storytelling, and silence, with nature as teacher and healer.

The Ojai Foundation
9739 Ojai-Santa Paula Road
Ojai, CA 93023
phone: (805) 646-8343
fax: (805) 646-2456
email: ojaifdn@fishnet.net
Website:
http://www.ojaifoundation.org/

A nondenominational land-based educational sanctuary located on a beautiful forty-acre semi-wilderness site at the foot of the Los Padres Mountains, ninety minutes north of Los Angeles. An educational sanctuary for youth and adults that unites learning and living, work in the world and spiritual practice, traditional and emerging wisdom. A learning community, a place for retreat, reflection, and healing; opportunities to participate in the creation of a caring, mindful culture; and a training center for bringing the Way of Council to the educational, business, and therapeutic communities. Rustic and simple accommodations, food preparation areas, pottery studio, meditation room, sweat lodge, two kivas with firepits, organic fruit orchard, and herb garden.

Organizations

The Reclaiming Collective
P.O. Box 14404
San Francisco, CA 94114
email: reclaiming@reclaiming.org
Website: http://www.reclaiming.org

Reclaiming is a community of women and men working to unify spirit and politics. Our vision is rooted in the religion and magic of the Goddess—the Immanent Life Force. Classes, workshops, and public rituals in the Bay Area, as well as Summer Intensives (Witchcamps) throughout the U.S., Canada, and Europe. Learn to deepen your strength, voice your concerns, and bring to birth a vision of a new culture. Reclaiming publishes a quarterly magazine and sponsors an events line (a telephone listing of Pagan events in the Bay Area): (415) 929-9249.

Global Fund For Women
2480 Sandhill Road, Suite 100
Menlo Park, CA 94025
phone: (415) 854-0420
Website: http://www.igc.apc.org/gfw/

An international organization that provides funding and support to women's groups around the world. It supports issues as diverse as literacy, domestic violence, economic autonomy, and the international trafficking of women, among others. Call for information on grant requirements.

Resource Center for Redesigning Education
P.O. Box 298
Brandon, VT 05733-0298
phone: (800) 639-4122

Books and videos available on alternative educational theories, research, and methods, including postmodern visions of education, student-centered learning, education and spirituality. Their catalog, "Great Ideas in Education," reviews titles on select themes or hot topics of debate. The Center also sponsors workshops, conferences, and retreats. A vehicle for linking those in the educational community who are looking ahead and in new directions.

Media Network
39 W. 14th Street, Suite 403
New York, NY 10011
phone: (212) 929-2663

This national organization enables women to tell their stories and get their messages out. Provides financial, legal, technical, and administrative support and tax-exempt status for women making issue-related films and videos. Promotes film and video made by women through seven subject catalogs that offer titles on everything from war and peace to health and community development. Produce a quarterly newsletter, *Immediate Impact,* and sells the book *In Her Image* which lists seventy films and videos made by and for women. $35.00/year membership.

Echoes of the Ancestors
4400 Keller Avenue #260
Oakland, CA 94605-4505
phone: (510) 639-7637
fax: (510) 482-1097
Website:
http://www.PrimoSounds.com/echoes/

A nonprofit organization founded by Malidoma and Sobonfu Somé, spokespeople for the Dagara tribe of Burkina Faso, West Africa. Let their graceful voices and spirits initiate you into the mysteries of their ancient ways. Free newsletter provides information on their books, tapes, training programs, special events, and work with the Dagara Water Project.

League of Women Voters
1730 M Street, NW
Washington, DC 20036-4508
phone: 202-429-1965
fax: 202-429-0854
email: lwv@lwv.org

Website:http://www.lwv.org/

The League of Women Voters is a multi-issue organization whose mission is to encourage the informed and active participation of citizens in government and to influence public policy through education and advocacy. Any person of voting age, male or female, may become a League member.

Study Circles Resource Center
P.O. Box 203
Pomfret, CT 06258
phone: (203) 928-2616

A support organization for small, informal discussion groups that meet occasionally or on a regular basis to discuss important topics of interest to the group. A leader usually prepares materials and helps facilitate the discussion, while the Center provides guides for organizing and conducting circles, and for specific themes.

Network for Attitudinal Healing
    International
33 Buchanan Street
Sausalito, CA 94965
phone: (415) 331-6161

Supports people participating in the process of attitudinal healing. Established in 1975, the Network places an emphasis on extending love and being of service to others and provides support to all types of people, from those dealing with long-term illness or bereavement to those coping with life's everyday challenges. Centers provide programs and workshops, educational outreach, and ongoing support groups.

GAIA Bookstore
1400 Shattuck Ave
Berkeley, CA 94709
phone: (510) 548-4172
email: gaiabkst@pacbell.net

GAIA Bookstore & Community Center specializes in books and other resources in the areas of inner development, health, psychology, creative arts, new paradigms of business and cultural evolution. GAIA holds nightly author readings, workshops, concerts and cultural events which provide a place for dialogue on the life of the soul.

Covenant of the Goddess
P.O. Box 1226
Berkeley, CA 94701
Website: http://www.cog.org

An international organization of cooperating, autonomous Wiccan congregations and solo practitioners. Holds educational and religious conferences, publishes a newsletter, and provides numerous other services to members. On their Website, you'll find information about the organization, activities, and the religious beliefs and practices of Wicca.

Feminist Spiritual Community
Box 3771
Portland, ME 04104
phone: (207) 797-9217

A diverse group of women that gathers to affirm spirituality, mark life passages, and build a women's community. Call or write for free information.

Community of Mindful Living (CML)
P.O. Box 7355
Berkeley, CA 94707
phone: (510)527-3751
fax: (510) 525-7129
email: parapress@aol.com
Website: www.parallax.org

Formed in 1983 to support mindfulness practice in the tradition of Vietnamese Buddhist teacher Thich Nhat Hanh, for individuals, families, and communities. Mindfulness means dwellng fully in the present moment, aware of what is going on within and around us. CML acts as a clearinghouse for over 200 local communities of friends, and a liaison for the Plum Village community in France, a mindfulness center for monks, nuns, laypeople, and Vietnamese refugees througout the world. CML publishes *The Mindfulness Bell* journal and is the home of Parallax Press, offering many books and tapes on socially engaged Buddhism. Journal subscription is $18 per year, three issues; $30 for two years. $35 membership in "Friends of Parallax Press" includes 10 percent discount on all orders for one year.

The World Business Academy
P.O. Box 191210
San Francisco, CA 94119-1210
phone: (415) 227-0106
fax: (415) 227-0854
email: wba@well.com

A network of spiritually oriented business executives and entrepreneurs whose common interest is to find the creative role of business in the changes taking place in the modern world. Publishes a newsletter and a quarterly journal and sponsors an annual international retreat and members' meeting, miscellaneous conferences, and local chapter meetings.

The Hartley Film Foundation
59 Cat Rock Road
Cos Cob, CT 06807
phone: (203) 869-1818
or (800) 937-1819
fax: (203) 869-1905
email: HartleyFilm@MSN.com
Website:
http://www.hartleyvideos.org/

A nonprofit membership and learning organization that promotes an understanding of humans and spiritual oneness that can ultimately lead to world peace. Also a small working foundation, funded solely by the sale and rental of our films. Has worked with some of the foremost spiritual leaders of our time, and offers a library of nearly 100 films. Website features stimulating video selection, links, membership information. Inquiries about any of our activities are welcome.

Intuition Network
369-B Third Streeet #161
San Rafael, CA 94901
phone: (415) 256-1137
fax: (415) 456-2532
email: intuition.network@intuition.org
Website: http://www.intuition.org/

The purpose of the Intuition Network is to help create a world in which all people feel encouraged to cultivate and use their inner intuitive resources. Offers opportunities for networking via phone, fax, newsletters, journals, and magazines, radio and television, small group gatherings, conferences on the Internet, conferences in hotels, and international travel and spiritual retreats.

Common Boundary
5272 River Road, Suite 650
Bethesda, MD 20816
phone: (301) 652-9495
fax: (301) 652-0579
email: connect@commonboundary.org
Website:
http://www.commonboundary.org/

A nonprofit educational organization dedicated to exploring the sources of meaning in human experience: the relationship among matters of the heart, matters of the mind, and matters of the soul; psychology, spirituality, and creativity; and individual growth and social change. Common Boundary encourages respect for the diversity and relatedness of all beings and serves as a nondogmatic, discerning companion for those on the journey of inner exploration. In addition to publishing the award-winning *Common Boundary* magazine, the organization holds an annual national conference exploring such themes as the connection between body and mind, the power of storytelling, and the sacred in everyday life. Magazine subscription $24.95 per year, six issues.

Arts and Healing Network
3450 Sacramento Street, Box 612
San Francisco, CA 94118
fax: (415) 771-3696
email: ahn@artheals.org
Website: http://www.artheals.org/

Works to enliven and strengthen the interface between art, healing, and the community and to promote the concept of the artist as healer. Serves as an international forum for artists who see their work as healing to themselves, the community, or the environment. Collaborates with several organizations, including JFK University, which houses their slide library of over 2,000 examples of healing artists' work. To visit the library call (510) 649-0499. Website features a calendar and photographs of arts and healing related events, a bulletin board, resources, and links to related organizations.

20/20 Vision
1828 Jefferson Place, NW
Washington, DC 20036
phone: (202) 833-2020
fax: (202) 833-5307
email: vision@2020vision.org.
Website: http://www.2020vision.org/

A national nonprofit advocacy organization dedicated to protecting the environment and promoting peace through grassroots action. At the heart of 20/20 Vision's mission is the revitalization of democracy by making it simple for citizens to participate in national and local policy decisions. Our motto: "Twenty minutes a month, twenty dollars a year, a vision for a healthy planet" is fulfilled by over 30,000 individuals who communicate with targeted decision-makers each month.

International Society for the Study of
    Subtle Energies and Energy Medi-
    cine (ISSSEEM)
356 Goldco Circle

Golden, CO 80401
phone: (303) 425-4625
fax: (303) 425-4685
email: 74040.1273@compuserve.com
Website:
http://www.vitalenergy.com/issseem/

A leader in the effort to synthesize traditional wisdom and shamanic knowledge about subtle energies with scientific theory and to study it with scientific method. A bridge between scientifically inclined intuitives and intuitively inclined scientists. Through conferences and publications, the Society seeks to stimulate theory, research, and discussion in the larger scientific community.

Center for International Cooperation
P.O. Box 36330
Tucson, Arizona 85740
telephone: 520/531-9343
fax: 520/531-9354
email: 71175.1715@compuserve.com
Website:
www.mindspring.com/~umcic/
cichome.html

The Center for International Cooperation (CIC) emphasizes traditional wisdom of indigenous peoples in its projects. Indigenous elders are often advisors and/or participants in CIC's educational partnerships. CIC is a nongovernmental organization on the Roster of the UN Economic and Social Council.

Tree of Peace Society
Chief Jake Swamp
Mohawk Nation
188C Cook Road
Hogansburg, NY 13655

The Tree of Peace Society holds ceremonial plantings of Trees of Peace around the world in honor of the Great Law of Peace, the Constitution of the Haudenosaunee (Iroquois Six Nations Confederacy)—which is one of the roots of the U.S.

Constitution—and in order to further world peace.

Association for Transpersonal
    Psychology
P.O. Box 3049
Stanford, California 94309
phone: (650) 327-2066

Based on observations and practices from many cultures, the transpersonal perspective is informed by modern psychology, the humanities, and human sciences, as well as contemporary spiritual disciplines and the wisdom traditions. Explore the transpersonal perspective and develop your personal, professional, and educational interests by participating in the activities and publications of the ATP. Members receive quarterly newsletter and subscription to *The Journal of Transpersonal Psychology*. Upon request, you can also receive a listing of professional members, schools, and programs, or members in your area. $75 per year general membership.

Buddhist Peace Fellowship
National Office
P.O. Box 4650
Berkeley, CA 94704
phone: (510) 655-6169
fax: (510) 655-1369
email: bpf@bpf.org
Website: http://www.igc.org/bpf/

An organization of meditating activists, the Buddhist Peace Fellowship is eighteen years old and 4,000 members strong. The national office provides information and support for members and BPF chapters around the U.S. and the world. Members are involved in disarmament work, environmental and human rights, including campaigns that oppose oppression of Buddhists in Bangladesh, Burma, Vietnam, and Tibet. Our journal, *Turning Wheel*, serves as a beacon for Dharma activists committed to transforming the world and themselves.

Membership does not require active status in a Buddhist organization, just a commitment to the spirit of our purpose. $35 per year general membership; $20 students, low-income. Includes journal subscription.

Circle of Seven
Glennifer Gillespie
email: glennifer@aol.com

Circle Technologies consists of presentations, workshops, and coaching in practices useful for women's circles. Assistance with starting a circle, deep listening, learning and practicing processes for creating community, working through difficult life challenges in the circle, developing witnessing and truth-telling skills, and practicing dialogue as a discipline to think and create together. Rites of Passage consists of presentations, workshops, and coaching in creating and conducting rites of passage processes for women moving into new life stages and adolescents moving through puberty into womanhood.

Spiritual Emergence Network
930 Mission Street, #7
Santa Cruz, CA 95060
phone: (408) 426-0902
fax: (408) 429-1614

A unique international service and volunteer organization that supports people experiencing psychospiritual crisis by offering educational materials and free referrals for appropriate counseling or emergency services. Referrals include psychiatrists, psychologists, counselors, psychics, shamans, medicine women, hospitals, clergy, healing centers, bodyworkers, and compassionate listeners. Published biannually, the *SEN Newsletter* nurtures active dialogue around psychospiritual transformation. Each issue features articles and stories from many points of view on selected themes, as well as reviews of books, audiotapes and videotapes. $35 membership includes newsletter.

Camphill Village Kimberton Hills
P.O. Box 155
Kimberton, PA 19442
phone: (610) 935-0300

A working community with disabled adults based on biodynamic agriculture and social therapy. Part of a worldwide movement.

New Farms
HC 69, Box 62
Rociada, NM 87742
phone: 505-425-5457

A rural development service group that offers bilingual education and demonstrations.

Resource Center for Nonviolence
contact: Anita Heckman
515 Broadway
Santa Cruz, CA 95060
phone: (831) 423-1623
fax: (831)423-8716
email: rcnv@rcnv.org
Website: http://www.rcnv.org

The Resource Center of Nonviolence in Santa Cruz, California, offers a wide-ranging educational program in the history, theory, methodology, and current practice of nonviolence as a force for personal and social change. Founded in 1976, the Resource Center has developed a variety of formats to explore the meaning of nonviolence and its prospects in shaping our daily lives and our work for social change. At the local/regional level, Resource Center public programs include talks, study groups, weekend workshops and occasional training programs of one to two weeks. Among the program emphases are Mexico/Latin America, the Middle East, Local Neighborhood Organizing, and Nonviolence in general.

The New Dimensions Radio
P. O. Box 569
Ukiah, CA 95482–0569

phone: (800) 935-8273
email: ndradio@igc.org
Website:
http://www.newdimensions.org

Since 1973, New Dimensions Radio has been interviewing the leading thinkers, creative artists, and social innovators on the planet. Hundreds of these intelligent, in-depth dialogues are available on audio-cassette—enriching, enlightening, and empowering conversations with such inspiring teachers as Joseph Campbell, Jean Houston, J. Krishnamurti, David Bohm, Alice Walker, H. H. the Dalai Lama, Thomas Moore, Ram Dass, Caroline Myss, Andrew Weil, and many more. New titles added regularly. Free catalog.

Other Books

In addition to the books by contributors listed in their biographies, you might be interested in the following:

Ecolinking by Don Rittner, 1992

Everyone's Guide to online environmental information. $18.95 paperback. ISBN: 0-938151-35-5. Peachpit Press.

The Need to Thrive
by Judy Remington, 1991.

An illuminating glimpse at women's organizations, particularly from the 1970s, that were motivated by the struggle to change the structure of society. This book will give you a new understanding of the organizations you may already belong to or will help to create in the future. $6.95 paperback. ISBN: 0-9629491-0-8. Minnesota Women's Press.

Women in Spiritual and Communitarian Societies in the United States by Wendy Chmielewski, Louis Kern, and Marlyn Klee-Hartzell, 1992

A study of various communitarian and spiritual societies from the 1700s. A fascinating glimpse at social experiements, functional communities, and women's experiences within them. $17.95 paperback. ISBN: 0-8156-2569-3. Syracuse University Press.

Wise Woman Herbal Healing Wise
by Susun Weed, 1989

The Wise Woman tradition is the way of nourishment and sustenance rather than "fixing" and "curing." This book introduces seven herbs, complete with food and medicine recipes, fun facts, and literary references. Includes detailed instructions for making your own herbal preparations. $11.95 paperback. ISBN: 0-9614620-2-7. Ash Tree Publishing.

Cybergrrl! A Woman's Guide to the World Wide Web by Aliza Sherman, 1998

An easy-to-understand explanation of the Internet, other women's stories of how the Web influenced their lives as well as listing sites geared towards women. Sherman's mission is to empower women through technology by removing barriers that keep them from the Web. Inspirational and instructional stories show women the relevance of the Web to their lives and where to begin their journey. $12.00 paperback. ISBN: 0–345423828. Ballantine Books.

Reclaiming Our Cities and Towns
by David Engwicht, 1993

New ideas and concrete examples of how to make cars part of a larger transportation picture that facilitates social and cultural exchange, as well as exchanges of information, goods, and services. $12.95 paperback. ISBN: 0-86571-283-2. New Society Publishers.

Economics As If the Earth Really Mattered
by Susan Meeker-Lowry, 1988

An incisive tool for using your money to create social change. Exposes many of the problems with our current money system, showing how local reinvestment in recycling, land trusts, and food co-ops can help communities enjoy self-reliance and diversity. $12.95 paperback. ISBN 0-86571-121-6. New Society Publishers.

The Overworked American
by Juliet Schor, 1992

Why do we seem to be working longer hours when technology should be making our lives more leisurely? Americans are caught in a vicious work-spend cycle like rats on a treadmill. The way out requires a change in our ethics of work and consumption. $12.00 paperback. ISBN: 0-465-05433-1. HarperCollins.

Streamlining Your Life
by Stephanie Culp, 1991

Personal organization should be about the way you live—not just how you manage your time. This book can help you evaluate your lifestyle and guide you through the adjustments necessary to streamline your life so you can live the way you want to, not the way you have to. $11.95 paperback. ISBN: 0-89879-462-S. Writer's Digest.

The Reading Group Handbook
by Rachel W. Jacobsohn, 1994

Provides tools for building your own book group, from the characteristics of good members and the art of discussion to suggested topics and complete listings of recommended readings. Create a space for people to share and discover each other's perceptions and knowledge. $10.95 paperback. ISBN: 0-7868-8002-3. Little Brown & Co.

The Nontoxic Home and Office
by Debra Lynn Dadd, 1992

A guide to ridding your home of nontoxic products and finding safe, cost-effective subsitutes. Analyzes many products you never thought of as dangerous, and includes recipes for homemade cleaners and personal care products. $10.95 paperback. ISBN: 0-87477-676-7. The Putnam Berkley Group.

Staying Well in a Toxic World
by Lynn Lawson, 1993

Thousands of chemicals have been introduced into the environment since World War II, and many people are unaware of their daily exposure to lesser known toxins. Provides a thorough list of organizations, books, and other resources to find information, support groups, or take legal action. $15.95 paperback. ISBN: 1-879360-33-0. The Noble Press.

Anxiety & Stress by Susan M. Lark, 1993

An outstanding resource to help women manage their stress, anxiety, and panic. Reviews the possible physical causes of anxiety and considers holistic strategies (herbal therapy, diet, supplements, relaxation techniques, exercise, acupressure) as well as pharmaceutical approaches. $12.95 paperback. ISBN: 0-917010-55-8. Westchester Publishing Company.

Sacred Living: A Daily Guide
by Robin Heerens Lysne, 1997

A 365-day guide to bringing spirit into your life. Organized by season, it offers an affirmation for each day, plus hundreds of simple ceremonies, suggestions, meditations, and holiday celebrations. $14.95 hardback. ISBN: 1-57324-099-0. Conari Press.

Voices from the Edge: Conversations with Jerry Garcia, Ram Dass, Annie Sprinkle, Matthew Fox, Jaron Lanier, and Others
Interviews by David Jay Brown and Rebecca McClen Novick, 1995

A sagacious sampling of leading-edge thinkers, influential spokesmen for the popular movements toward higher and wider consciousness in the past three decades. Includes interviews with Marija Gimbutas, Jean Houston, and Francis Jeffrey. *"Anyone aspiring to understand the new millennium we are entering will have to read this book."* —Robert A. Wilson. $14.95 paperback. ISBN: 0-89594-732-3. The Crossing Press.

Raising Spiritual Children in a Material World: Introducing Spirituality into Family Life
by Phil Catalfo, 1997

Through the stories of nine families, the author explores the challenges and opportunities of raising children with an understanding of the sacred. Discover the power of prayer, the importance of tradition, the richness of blending traditions, the need for making spiritual practice relevant to contemporary life, and the significance of community. Learn through your children how parenting and family life can be a spiritual practice in themselves. $12.00 paperback. Berkley Books.

Stone Soup for the World: Life-Changing Stories of Kindness & Courageous Acts of Service.
Edited by Marianne Larned; foreword by Colin Powell.

Highlights hundreds of organizations and individuals making a difference in the world through community service. Offers a directory to link readers to a vast array of community-building organizations. $15.95 paperback. ISBN: 0-57342-118-0. Conari Press.

Poetic Diction: A Study in Meaning
by Owen Barfield, 1973

Barfield's insights into the deep structure of metaphors as the real engine of a given language's history are only now being studied in laboratories dedicated to mapping language functions in the human brain.

$16.95 paperback. ISBN 0-819560-26-X. Wesleyan University Press.

The Reinvention of Work: A New Vision of Livelihood for Our Time by Matthew Fox, 1995

Job dissatisfaction afflicts more than 90 percent of American workers; The Reinvention of Work thoughtfully explores the causes of and cures for this malaise. $14.00 paperback. ISBN: 0-060630-620. HarperSanFrancisco.

A Brief History of Everything by Ken Wilber & Tony Schwartz, 1996

An altogether friendly and accessible account of men's and women's place in the universe of sex, soul, and spirit, this vivid summary of the new and emerging American wisdom provides radical commentary on hot topics of the day, from political correctness to spiritual enlightenment. $14.00 paperback. ISBN: 1-570621-87-X. Shambhala Publications.

Building a Win-Win World: Life Beyond Global Economic Warfare by Hazel Henderson, 1997

World-renowned futurist Hazel Henderson extends her twenty-five years of work in economics to examine the havoc the current economic system is creating at the global level, examining how jobs, education, health care, human rights, democratic participation, socially responsible business, and environmental protection are all sacrificed to "global competitiveness." She then outlines a new economic architecture based on positive, sustainable systems. $19.95 paperback. ISBN: 1-576750272. Berrett-Koehler.

The Resurgence of the Real: Body, Nature, and Place in a Hypermodern World by Charlene Spretnak, 1997

Our globalized, "virtual," and hyper-rationalized world is built on denial of the fundamental human connection to nature; a sense of place; and an understanding of the body, says Spretnak, who explains why the fall of communism and the triumph of capitalism have not come close to establishing a new world order, and how, until we face the failure of modernism, nothing will change. $22.95 hardcover. ISBN: 0-201-5341-93. Addison-Wesley.

Sacred Circles: A Guide to Creating Your Own Women's Spirituality Group by Sally Craig & Robin Deen Carnes, 1998

A guidebook for women longing for a powerful community in which to thrive spiritually, as well as a supportive, female-centered atmosphere of discovery. $16 paperback. ISBN: 0-06-251522-5. HarperSanFrancisco.

Wisdom Circles : A Guide to Self-Discovery and Community Building in Small Groups by Charles A. Garfield, Cindy Spring, Sedonia Cahill, 1998

This practical, inspirational guide shows readers how to use the power of small circles to effect changes in their lives and in their communities. $21.95 hardcover, ISBN: 0-786862769. Hyperion.

True Work: The Sacred Dimension of Earning a Living by Justine Willis Toms and Michael Toms, 1998

Does your job enhance your soul life? From the husband and wife creators of the weekly radio program, "New Dimensions," comes a book about how to live your dream on a daily basis. Encompasses the insights gleaned from everyone from H.H. the Dalai Lama, the late mythologist Joseph Campbell, inventor and scientist R. Buckminster "Bucky" Fuller to activist Alice Walker, physician Deepak Chopra, and philosopher Sir Laurens van der Post. $21.00 hardcover. ISBN: 0-517705877. Bell Tower.

Women's Bodies, Women's Wisdom: Creating Physical and Emotional Health and Healing by Christiane Northrup, 1998

The new classic guide to women's physical and emotional well-being, bringing together the best conventional treatments and the full range of alternative therapies with the individual's own natural healing power. $17.95 paperback. ISBN: 0–553–37953–4. Bantam Doubleday Dell.

Our Bodies, Ourselves for the New Century: A Book by and for Women by The Boston Women's Health Collective, 1998

A newly revised and updated edition of a classic. Designed for women of all ages and ethnic groups, this book encompasses such controversial issues as "managed care" and the insurance industry; breast cancer treatment options; recent developments in contraception; and much more. $24 paperback. ISBN: 0–684842319. Touchstone Books.

Journals, Magazines, Newspapers

Indigenous Woman
Lea Foushee, Editor
Indigenous Women's Network
P.O. Box 174
Lake Elmo, MN 55042
phone: (612) 770-3861

Provides a platform and a voice to empower Native women to preserve their cultures and communities. Stories and accounts of strong, competent women determined not to sit back and endure an existence of quiet suffering and cultural disintegration. Magazine subscription is $10.00 per year, two issues; membership is $25.00 per year, including magazine.

In Context
Robert Gilman, Editor
Context Institute
P.O. Box 11470
Bainbridge Island, WA 98110
phone: (800) 462-6683

Provides alternative visions of what money means, along with ideas and tools to construct different frameworks for leading our lives. Promotes financial sufficiency and a sane existence based on the quality of our time rather than the quantity of our earnings. $24.00 per year, quarterly.

Community Jobs
Ingrid Johnson, Editor
ACCESS
30 Irving Street
New York, NY 10003
phone: (212) 475-1001

This newspaper offers solid advice for people seeking employment with nonprofit agencies. Covers a wide range of topics and services for the "make a difference" professional, from information on jobs, organizations, services, and books to starting your own nonprofit business. $69.00 per year, twelve issues.

Earth Work
Lisa Younger, Editor
Student Conservation Association
P.O. Box 550
Charlestown, NY 03603
phone: (603) 543-1700

A job listing for the environmentally conscious, specifically geared to those who want to volunteer in the environmental sector. $29.95 per year, six issues.

Whole Earth Review
Howard Rhinegold, Editor
P.O. Box 3000
Denville, NJ 07834
phone: (800) 783-4903

Information on everything from sheep farming to counterculture, with an emphasis on self-sufficiency and community building. $27.00 per year, quarterly.

Heresies
280 Broadway, Suite 412
New York, NY 10007
phone: (212) 227-2108

This feminist publication stimulates thought about the political and social realities experienced by women every day. Each issue focuses on a central theme and features poetry, prose, interviews, and commentary, along with photographs, paintings, and sculptures. $27.00 per year, quarterly.

Crone Chronicles
Crone Corporation
P.O. Box 81
Kelly, WY 83011
phone: (307) 733-5409

An open forum for women exploring the wisdom and spiritual gifts of aging. Provides nourishing and exciting food for thought in the form of interviews, essays, poetry, reviews, fiction, and art. Reclaims the archetypal meaning of the "crone" as an aspect of the Triple Goddess. $18.00 per year, quarterly.

Circle Network News
Box 219
Mt. Horeb, WI 53572

One of the most important resources for information about the Neo-Pagan, Wiccan, and Goddess community, published by Wiccan priestess Selena Fox. If you want to contact Pagan or Wiccan groups, this is a great place to start! $9 per year, quarterly; $3 sample.

The Wise Woman
Ann Forfreedom, Editor
2441 Cordova Street
Oakland, CA 94602
phone: (510) 536-3174

Witness the meeting of spirituality and politics in this journal full of savvy and irreverent political commentary on feminist issues. Special focus on Goddess lore, feminist spirituality, and feminist withcraft. $15.00 per year, quarterly.

The Journal of Transpersonal Psychology
P.O. Box 3049
Stanford, California 94309
(650) 327-2066
Website:
http://www.igc.org/atp/journal/journal.html

For general readers, professionals, educators, and students who are interested in the study and open communication of transpersonal experiences, concepts, and practices that connect contemporary educational, scientific, and clinical methodologies with personal, social, and spiritual understanding. $24.00 per year subscription, two issues.

IONS: The Noetic Sciences Review
The Institute of Noetic Sciences
475 Gate 5 Road, Suite 300
Sausalito, CA 94965
phone: (800) 383 1394
Website:
www.noetic.org/publications.html

A quarterly magazine featuring literary-quality essays that chronicle the growing edge of consciousness studies and societal change. Free subscription with membership; rates for basic membership are $35 annually.

Orion Magazine
195 Main Street
Great Barrington, MA 01230-1601
(413) 528-4422
email: orion@orionsociety.org
Website:
www.orionsociety.org/orion.html

Orion uses writing from scientific and artistic viewpoints to explore and heal the roots of humanity's estrangement from nature. Free subscription with membership; basic membership fee is $25 per year.

Resurgence
Walt Blackford
P.O. Box 404
Freeland, WA 98249
email: waltb@whidbey.com
Website:
http://www.gn.apc.org/resurgence

An international forum for ecological and spiritual thinking printed in the U.K. Annual subscription fee for the U.S. is $50 to receive via airmail and $40 for surface mail.

Audio & Videotapes

New Era Video
P.O. Box 7180
Los Osos, CA 93412
phone: (800) 549-4754
email: neweravid@aol.com

A membership organization and unique library of inspiring videotapes. In-depth interviews, talks, workshops, and insightful documentaries with leaders and thinkers of the new paradigm. New titles are added regularly. Members receive special prices on many of the videos and can rent them for a week at very low rates. Enjoy the best of both worlds: rent a video, and if you decide to buy it, we'll credit the rental fee to the purchase price. $25 lifetime membership.

Sounds True
P.O. Box 8010
Dept. W11B
Boulder, CO 80306-8010
phone: (800) 333-9185

A selection of over 300 audio, video, and sacred music programs for adult learn-ers and seekers. Listen to the inspired voices and words of gifted teachers, trailblazers, and allies to enhance your inner life, and find your own inspired voice. Each program is designed to be a learning experience you can return to again and again.

ZBS Foundation
RR1 Box 1201
Ft. Edward, NY 12828
phone: (800) 662-3345 from 9am-4pm
    EST
or (800) 395-2549 other times
fax: (518) 695-6406
Website: http://www.zbs.org/zbs.html

Wonderful audio adventures with spiritual and humorous storylines that have won international awards. Their CDs and tapes will make your life richer and less stressful and provide valuable information as well as hundreds of hours of great listening.

Serpentine Music
P.O. Box 2564
Sebastopol, CA 95473-2564
phone: (707) 823-7425
fax: 707) 823-6664
email: annehill@serpentinemusic.com
Website:
http://www.sonic.net/serpentine/

The only place online or in print where you will find extensive listings of Pagan music in all genres, biographies, and information on the artists and Pagan culture that puts it all in context. Also includes books, video, and spoken-word tapes.

New Medicine Tapes
1308 Gilman Street
Berkeley, CA 94706
phone: (800) 647-1110
Website: http://www.newmed.com

Audio and video cassettes of transformative messages by noted shamans and healers. Offering the most inspiring and heart-opening presentations from conferences and retreats throughout the world.

Let these master teachers from the great spiritual traditions empower your journey to a new way.

Women & Spirituality Series
by Donna Read, 1990
Direct Cinema Limited
P.O. Box 10003
Santa Monica, CA 90410-1003
phone: (800) 525-0000

Goddess Remembered is a poetic look at ancient goddess cultures and an exploration of contemporary, goddess-centered spirituality; *The Burning Times* recounts the evolution of European society and the witch craze that took millions of lives; and *Full Circle* explores the role of goddess-centered spirituality in the modern world. Honoring the Goddess connects us with our past, the earth, and each other. $34.95 per video.

Conscious Evolution: Awakening Our Social Potential
by Barbara Marx Hubbard
Conference Recording Service
phone: (800) 647-1110
Website: http://www.newmed.com

One of the keynote tapes from the Institute of Noetic Science's 1997 Questing Spirit Conference, *Conscious Evolution* offers a dramatic presentation of a new worldview and vision of the future equal to our spiritual, social, and scientific capacities. $9.95 cassette (ACE-C001).

Thinking Allowed Videos
2560 Ninth Street, Suite 123
Berkeley CA 94710
order: (800) 999-4415
fax: (510) 548-4275
email: thinking@thinking-allowed.com
Website:
http://www.thinkingallowed.com

Possible Human, Possible World
by Jean Houston, 1992

In Part One of this ninety-minute program, Jean Houston describes the range of human capacities that are found in different cultures. We are living at a unique historical moment when the cultures of the entire world are available to us, and we are challenged as we have never been before. In Part Two, she expands upon the learning experiences she had with Margaret Mead, elaborating on her own experiences working with different cultures. She also presents exercises to promote a new vision of human potential. $49.95 (W175).

Archetypal Psychology
by Jean Shinoda Bolen

Jean Shinoda Bolen suggests that the images of the ancient dieties represent powerful projections of the psyche. By studying the myths of the gods from a psychological perspective, we can learn much about ourselves. It is by facing the truth of our lives that we can die to our past ways and enter into a new order of being. $49.95 (W204).

Reclaiming Our Past, Recreating Our Future: Reflections on The Chalice and the Blade
by Riane Eisler

At the dawn of modern civilization, says Riane Eisler, humanity shifted from a partnership model of social interaction to a dominator model, and warfare and male domination became established social institutions. Since that time they have been such an integral part of our culture that we rarely imagine things could be otherwise. Yet in a partnership model, men and women treat each other as equals. $49.95 (W035).

Planetary Birth
by Barbara Marx Hubbard

Barbara Marx Hubbard presents her vision of a positive future, involving a quantum change in consciousness to a higher state in which all humans will function with a fuller awareness of the larger planetary being. She suggests that the great religious leaders of humankind offer templates of future evolution. $34.95 (H345).

Archetypal Forms and Forces
by Angeles Arrien

Archetypal energies beckon us to live a larger life. We are all healers, warriors, visionaries, and teachers, but often these potentials remain in latent form. Through song, dance, storytelling, and meditation we can activate these archetypes. $34.95 (H130).

Embodying Buddhism
by Sylvia Boorstein

Sylvia Boorstein presents the essence of the eightfold path and the four noble truths of Buddhism. She discusses Vipassana—or mindfulness—meditation which entails detaching from the thoughts, cravings and aversions that pass through the mind. Through this practice one gains insight into the impermanence of all mental states. $34.95 (H270).

African Ritual and Initiation
by Malidoma Patrice Somé

Somé describes his childhood among the Dagara people, focusing on their use of ritual as a means of establishing an ongoing relationship with the worlds of their ancestors and of the spirits. He also describes his own shamanic initiation. He suggests that the elders of the Dagara community were skilled in creating doorways through which practitioners could pass into other dimensions of reality. $34.95 (H320).

Carnival of the Spirit by Luisah Teish

Luisah Teish's work engages every aspect of life, from singing, dancing, and storytelling to rituals observing the cycles of life. She describes the religions of the African diaspora, noting that they survive in the West by blending with the dominant

Christian faith. Luisah Teish is priestess of Oshun, the African Yoruba goddess of love. $34.95 (H110).

An Evening with Joan Borysenko
by Elda Hartley

Borysenko, cofounder of the Mind/Body Clinic at the Harvard Medical School and head of Mind/Body Health Sciences, Inc. in Boulder, Colorado, explains the latest findings in mind-body research. She provides successful techniques for helping people regain control of their physical and emotional well-being. Borysenko was drawn to the field of mind-body health as a result of a two-year illness. The video tells the story of her recovery, and how with meditation she was able to get back on track. $29.95. Hartley Videotape 60 minutes VAE-V001. (800) 383-1586.

Catalogs

Seventh Generation
49 Hercules Drive
Colchester, VT 05446
phone: (800) 456-1177

"You don't have to give up value and performance to help the environment."

Green products for any household or personal use imaginable, as well as an extended section of GreenCotton clothing and linens. From cover to cover of its recycled pages, Seventh Generation pays close attention to the health of the planet. Free catalog.

Mountain Spirit
P.O. Box 368
Port Townsend, WA 98368
phone: (360) 385-4491

A woman-owned and operated mail-order company dedicated to the health and well-being of their customers. Offering a selection of fresh, hand-prepared oils, herbs, tinctures, teas, salves, and more. All blends are made the wise woman way, using fresh organic or wild-crafted herbs.

Femail Creations
2925 East Patrick Lane
Suite O
Las Vegas, NV 89120
phone: (800) 969-2760

Chock full of wonderful resources for and by women including cards, sculptures, clothing, posters, etc.

Ladyslipper Catalog
P.O. Box 3124
Durham, NC 27715
phone: (919) 683-1570
fax: (919) 682-5601
orders: (800) 634-6044
Website:http://www.ladyslipper.org

A nonprofit organization and a small independent label whose purpose is to heighten public awareness of the achievements of women artists and musicians, to further new musical and artistic directions for women musicians, and to expand the scope and availability of recordings by women. Comprehensive catalog of over 1500 titles lists a variety of female musicians, writers, performers, and composers, musical contributions by nonsexist men, as well as video recordings, songbooks, and music-related books. Online catalog also features hundreds of music samples for listening.

Young Living Essential Oils
Contact: Neela Ford
535 W. Cordova Road, Suite 820
Santa Fe, NM 87501
phone: (505) 466-1821
fax: (505) 466-3908

Essential oils are the best preventative medicine for any body. They can also provide emotional upliftment and relief from the many energetic problems and changes related to spiritual awakening, such as migraines, menopause, chronic fatigue, and superwoman syndrome.

Dharmacrafts
405 Waltham Street, Suite 234
Lexington, MA 02173
phone: (617) 862-9211

An excellent catalog for anyone who meditates, plans to mediate, or just enjoys esoteric Eastern paraphernalia. Everything from cushions, mats, and benches to fine incense, books, and statues of Buddha and Hindu deities. $2.00 per catalog.

Hazelden Publishing and Education
Hazelden Educational Materials
P.O. Box 176
Center, City, MN 55012-0176
phone: (800) 328-9000

Provides a variety of products and services related to addiction and recovery, from books, workbooks, and study guides, to audio and video tapes, and teaching aids. Emphasizes the basic 12-step approach, including the spiritual dimensions of recovery. Free catalog.

Sacred Spirit Music
Box 1030D
Shaker Road
New Lebanon, NY 12125
phone: (518) 794-7860

Mail-order catalog with a hand-picked selection of CD and audio cassettes focusing on sacred and religious music, world music, and music for meditation, healing, enjoyment, massage, and relaxation. Features low-cost samplers with selections from their most popular albums, and includes a special section on sacred music for children.

Dharma Seed Tape Library
P.O. Box 66
Wendell Depot, MA 01380
phone: (800) 969-7333

Great source for Dharma tapes and books, personally recommended by Sylvia Boorstein.

Directories

City Spirit Publications
7282 Sir Francis Drake Blvd.
P.O. Box 267
Lagunitas, CA 94938
phone: (415) 488-8160; (800) 486-4794
fax: (415) 488-8167; (800) 211-6746
email: CitySpirit@aol.com

22 Prince Street, Suite 411
New York, NY 10012
phone: (212) 966-8842
fax: (212) 941-6302

A free, easy-to-use regional directory that works like a holistic Yellow Pages, full of community resources for natural living. Publications include: *Bay Area Naturally, New York Naturally, Long Island Naturally, New Jersey Naturally,* and *Connecticut Naturally.* A networking resource and support whether you're already living a natural lifestyle or are in transition, seeking a new experience.

Common Ground
305 San Anselmo Avenue, Suite 313
San Anselmo, CA 94960
phone: (415) 459-4900
fax: (415) 459-4974
email: comngrnd@ix.netcom.com
Website: http://www.comngrnd.com.

A free seasonal directory providing access to resources for personal transformation primarily in California. Also features interviews and articles, book and music reviews, and a calendar of events. Resources listed include the people as much as the goods and services they offer.

The National Women's Mailing List
P.O. Box 68
Jenner, CA 95450
phone: (707) 632-5763

A voluntary listing of over 70,000 individuals and links with more than 12,000 women's organizations. Fill out a questionnaire indicating your interest areas, and within six weeks you will begin receiving information on books, organization, magazines, and events. A great way to gain access to resources and information in the women's community nationally. Call or write for free brochure.

A Directory of National Women's Organizations
The National Council for Research on Women
530 Broadway, 10th Floor
New York, NY 10012
phone: (212) 274-0730

The largest national directory dedicated exclusively to women's organizations. A great place to start if you want to hook up with others, professionally or personally, who share your interests, and a good source for fundraising. Every library, women's organization, and university can benefit from it. $44.00 paperback.

The Women's Information Exchange National Directory, edited by
Deborah Brecher & Jill Lippitt
Avon Books
Box 767
Dresden, TN 38225
phone: (800) 238-0658

A listing of 2,500 services, organizations, institutions, and programs for women. A variety of subjects including women's periodicals, bookstores, colleges, and universities. $10.00 paperback.

Communities Directory: A Guide to Cooperative Living
Communities Directory
Route 4, Box 169
Louisa, VA 23093
phone: (703) 894-5126

Over 540 listings and profiles of intentional communities, identifying the philosophy, schooling, housing, and economics of each. All communities listed align themselves with a philosophy of nonviolence, and members are free to leave at any time. Fellowship for International Communities & Communities Publication Cooperative, 1995. $20.00 paperback.

Shopping for a Better World, 1992
The Council on Economic Priorities
30 Irving Place
New York, NY 10003
phone: (800) 729-4237

An annually updated guide that rates companies and products for social responsibility. Among their criteria are: the advancement of women and minorities, charity, environmental policy, animal testing, workplace issues, family benefits, and childcare policies. $5.99 paperback. Book included with $25 annual membership for The Council on Economic Priorities.

Online Resources

Women's Wire
http://womenswire.com

Features news, interviews, comics, surveys, forums, and an extensive list of hyperlinks to women all over the Web.

FeMiNa
http://www.femina.com

FeMiNa is the only Website of its kind, providing women with a comprehensive, searchable directory of links to female friendly sites and information on the World Wide Web.

Cybergrrl
http://www.cybergrrl.com

This eclectic site—one of the first to focus on women—contains a collection of links on various women's issues in addition to a general Webguide, a survey of women

on-line, and information on Webgrrls—a nationwide "real-world, face-to-face networking group for women in and interested in new media" that provides a "forum for women to exchange information, give job and business leads, learn about new technologies, mentor, intern, train, and more!" Members can post to message boards and participate in future chats.

The Phenomenal Women of the Web
　Resource Network/Resource
　Health Network
http://www.spydersempire.com/
network/

These Websites are places where women can come to find information and knowledge on things that affect our everyday lives. The links provided within the categories represent the most comprehensive the Internet has to offer.

Wild Wolf Women
http://www.wildwolfwomen.com/

A group of women who meet regularly on the Internet to talk about their thoughts, emotions, pain, strength, and the themes of the book *Women Who Run with the Wolves* by Clarissa Pinkola Estes. Participants cross the boundaries of language, religion, culture, and race because of their common base as wild women. Includes pages of links to poetry, stories, artwork, books, etc. for a full and healthy Wolf Life on the Web.

The Jamie Sams Web Page
http://www.jamiesams.com/nat

Information on all her books, tapes, and audio adventures as well as links to documentaries, other books, and the videos she's participated in.

EnviroLink
http://envirolink.org/

A nonprofit organization and online grassroots community that unites hundreds of organizations and volunteers around the world with millions of people in over 130 countries. The largest online environmental information resource on the planet, dedicated to providing the most comprehensive, up-to-date environmental resources available.

EVE Online
http://envirolink.org/orgs/eve/

A Website dedicated to promoting all aspects of ecofeminism, based on the premise that the domination of women and the domination of nature are fundamentally connected. Contributions from environmentalism, alternative spirituality, animal rights, and other progressive affiliations have all influenced ecofeminist theory and action. Peruse EVE Online to get a feel for ecofeminism through the exploration of issues, ecofeminist writings, a bibliography, and links to allied organizations.

New Dimensions Radio
http://www.newdimensions.org

An independent, listener-supported producer/distributor of public radio programs, New Dimensions is dedicated to presenting a diversity of views from many traditions and cultures, and strives to impart practical knowledge and perennial wisdom. An international forum for some of the most innovative ideas expressed on the planet, New Dimensions has reached millions of listeners with its practical and provocative views of life and the human spirit. New Dimensions fosters the process of living a more healthy life of mind, body, and spirit while deepening our connections to self, family, community, and the environment. Exciting Website features library, articles, audio programs, dialogue groups, links, radio stations, online ordering, membership, and more.

Thinking Allowed
http://www.thinkingallowed.com

A national public television series and an extensive video library featuring the world's leading writers, teachers, and explorers in the areas of consciousness research, psychology, philosophy, personal and spiritual development, health and healing, intuitive arts, and the frontiers of science. Website features a video catalog, a sampling of complete transcripts, broadcast information, broadcast information, links, discounts, new video releases, and much more.

Online Noetic Network
http://www.wisdomtalk.org/

An e-mail magazine focusing on spirituality and inner experience. Become a member of the Online Noetic Network and join our discussion about Noetic Vision, the perspective that sees the importance of awareness and life itself. ONN e-mails twelve articles a month by your favorite speakers and authors, so you can respond with your questions and comments directly to the experts. Join ONN and talk with other people who are passionate to know spirit and self!

The Co-Creation Website
http://www.cocreation.org/

This site was created by the Foundation for Conscious Evolution in order to forge community and disseminate social innovations in all fields. Co-Creation scans for solutions and categorizes and connects projects to create a positive future. You can place your projects on the Website, identify vital teammates and resources, and learn about model projects that are already successful. The pragmatic creativity of individuals and groups working collectively is a mighty force for a sustainable, compassionate, life-enhancing, and option-rich world.

Alternative Therapies in Health and Medicine
http://www.healthonline.com/scripts/pagesrv.exe?ALTTHER

A peer-reviewed journal and forum for sharing information concerning the practical use of alternative therapies in preventing and treating disease, healing illness, and promoting health. Encourages the integration of alternative therapies with conventional medical practices and promotes the evaluation and appropriate use of all effective approaches from the physical to the transpersonal. Publishes a variety of disciplined inquiry methods, including high-quality scientific research. Website features articles, back issues, electronic bulletin board, information by topic, products, and links.

Art As A Healing Force Web
http://www.artashealing.org/

A center of art and healing energy on the web. As creativity, art, and healing merge, the fields of art and medicine are changing. Making art frees the body's healing mechanisms, uniting body, mind, and spirit. Here the creative process is seen as the healer and art is transformational in itself. Website offers information about how art heals, the history of art and healing, how to heal yourself with art, music, and dance, art programs in hospitals, and people making healing art to heal themselves, others, and the earth. Links to other sites on art and healing, the earth, ritual healing, art therapy, and expressive arts.

In the Spirit
http://www.inthespirit.com

The online home of *Free Spirit* magazine, published and distributed in New York City, Los Angeles, and Orange County. Features engaging and enlightening articles, columns, interviews, a daily calendar, and a marketplace full of healthful services and products. *In the Spirit* illuminates the many paths to self-empowerment that are available in our time. An invaluable, inclusive resource for people who are motivated to realize their greatest potential—physically, mentally, emotionally, and spiritually.

Images of Divinity (IOD)
http://www.imagesofdivinity.org

An independent research project currently under the sponsorship of the Graduate Theological Union's Center for Women and Religion in Berkeley, California. IOD evolved from the literary works of China Galland, Lucia Chiavola Birnbaum, and similarly interested scholars, as well as artists, performers, painters, photographers, and curators working with this imagery. See also The Black Madonna Group and The Black Madonna Network, http://www. blackmadonna.org.

Institute for Global Communications
http://www.igc.org/igc/

A unique, global community of progressive individuals and organizations. Our mission is to expand and inspire movements for peace, economic and social justice, human rights, and environmental sustainability around the world by providing and developing accessible computer networking tools. IGC's five on-line communities of activists and organizations (PeaceNet, EcoNet, ConflictNet, LaborNet, and WomensNet) are all gateways to articles, headlines, features, and Weblinks on progressive issues. Site also features directory of member organizations, Internet products and services, and descriptions of IGC special projects.

Empowerment Resources Online Bookstore
http://www.empowerment resources.com/

Offers over 320 top quality empowerment resource books and more than seventy links on many topics related to personal growth, social change, and ecology. Most books are discounted 20 to 30 percent. Promotional and networking opportunities to publicize your resources, issues, group, or Website.

Women, Ink
http://www.womenink.org/

The largest international distributor of books on women and development. A project of the International Women's Tribune Centre to market and distribute books on women and development worldwide. Its large selection includes books from the United Nations Development Fund for Women (UNIFEM) and the NGO Forum on Women, as well as hard-to-find primary materials from the Global South.

DharmaNet
http://www.dharmanet.org/

An Internet gateway to Buddhist resources throughout the world. Features links to centers and practice groups, Buddhist studies resources, personal ("non-organizational") pages, online libraries of text, art, and multimedia, a newsstand, a meditation retreat calendar, a Buddhist e-mail directory, geographic databases, newsgroups, lists, and chat lines, a Who's Who of teachers, information about Engaged Buddhism and co-creating a better world, service opportunities, classifieds, a virtual community bulletin board, and a marketplace of publishers, bookstores, products, and services.

INDEX

Conari Press, established in 1987, publishes books on topics ranging from spirituality and women's history to sexuality and personal growth. Our main goal is to publish quality books that will make a difference in people's lives—both how we feel about ourselves and how we relate to one another. Our readers are our most important resource, and we value your input, suggestions, and ideas. We'd love to hear from you—after all, we are publishing books for you!

For a complete catalog of our titles, or to get on our mailing list, contact:

CONARI PRESS

2550 Ninth Street, Suite 101, Berkeley, CA 94710
800–685–9595   FAX: 510–649–7190
email: conaripub@aol.com